ART IN
MEDIAEVAL
FRANCE
987–1498

———

A Study in
Patronage

Oxford University Press, Amen House, London E.C. 4

GLASGOW NEW YORK TORONTO MELBOURNE WELLINGTON
BOMBAY CALCUTTA MADRAS CAPE TOWN

Geoffrey Cumberlege, Publisher to the University

The Virgin. Detail from the Nativity. Painted by the Maître de Moulins for
Cardinal Jean Rolin, Bishop of Autun. *c.* 1470.

(Phot. Bulloz.)

ART IN MEDIAEVAL FRANCE

987–1498

BY

JOAN EVANS

GEOFFREY CUMBERLEGE
OXFORD UNIVERSITY PRESS
LONDON NEW YORK TORONTO
1948

TO THE
ARCHAEOLOGISTS AND ANTIQUARIES
WHO FOUGHT FOR FRANCE
1939–1945

✳

Beneoiste soit France et de Dieu absolue
Que tant de bone gent en est de li issue
Cil conquisent la terre sor la gent mescreüe . . .

LA CHANSON D'ANTIOCHE

NOTE

THE materials for this book have been gathered over so many years that it is hardly possible to enumerate all those to whom my gratitude is due. I should like briefly to express my thanks to the Museum authorities who have given me information and have allowed me to reproduce objects from their collections, and to Professor Kenneth Conant, Mr. Arthur Gardner, Mr. Ellis Waterhouse, Mr. Christopher Norris, Monsieur Pierre Verlet, Monsieur Oursel, Monsieur Élie Lambert, Monsieur Jacques Dupont, and the Directors of the Art Institute of Chicago and of the National Museum, Copenhagen, for gifts of photographs. I remember with gratitude those who have encouraged me to write this book, and not least among them my friends Monsieur J. J. Marquet de Vasselot and his daughter Madame Claude Carnot. I thank those of my friends who have had the patience to read and criticize the book in manuscript, especially Mrs. Murdo Mackenzie, Miss Louise Stone, Dr. Margaret Whinney, and Mr. T. S. R. Boase, the President of Magdalen. To all of them I am greatly indebted.

J. E.

WOTTON-UNDER-EDGE

PREFACE

THE best of French mediaeval art is so beautiful that it can be, and should be, enjoyed from a purely aesthetic point of view. Yet the best has to be picked out by each observer from among a surprisingly large amount of good art; so large an amount, indeed, that it becomes overwhelming unless a sense of historical development brings order into the mass. It is this historical development, and not that of technique or style, which is the subject of this book.

My whole endeavour, indeed, is to show that French mediaeval art took the forms it did because of the needs of the men who commissioned it. For this reason I have taken the different classes of society—monks, bishops, canons, friars, kings, nobles, citizens, and the rest—and have described the art that was created to meet their needs. As a picture of mediaeval society my book cannot be altogether in proportion, for it necessarily lays too much stress on those with money to spend on works of art or skill enough to create them; but as a study of cause and effect it may help to show mediaeval art as the expression of a society. We falsify history if we regard any kind of art as a series of specimens ranged in museums, impersonal and without reason or background.

The deliberate study of French mediaeval art is the more necessary because much of what has survived has lost its purpose. The Hundred Years War and the Wars of Religion destroyed much beauty, but did not change the significance of what survived. The Revolution, however, succeeded in overturning both the religious and feudal bases of French society, and subsequent governments have only added to the overthrow. The mediaeval art of France has to be studied in castles where no one lives, monasteries where none takes his vows, and, often, in churches where no one prays. Only by an effort of the historical imagination can we endow them with their true significance; but the effort will make the stones live.

The limits of the book in time and space were more difficult to determine than the limits of its subject-matter. The day is past when the historian of French art could assume that it blossomed suddenly from the bare ground, like a crocus in autumn, somewhere about 1100. We now see the hundred years before this as the time of growth: we can study the first springing of the leaves, and the first forming of the bud, of a plant in no wise ephemeral.

The history of France may be said to begin at the Battle of Fontanet in 841, when the land was freed from the yoke of the Holy Roman Empire; but it was a century and a half before the continuous development of a national art began, and I have preferred to take the accession of Hugues Capet as the initial date. The geographical field has been yet more difficult to delimit. The Rhône pilots still call the right bank of their river *Riaume* and the left *Empi*; and the feudal division between *Royaume de France* and *Saint Empire* seemed the only possible distinction and has remained a primary one.[1] Thus the extent of English occupation, except for the study of possible English influence, is of little importance, for the land remained feudally speaking part of the Kingdom of France; but other provinces, that we think of as essentially French, did not come under French allegiance until later in the Middle Ages. Auvergne was not technically French until 1196, Normandy not definitely until 1205, Provence not until 1246, Lyons not until 1274; yet Flanders was French for most of the Middle Ages (though Brabant and Hainault were not), and the county of Barcelona depended on the *couronne des fleurs de lys* until 1258. Civilization, however, is not a matter only of government and allegiance. The earlier monastic architecture of Normandy drew its inspiration from France; Auvergne was a creative centre for the French Romanesque style; Provençal art is by the first half of the twelfth century inseparable from French art. On the other hand, Catalonia has always had an art of its own, as Flanders has had at least since the thirteenth century. I have therefore compromised with history: Catalonia, Roussillon, and Cerdagne are omitted; Flanders is excluded for the later Middle Ages; and *terres d'Empire* that at some subsequent time became French have not been included. In the history of art the ultimate territorial test must be one of civilization.

It is only when one travels in France at leisure that one discovers how much of the Middle Ages still exists for anyone who has time to look at it. I have seen cider-carts like those of the Bayeux Tapestry in the streets of that city; I have watched barley threshed with flails at Brioude and waited while oxen, hung in slings, were shod at Mesvres. Ploughing and sowing, reaping and binding, pruning and vintage, all the mediaeval labours of the months have passed before my eyes; and within the churches the unchanging ritual of the Mass has waked the echoes of the Middle Ages. I have seen the bishop wash the choir-boys' feet on Maundy Thursday at Auxerre; I have followed the relics of Saint Edme round Provins, of Saint Bernard round Comminges, and of Saint Junien round Nouaillé. I have attended the ancient fair of the Grande Guibraye, that has been held since William the Conqueror founded it; and have been to the monthly markets that still take place in the shadow of the abbey of Cluny. I have found myself travelling from one *pays* to another, and have found the ways of roofing houses and stacking corn change as I travelled. No bureaucracy can alter the frontiers of the innumerable *pays* of France, ghosts of the *pagi* of the Carolingian empire and sometimes of the territory of a Gaulish tribe. These are, and will remain, the true units of local life.

Yet in many walks of life mediaeval tradition has ended in living memory.

[1] For this reason I have permitted myself to use 'France' as a geographical expression even when speaking of times when it did not exist as a political entity.

When I first went to France as a child the women still wore the characteristic caps of their provinces, and the men the traditional garb of their craft or calling: now power-driven machinery produces uniform clothing for all. Then, traditional forms of lamps and pots, saucepans and cans, were still in use, and varied from province to province; now the Bazar sells uniform types to all. It is now only the exceptional man who inhabits a mediaeval world: the hedger or the shepherd who does not leave his farm, the gardener or vinedresser who labours in some remote corner of the country, the Benedictine who lives by the sun and the feasts of the Church. They alone are dominated by the mediaeval cycle of times and seasons, traditions and beliefs. We, who move easily from one place to another, who no longer find light and warmth pressing problems of existence, who seek immediate cause and effect rather than the ultimate reason of things, live in another world. The modern tendency to approximation, the democratic ideal of mediocrity, the monotony of an age of mass production, make it harder for us than for our ancestors to apprehend the Middle Ages. To us the unchanging mediaeval distinctions between class and class, occupation and occupation, and even province and province, are hard to understand. An art of which the form, and often the detail, is dictated not by the artist but by his patron, is likewise strange to us. A study of mediaeval art, indeed, may teach us that the basis of artistic production is not so entirely a matter of self-expression as the modern artist is apt to believe.

I wrote the greater part of this book at a time when an estranging sea of war isolated England from France, and part of the suffering of each country was that its suffering could not be shared. Many of the buildings of which I wrote were being damaged or destroyed even as I was writing of them. Now the full story of destruction is beginning to be told; some links in the golden chain of beauty are for ever broken. Yet by force of memory and imagination and love we may mend the shining chain: not France, nor her history, nor the memorials of that history, can die.

CONTENTS

LIST OF ILLUSTRATIONS

When no other source is indicated the photographs come from the Archives
Photographiques d'Art et d'Histoire, Palais-Royal, Paris

The Virgin. Detail of the picture painted by the Maître de Moulins for Cardinal Rolin, Bishop of Autun, c. 1470. Musée d'Autun. Phot. Bulloz. *Frontispiece.*

b

LIST OF PLANS

THE DAWN OF THE MIDDLE AGES

FRANCE in 987 was a country which already had a long tradition of continuous civilization. Its Dark Ages had been darkened by warfare, destruction, and bloodshed, but they had been neither barbarous nor barbarian. The uses of Roman speech had survived; the traditions of Roman institutions were not wholly dead. The memory of Roman occupation had outlived the five centuries since Syagrius had left Gaul; thousands of estates still represented and still kept the name of a Roman villa, hundreds of settlements still had the name of a Roman town. Cities as far north as Autun and Langres still had their Roman gates, and Bourges its Roman walls. The humblest farmer, when he ploughed his land, might find treasure of red pottery and thin glass, sculptured marble and engraved stone, black silver and green bronze, or gold coins thick and round as seals. The barbarian tribes that had come after the Romans—Visigoths, Ostrogoths, Burgundians, and Saxons—had left little behind them but graves with other treasures of buckles and brooches. The Franks had overrun everything, and had made the land permanently theirs; but the Franks had come not to destroy the Roman Empire but to settle in it and to enjoy its riches; what they maintained was in many ways more significant than what they destroyed. The generation of Hugues Capet inherited from them not only the germ of a national consciousness, but also a civilization.

That civilization was fundamentally Christian. Most of France had been evangelized in the third and fourth centuries, and the memory of those who had brought the gospel had been perpetuated by their veneration as local saints: Saint Cydroine round Joigny, Saint Martin, Saint Gatien and Saint Brice at Tours, Saint Eutrope at Saintes, Saint Sernin and Saint Exupère at Toulouse, Saint Maurin, Saint Savin, and Saint Orens in Gascony, Saint Martial and Saint Aurélien at Limoges, Saint Hilaire, Sainte Radegonde, Saint Junien, and a host of others in Poitou, Saint Ursin, Saint Satur in Berri, Saint Austremoine, Saint Allyre, Saint Prix, and a score more in Auvergne, Saint Bénigne, Saint Andoche, and Saint Seine in the Dijonnais, Saint Denis and Sainte Geneviève at Paris, and hundreds more who might have been forgotten had not some place-name or tomb perpetuated their memory. The earliest of them had died at Roman hands, the next at the hands of the Arian Visigoths; but the baptism of Clovis in 496 had sealed the land as Christian and Catholic. In the centuries that followed, invasion, warfare, and the eternal strife between the rival Merovingian kingdoms of Neustria and Austrasia had weakened the civil and political life of the country, but the Church had continued, unchanging and strong. Consequently the chief monuments of Frankish civilization were religious.

Already, indeed, the great institutions of medieval Christianity were not only established in France, but had created their artistic traditions. The dioceses of France, first represented at the Council of Arles in 314, were still organized in ecclesiastical provinces that corresponded with the civil provinces of Gallo-Roman times. Of the seventeen metropolitan churches of the Carolingian Empire seven—Rouen, Tours, Sens, Rheims, Bourges, Bordeaux, and Éauze—continued to be within Capetian France or within the duchies of Burgundy, Toulouse, and Normandy, and the counties of Blois, Troyes, Champagne, Anjou, and Maine that to some extent depended upon it.[1] In 811 Charlemagne had endowed these sees; dividing his wealth into three parts he had given two of them to the twenty-two metropolitan churches of his Empire. Each of these archbishoprics and bishoprics represented not only a centre of ecclesiastical organization but also a great church: a church, it might well be, ruined and roofless, burnt by Danes or Saracens or Hungarians, but still a link in a tradition of splendid building that went back to the temples of Rome.

The marble Corinthian capital, the stamp and hall-mark of Roman architecture, had been continuously in use in France from Roman times until the eighth century. Then Saracen invasions from the south-west had broken up the Aquitanian school of marble sculpture for a time, and made a gap in the tradition; but before the accession of Hugues Capet such capitals were again being imitated, however crudely, in stone. Before his accession, too, the plans of cathedrals had received new development. The classic basilican plan with a triple apse had already been enriched in new and characteristic fashion. When the cathedral of Chartres had been rebuilt by Gislebert after the Normans burnt it in 858, the aisles had been prolonged round the apse as a narrow passage, forming a rudimentary ambulatory.[2] When the cathedral of Clermont had been rebuilt in 946 by Bishop Étienne[3] he had planned it with an ambulatory from which chapels radiated,[4] and had thus established a tradition destined to be as fruitful a source of inspiration as the basilica had been before it. At Clermont, too, the same bishop had ordered Aléaume, his clerk of the works, to make a statue of the Virgin, of wood covered with gold, to hold relics, to be

[1] On these depended the bishoprics of Avranches, Bayeux, Coutances, Évreux, Lisieux, Séez; Angers, Le Mans; Auxerre, Chartres, Meaux, Nevers, Orléans, Paris, Troyes; Amiens, Beauvais, Châlons-sur-Marne, Laon, Senlis, Soissons; Albi, Clermont, Cahors, Javols (Mende), Limoges, Rodez, Le Puy; Agen, Angoulême, Périgueux, Poitiers and Saintes; nine small Gascon bishoprics under Éauze; and Autun, Langres and Chalon on the archbishopric of Lyons, most of which lay in *terre d'Empire.*

[2] Bréhier, p. 143. The plan was revealed by excavation in 1904.

[3] Hubert, p. 149.

[4] Bréhier, p. 140. The crypt survives.

set at the great feasts upon the altar.[1] It was one of the first of a series of such reliquary statues, destined to become the objects of pilgrimage. If a church could not afford a 'majesty'—for so these statues were called—plated with gold or silver, it had a simpler statue of stone or wood. These were sometimes given the prestige of an immemorial antiquity: woodmen, it was said, had found them beneath the roots of oak-trees; shepherds by a dolmen or a fairy spring. Already the Church of France was sufficiently conscious of its history to demand antiquity in the material objects of its cult.[2]

The cathedrals already had their treasures: silks from Syria, ivories from Byzantium; shrines and chalices[3] inlaid with garnets like the brooches and sword-hilts of Frankish warriors; and, it might be, treasures of gold[4] and hard stone that dated from Roman times.

France was already rich in other churches than cathedrals. The fourth and fifth centuries had been times of evangelization, when baptisteries had risen in most of the greater urban centres: buildings for the most part polygonal or circular in plan, roofed by cupolas on columns, of a type derived from the East.[5] With the gradual grouping of *villae* into villages the parish had been created as a basis of rural life, and from the middle of the seventh century onwards France had been scattered over with parish churches. These had tended to perpetuate the Roman temples in their plan, if in the simplest and most barn-like form,[6] and had often been enriched with mosaic floors that in style and subject alike were Roman.[7] Some, indeed, were traditionally supposed to be on the site and foundations of ancient temples; others enshrined the tomb of the man who had evangelized the district. Saint Chalan, the disciple of St. Patrick who had brought the gospel to remote parts of Berri in the seventh century, lay at Charenton-sur-Cher in a stone sarcophagus[8] chiselled with linear representations of Daniel in the lion's den and a chalice between two griffins, in the same style as the ornament on the buckles of the tribe he had converted; Saint Drausin lay at Soissons in a coffin carved with vines; Saint Bonnet's bones lay in an oaken shrine covered with copper chased in low relief and gilt, and

[1] Ibid., p. 240.

[2] At Chartres and Longpont an undatable tradition makes the cult of the Virgin a continuation of a Druidic cult of a Virgin Mother.

[3] e.g. that at Chelles attributed to Saint Éloi.

[4] Like the plate given to Auxerre by Bishop Didier *c.* 560. Labarte, *Histoire des arts industriels*, i. 426.

[5] Surviving examples are the Temple-Saint-Jean at Poitiers, fourth century with seventh-century additions, and the Baptistery at Fréjus, fifth century.

[6] e.g. Saint-Martin de Moissac, built probably in the sixth century, possibly on Gallo-Roman foundations. It was partly rebuilt in Carolingian times and again restored in the fourteenth century. Another plain and early church is Notre-Dame de la Vallée Française, near Saint-Jean-du-Gard.

[7] e.g. the early church of Saint-Geniès de Thiers, built in 575. The mosaics have medallions with a stag, a lion, a man riding a sea monster, a snail, a basilisk, and a peacock.

[8] Now in the Musée du Berry at Bourges.

set with a cross inlaid with garnets, on the altar of his church at Saint-Bonnet Avalouze;[1] Saint Alain rested at Lavaur in a marble tomb carved with panels of foliage:[2] and these were but four in a noble army of martyrs.

The churches of France had for the most part been built or rebuilt in Carolingian times, with walls of *petit appareil*: small stones set close and held together by courses of larger stones. The decoration lay in the patterns made by the stonework, which was sometimes elaborated into decorative inlays, and in the accentuation of the courses of larger stones, which were sometimes developed as a projecting string course with gable-like triangles between the windows.[3] Sculpture was rare; when it occurred it usually copied in low relief the Irish interlaced patterns which monks were using to adorn their illuminated manuscripts in the new monasteries of France.[4] Exceptionally a church might follow the domical plan generally reserved for baptisteries. When the abbot of Fleury rebuilt the church of Germigny-les-Prés between 798 and 818, he designed it as a square with an apse in each side and lesser compartments at the angles, with a central cupola: a thoroughly Eastern plan.[5]

Important as were the cathedrals, and numerous as were the parish churches, they took second place in French civilization to the great monasteries of the land. Monasticism had reached Gaul in a primitive and oriental form as early as the fourth century; and though by Capetian times the south-eastern centres of the Île de Lérins and Saint-Victor de Marseille were in Imperial territory, Ligugé, that had been founded in 360, Marmoutiers, founded in 371, and Saint-Martin de Tours lay in the heart of France. These primitive foundations had been increased by such royal endowments as Saint-Vincent at the gates of Paris (later to be known as Saint-Germain-des-Prés), Saint-Médard at Soissons, and Sainte-Croix at Poitiers. In 585 St. Columban had come to Gaul with twelve monks from Bangor and had founded four monasteries of which Luxeuil was the greatest. His coming had initiated a great era of monastic building; in the hundred and fifty years that followed nearly two hundred abbeys had been built. Mont-Saint-Michel had been founded because St. Michael appeared to Saint Aubert, Bishop of Avranches, bidding him build a church on the island of Mont Tombe, where an ancient tradition held that the souls of the dead rested

[1] It dates from the first half of the seventh century. In 722 the body of Saint Bonnet was borne from the abbey of Saint-Pierre de Lyon to Clermont-Ferrand, and every village where the procession stopped took the saint's name.

[2] Now in the hospital at Lavaur.

[3] These are now best represented by Savenières, Distré, and Gennes in the department of Maine-et-Loire, and by Cravant, Saint-Généroux, Chanceaux, and parts of Azay-le-Rideau, Indre-et-Loire.

[4] e.g. a sculptured door-jamb at Cravant, and a square pillar in the crypt of the abbey church of Flavigny. On the later capitals in the style see Courajod, i. 234.

[5] The church was cruelly restored in the middle of the nineteenth century, and the inscription giving its dedication date is false. See Bréhier, p. 129.

in eternal sleep. Some monasteries had risen, like Cluny, on land that had been given by a feudal lord whose conscience was uneasy; many, like La Voulte Chilhac and Saint-Michel de Tonnerre, on the ancestral estates of a man who had entered religion and brought his property with him into the community. A priory dedicated to Saint Honorat of Arles had been founded among the ruins of a Roman thermal station, Aquae Nisincii, in the Nièvre [1] An abbey had become attached to the great Visigothic church of Sainte-Marie at Toulouse, called La Daurade from the golden background of its mosaics. Sometimes monasteries had grown up beside Merovingian oratories or basilicas that had been raised over the tombs of saints: such were the houses of Saint-Germain at Auxerre, Saint-Bénigne at Dijon, Saint-Martial at Limoges, Saint-Médard at Soissons, and Saint-Rémi at Rheims. Most often, however, the monasteries had been built *de novo*, with churches on a basilican plan, wooden-roofed, with the traditional single or triple apse lengthened by a bay to give room for the *chorus psallentium*.

These monasteries resembled the great monasteries of Syria, such as Qalaat Seman, rather than any group of Roman buildings.[2] The greatest of the numerous churches which each monastery included usually had its basilican plan modified into a cruciform scheme with a cloister between two of the arms: a plan found at Qalaat Seman itself. Their infirmary chapels and lesser oratories;[3] their gables and towers[4] and wide enclosures, all went back in tradition if not in actual style to the coenobite communities which had held both the world and alien enemies at bay on the barren hill-sides of North Syria. The rule which was followed within their walls was based on the Eastern rules of Pachomius and Basil, as well as on the reforms of Benedict; and like the Syrian houses they

[1] Now Saint-Honoré-les-Bains.

[2] The analogy was first pointed out by the Marquis de Vogüé, *La Syrie centrale*, p. 21.

[3] These secondary chapels continued to exist in many monasteries in the Romanesque and Gothic periods. Cluny is a notable example. The seventeenth-century illustrations of the *Monasticon Gallicanum* show secondary chapels still existing at the Benedictine monasteries of Saint-Pierre-sur-Dive, Saint-Pierre de Ferrières, Saint-Nicolas d'Angers, Saint-Sauveur-de-l'Évière d'Angers, Saint-Jean de Château-Gontier, Saint-Clément de Craon, Saint-Maur-sur-Loire, Saint-Maur-de-Glanfeuil, Saint-Florent de Saumur, La Couture du Mans, Saint-Vincent du Mans, Saint-Melaine de Rennes, Cormery (three chapels), Marmoutiers, Saint-André de Villeneuve-lès-Avignon, Bassac, Saint-Allyre de Clermont (two chapels), Saint-Bénigne de Dijon, Ambronay, La Trinité de Vendôme, Notre-Dame de Coulombs, Saint-Pierre de Rebais, Saint-Germain-des-Prés, Corbie (two chapels), Saint-Valéry-sur-Mer, Saint-Jean de Laon, Saint-Nicolas-aux-Bois, Mont-Saint-Quentin, Saint-Vigor de Bayeux, Saint-Taurin d'Évreux, Notre-Dame d'Ivry, Notre-Dame de Lyre, Bec, La Trinité de Fécamp, Jumièges, Saint-Ouen de Rouen, Saint-Michel du Tréport, and Saint-Wandrille (four chapels). In some cases a subsidiary chapel had come to be used as a parish church; in others (not included in this list) it had been rebuilt as a Lady Chapel attached to the abbey church.

[4] Though towers are found in the monasteries of Syria (e.g. at Kasr-el-Banat, and on the façade of Qalaat Seman) the use of them for bells is regarded as a French invention of the fifth century. Hubert, p. 83.

had armed enemies as well as the contagion of the world from which to defend themselves.

These monasteries were for the most part on a large scale, like their Eastern prototypes. When Queen Bathilde founded Jumièges in 654, Saint Philibert, who likewise built Noirmoûtier and Saint-Michel-en-l'Herm, planned it with three churches: a cruciform basilica dedicated to the Virgin, with a lesser church to the south dedicated to St. Peter and another to the north dedicated to Saint Germain and Saint Denis. There were two dormitories two hundred and ninety feet long and fifty feet wide, to house seventy monks, with refectories and kitchens beneath. When Fontenelle was rebuilt between 807 and 883 it had a great church dedicated to St. Peter, a lesser church, and a burial church and several oratories outside the actual cloister but within the enclosure. Corbie in Picardy was built in the ninth century on a yet grander scale. A great wall enclosed the precincts, which were wide enough to give shelter to the abbey vassals when danger threatened. The monks had three basilicas for their worship and four oratories for their prayers. They had quarters for between three and four hundred monks and a hundred and fifty lay brethren: chapter-house, cellars, kitchens, refectories, and guest-house with quarters for bishops, lords, monks, clerks, and wayfarers, with a separate oratory for each. The monks had their own workmen: cobblers and fullers, smiths and harness-makers, masons and carpenters, founders and woodcarvers, brewers and gardeners.[1] The monks prepared their own parchment and copied and illuminated the books for their own library.

Such monastic scriptoria, indeed, were the chief centres of artistic creation in Carolingian times. Every great monastery had its writing-room,[2] where manuscripts were produced that not only perpetuated the texts of classical and patristic authors but also established a Carolingian artistic style: a style of rather ungainly magnificence, with Eastern glories of transparent purple and burnished gold, in which the rival influences of Byzantium and Syria and Rome and Ireland seem to be for ever at war. The style of such manuscripts was reflected in the decoration of the monastery churches: in such wall-paintings as the allegorical figures of the earth and the winds that were painted on the refectory walls at Fleury;[3] in such mosaics as the cherubim with the ark of the covenant that the Abbot of Fleury set in the church of Germigny-les-Prés; in such shrines as that called

[1] Farther south the monks cultivated their own vineyards and vintaged their own grapes; the famous *vigne du Clos de Bèze* had been tended since 630 by the members of the abbey of Bèze.

[2] Important centres in France were Ferrières, Saint-Josse-sur-Mer, Saint-Bénigne de Dijon, Saint-Martin de Tours, Marmoutiers, Saint-Denis, Fleury, Rheims, Corbie, and Luxeuil.

[3] Focillon, p. 10; cf. the hanging with the same subject given to Saint-Denis by Adelaide wife of Hugues Capet. Muntz, p. 84. Mid-ninth-century paintings of St. Stephen and of bishops still survive in the crypt of Saint-Germain d'Auxerre. Hubert, p. 120. There is some evidence to suggest that the greater Carolingian monasteries had windows filled with stained glass. Ibid., p. 127.

Saint Mommole's at Fleury with more cherubim; and in long inscriptions in
leonine verse that were like the pages from a manuscript that had been transferred to a wall.

The chief building of a Carolingian monastery was always and necessarily
the abbey church, as the home of the liturgical prayer that was the reason of
the community's being. Most of such churches were true basilicas such as still
survive in Rome, with aisles and a triple apse. The church of the abbey of
Saint-Martin d'Autun, that was built between 589 and 600 and survived up to
1714, may serve as an example. Its aisles were divided from the nave by four
antique marble columns on either side; its wooden roofs were handsomely
carved and painted within; its walls, made like the Roman gates of Autun of
dressed stone clamped together without mortar, were covered inside with
mosaics.[1]

Until the middle of the eighth century such churches had been adorned with
capitals, bases and columns drawn from the ruins of Roman buildings.[2] When
the abbot rebuilt Saint-Germain d'Auxerre in 850 he had to send monks as far
as Arles and Marseilles to find the necessary ancient marbles. As the supply of
Roman material became exhausted, men had to learn to hew and carve anew;
and as new work, fitted to its particular use, became a possibility, the re-use of
old sculpture and cut stone gradually went out of fashion. When the apse of
Saint-Denis had been rebuilt between 623 and 625 it had been constructed
almost entirely from ancient remains; but when the whole basilica was renewed
by Abbot Fulrad and Pepin the Short about 750, it was, but for its marble
columns, built of new dressed stone, with a wooden roof and a sculptured
cancellum, high and dark, to shut off the choir.

The treasures of this church had in Carolingian times been among the richest
in France,[3] and these riches survived into the Capetian age. The chief altar in
the old apse was sheltered by a great ciborium given by Abbot Fardulf, beneath
which hung a golden lamp given by Charles the Bald. The altar frontal,[4]

---

[1] Hubert, pp. 12, 47. I regret that I cannot follow M. Bréhier (p. 202) in accepting the head of
Christ, now in the church of Saint-Pantaléon at Autun, as that of the Crucifix of Saint Odo from
Saint-Martin's. It is, I think, Spanish, and some century and a half later than Saint Odo.

[2] e.g. the crypt of Saint-Paul de Jouarre, 630-4. A late example is the oldest part of the crypt of
the Couture du Mans, begun in 995 and finished in the eleventh century. On exceptional sites the
practice continued even into the Middle Ages. The chapel of Notre-Dame du Haut Solier, near Saint-
Paulien in the Velay, was built in Romanesque times out of the fragments of Roman buildings, and
Saint-Lubin Suèvres, in Touraine, was built over the ruins of a Roman temple and with its stones.

[3] See L. Levillain in *Mém. Soc. Hist. Paris*, 1909, xxxvi. 143; W. M. Conway in *Archaeologia*, lxvi
(1915), p. 104. A further study of the treasure of Saint-Denis is promised by Comte Blaise de Montesquiou Fezensac. Some may have been made within the abbey itself; a letter written by Loup, Abbot
of Ferrières, in the first half of the ninth century, expresses his gratitude for the admission of two
of his young monks to the goldsmiths' school of Saint-Denis.

[4] Represented in the picture by a fifteenth-century French master, *The Mass of St. Giles,* in the

likewise his gift, was of richly jewelled gold, with figures of Christ seated in glory between figures of apostles under arcades. On the altar itself stood a strange votive gift, the *Escrin de Charlemagne*: a kind of high arcaded frame, richly jewelled and set with antique cameos and intaglios, that served to display their riches and to crown a reliquary.[1] A second altar, in the new apse, was faced with porphyry; over it hung seven lamps of gold. The tomb of Charles the Bald, to whose generosity the greater part of these riches was due, stood between the two altars, surmounted by an enormous jewelled cross. The lectern was an eagle of gilt bronze. The monks' stalls were of marble and bronze: magnificent, but cold. Every ritual necessity of the church, vestments and hangings, gospel books and the vessels of the Mass, reliquaries that on feast days lay upon the altar, were stored in the sacristy in unparalleled magnificence. The riches of the Carolingian Empire lay piled there: silks from Persia and Syria, ivories from Byzantium, unicorn's horns from Harun al Raschid's treasury, loot from the palaces of Sassanian kings, pearls and emeralds from India, carved stones that had survived the Roman Empire, and glass and porphyry and crystal that had been taken from the tombs of Egypt.

The stormy time that lay like a gulf between the France of Charlemagne and the France of Hugues Capet did not destroy everything. The Normans had first taken Rouen in 841, two years before Charles the Bald had been crowned as the first King of France; by 844 they had reached Toulouse, and in the next year had sacked Paris. For more than seventy years they ravaged France, but they did not ravage all France. With their conversion to Christianity after 911 civilization began to return to the north. The ninth century had witnessed an almost total extinction of trade: Arab invasions, Breton and Aquitanian revolts had aided the conquering Northmen in their destruction of the highly organized framework of Carolingian society. Yet on the self-sufficing monastic estates life had gone on, and had gone on with a clear recollection of past grandeur. Fleury, that had saved the body of Saint Benedict from the invaders of Monte Cassino, was even rich. Tournus, that had sheltered the body of Saint Philibert from Noirmoûtier, was at least prosperous.

Cluny, that had been founded in 910, was becoming a great reforming force; between 936 and his death in 944 its abbot, St. Odo, had revived no less than nine ancient monasteries in France, and between 954 and 994 his successor, Saint Mayeul, had reformed six more and died on his way to reform Saint-Denis itself. The Magyars had ravaged Burgundy and the valley of the Saône in 955, but they did not touch the monasteries that lay off the main highways. Even

National Gallery. Similar frontals were by the end of the ninth century likewise owned by the abbey of Saint-Germain-des-Prés, Luxeuil, Saint-Germer-de-Fly, Saint-Wandrille, Saint-Sauveur de Redon, and Saint-Rémi de Reims. Hubert, p. 130.

[1] A fragment survives in the Bibliothèque Nationale with an intaglio of Julia, daughter of Titus.

the monasteries that were materially destroyed were capable of rebirth. Their churches might suffer swift and dreadful destruction by fire, and the slower and more inevitable destruction of their ruins by time. The cubes of mosaic might slip away into the nettles beneath, the painted plaster flake off like bark from a dead tree, winter snow and summer thunderstorm bring down each year more of cornice and apse; but one day the monks would come back from the distant house where they had taken refuge, their black robes dusty from the roads, their skirts stained by the rank wayside weeds, but the saint's shrine in its travelling-case of leather safely borne, like a corpse upon a bier, upon their shoulders. The soundest part of the old church was soon repaired with boughs and hurdles to give the relic shelter; and then the abbot and the mason, who might be no more than a builder of farm walls, would set about prodding and probing, designing on a scrap of parchment and with sticks and strings upon the ground, to determine how the new church should lie: mended or built anew, smaller or larger, on the old plan or on some new scheme that the abbot had seen or heard of on his travels. Sometimes, indeed, the very expulsion of the monks from their home led to the foundation of a new monastery, that lived on as a dependency when the community returned to the mother house: Chablis was thus founded when the monks of Tours had to fly before the Normans with the body of Saint Martin.[1] More rarely the monastery that had given shelter to a shrine in exile refused to give it up: Vézelay had sheltered the relics of the Magdalene that had been brought into Burgundy from Saint-Maximin in Provence to escape the Saracen invasion; the abbey kept them, and grew to be a great centre of pilgrimage in virtue of their possession.

All told, from the French side of the Pyrenees to Normandy, there were four hundred and seventy-four abbeys and collegiate churches in France at the end of the tenth century, and of these only sixty were still ruined. The dioceses most richly endowed with such foundations were Rheims, Limoges, and Autun, each with fifteen, Paris, Clermont, and Bourges, each with twenty-one, and Le Mans, Langres, and Tours, each with sixteen.[2] The great barons, still unsubdued in power and undiminished in wealth by monarchical supremacy, seconded the efforts of the ecclesiastics in restoring and rebuilding the churches of France. When Foulques Nerra succeeded to the county of Anjou in 987 the cathedral

[1] The church door at Chablis is still studded with horseshoes dedicated to the saint by pilgrims and travellers safeguarded by his protection.

[2] Lot, p. 427. The diocese of Amiens had 11, Beauvais 6, Châlons-sur-Marne 5, Laon 6, Noyon 7, Rheims 15, Soissons 12, Auxerre 13, Chartres 13, Meaux 12, Nevers 9, Orleans 12, Paris 21, Sens 14, Troyes 8. In Normandy Avranches had 1, Bayeux 3, Coutances 4, Évreux 2, Lisieux 2, Rouen 12, Séez 1. In Touraine Angers had 7, Le Mans 16, Nantes 2, Rennes 2, Tours 16. Autun had 15, Chalon-sur-Saône 8, Langres 16, Macon 7, Bourges 21, Cahors 4, Albi 4, Clermont 21, Limoges 15, Mende 3 (all ruined), Le Puy 5, and Rodez 4. There were 38 in the province of Bordeaux, 24 in that of Auch, and 55 in the Narbonnais on the French side of the Pyrenees.

of Angers was in ruins and most of the monasteries were in a parlous state. He and his successor helped to rebuild the cathedral and to re-establish the monasteries of Saint-Maur-de-Glanfeuil, Chalonnes, Saint-Serge d'Angers, Saint-Florent de Saumur, and Saint-Florentin d'Amboise. Furthermore he and his son founded new abbeys at Beaulieu near Loches, Saint-Nicolas d'Angers, the Trinité de Vendôme, and a collegiate church at Saint-Laud d'Angers, while his wife founded a great nunnery at La Ronceray d'Angers.[1]

Similar restoration and rebuilding were taking place everywhere in the tenth century: in the south at Saint-Barnard-de-Romans, at Cruas, at Notre-Dame de Vallée Française, at Le Puy; in the west at La Réole, rebuilt in 977 after its destruction by the Normans; in the north at Saint-Pierre de Jumièges in 930 and at Montier-en-Der between 900 and 922; in the centre, at Cluny and Charlieu and Souvigny.

These monasteries marked the beginning of a new era in the history alike of architecture and of monasticism. In every instance the new building bore witness that the Benedictine ideal of the monastic family had vanquished the oriental ideal of the monastic town. Instead of a multiplicity of churches and oratories there was a single abbey church; the monastery might or might not have a hospital chapel and a single oratory as separate buildings. Consequently this abbey church tended to be much larger, and its architecture, however simple, had an experimental quality that held possibilities of progress. At Jumièges and Montier-en-Der the heavy square piers are surmounted by little galleried recesses, that are the ancestors of the triforia of the Middle Ages, and have crude Corinthian capitals, that prefigure the sculptured enrichments of the Romanesque style. At Marcilhac, in the second half of the tenth century,[2] the reticulated work above the door was set with small sculptured slabs of stone, carved with figures of Christ blessing, between the sun and moon. Below are angels, and at the bottom St. Peter and St. Paul, the patrons of the monastery. The carving is ludicrous in its crudeness; the composition is as incoherent as dominoes scattered on a table; yet in this triangular composition with Christ enthroned in the centre lies the germ of all the great Gothic portals.

So, too, the foundations of France's literary history were being laid. Towards the end of the tenth century churchmen once more had time to turn to literary studies,[3] and even to humanistic learning; and these studies inspired them to literary creation. Abbot Odo of Cluny wrote hymns and sermons in verse and prose, and he was but one of a host of Benedictines who essayed composition in

---

[1] Halphen, pp. 81 et seqq.

[2] After examining the sculptures I cannot accept the view of MM. Deshoulières and Deschamps that they were carved *après pose*.

[3] See Adhémar, p. 16.

Latin. French itself was taking form as a literary language with poems on the Passion and lives of Saints that were the vernacular equivalent of such Latin works.

With the coronation of Hugues Capet in 987 this new national basis of French civilization received, unconsciously enough, its political expression. The shadowy rule of the Carolingian kings had marked the decline of an empire; the hardly less shadowy rule of Hugues differed chiefly because it marked the beginning of a kingdom. It has been said that the tenth century produced no great men. Hugues Capet is not one in the judgement of history; but he was great enough to be elected King of France on grounds not of heredity, but of merit; and down to 1792 his descendants ruled France in virtue of that election.

He was a feudal baron, *oint des saintes huiles*, at the head of a feudal system of a traditional complexity that had given up the conception of personal vassalship and was settling down on a new basis of feudal duty based on the possession of land. He was the head of a state as yet inchoate; it had a literature and an art that were as yet not national, but were capable of national development. The land had hardly emerged from a stormy era of invasion; but Normans and Hungarians had both been baptized Christians and had both made their chief centres outside France. That other menace, Arab Spain, was beginning to break up. Two years after the accession of Hugues Capet the first Peace of God was proclaimed to check the ravages of feudal war.

The time had come when prosperity could once more spin the thin thread of French civilization, tangled, knotted, yet unbroken, into full roundness and strength. The architectural style that France already shared in common with the civilized parts of western Europe could develop as French Romanesque. Carolingian elements were still dominant: cathedrals and monasteries still had their towers; the small stones set endwise and the abundant mortar of *petit appareil* were still in common use, though the courses of larger stones were given less decorative importance; interlaced ornament was still widely used, as it was to be for a century more in such districts as Berri; a chevron moulding, based on the familiar Carolingian triangular decoration, was everywhere employed, sometimes chipped on the edge of a square member, sometimes simple and sometimes elaborate in profile, single, double, triple, or quadruple, in increasing elaboration with the progress of time. Already, however, the provinces were beginning to show their local styles. In the centre and south Roman models encouraged men to attempt the sculpture of human figures and leafage; in Normandy there was a liking for strange mouldings of birds' heads like the decoration of northern brooches;[1] in Champagne and Burgundy there was a more experimental attitude to pure architecture than elsewhere; in Auvergne

---

[1] Cf. the later examples at Rots and Saint-Contest, Calvados.

petit appareil was being developed as a decorative inlay;[1] in the valley of the Loire the elements of Carolingian classicism still lingered on. Everywhere men were planning and measuring, hewing and planing, for the abbeys and churches that were to house God in His land of France.

[1] For other classical and Gallo-Roman survivals in Auvergnat Romanesque see Bréhier in *Revue d'Auvergne*, xl, Clermont-Ferrand, 1923, p. 53.

II

THE BENEDICTINES

1. THE BENEDICTINE CHURCH

IN 670[1] the Council of Autun decreed that all the monasteries of France should follow the Benedictine Rule. This was already accepted at Saint-Rémi de Reims, Marmoutiers, and Saint-Denis; but elsewhere, at Limoges, at Saint-Symphorien d'Autun, at Jumièges, and at Fleury, the rules of Cassian or Basil or Anthony or Colomban, or some combination of them,[2] had as yet hardly been modified by Benedictine influence. Such influence, indeed, proved slower in its action in France than it had been in Italy. At last the Carolingian desire for uniformity led to a codification of the rule, at the hands of St. Benedict of Aniane, and the Council of Aix-la-Chapelle in 817 imposed this code upon the monasteries of the Empire. Even then the ninth-century invasions undermined this uniformity. When in 909 Odo and his friend Adhegrin set out from Tours to find a monastery where religious fervour still glowed, where the Benedictine vows of poverty, chastity, and obedience were still kept, they had to travel as far as a remote valley of Jura before they found at Baume the community they sought.[3]

It was Berno, the Abbot of Baume, who in 910 was summoned to the foundation of Cluny by William of Aquitaine; it was Odo who in 926 succeeded him as abbot. Cluny was poor; it had no ancient history; it lay on no great route of trade or pilgrimage; but in virtue of the greatness of its abbot, the strictness of its rule, its temporal freedom and its spiritual aristocracy, it gave new life to Benedictine monachism up and down France. Abbot Odo was called upon to reform or revive the monasteries of Saint-Austremoine at Clermont, Saint-Pierre-le-Vif at Sens, Saint-Martin at Tulle, Saint-Pierre at Lézat, Saint-Sauveur at Sarlat, Saint-Martial at Limoges, Saint-Sore at Genouillac, Saint-Benoît at Fleury, Saint-Julien at Tours: the thin and stunted little man, with a few books hung in a bag at his saddle-bow, rode on his mule from province to province with a couple of monks in dusty black for escort, and restored the whole monastic system.

The next abbot, Aymar, had to devote himself to the affairs of his own abbey, but his successor, Mayeul, continued Odo's work of reform. Some of the monasteries, already reformed by Odo, had slipped back, and were once more given new life; Marmoutiers, Saint-Germain d'Auxerre, Saint-Maur-des-Fossés, and Saint-Bénigne de Dijon were added to the number. Mayeul died at the Cluniac monastery of Souvigny on his way to reform Saint-Denis.

---

[1] Or possibly 663.   [2] See Leclercq, pp. 28 et seqq.   [3] See Joan Evans, *Mon. Life*, p. 1.

The reign of Hugues Capet thus witnessed the completion of a Benedictine revival and the beginning of a great age of monastic building. Much of this building was encouraged by royal benefactors: Hugues Capet advised his son Robert 'never to displease that sure friend, the great St. Benedict'.[1] At first men were haunted by the memory of the glories that had been, and began to build on a scale so magnificent that it could not be sustained. In 1005 Abbot Airard planned and began a new church for Saint-Rémi de Reims that should have rivalled the greatest Carolingian basilicas; but his successor, knowing that it was hopeless to try to complete it, had it pulled down and built more modestly, using the columns and hewn stone afresh.[2]

The Benedictine Rule had never rigidly prescribed the form that monastic buildings should take, but an ancient tradition and the immutable ways of Benedictine life had already established a classic plan of church, chapter-house, refectory, kitchen and cellars, dorters, hospital, and guest-house.

The whole framework of the Benedictine day reposed on the obligation of liturgical prayer. The Regular Hours were sung in the abbey church at times measured from the dawn, varying only when the seasons compelled it: Matins, ending at sunrise, Lauds, beginning then, Prime an hour after, Terce two hours later, Sext three hours later, Nones three hours after that, Vespers at sunset, Compline at nightfall, and Nocturns and Vigils in the course of the night. The abbey church was thus always and necessarily the centre of community life; it had to hold the choir of monks at every canonical service, and a general congregation might be admitted to part of the church outside the claustral enclosure on feast days. Consequently its chief development was all at the eastern end of the church, where the monks sat, and the development of the nave was a matter that depended on local conditions.

The design of such abbey churches was thus partly dictated by tradition and partly by use; the final word rested with the abbot and his chapter. There does not seem to have been any attempt at symbolism in the actual plan of the church. In 1029 Adémar de Chabannes preached a sermon at Saint-Martial de Limoges on the dedication festival of the church of Saint-Sauveur. His theme was the symbolism of Christian architecture. He spoke first on the symbolism of the dedication, then on the twelve hanging lights as symbols of the Apostles; but he said nothing of a possible symbolism in the actual building.[3] More than a hundred years later Abbot Suger, rebuilding his great church at Saint-Denis, found no more symbolic meaning than that the twelve great columns signified the apostles and the lesser ones the prophets their forerunners.[4]

The work of building was carried out by lay masons and stonecarvers, not

---

[1] Chénesseau, p. 16.   [2] Lasteyrie, *Arch. Rom.*, p. 158.
[3] Mortet, i. 80.
[4] *De consecratione ecclesiae S. Dionysii*, § 5.

by the monks, but monastic direction sufficed to set a characteristic stamp upon the plan of the building and the iconography of the ornament. On the technical side, however, the style both of building and sculpture was normally that of the locality. In the course of the tenth and eleventh centuries bodies of artisans came to settle 'under the monastery', holding only their house and garden and labouring not in fields but in workshops; thus most monasteries had local labour to call upon, or could invite settlers for the purpose. An eleventh-century contract between the Abbot of Saint-Aubin d'Angers and a serf, Fulk, belonging to the abbey, agrees that Fulk is to paint the whole church as the chapter shall direct, and to make glass windows for it. In return he is to become a freeman and a lay brother, and to have possession of an acre of vineyard and a house for his life, with a possible extension if he has a son who knows the art and can serve Saint-Aubin in the same way.[1]

It was the Benedictine ideal to be self-supporting: a reasonably endowed monastery bought nothing but cheap cloth of local manufacture for the monks' habits. Similarly it called upon local builders to erect a church, but since what they built was a house of God, it demanded their finest work. Exceptionally a team of workmen moved on from one abbey church to another; those from Saint-Bénigne de Dijon were sent on at the abbot's request to Fécamp. The Benedictine Rule decreed: 'artifices si sint in monasterio cum omni humilitate faciunt istas artes': there are a few instances of such monkish workmen being engaged on work, usually wall-painting, in an abbey church, but they remain exceptions.[2] Workmen, however, were often lodged in special quarters in an abbey when they were working for it, and such buildings are mentioned in the early descriptions of Cluny. Weavers were engaged by the Abbot of Saint-Florent de Saumur in 990 to weave woollen hangings for the church, adorned with elephants and lions and birds, and were lodged by the abbey. In the absence of the abbot the cellarer refused them their customary ration of wine, and they wove the patterns awry in protest.[3]

The traditional basilican plan of an aisled church with a triple apse was that commonly used in the Benedictine Order in the early Middle Ages. The two towers, that already formed part of the traditional plan, continued to give dignity to the western end and support to the high gable of the nave (Fig. 1). At Jumièges, for example, when they had their steeples, they were more than a hundred and sixty-five feet high on a base some twenty-eight feet by twenty-two. Their base is a fortress, but the summit rises like a prayer. Another tower

[1] Mortet, i. 264; drawn up between 1082 and 1106.

[2] See Swartwout, p. 54. When Fleury was rebuilt after a fire in 1026, many workmen, whose names have been preserved, suffered from accidents and were healed or saved by the power of St. Benedict. Among them there is only one undoubted monk, Odolric of Saint-Julien de Tours, who fell from the scaffolding when painting the vaults of the church.

[3] Hubert, p. 125.

usually rose over the crossing,[1] and in exceptionally large churches there might be subsidiary towers in the transept, making five in all.[2]

The central apse was very considerably lengthened to hold the choir of monks, and the side apses, almost equally long, were linked to the central apse by an arcade in the dividing walls. The extended *chevet* was generally entered from a transept which might or might not have subsidiary absidioles.[3] This Benedictine plan was arrived at by a series of experiments. The church dedicated at Souvigny in 920 or 921 had instead of an arcade a curious arrangement of semicircular niches in the choir; at Saint-Jean d'Abbetot there are some seats in an arcade; at the second church at Cluny, begun about 955 and dedicated in 981, there were additional rectangular chapels in the angles between the apse and the transept.[4] At Notre-Dame de la Ronceray at Angers,[5] consecrated in 1028, at Bourbon-Lancy, built in about 1040, and in the contemporary church of Champvoux, the plan is typical and complete[6] (Fig. 2). In a simpler form—as for instance at Saint-Cydroine—it has an aisleless nave.

It was a plan that, wherever it was first conceived, received the approval of the Cluniac reformers. William of Volpiano, the Lombard monk of Cluny who was sent with eleven brethren to reform Saint-Bénigne de Dijon, used it for all the purely monastic churches that he built: slightly simplified at Salmaise, soon after 1010, and at Saint-Mesmin;[7] enriched with two absidioles in each arm of the transept at Bernay about 1025; and, it may well be, in the new church of Saint-Germain-des-Prés at Paris, rebuilt at this time after having been five times destroyed by the Normans. At Jumièges, likewise reformed by Abbot William, the rebuilding of the church was not begun until nine years after his death in 1031.[8] Robert Champart, the abbot, began at the east end, but the choir was rebuilt in the thirteenth century.[9] The nave remains (Fig. 3) remarkable for its height in three stories, its plan in bays each of two units, and the

[1] Morienval has one at the façade and one each side of the central apse, but this is not a common arrangement.

[2] e.g. Saint-Germain-des-Prés, 1005.

[3] See Lefèvre-Pontalis in *Bull. Mon.* lxxvi, 1912, p. 440.

[4] I follow Professor Conant's reconstruction which he generously allowed me to reproduce in *Rom. Arch. Ord. Clun.*, p. 63. These side-chapels may be reflected in the flat ends to the flanking apses at Lessay and Cérisy-la-Forêt.

[5] Always a 'noble' house, its members, though they took Benedictine vows, were not strictly enclosed.

[6] As it is outside France in the Cluniac churches of Romainmôtier in Switzerland, before 1026, and Gigny in the Jura, mid-eleventh century. Later instances in France are Saint-Martin d'Angers, Mauriac (founded 1053), Peyrusse-Grande, Blet, Châteaumeillant, Plaimpied, La-Celle-Bruère, Saint-Genou, and others.

[7] See *Bull. Mon.* lxxx, 1921, p. 18.

[8] It was dedicated in 1067.

[9] The eleventh-century choir seems to have had a kind of ambulatory like that of the second church at Cluny. See *Bull. Mon.* lxxvii, 1928, p. 108.

noble simplicity of its design. The aisles and the triforium over them have vaults of groin-vaulted stone;[1] their solidity makes the lofty walls of the nave possible, for these are crowned only by a wooden roof. There is little sculptured decoration, yet it is hardly missed. The same bare beauty is visible in the two great abbeys at Caen which William the Conqueror founded in 1061 when a Truce of God brought peace to Normandy:[2] the Abbaye aux Hommes, dedicated to St. Stephen, and the Abbaye aux Dames, dedicated to the Trinity. Lanfranc, who was Abbot of St. Stephen's, planned it on a yet grander scale than Jumièges. Its scheme is more elaborate; its arches and string-courses are enriched with sculptured mouldings; its height is yet more impressive.[3] At La Trinité even the crypt has fine sculptured capitals, more or less Corinthian in scheme; but in spite of such enrichments the essentials remain unchanged.

Such churches were planned from the high altar outwards; their exterior was of an extreme simplicity. Buttresses, arcades, pilaster strips, and cornices might be stressed to give proportion to the whole, but down to 1100 there was an almost total absence of external ornament in Benedictine churches.

Already there were schools of workmen who could be called upon for buildings on this great scale and men experienced in the planning of them. When Saint-Rémi de Reims was rebuilt between 1005 and 1049 *viri architecturae periti* were employed by the abbot.[4] When William, Abbot of Le Monastier Saint-Chaffre between 1074 and 1086, wished to rebuild his church, he asked Abbot Hugh of Cluny for advice, and summoned skilled craftsmen from various regions to execute the plans.[5] Since each Benedictine abbey was autonomous and independent the variety in architectural and sculptural style was considerable. Gradually, however, Cluny, that from the beginning had reformed other abbeys, came not only to own a number of newly founded priories but also to absorb a number of older abbeys into what had become an order of Cluny within the greater Order of St. Benedict. The tendency first became evident under Mayeul's successor, Odilo, abbot from 994 to 1049, and reached its height under Hugh, abbot from Odilo's death until 1109.[6] Each of these subsidiary

---

[1] Such stone vaults had come gradually back into use by way of the crypts; one of the earliest surviving is that in the crypt of Saint-Paul de Jouarre, *c.* 847. Other early examples are the crypts of Saint-Médard de Soissons; the sacristy of Senlis; the crypts of Flavigny, Saint-Andoche d'Autun, Saint-Savinien de Sens, Saint-Geosmes, and Saint-Seurin de Bordeaux. Several of these make use of antique columns and capitals. See Bréhier, p. 138.

[2] They were an expiation for his having married within the prohibited degrees without papal dispensation.

[3] A later vault has taken the place of the original wooden roof. The triforium has here a half-barrel vault. The choir was rebuilt in the thirteenth century.

[4] Mortet, i. 40.   [5] Mortet, i. 235.

[6] See Joan Evans, *Mon. Life*, p. 10. The practice was confirmed and sanctioned by Pope Paschal II in 1100.

C

priories owed allegiance to Cluny and obedience to its abbot; and as a consequence a certain uniformity began to appear as a spontaneous expression of this
common allegiance. The second abbey church at Cluny, the work of Saint
Mayeul, served to crystallize the Benedictine plan, and in a simplified form
inspired the churches of the whole Order. The smallest priories had single
apses, the larger triple apses, the next greatest quintuple, and La Charité, the
finest church of all, a sevenfold apse[1] (Fig. 4). This development had a wide
influence outside the Order of Cluny: fivefold apses appear in the Benedictine
churches of Méobecq, Chezal-Benoît, Saint-Amand-de-Boixe, and La Sauve;
and sevenfold ones at Châteaumeillant and Saint-Sever.[2]

Already sculptors were prepared both to imitate the remains of antiquity and
to translate the miniatures of the abbey manuscripts into stone. The monasteries of central and southern France were more dependent on such adornments
than those of the north, for the architectural tradition of their provinces lay
closer to classical architecture. The interlaced ornament of Carolingian times
still continued in use;[3] rough imitations of Corinthian capitals of a debased kind
were attempted;[4] and human and animal figures of one sort and another were
carved with gradually increasing skill. At Champvoux there is a capital with
a flute-player; at Saint-Germain-des-Prés, built between 990 and 1014, one
with Christ in Majesty,[5] obviously copied from a manuscript, and another with
centaurs; at Saint-Maur-de-Glanfeuil, dedicated in 1036, capitals with beaked
birds like those used to form initials in contemporary illuminations. The
capitals incrusted with stucco from Saint-Rémi de Reims, that date from
between 1034 and 1049, represent Samson and the lion and Samson carrying
off the gates of Gaza,[6] subjects that are illustrated in the Catalan Bibles of the
time.[7]

Such sculptured capitals, like all the decoration of the churches, were richest
round the high altar. The choir was the vital centre of the church, and the high
altar was the heart of the choir and the chief reason of its being. Colour was concentrated round it, in the frescoes or mosaics of the apse and in the embroidered
curtains that hung behind it on feast days; light was concentrated on it, in the
hanging lamps and circles of lamps that glimmered above it; and riches were
concentrated upon it, in all the treasures that the abbey accumulated for the

---

[1] See Joan Evans, *Rom. Arch. Ord. Clun.*, chap. i.

[2] See *Bull. Mon.* lxxvi, 1912, p. 464, and lxxx, 1929, p. 35.

[3] e.g. at Ris, built by Abbot Odilo of Cluny, and the eleventh-century parts of the tower of Brantôme.

[4] e.g. at Champvoux, Saint-Germain-des-Prés, piers of crossing (1047) at the Abbaye-aux-Dames,
Saintes.   [5] Now in the Musée de Cluny, Paris.

[6] See Deshoulières, *Au début de l'art roman*, p. 63.

[7] See W. Neuss, *Die katalanische Bibelillustration in der Wende des elften Jahrhunderts*, Bonn and
Leipzig, 1922, p. 51.

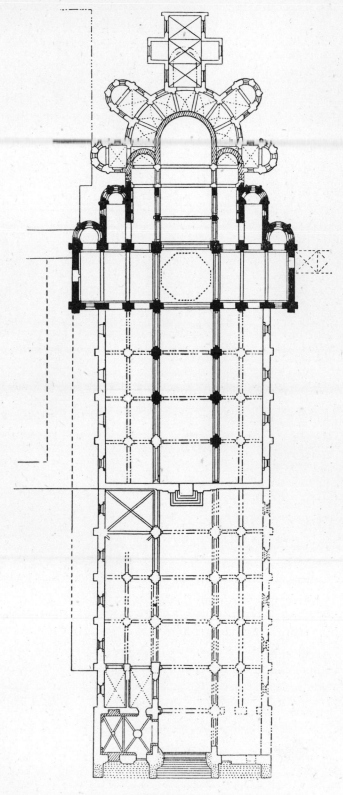

PLAN 1

Cluniac abbey church of La Charité-sur-Loire, Nièvre. Consecrated 1107, the apse
modified in the middle of the twelfth century. After Beaussart

ritual uses of its service. Exceptionally, as in the second church at Cluny, a great ciborium of precious metal rose like a canopy above it[1] and altar frontals and *tabulae* of wrought gold or silver glorified it on feast days.

2. MONASTERIES OF PILGRIMAGE

The high altar in its glory, with a dark background of parallel apses behind it, and the *chorus psallentium* enclosed before it, remains the most typical expression of Benedictine monasticism. Yet this plan, logical, lucid, and beautiful though it was, met only the narrower needs of a monastic community. From the beginning of the Middle Ages the great Benedictine houses that enshrined the body of a saint followed another scheme, for besides being monasteries they were also places of pilgrimage.

The abbeys of Saint-Germain at Auxerre, Saint-Bénigne at Dijon, Saint-Martial at Limoges, Saint-Médard at Soissons, Saint-Rémi at Rheims, and Saint-Martin at Tours had enshrined the bodies of their patron saints for many generations; but the true cult of such relics was a development of the ninth, tenth, and eleventh centuries. Not until the end of the eighth century was it permitted to put reliquaries upon the altar itself;[2] not until two centuries later[3] were saints formally canonized. Already, however, a monastery was recognized as being in some sense the personal possession of the saint who lay there. When about 986 the Abbot of Fleury and the Bishop of Orleans quarrelled over the possession of a vineyard, the monks came out in procession with the relics of St. Benedict, the episcopal guardians of the vineyard made way for the saint, and the monks harvested their vintage in peace.[4]

This strong sense of the saint as a living person was undoubtedly fostered by the fact that his relics were often enclosed in a statue. The earliest recorded is one of the Virgin, made of wood, covered with gold, that was ordered for Clermont Cathedral by Bishop Étienne soon after 946.[5] Étienne, a pluralist after the manner of his day, was also abbot of the monastery of Conques, which at the end of the ninth century had acquired the relics of Sainte Foy by a simple process of theft from a monastery at Agen. Étienne proceeded to enshrine them in his turn in a magnificent statue of gold (Fig. 5), representing the saint holding the bed on which she suffered martyrdom.[6] By one of the miracles of

---

[1] None survives in France, but there is still a Romanesque silver ciborium in the Treasury of Gerona in Catalonia. Unfortunately there is no clear distinction in verbal use between a ciborium-vessel and a ciborium canopy that shelters it; both are indiscriminately called ciboria.

[2] Bishop, *Lit. Hist.*, p. 25.   [3] In 995.

[4] Chénesseau, p. 19.

[5] See Bréhier, p. 185.

[6] See *Bull. Mon.* lxxxiv, 1925, p. 5. This statue too was borne in solemn procession round the abbey lands whenever the boundary was in dispute.

history the statue still survives. Ugly and magnificent, it has a strange force and conviction. It is easy to see why men believed that it worked miracles: that a vision of it restored sight to Vuitbert, who was blind; that it appeared as a terrifying apparition to the monk Gerbert, who had kept a little gold that had stuck to a mould in the saint's own workshop; and that it appeared in a dream to Bernard of Angers to demand two golden doves to adorn its throne. Bernard of Angers, indeed, owed some reparation to the saint. When he visited Conques in 1013 he was struck by the likeness of the image to a pagan idol, and wondered whether Sainte Foy and the similar golden Saint Géraud of Aurillac were indeed fit for a Christian church, especially as he saw peasants reverencing them, praying to them, and laying offerings before them. Such scruples carried no weight before the steady and considerable revenues which pilgrims brought to a monastery that could show them something so rich and so remarkable. 'Men's eyes', said the Abbot of Saint-Denis, 'are set under a spell by reliquaries. . . . They see the shining image of a saint and in the imagination of the people his saintliness is proportioned to its brilliance.'[1] The image of Sainte Foy became encrusted with the jewels and brooches, bracelets and belts, that pilgrims had dedicated at her shrine; and the fashion for statue reliquaries spread from Auvergne to other parts of France. A statue of gold of Saint Martial was made for Limoges in 952; he was represented seated, blessing with the right hand and holding a book in the left. The type was that, if not of Christ in Majesty, at least of an apostle; and in a few years the monks of Saint-Martial had invented a legend that their saint had been sent by St. Peter to convert the Limousin. The legend was fought by many rival monasteries, but was finally accepted by the council of Limoges in 1031.[2]

Sometimes a benefactor would give such a shrine to a saint and his monastery. King Robert and Queen Constance decided early in the eleventh century to make such an offering to Saint Savinien at Sens. A monastic goldsmith from Sens was entrusted with the work and travelled thence over the rough and muddy winter roads to the royal court at Dreux. There he was given thirteen *sols* of gold as material for his work. Though miraculously increased, it was still not enough, and the shrine had to be finished with the aid of a gift of precious metal from the monastery. When it was complete the king was so much pleased that he gave thirty-three *sols* of pure silver for a shrine for the brother saint, Saint Potentinien.[3]

It was not long before all the great churches that enshrined the body of a saint encouraged the pilgrimage of the faithful by exposing the precious relic on feast days either in a statue or reliquary or in some other equally splendid

[1] Suger in Migne, *Pat. Lat.* clxxii, col. 915.
[2] Lasteyrie, *Saint-Martial*, p. 1.
[3] Swartwout, p. 55.

fashion.[1] When the Synod of Rodez was held in 1161 tents were set up in a field to shelter four such statues, called Majesties, that had been brought to grace the festival: Saint Marius of Vabres, Saint Amand of Rodez, Sainte Foy of Conques, and the Virgin of Saint-Sernin of Toulouse. The visitor to Le Monastier Saint-Chaffre will to this day find a silver Saint Chaffre of the eleventh century set upon the altar for his veneration, holding a bunch of the last harvest's corn.

Times were already more secure. The monks had no longer to keep their relics so that they could be carried away quickly before the threat of invasion. Instead, people were free to come long distances to pay homage to the saint. The knights in their bright surcoats, their ladies with wide sleeves of crimped linen beneath great travelling-cloaks of fine cloth, comfortable town priests with a train of no less comfortable penitents; farm labourers so old that at last they had a holiday to bring a grandchild to see the saint; dusty and tired folk going from shrine to shrine on their way to Rome or Compostella; a few men coming with a mixture of pleasure and dread to worship at a shrine where they felt a growing vocation to serve: each and all brought something to the shrine, enthusiasm and devotion as well as gold. Sometimes, if the church were unfinished, a pilgrim might even give a capital. At Volvic, which had a local pilgrimage to the shrine of Saint Projet, there is one (Fig. 6 B) that shows a certain Guillaume de Bez handing over the column and its capital to the prior for the good of his own and his wife's souls.

Such pilgrimages needed another setting than that of the typical monastic church, built to serve the needs of a small enclosed community. More space was needed in the nave to accommodate the crowds at festivals; the aisles had to be developed and extended round the choir to make it possible to hold processions with some at least of the relics; and the altars of the church needed to be multiplied so that more masses could be said.

The first of the French monasteries to attempt to meet the particular architectural needs of a pilgrimage church by a modification of the basilican plan was Saint-Martin de Tours. The abbey church was built early in the tenth century; the plan is not exactly known, but there is a reasonable certainty that it had an ambulatory and radiating chapels.[2] It probably formed the model for the cathedral of Clermont, consecrated in 946, that is known to have had an ambulatory with radiating chapels, double aisles, and an aisled transept. The plan was copied not only in the cathedral of Orléans but also in the second church of

[1] Fleury, besides the body of St. Benedict, seems also to have had a statue reliquary of the Virgin, which is represented in an early thirteenth-century manuscript from the abbey, *Bibliothèque d'Orléans*, p. 13. Chénesseau, p. 76.

[2] It may have been based on the cathedral at Chartres as rebuilt in 858. Part of the plan has been revealed by excavation; see Lasteyrie in *Mém. Acad. Inscr. et belles lettres*, xxxiv, pt. i, p. 1.

Saint-Martin de Tours, rebuilt between 997 and 1014 in consequence of the growing importance of the pilgrimage to Saint Martin's shrine. This served to make the plan a classic one, to be followed by the greatest shrines of France. The abbey of Conques had so far been satisfied with a typical wooden-roofed Benedictine church, finished about 980, with the golden statue in the nave behind the grille made from the chains of prisoners whom Sainte Foy had delivered. Now this was no longer enough. Between 1041 and 1052 Abbot Odolric began a new church, on the plan of Saint Martin's. Saint-Martial de Limoges, that had several times been burnt but had always been rebuilt on the old plan, with the old Roman stone, became Cluniac in 1063 and was immediately rebuilt as another great pilgrimage church of the new design. Saint-Sernin de Toulouse, that had been rebuilt in the first quarter of the eleventh century, was again rebuilt to the new plan under Bishop Izarn between 1071 and 1105.[1] Finally, at the end of the pilgrimage road through Spain, Santiago of Compostella was begun on the same plan about 1078.[2]

Nothing remains of the church at Tours; but Conques, hidden in the green shade of a remote and depopulated valley of the Rouergue, still survives with but little change. Like Tours, it has an aisled transept and an ambulatory, making it possible to have the most effective of processions round the church; but, since its quiet valley could not hope to gather so many pilgrims as the highway of the Loire, it is on a smaller scale: there are three radiating chapels instead of five, single not double aisles, and a nave that seems rather short in comparison with the great transept. The façade has the two towers that befit a Benedictine abbey, but there is no narthex. The exterior remains equally Benedictine in its extreme simplicity; it may fairly be said to strive after nothing but decency and has no ornament but the necessary buttresses and cornice. Yet, architecturally, the church is remarkable as having a vaulted nave; the thrust is taken by a triforium over the aisles.[3]

Saint-Martial de Limoges has disappeared, but an eighteenth-century plan[4] shows it to have been much more magnificent in scale than Conques, as befitted a greater centre of population. It had, like Tours, five radiating chapels, and though its aisles were single, the nave extended for nine bays. The scheme was yet more splendidly carried out at Saint-Sernin de Toulouse (Fig. 7), which has the double aisles and five radiating chapels of Tours and double absidioles in

[1] Rey, p. 16, thinks it was planned as early as 1060. The history of the church goes back at least to the fourth century, when a basilica was built in place of the chapel that covered the saint's tomb. The foundation was sometimes Augustinian, sometimes Benedictine, but the existing building undoubtedly bears the Benedictine stamp.

[2] The tomb accepted as that of St. James had been discovered in 830.

[3] There seems to have been difficulty with the nave roof; work on it was still going on about 1090.

[4] C. de Lasteyrie, Plate II.

each arm of the transept. This church survives in its entirety;[1] no one who has
seen it can fail to have a profound respect for French Benedictine monachism
of the eleventh century. It is older than the first Crusade, older than the *Chanson
de Roland*; it is inspired by an epic majesty that ennobles the age that produced
it. It has the archaic and headstrong beauty—
ἀρχαϊκὸν Δέ τι καὶ αὔθαΔες κάλλος—that was
once ascribed to the style of Thucydides. Its
mere size would be impressive—it is just over
three hundred and seventy-seven feet long outside—were it not so homogeneous and so
complete that it transports us to a world of
unquestioning faith with values of its own.

The pilgrimage churches had a great influence
on other monasteries. These, too, had relics and
soon began to hope that they might find new
prestige and new revenue by developing their
churches as places of pilgrimage. Their relics
had hitherto been housed in small box-like
portable shrines, *capsae*, or in even smaller hanging reliquaries called phylacteries, which were
borne in procession on the great feast days hung
round the necks of the senior monks[2] (Fig. 6 A).
About the middle of the eleventh century reliquaries on a larger scale were adopted in many
abbeys: Cluny had a golden seated image of St.
Peter, worthy to be set beside Sainte Foy herself.
A little later Beaulieu boasted a silver statue of
the Virgin; Souvigny and Vézelay and a host
of other monasteries acquired wooden statues of
Our Lady, that might be painted and gilt until they rivalled their prototypes
in precious metal (Fig. 8). In parts of the south the tradition of the
sarcophagus lingered; Sainte Maignance lay in one of sculptured stone; at
Saint-Hilaire in the Aude the saint reposed in an eleventh-century marble
sarcophagus that is a frank imitation of a Gallo-Roman tomb. At Saint-Gilles
the abbot had a shrine made for his saint of this form, with figures in relief on

PLAN 2

Cluniac Abbey of Saint-Martial
de Limoges. Reconstruction Plan.
Consecrated 1095. After C. de
Lasteyrie

---

[1] Begun *c.* 1077, the choir consecrated by Urban II in 1096; the transept begun *c.* 1090 and the
nave *c.* 1125.

[2] See Dr. Rose Graham in *Archaeologia*, lxxx, 1930, p. 149. Good examples survive at Bar-sur-
Aube (Fig. 6. *a*) and at Saint-Nicolas d'Arras, both now mounted on pedestals of later date. A later
example is the phylactery reliquary of the Holy Blood, formerly in the cathedral of Boulogne and now
in the Treasury of Saint-François-de-Sales' church there.

every side and a gabled roof of scale work.[1] At Grandselve the shrine of Sainte Libaude (Fig. 9) was of this form; a tower was later added to make it like a church.[2] At Avenas, Saint Vincent had a tomb in stone, carved with Christ and the Apostles, the life of the Virgin, and Louis VII offering the church to the saint. Such shrines and tombs were no longer hidden in a crypt or *confessio* but were raised high where all men might see them, above, upon, or below the high altar of the church.

With these to attract pilgrims, modifications were introduced into the 'Benedictine plan' to make it better fitted for the crowds of pilgrims and their processions round the church.[3] Lesser monasteries could not afford to imitate the whole scheme of the great pilgrimage churches, but each copied one or more of its characteristic features. The abbey of Tournus, that enshrined the body of Saint Philibert, was rebuilt by Abbot Étienne about 970. He had been prior of Saint-Pourçain in Auvergne[4] and copied Clermont Cathedral in an ambulatory with radiating chapels of angular design.[5] Saint-Rémi de Reims, that held the body of its patron saint, was rebuilt between 1015 and 1040 with an aisled transept and an ambulatory with chapels.[6] Fleury, that had the body of St. Benedict, was rebuilt in its turn, the work beginning between 1067 and 1080 (Fig. 10). This follows the plan of the pilgrims' churches in its ambulatory and radiating chapels.[7] Here effect was added to the processions by subtle effects of perspective: the ambulatory arches are highest by the altar and decline towards the sides; the choir floor is steeply ramped, like a stage, and there are many steps up to the altar. At Cluny, an abbey rich in relics, the abbey church was rebuilt by Abbot Hugh on a plan that owed its ambulatory and radiating chapels and double aisles to the pilgrimage churches, though its double transept was its own.[8] Its peculiar beauty lay not only in the immense length of the nave and the proportion of its pointed arches, but also in the extreme elegance of its apse, of which the capitals alone survive. It was the largest and most sumptuous church in Christendom, with a great nave of eleven bays, and served as a model to innumerable Benedictine churches built within and without the Order of Cluny.[9] Professor Conant's restoration well shows its overwhelming magni-

---

[1] For a description see Vielliard, p. 41.

[2] The same scheme was followed for the other shrines of the abbey, that of the Crucifixion, and of Our Lady. All are now in the church of Bouillac, Tarn-et-Garonne.

[3] Just as Rome had its *Mons Gaudii* and Jerusalem its Montjoie from which the cities were first seen, so Vézelay and Mont-Saint-Michel had their Montjoies.

[4] See Bréhier, p. 152.   [5] On the dates of the whole church see Oursel, pp. 33 et seqq.

[6] Deshoulières, *Début*, p. 60.

[7] Fleury encouraged the Compostella pilgrimage; the 'Great Legend of St. James' was written there in 1005. See G. G. King, *Way of St. James*, i. 99.

[8] At Fleury the outermost radiating chapels are set at right angles, making a kind of false transept in the apse.

[9] See Joan Evans, *Rom. Arch. Ord. Clun.*, pp. 67 et seqq.

ficence (Fig. 11);[1] Paray-le-Monial survives as a much reduced copy to give some idea of the beauty of its detail.

Churches of an average size had three radiating chapels,[2] the more important five.[3] The abbey of Saint-Léonard in the Limousin, that succeeded in making its saint's shrine an important place of pilgrimage, had seven. Existing churches, too fine and too new to be rebuilt, were modified to make them more like the pilgrimage churches. In the last quarter of the eleventh century five radiating chapels were added to the apse of Saint-Savin, that enshrined the body of the saint behind the altar. Early in the twelfth century, La Charité had radiating chapels added to its apse, and Souvigny, that fostered a pilgrimage to the shrine of Saint Mayeul, added a second aisle to the nave and a second transept to the east end.[4]

A few of these churches[5] attempted to imitate the triforia of the pilgrimage churches, but developed schemes of their own. Their variety is testimony to the vitality of local style, at a time when the demand for much building on a monumental scale had everywhere developed true schools of architecture. The lofty storied scheme of Jumièges and Caen, capped by a wooden roof, has little but the essentials of ground-plan in common with the classical colonnades and vaulted roofs of the abbey church of Saint-Savin in Poitou (Fig. 13), which are probably only a decade later than the consecration of Jumièges and almost contemporary with the consecration of Saint-Étienne de Caen.[6] At Saint-Savin a windowless nave of eight bays, round pillars with rather shallow foliage capitals, a lofty barrel vault, with groin vaults in the aisles, a very high cul-de-four apse, with a transept out of which two deep apsidal chapels open on either side, seem to carry on the traditions of the Roman basilica; but, if the ground-plan is examined, it is the familiar Benedictine plan modified by the adoption of an ambulatory and five radiating chapels. At Cluny, again, the plan was familiar in its essentials, but its aspect was changed by complex piers, a false triforium with windows above, and the utmost richness of sculptured decoration; whereas

---

[1] I should like to express my thanks to him for allowing me to reproduce this.

[2] Cluniac: Paray-le-Monial, Monstierneuf de Poitiers, Beaulieu, Souvigny, Chambon, Arnac, Saint-Sauveur de Figeac, Saint-Hilaire de Melle, Saint-Eutrope de Saintes, Benedictine: Fontgombault, Saint-Pierre de Chauvigny, Airvault, Saint-Jouin-de-Marnes, Lesterps, Saint-Nectaire, Fécamp, and others.

[3] The Benedictine priory of Le Montet copied the Cluniac church of Souvigny, with an ambulatory, five radiating chapels, and absidioles in the transept, before 1095. The likeness is so close as to suggest that a team of masons moved on.

[4] Deshoulières in *Bull. Soc. Antiq. France,* 1916, p. 263.

[5] e.g. Saint-Étienne de Nevers, Châtelmontagne, Mont-Saint-Michel, and Saint-Sauveur de Figeac.

[6] See Maillard; the church was begun earlier, at the choir end. It may be compared with the church of Lichères, which has narrow aisles, massive columns, and extremely classical capitals with volutes.

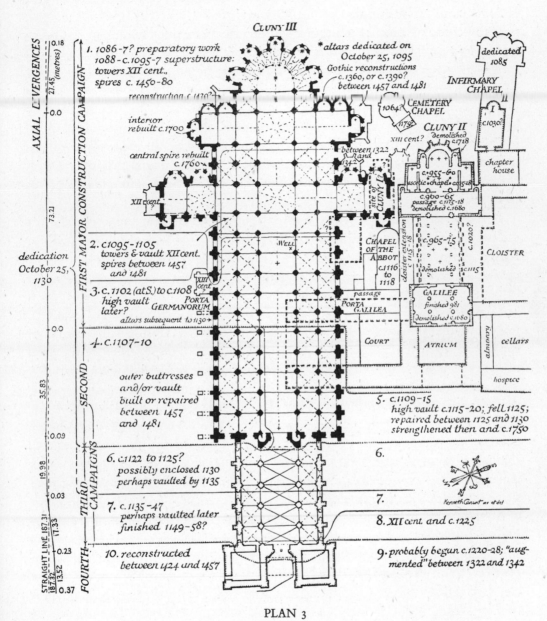

PLAN 3

Third Abbey Church of Cluny, showing stages of construction.
By Professor K. J. Conant

at Vézelay the stress is on horizontal line and the arches of the roof (Fig. 14). In Normandy, for example at Saint-Georges-de-Boscherville, the pier is of an extreme complexity of plan and decorative effect is gained not from sculpture but from a multiplicity of columns and colonnettes.

The adoption of radiating chapels led to a great change in the external aspect of Benedictine churches. The outward simplicity of such abbeys as Conques and such priories as Chamalières was necessarily modified by the picturesque grouping of the apse and its attendant chapels, that seemed in themselves to invite ornament. Constant though the ground-plan was, the elevation could be infinitely varied by the relation of the height of the apse and the chapels and by the complication of their ornament (Figs. 15, 16). Few architectural schemes have ever been more fruitful or more satisfying.

The monastic churches which aspired to become pilgrimage churches, yet did not have great aisled transepts, provided for the crowds of pilgrims whom they expected on feast days by the erection of a narthex or galilee before the church. The earliest galilees, like the tenth-century one at Chamalières,[1] were little more than fortified porches; but the *Customs* of Cluny,[2] written between 1030 and 1048, describe a *galilea* sixty-five feet long, with the two western towers of the monastery incorporated in its façade: presumably the galilee of the second abbey church, consecrated in 981. A surviving narthex of the kind is that of the abbey of Tournus, fairly certainly of the end of the tenth century.[3] This is already a lesser church of three bays with aisles. Church-galilees of the same type appear before many of the eleventh-century abbeys that had some claim to be places of pilgrimage: Mozac, Fleury, Souvigny, Saint-Eutrope de Saintes, and Airvault. The greatest surviving is that added to Vézelay (Fig. 17), that bore the significant name of *ecclesia peregrinorum* and served to provide an annexe to the nave for the thousands of pilgrims that visited the Magdalene's shrine at Easter, Pentecost, and her feast day of 22 July.

By the first quarter of the twelfth century nearly all the great monasteries of France had thus become in some degree pilgrimage churches. The famous *Liber Sancti Jacobi*[4] that guides the pilgrim to the shrine of St. James of Compostella, made accessible to French pilgrims by the Spanish Crusades of the eleventh century, gives a choice of itineraries that combine as many as possible of these churches into four routes from which the traveller may choose: one by Saint-Gilles and Saint-Sernin de Toulouse, one by Le Puy, Conques, and Moissac; one starting from Vézelay and one from Saint-Martin de Tours. The

---

[1] See Bréhier, p. 145.

[2] *Consuetudines farfenses,* ed. Albers, p. 137.

[3] Puig y Cadafalch, pp. 107 and 112, dates it in the first half of the eleventh century.

[4] The best edition is that of Jeanne Vielliard, Mâcon, 1938. She dates it about 1139, the year of the last miracle it records.

book was clearly written under monastic direction, and it represents, at least for the French part of the itinerary, the final organization of the pilgrimage by the monks rather than any very ancient tradition.[1]

3. SEPULCHRE CHURCHES

The architectural impulse that created the church of Compostella came along the *camino francés* from Tours. Another and yet greater pilgrimage road gave passage to an architectural influence in an inverse direction: an influence that started from the Church of the Holy Sepulchre at Jerusalem and came into France and beyond. Even in the tenth century lords and prelates had painfully made their way to the Holy Land to save their souls; and if they had the good fortune to come safely back, came with relics for oratory, abbey, cathedral, or parish church. The characteristic plan of the most sacred church of Christendom, of a rotunda for the Sepulchre and a basilica for the Martyrium, is inevitably recalled in that adopted for Saint-Bénigne de Dijon when Abbot William of Volpiano began to rebuild it in 1001.[2] The likeness existed before his time, for a basilica over the saint's tomb had been built as early as 535, with a separate oratory to the east, and these had been united by a long nave in 870. Abbot William, however, transformed it all, turning the nave into a great round church with a double aisle and double triforia.[3]

The Church of the Holy Sepulchre at Jerusalem was destroyed in 1009, and for some twenty years pilgrimage thither was impossible. Then for a time it was permitted and indeed encouraged; the church of the Sepulchre was restored and its influence was once more felt. The master mason might never have seen the prototype; but someone who had reached Jerusalem carried an ineffaceable memory of it, which had, however inaccurately, to be reproduced. The church of the Benedictine abbey of Sainte-Croix de Quimperlé was begun soon after 1029 as a rotunda with three absidioles and a porch, with a circular aisle;[4] a similar plan was followed in the contemporary church of Lanleff near Paimpol. Before 1038 the abbey church of Flavigny was built, as an aisled octagon. Neuvy-Saint-Sépulcre was yet a more obvious imitation: it was founded in 1045 by a viscount of Bourges *ad formam Sancti Sepulcri Ierosolimitani*, on his return from the Holy Land. By 1079 it actually depended on the church of the Sepulchre at Jerusalem and paid it the *cens*.[5] The rotunda and basilica were here

---

[1] M. Bédier in his *Légendes épiques* has pointed out the connexion between this organization of the pilgrimage and the organization of epic matter into *chansons de geste*.

[2] Mortet, i. 27. It was consecrated in 1016. M. Jean Hubert does not accept the theory of its inspiration by the Holy Sepulchre, but prefers to derive it from the tradition of funerary chapels.

[3] It was destroyed except for the crypt in 1792. Plancher's drawing of it is reproduced in Lasteyrie, *Arch. rom.*, p. 278.

[4] It has been partly rebuilt but preserves the original plan.

[5] Ebersolt, p. 86. It later became a house of canons regular. Its dedication was to St. James.

originally separate. The rotunda had a cenotaph in imitation of the Sepulchre in the centre; its roof, now vaulted, may originally have been of wood.

Sometimes, too, the shrine at Jerusalem was imitated on a smaller scale. The abbey of Saint-Rémi de Reims had a sepulchre in a chapel of the Trinity that was supposed to be a model of the most sacred shrine in Christendom; it was consecrated in 1049. It was imitated at the near-by abbey of Saint-Thierry, in the crypt, consecrated in 1115; here it was accompanied by figures of the angel guardian of the Tomb and of the Holy Maries.[1]

At the end of the eleventh century the Seljuk invasion of Palestine, and the growing impulse to crusade, gave new force to the idea of the Holy Sepulchre as a symbol to be fought for. The church of the Benedictine abbey of Charroux, consecrated in 1095, the year in which Urban II preached the Crusade, remains the most magnificent adaptation of the Sepulchre plan. The rotunda, of which only the centre survives (Fig. 18), had two circles of pillars and an inner ring of quadrilobed piers. This served as a choir; a sanctuary with five radiating chapels projected to the east and the nave extended for eight bays to the west. The contemporary priory churches of Villeneuve-d'Aveyron and Rieux-Minervois are lesser instances of monastic churches influenced by the Sepulchre scheme.[2]

To some extent the Crusades, 'pilgrimages under arms', robbed all other pilgrimages of their prestige. They might bring relics to the abbeys of France, but they brought no revenue. Consequently monastic interest in the Sepulchre type of church waned and vanished. Even in 1053, when a count of Rouergue founded the monastery of Mauriac in fulfilment of a vow made in Jerusalem, the church was built on the familiar Benedictine plan with a triple apse; and after the Crusade had been preached in 1095, I do not know of a single monastic church which followed, or tried to follow, the plan of the rotunda of the Sepulchre at Jerusalem. About 1140 Abbot Suger put up a window in Saint-Denis[3] with ten episodes of the First Crusade, then barely forty years old; but it was rather a tribute to Louis VII, profoundly interested in the Second Crusade preached in 1146, than an expression of any identity of interest between the Benedictines and the Crusaders.

4. BENEDICTINE ART

The simplicity of decoration of the early Benedictine abbeys was modified in the course of the eleventh century as their architectural splendour increased. Such buildings as remain of the first half of the century—for example Ris

[1] See p. 42.

[2] The abbey of Saint-Bertin at Saint-Omer had an octagonal building linked to the apse by a passage that may have been another instance of the scheme.

[3] Now destroyed, but reproduced in Montfaucon, *Monumens de la monarchie française*, p. 385, plates l to liv.

and Bourbon-Lancy—have a few sculptured capitals in the classical or Carolingian tradition. By the middle of the century the demand for sculptured and
painted ornament began to increase, and by the end carving and painting were
used to adorn the entire building. The exteriors, that had had simple architectural arrangements of buttress and cornice, now had their apses adorned with
sculptured arcades and friezes[1] (Fig. 19), their façades with yet more elaborate
sculpture or with magnificent portals (Fig. 21), their towers with cusped ornaments and statues set like watchmen at the corners.[2] At Saint-Amand-de-Boixe
even the transept wall is richly sculptured; at Nouaillé, the nave. Interiors, that
had once had a few carved capitals in the choir, now had every column and
every arcade thus adorned; at Saint-Sernin de Toulouse there are more than
five hundred such capitals, at Cluny there must once have been over a thousand.
The half-cupola of the apse was almost always frescoed, and sometimes the
walls of the entire church were covered with paintings.

The universe outside the abbey enclosures was still a stern and austere place,
in which the necessities of use or defence dictated architecture, and ornament
was almost unknown. Its beauty lay in great forests and wide heaths, in tilled
fields and shining rivers. Those who entered a Benedictine abbey found themselves in another world. Struggle and danger were shut out, and with them
natural beauty, except for such a prospect as might be seen from the abbey
garden. The monks lived in a gracious world of stone, splendidly planned and
finely built, ornamented with sculpture and burnished bronze, bright with gold
and colour, sweet with incense. Their hands were busy with neither sword nor
spade, but with quills and parchment; their minds occupied not with talk of
ordinary things, but with the thoughts expressed in serried lines of crabbed
Latin. Their day was ruled not only by sun and seasons, but also by the chants
of the canonical hours and the succession of the liturgical feasts. They conceived of beauty as a part of worship; and the beauty they achieved was altogether different from any to be found in the world outside.

The extent and subject of the sculptures and paintings that adorned the abbeys,
like the plan of the church, were determined by the abbot and the great officers
of the abbey. The ruling of the Second Council of Nice still held good: 'the
composition is not the invention of the artist, but a product of the legislation
and tradition of the Catholic Church. The art alone is the artist's; the choice
and arrangement are of the fathers who build the churches.' Certain types of
capitals were part of the mason's tradition, and these continued in use, especially
in the parts of the church farthest from the high altar. The Corinthian acanthus

---

[1] e.g. Saint-Paul-lès-Dax, Apostles and Last Supper, early twelfth century; Selles-sur-Cher, Life
of Christ.
[2] e.g. Saint-Philibert de Tournus, on the upper story of the north tower, probably built before
1108; *Cong. arch.*, 1928, p. 383.

and the Doric volute were still familiar,[1] and appear in a crude form in the eleventh-century capitals of the crypt of Saint-Aignan at Orleans, built between 989 and 1029 (Fig. 23 A), and in the slightly later capitals of the Ronceray of Angers. In the second half of the century the Corinthian capital developed into real elegance and beauty: the narthex and nave of Fleury, the choir of Sainte-Radegonde de Poitiers, the churches of Saulieu and Thil-Châtel, show the efforts of the masons to copy the antique models that the neighbourhood provided,[2] and culminate in the splendid capitals from Cluny (Fig. 23 C). Exceptionally, other forms of classical capitals served as models: the abbeys of Mozac (Fig. 23 D) and Saint-Nectaire and the remote priory of Langogne in the Velay have capitals with winged genii. Others seem to be inspired rather by sarcophagi than capitals: there are some with masks at the angles at Souvigny and Mozac; one with gorgon heads at Nouaillé; the familiar motive of griffins with a vase between them appears at Souvigny, Saint-Menoux, Charonton-sur-Cher, and Mozac. The cockfights on capitals at Autun and Saulieu and the scenes of the chase at Fleury, Vézelay, and Saint-Hilaire de Melle are probably likewise imitations of Roman tombs.[3] On other parts of the building the classical tradition was less consistently maintained: at Châteauneuf-sur-Charente, for example, the cornice is composed of classical rosette-metopes separated by consoles carved with barbaric figures. Exceptionally, too, larger works of sculpture were inspired by classical models: there is an obvious relation between bas-reliefs from Saint-Sernin de Toulouse, with women holding a ram and a lion, and certain Gallo-Roman stelae.[4]

Outside this traditional repertory the stone-carver depended on the abbot or his deputy for a model. The abbot was not himself an artist, and could not create it; instead, he had to choose one from the limited repertory of the monastery's possessions or the monuments of the locality. It was very rarely classical: the abbot was often familiar with works of classical art,[5] but he was as conscious of their pagan character as he was of the pagan character of Horace and Virgil. At Saint-Ursin de Bourges, it is true, the tympanum has a hunting scene copied from a Roman sarcophagus, but it was a sarcophagus sanctified by its use as the tomb of Saint Ludre at Déols.[6] More often the design might come from one

---

[1] Roman sites continued to be adapted to monastic use, though much less often than in the earlier period. Mauvinard, near Nouaillé, was built over the remains of a Roman temple on the old road from Poitiers to Limoges; and Notre-Dame de Melun over a temple of Mercury.

[2] Consequently the models are of different dates: at Saulieu the chiselled acanthus of Rome and the drilled acanthus of Byzantium appear side by side.   [3] Adhémar, p. 160.

[4] See, for example, Espérandieu, *Recueil des bas-reliefs de la Gaule romaine,* iv. 2769 and 2793.

[5] The famous diptych of the Nicomachi and the Symmachi, for example, now divided between the Victoria and Albert and Cluny Museums, belonged to the abbey of Montier-en-Der.

[6] Adhémar, p. 165. At Fleury there is an early eleventh-century relief of Romulus and Remus on the north face of the tower, and at Vézelay, Sainte-Eulalie-de-Benêt, and Saint-Pierre de Melle versions of the Spinario. Ibid., p. 190.

of the oriental brocades that were treasured in the sacristy.[1] A stuff like the tenth-century silk that wrapped the bones of Saint Josse (Fig. 24 A) inspired the sculptors who carved capitals with elephants at Caen, Saint-Cydroine, Vézelay, and Monstierneuf (Fig. 24 B). Graville-Sainte-Honorine has a capital with affronted horsemen remarkably like those of a Sassanian brocade. The Byzantine silk that covered the relics of Saint Germain at Auxerre[2] inspired capitals with eagles in the Cluniac priories of Moissac, La Charité, and Saint-Révérien; and at Moissac and Saint-Révérien two capitals appear to draw independent inspiration from a brocade with birds and trees.

Usually, however, the painter's and the sculptor's model was provided by the illuminated manuscripts in the abbey library. Had the Romanesque churches of France still their medieval wall-paintings we should realize yet more clearly how strong was the dominance of manuscripts over Benedictine art. As it is, a tithe, or less, of the manuscripts survive; hardly more of the sculptures; and not a hundredth part of the paintings that would have served to link the two.

To the illuminated manuscripts nine-tenths of the sculptural innovations of the second half of the eleventh century can be directly traced. The link was more obvious then than it is now; it is as hard for us to remember that Romanesque sculpture was coloured as that the *Chansons de Geste* were sung. Sculpture in stone was not then an art of statues in marble or bronze made remote by their want of colour, but an art primarily of coloured reliefs; such free-standing work as existed was either in metal diversified with jewels and enamels or in wood brightly painted and gilt. Painting and sculpture performed similar decorative functions and the transition from one to another was easy. Even the fields appropriate to the one might be taken by the other: at Saint-Étienne de Nevers there is hardly any sculptured ornament, but its portal was once painted with ribbon meanders, birds, and other decorative motives, and its plain capitals are obviously intended to serve as a field for decorative painting. In some abbeys, for example Beaulieu and Figeac, plain capitals, intended for painting, occur among sculptured capitals that were once coloured.

Time and the energy of restorers have destroyed nearly all the colouring of Romanesque sculpture. At Cluny the recently excavated fragments of the portal show that the sculpture in fine stone had little colouring, but that the work in soft stone was painted in orange, red, ochre, yellowish-green, and blue. The capitals at Mozac and Saint-Nectaire and the tympanum at Conques are still bright enough to give an impression of the decorative effect. A head from the church of Saint-Rémi de Reims has the cheeks slightly reddened, the lips red, the eyes blue, the hair, beard, and eyebrows brown, and a crown painted

[1] Some of these were imported from Apulia, like the silks that Ordericus Vitalis records the abbot of Saint-Évroult to have brought thence to make copes.
[2] See Joan Evans in *Pantheon*, x, July 1932, p. 221.

D

yellow and partly gilt. Such sculptures formed part of an ensemble that was no less brilliant. At Châtelmontagne the late Romanesque paint on the architectural details remained clear until some ninety years ago: the columns were diapered with yellow lozenges each containing a pink flower on a greyish ground, the background of the capitals was alternately red and yellow, with a yellow or red astragal, and the triforium had bands of ribbon meanders and stylized leaves and flowers like the ornaments of a manuscript.[1]

The eleventh century witnessed a true revival of manuscript illumination in France. The texts transcribed were nearly all religious in subject and intention, and it was felt to be fitting that they should be beautiful. Baudry, Abbot of Bourgueil between 1079 and 1107, had not only a skilled copyist to write out his verses, but also an illuminator, Gerard of Tours, to beautify them. He wished the manuscript to be fair to the eye:

> Praecepi fieri capitales aere figuras,
>   ut quod non sensus res tribuat pretium.
> Ad nos miserunt Arabes huc forsitan aurum,
>   materiarum quo signa priora micant;
> Introitus alios minio viridique colore,
>   ut mirabilius omne nitescat opus . . .[2]

Skilful scribes were almost insensibly driven into ornament. Their days were ruled by an inexorable routine; their writing by the inevitable duty of copying a familiar text; actual illustration was confined to extremely few books and was limited by a traditional code; only in the decoration of their manuscripts with ornamental initials could they exercise their fancy. It is not without reason that the centuries of the greatest Benedictine austerity produced the most rich and fantastic initials.

Such initials, indeed, were themselves decorative enough to serve as models for the sculptor. A typical Q (Fig. 25) from a text of Josephus written at Moissac about 1070 shows interlaced bird-beasts, a lion with his head turned back, and a half-free, half-symmetrical arrangement of the whole. A capital from Layrac (Fig. 26 A), a priory church built by the man who was abbot of Moissac between 1072 and 1085, shows the same bird-beasts, the same lion, and the same type of composition. Capitals at Fleury (Fig. 26 B) are clearly inspired by initial decorations of a similar kind. Other small symmetrical initials with birds and beasts (Fig. 27 A) were ready-made designs for capitals: many of the more than five hundred capitals of Saint-Sernin de Toulouse, with pairs of griffins, lions, goats, monsters, eagles, and doves, follow a similar scheme. Many manuscripts (Figs. 28, 31) had initials decorated with twining foliage in pen-

---

[1] *Cong. arch.*, 1854, p. 166.
[2] Raby, *Christian Latin Poetry*, p. 281.

work; similar foliage decorates hundreds of capitals in monastic churches (Figs. 29, 32). Another type of initial is of coiled foliage work, with beast or bird figures among the coils (Fig. 30 A); this type in its turn is represented on sculptured capitals (Fig. 30 B)[1] in which such figures as there are play a secondary part among coiling leafage.

Initials served as models for larger works of sculpture than capitals. The beginning of St. Matthew's Gospel in the Bible of the Benedictine abbey of Saint-Martial de Limoges (Fig. 33 B) has an initial L filled with grotesque beasts and birds and little climbing figures, and a formal picture of the saint standing under an arcade. Sculptural parallels to both these subjects can be found in Benedictine houses. At Souillac (Fig. 33 A) the pillar of the door is carved with a fantastic assemblage of birds, beasts, and men that closely recalls the initial; at Moissac a pier in the cloister has panels on its sides sculptured with figures of three apostles and the abbot that could easily be translated back into such miniatures as the St. Matthew.

These initials and these small pictures, however, could rarely provide a subject for sculpture on a large scale. For monumental work much larger exemplars were needed, such as only full-page miniatures could provide. The number of books with large illustrations was, in the eleventh century, extremely small. The manuscripts of the Commentary of Beatus on the Apocalypse, a book which must have been in all the great monastic libraries of France, represent the most important. Its author, Bishop of Liebana in the Asturias, wrote the book in Spain about 780. A century later it was already being copied in Spanish scriptoria with abundant illustrations; it was generally bound up with the commentary of Jerome on Daniel, similarly illustrated. By the eleventh century copies of the manuscript were widely distributed among the Benedictine houses of France, south of the Loire. The finest surviving French copy is that from the abbey of Saint-Sever-sur-Adour, written and illuminated in Gascony between 1028 and 1072, in the abbatiate of the Spaniard Gregory of Montana.[2] A lost Limousin or Poitevin version of it furnished models for a great part of the paintings that at one time covered every mural surface of the abbey church of Saint-Savin-sur-Gartrempe.[3] The whole porch, and part of the nave, is still painted with apocalyptic scenes that seem a transcription from such a manuscript. Their colouring and technique—brownish-red, yellow, green, and white in a strong brown outline with no shading—is that of illumination. Here it is less a question of influence than of exact copying on a large scale. In sculpture imitation had evidently to be less exact and more selective, but it was none the less considerable. It is from these Commentaries, with their fantastic subject-

[1] The capital illustrated has another interest: it provides a very close parallel with a part of the lintel of the Church of the Holy Sepulchre at Jerusalem.

[2] Bib. Nat. lat. 8878.   [3] See E. Maillard, *Petite monographie*.

matter and their Spanish background of literal mysticism, that Romanesque sculpture derives that supernatural intention which sometimes disquiets the modern observer, and that force and exaggeration of reality which nothing but blind faith can inspire.

The Jesuits of later centuries have set *Ad Majorem Dei Gloriam* on every façade and every frontispiece. The Benedictines of the eleventh and twelfth centuries carved Christ in glory over their portals.[1] One of the finest of the illuminations of Beatus' Commentary is a double-page illustration of Christ as he is described in the fourth chapter of Revelation: 'One sitting upon the throne, and round about the throne four and twenty elders' thrones and upon the thrones four and twenty elders sitting arrayed in white garments and on their heads crowns of gold . . . and round about the throne four living creatures . . . the first creature like a lion, and the second creature like a calf, and the third had a face as of a man, and the fourth like a flying eagle . . . having each one of them six wings.' The Apocalypse of Saint-Sever depicts the elders, each upon a throne of a different pattern, in broken rank. Each holds a lute and a golden cup; as the Vulgate describes them: 'habentes singuli citharas et phialas aureas plenas odoramentorum, quae sunt orationes sanctorum.'

The scheme not only inspired wall-paintings that are now lost[2] and a magnificent set of embroidered wall-hangings which Matthew, Abbot of Loudun from 1128 to 1155, had made for his church,[3] but also sculpture on a grand scale. The composition had monumental qualities which soon caused some abbot to choose it as a model for a tympanum. The earliest of such tympana that survive is that of Moissac (Fig. 34), which must once have formed part of a great door at the end of the church.[4] The accomplishment of the whole suggests that this was not the first experiment, though its precursors no longer exist; yet even so the effect is crowded to the verge of incomprehensibility and the scheme gives the impression of having been imposed upon the sculptor by someone who had not himself to carry it out.[5] None the less there are some modifications of the manuscript scheme. Christ is represented on a proportionately larger scale; the glory round him is less important; the beasts have only single pairs of wings; and fourteen of the elders are seated to form a frieze at the base. The

---

[1] The subject had already been painted in the cupola over the altar in Charlemagne's basilica at Aachen and in a church in Gaul described by Alcuin. Hubert, p. 120.

[2] One of about 1120 survives at Saint-Martin-de-Fenouilla, Maureillas, Pyrénées-Orientales, just outside the geographical scope of this book.

[3] Mortet, i. 22.

[4] A fifteenth-century chronicler, Aymeric de Peyrac, says that it was made in the time of Abbot Ansquitil, who died in 1115. A little later it was removed and reset as part of a great porch to the side of the church, with additional sculptures made after the death of Abbot Roger in 1132.

[5] At Fleury about 1095 an unfortunate sculptor had to attempt to put the whole Last Judgement on a capital.

Heavenly Host is reduced to two figures, nearly as great as the Christ beside whom they stand.

Evidently the scheme was not wholly satisfactory, because it was not wholly monumental. A simpler and more suitable version was provided by the many eleventh-century sacramentaries which have a page with a highly stylized Christ in glory with the four beasts in the angles. A manuscript of Caesar from Fleury[1] has on the end page a sketch for a differently spaced composition of the kind, which may even have been drawn as a sketch for a sculptor to work from (Fig. 35 A). It was the classic theme for apsidal painting; it occupied the great apse of the third church of Cluny and is reproduced on a small scale in the chapel of the Cluniac grange at Berzé (Fig. 36). The scheme is repeated on the tympana of many Benedictine houses,[2] and passed thence into the iconography of the cathedrals.

The page of the Commentary of Beatus that records that John fell at the feet of the angel before receiving the commission to the Seven Churches of Asia is headed in the manuscript from Saint-Sever by a representation of Christ enthroned in a circular glory upheld by angels, who are rather standing than flying (Fig. 37 A). This subject inspired the design of many tympana in the Benedictine churches of Burgundy.[3] It is closely copied, with even more static angels, on the door of the priory church at Charlieu consecrated in 1094; it reappears, with six-winged angels as in certain copies of Beatus, in the slightly later tympanum of the Benedictine priory of Perrecy-les-Forges (Fig. 37 B). A rough sketch on a blank space of a manuscript from Saint-Martial de Limoges,[4] that again may have been drawn to serve as a sculptor's model (Fig. 35 B), shows *angelus domini* very much as the angel appears in another group of Benedictine tympana, in which it seems as if the weight of the glory were too heavy for the angels to bear.[5] In a later tympanum at Saint-Julien-de-Jonzy (Fig. 38 A) the angels come forward with dancing feet and fluttering wings.

These two schemes, Christ in a mandorla with the four evangelistic beasts, and Christ in a mandorla upheld by angels, were combined in a third which appears to be characteristically Cluniac. The finest example, if not the archetype, was the tympanum of the great door of the third abbey church at Cluny,

---

[1] Bib. Nat. lat. 5763. The sketch appears to be of the twelfth century.

[2] e.g. the priory of Cervon, Nièvre.

[3] The earliest instance, and closest imitation, is a lintel of the church of Saint-Genis-des-Fontaines datable to 1020-1; but it is in Roussillon (Pyrénées-Orientales) and so outside the scope of this book.

[4] Bib. Nat. lat. 2826, fol. 157.

[5] One is from Anzy-le-Duc, and is now in the Hiéron du Christ Roi at Paray-le-Monial. It is sometimes interpreted as an Ascension scene, since the lintel has figures of the Virgin and the Apostles; but the Christ is seated. I should take His seated or standing posture as the test whether such a composition represents Him in glory or ascending to Heaven. A second tympanum of the kind is at Bellenaves, Allier.

of which a reconstruction has now been made from the fragments recently excavated.[1] The tympanum was very large, and evidently the four beasts or the two angels would alone have hardly sufficed to fill the angles of the lunette. Christ in a great mandorla was represented upheld by four angels, two flying in an upright position and two head downwards with clouds about their feet. The evangelistic beasts filled the spaces towards the edge. The composition seems to have been imitated in the destroyed tympanum of Avallon, and certainly inspired those of the abbey of Saint-Bénigne de Dijon (Fig. 39),[2] of Thil-Châtel,[3] of the narthex at Charlieu,[4] and of the Cluniac church of Semur-en-Brionnais.

The remaining important representation of Christ in glory in the Beatus manuscripts is that which represents Him coming with the clouds. This depicts Him standing, surrounded by a glory of irregular form, with circles nimbing the head and feet and an oval to surround the body. Four angels fly round the figure but do not touch the aureole. On the ground beneath stand seven men in attitudes of wonder and dismay.

This, doubtless through a series of iconographic experiments now lost to us,[5] ultimately inspired the great tympanum of the Benedictine abbey of Conques (Fig. 40). The angels still surround the cloudy aureole, but the figure it contains is given an altogether new significance by the great Cross that rises behind it: Christ appears not only as Judge but also as Saviour. The rest of the tympanum is occupied by the first great representation known to us in sculpture of the elect and of the damned. On Christ's right the elect approach, led by the Virgin, St. Peter, and the pilgrim St. James. Above their heads angels hold scrolls bearing the names of the Virtues. On the other side are angels carrying book, censer, sword, and lance, and beyond these are carved the tortures of the damned. The two gable-shaped lintels below represent Heaven, with Abraham holding the souls of the righteous in his bosom, and Hell, with Satan presiding over its torments.[6] The whole must have been at once more lucid and more decorative when it glowed with the colour of which traces still survive.[7] Though it seems an original composition and not a transposition from manuscript into sculpture, everything is labelled, down to the sun and moon, the

[1] Excavations conducted by the Medieval Academy of America under Professor K. J. Conant; reconstruction by Dr. Helen Kleinschmidt; to both of them my thanks are due for allowing me to see the reconstruction before its publication.   [2] Now in the Musée archéologique, Dijon.
[3] This is signed PETRVS DIVIONENSIS FECIT LAPIDEM ISTVM and may be by the same sculptor as the Dijon tympanum.   [4] Apparently by the sculptor who worked at Saint-Julien-de-Jonzy.
[5] One survives in the late eleventh-century wall-painting of the Baptistère Saint-Jean at Poitiers. Others occur in manuscripts of the School of Reichenau.
[6] The process of dissemination through dependent houses can here be studied. Perse, near Espalion, was a dependency of Conques and has a crude small version of the Conques Judgement on its tympanum.   [7] See the coloured cast in the Musée des monuments français.

lance and the nails, as it might be by some conscientious illuminator. Yet the time had come when the tradition was handed on not only from manuscripts to sculpture, but also from tympanum to tympanum. At Beaulieu the Cross of Conques reappears, but there is no mandorla. There are still four angels; two blow the trumpets of Resurrection and two uphold the Cross. The Saviour's hands are no longer raised in blessing, but are stretched out in the attitude of Crucifixion. Beatus seems to be forgotten; but below the main group there is a double frieze of animals exactly copied from those that appear on another page in most of the manuscripts of his Commentary. At Vézelay (Fig. 41) the theme finds its next modulation: Christ appears not as Redeemer-Judge but simply as Redeemer. The great tympanum shows Him between the spring of the Water of Life and the tree whose leaves are for the healing of the nations,[1] with streams of visible force falling from His hands upon the Apostles beneath. They may be streams of Grace; they are probably streams of Blood;[2] but the theme is unmistakable.[3] The lesser compartments are filled with figures who represent those to whom the Gospel shall bring healing: the halt and blind, who shall receive physical healing, and the heathen nations, dog-headed men from India and other strange folk, to whom it shall bring spiritual salvation. On the lintel the procession continues with men who sacrifice to idols, skiapods, big-eared Scythians, and the rest. The voussure shows the zodiac that encompasses the world; the mullion the figure of St. John bearing the Lamb, as the symbol of Baptism through which the Church must be entered. The portal was erected when Peter the Venerable was Abbot of Cluny, the mother house of Vézelay. Much of his life's work and most of his writings were devoted to refuting the errors of Jews, Mohammedans, and heretics that he might bring them within the Christian fold; and in the portal we can recognize the influence of a man great enough to turn a traditional scheme into a magnificent expression of his vocation as an evangelist. Finally, at Saint-Denis the much restored tympanum of the west door keeps the irregular aureole and the four angels of the Beatus tradition, but Christ is represented actually crucified. At Conques the Cross appeared behind him; at Beaulieu his arms held the gesture of crucifixion; at Vézelay blood streams from His wounded hands; here they are actually nailed to the Cross.

The Second Coming of the Lord portrayed in the Beatus illustrations also provided a model for the representation of the Ascension.[4] The scene was

[1] Rev. xxi. 6. [2] Cf. a contemporary fresco at Saint-Gilles de Montoire. R. Gérard, *Saint-Gilles de Montoire*, 1935, p. 55.

[3] It is often interpreted as the Commission of the Apostles, but the spring and tree would have no place in this theme.

[4] It seems first to have been followed in liturgical manuscripts, e.g. the eleventh-century sacramentary of Saint-Bertin. The Ascension does not seem to have been dramatically represented in French churches before the twelfth century, at Soissons. Young, i. 483.

carved soon after 1100 above the side door of Saint-Sernin at Toulouse in the familiar Beatus scheme; every fold of the sculptured drapery is linear and two-edged and represents the pen-stroke of an illuminator. At Saint-Gilles de Montoire it inspired a magnificent wall-painting that glorifies the apse of the priory church. At Collonges the four angels and Christ in an irregular mandorla stand in the tympanum above an arcaded frieze with the Virgin and the Apostles; at Montceau-l'Étoile (Fig. 38 B) Christ bears the Cross of victory and the angels that bear the mandorla are clearly flying upwards. There is no lintel line; the gesticulating hands of Virgin and Apostles bring them into the general composition. At Mauriac, however, the lintel line is used with considerable effect, for the mandorla breaks it, and so helps to give the necessary ascending movement;[1] but the originality is more apparent than real, for in the Beatus illustrations the colour of the ground changes exactly at the point where the line of the lintel is here introduced.

These are the great scenes that are derived from Beatus' Commentary on the Apocalypse. There are a host of lesser ones: the angel who sounds a trumpet on a capital of the narthex at Vézelay; the devil chained and unloosed on a capital at Moissac; *Babilonia magna* on capitals at Moissac and Chauvigny; the Son of Man appearing to St. John between the seven stars and the seven candle-sticks on a capital at Fleury and a tympanum at La-Lande-de-Cubzac; the Four Horsemen letting loose the plagues on the world on capitals at Fleury and Saint-Nectaire.

Enough has been said to show that the sculptor was provided with a design for his work by his monkish patron, who found that design in the illuminated manuscripts of his monastery. Sometimes, but much more rarely, the sculptures of a church were inspired by the relic that it contained. At Saint-Jouin-de-Marnes a frieze was sculptured about 1135 right across the gable, with a procession of pilgrims coming from either side towards the statue of the Virgin.[2] At Mozac the image is carved on the lintel with a train of saints and abbots on either side to worship it. Another reminiscence of pilgrimage is the figure of Constantine, possibly inspired by a pilgrim's sign[3] that commemorated the statue thought to be his outside the Lateran in Rome, which appears carved on the façade of many Benedictine churches up and down France[4] and painted on the walls of Saint-Jean de Poitiers.[5]

[1] See A. Gardner, *Med. Sculp.*, fig. 101.
[2] Another version of the same theme occurs on the façade of Loupiac, Gironde.
[3] See Adhémar, p. 215.
[4] Parthenay-le-Vieux, Notre-Dame-de-la-Coudre, Riez, Saint-Jean de Poitiers, Notre-Dame de Saintes, Saint-Gildas-de-Rhuys, Saint-Hilaire de Melle, Saint-Eutrope de Saintes, Airvault, Déols, &c. See Mâle, *Art rel. XIIe siècle*, p. 347, and Adhémar, p. 207.
[5] It is an argument against the monastic origins of the *Chansons de Geste* that their matter does not form a part of monastic iconography, except for one or two very doubtful instances; for the matter of

In the scriptoria the old traditions were being slowly enlarged to include fresh illustrations, and the same creative power is evident in sculpture. Some attempt was made at original historical illustration; a manuscript cartulary of Saint-Pierre de Vierzon, written soon after 1100,[1] shows Ambran sieur de Vierzon with his wife, making a donation to the abbot. Similarly a capital in the choir of Fleury shows Hugues de Sainte-Marie, who wrote a book of miracles of St. Benedict about 1120, offering a copy to the Virgin.[2]

The sculptor, too, had acquired enough skill to create his own version of a subject; as this capacity developed there was a growing use of text rather than illustration to provide him with a model. The development of pilgrimages had produced a considerable literature of lives of local saints. Hardly any of these manuscripts were illustrated, yet their subject-matter provided material for a number of sculptures and paintings.

At Fleury, which enshrined the body of St. Benedict, a whole series of capitals depicted his miracles and the stories of his friends Maur and Galla; the lintel of the door was carved with the discovery of his relics.[3] At Saint-Savin there are paintings of the lives of Saint Savin and Saint Cyprien; at Berzé-la-Ville of St. Laurence and St. Blaise. The life and miracles of St. Hilary were once visible on the walls of Saint-Hilaire de Poitiers.[4] At Vézelay there is a capital showing St. Martin commanding the pagans to cut down a sacred tree, and at Saint-Nectaire there are others with scenes from the life of the same saint. At Semur-en-Brionnais there is a lintel with the story of Saint Hilaire; at Souillac part of the portal has the story of Theophilus; at Dijon a tympanum once told the story of Saint Bénigne.[5] At Vézelay a whole series of capitals tells the story of St. Benedict and of the Egyptian hermits St. Antony and St. Paul.

Further inspiration was drawn from a new form of literary composition, the liturgical drama, which grew out of the Gospels, anthems, and special versicles used at the great feasts. These brief Latin dramatizations made their appearance in some of the great Benedictine abbeys as part of the ceremony of the Mass at the very end of the tenth century, but do not seem to have been widespread until the beginning of the twelfth century. They grew almost unconsciously from a natural need to emphasize the dramatic character of the liturgy, and owe nothing to classical drama.[6]

The earliest known is an Easter play with the altar as its centre, *quaedam assimilatio sepulchri*.[7] A monk in a white alb came and sat beside it, in the character of

the lives of Saints and the liturgical dramas, the undoubted products of the cloister, are well represented in the surviving monastic sculpture and painting.   [1] Bib. Nat. lat. 9865.

[2] A similar historical intention is shown on capitals at Souvigny and Saint-Georges-de-Boscherville which show monks striking money in commemoration of the abbey's right of mint.

[3] Mâle, *Art rel. XIIᵉ siècle*, pp. 232 et seqq.   [4] Ibid., p. 205.   [5] Ibid., p. 219.

[6] See Young for an admirable account.

[7] In 1160 a version of the play was performed at the Holy Sepulchre itself. Young, i. 239.

the angel watching beside the tomb. Then three other monks in women's long cloaks came slowly and hesitatingly forward, censer in hand. They were the Holy Women, the three Maries. The brief dialogue tells all. The angel speaks:[1]

'Quem queritis in sepulchro, O Christicole?'
'Ihesum Nazarenum crucifixum, O celicole.'
'Non est hic, surrexit sicut ipse dixit; ite, nunciate quia surrexit.'
'Alleluia, resurrexit Dominus, hodie resurrexit leo fortis, Christus, filius Dei; Deo gratias, dicite eia!'—

and so the drama merges into the Alleluia. None of the surviving manuscripts is illustrated,[2] but the scenes of the Easter play appear in many Benedictine sculptures and in some of the paintings at Saint-Savin. The Cluniac priory of Chalais has on its façade a relief of the half-open sarcophagus and the three Maries approaching it; there are similar representations at Dax, Arles, Saintes, and Cognac. The angel by the empty tomb and the three women appear on capitals of the Benedictine priory of Lesterps and of the Cluniac churches of Saint-Pons-de-Thomières, Mozac (Fig. 42), and the Daurade of Toulouse. The Easter play was performed with the altar of the church for Sepulchre,[3] and the fact is reflected in the altar-like form of the Sepulchre in these representations, and sometimes by the occurrence of a ciborium-like erection over it.

On the Tuesday in Easter week the monks enacted in some abbey churches[4] a drama of the meeting of Christ and the Disciples on the road to Emmaus. The text describes the Disciples, cap on head and staff in hand, meeting the risen Christ dressed as a pilgrim. Just such a scene appears on one of the lesser portals of Vézelay,[5] and on a capital from the Daurade of Toulouse.

It seems to have been through the liturgical drama that the actual cult-image of the church was most often represented in sculpture. In dramas representing the Adoration of the Magi, for example, it was naturally set upon the altar to represent the Virgin and Child: and it is because of this that they are figured in such strangely formal guise on a tympanum at Saint-Gilles and on a capital at Chauvigny (Fig. 43B). At Donzy-le-Pré (Fig. 43 A) the relation with the liturgical drama is yet clearer, for the cult-image of the Virgin is represented between figures of a censing angel and a prophet, such as occur in a Limoges drama in which the prophets appear to testify to the coming of Christ.[6]

Another type of liturgical drama was that of the Wise and Foolish Virgins.

[1] I follow the version used at Saint-Martial de Limoges. Young, i. 210.
[2] At the same time it must be remembered that the Maries at the Tomb had been represented in East Christian art as early as the third-century frescoes of the church of Doura Europos.
[3] Every altar contained relics, and each was thus in a sense the sepulchre of a saint.
[4] See Young, i. 451.
[5] A rather later and very complete version of the Easter cycle will be found on the piers of the cloister of Saint-Trophime d'Arles.   [6] See Mâle, op. cit., p. 143.

The early twelfth-century version of Saint-Martial de Limoges, that may come from the version played at Saint-Amand-de-Boixe, shows how moving and beautiful a dramatic composition this could prove.[1] The text says that the Foolish Virgins had spilt their oil: a capital from Saint-Étienne de Toulouse portrays them holding their chalice-shaped lamps upside down to show their emptiness.

Direct illustration from the New Testament is hardly found before the twelfth century,[2] apart from a few subjects which are derived from Beatus illustrations. Even after 1100 such illustrations come chiefly from Languedoc, from the area of Albigensian heresy, and seem to have had a homiletic and evangelistic purpose. Capitals from Sainte-Marie-la-Daurade at Toulouse are carved with the story of John the Baptist, Christ washing the Disciples' feet, the Last Supper, Christ speaking with the Disciples in the Garden of Gethsemane, the whole scene of the Betrayal of Judas, the Descent from the Cross, the laying of Christ in the tomb, the Resurrection,[3] Christ's descent into Hell, the Ascension, and Pentecost.[4] This desire to illustrate the gospel for didactic purposes is not unnatural in a province menaced by heresy; it is rare in the more orthodox part of France in the first half of the twelfth century.[5] More significant still is the representation for the first time on a capital from Saint-Pons-de-Thomières and on one of the tympana of Saint-Gilles of the actual scene of crucifixion.[6] At Saint-Gilles it has a peculiar appropriateness. It was in the square there that Pierre de Bruys was burnt as a heretic in 1143; and there, at much the same date, Christ appears on the most public part of the church, upon the Cross which Pierre de Bruys and his heretical followers had mocked.

A time came when subjects were taken from manuscript illuminations and literary sources and given a new intellectual force in monumental art. The

[1] See Young, ii. 360.

[2] The flight into Egypt is found in Burgundy at Saulieu and Bois-Sainte-Marie, and paintings of the childhood of Christ at Vic, a priory of Déols. By analogy with the temptations of St. Benedict and St. Antony, the temptation of Christ with the stone to be made into bread appears at Saulieu and Chauvigny.

[3] The figure of the risen Christ was not included in the Easter play before about 1160. See Young, i. 369.

[4] Mlle Marie Lafargue has lately been able to show how closely these are based on a manuscript like that of the Bible of Avila. *Les Chapiteaux de Notre Dame la Daurade*, 1940. Most of these subjects will be found in the paintings at Vic of the middle of the century, and in the later paintings of Saint Savin. The nave paintings there, of the second half of the century, represent direct illustration from the Old Testament (Genesis and Exodus) and are probably derived from a Catalan Bible manuscript.

[5] A series of capitals with the life of Christ occurs in the Cluniac priory of Lubersac, Corrèze. Instances of the second half of the century were probably influenced by the *mystères* acted on saints' days outside the church. A late twelfth-century manuscript from Fleury (Orléans, 201) had ten such plays, including the Nativity and Resurrection. Chénesseau, p. 78.

[6] It also occurs at Champagne, Ardèche, Saint-Jean-de-Vaux (Saône-et-Loire), and on the external frieze of Saint-Paul-lès-Dax. No dramatic representation of the Crucifixion is known before the beginning of the thirteenth century. Young, i. 492.

strange races, skiapods and Scythians and Ethiops, described by Isidore of Seville and Honorius of Autun; the monsters and legendary beasts of the bestiaries; the signs of the zodiac and the labours of the month of the calendars, were all put together with a new appropriateness on the shaft of a sundial at the Cluniac priory of Souvigny. The same power of assembling old and familiar subjects into a new whole is evident in the surviving tympana at the Cluniac priory of La Charité. On one the Beatus scheme of Christ in glory upheld by angels is given new significance. Our Lord sits sideways to receive the Virgin, who is floating up to Him holding the aureole's jewelled rim: it is an Assumption unique in the art of the early twelfth century. Behind the Virgin kneels the prior of La Charité. Beneath, indications of the crystal sea and of the trees of Paradise show that no Ascension from earth is represented, but a scene of fulfilled glory in Heaven. The lintel is integrated with the tympanum: it shows the great events of the Nativity cycle, in virtue of which the Virgin is received into Heaven by her Son: the Annunciation, Visitation, Nativity, and the angel appearing to the shepherds.[1] The second tympanum makes a pendant to it: if one is to the glory of the Virgin, the other is in honour of her Son (Fig. 44). The theme is Christ held up for adoration. On the lintel the pagan world worships Him, as the Magi hasten forward to greet Him, enthroned in his Mother's arms. The church of the Ancient Law accepts Him, as Simeon takes Him from the Virgin; and in the lunette He appears for the adoration of all Christians transfigured between Moses and Elias.

This integrating quality is characteristic of much of the surviving work executed for the Order of Cluny in the fifty years that lie between 1090 and 1140. So much of it has been destroyed that it is hard to estimate the exact contribution, yet this quality seems the hall-mark of what remains. The Order was remarkably homogeneous in culture as in administration. Its intellectual standards were high; there was much reading and much copying of manuscripts, and the absence of heavy manual labour tended insensibly to produce a community of scholarly thinkers. The art of the great Cluniac churches could therefore be allusive and literary, intended for a limited public with an advanced special training in the understanding of religious symbolism. It did not need to be a Bible of the Poor; it was a philosophic commentary for the learned.

The integrating and symbolic tendency is marked in the work designed for the third abbey church, begun in 1088, of which the decoration represented as great an advance as did the scale and boldness of its architecture. Radulphus Glaber the chronicler, who ended his days as a monk of Cluny, began the five books of his *Histories* which he wrote about 1047 with a philosophical view of the cosmos. 'God,' he wrote, 'Creator of all things, distinguished what he made

---

[1] At Vézelay the Virgin's door has the Magi in the tympanum and the Annunciation, Visitation, Nativity, and Shepherds on the lintel.

by manifold forms and appearances, that through what the eye perceived or the mind apprehended, he might raise the learned man to the simple intuition of the Godhead.' Through this perception, apprehension, and intuition the Greek Fathers had arrived at the conception of the quaternities of the world. There are four gospels which build up in our minds the upper world, and four elements which build up the lower. Similarly there are four dominant virtues and four chief senses: touch is less subtle than the rest and is only intended to serve them. There are four gospels and four rivers of Paradise which are mystically analogous with the elements and the virtues. So too are the four ages of history: from the Creation to the Flood, an age of Prudence; the age of the Patriarchs, an age of Temperance; the age of Moses, an age of Fortitude; and finally the age of Christ, when Justice has come down to rule the earth.

The capitals of the ambulatory of Cluny represent these quaternities in a yet more elaborate scheme. The engaged capitals at the end seem to have represented the Four Ages of History; at all events two of them represent the Fall of Man and the sacrifice of Isaac. Another capital (Fig. 45) has at each corner one of the Four Rivers of Paradise: nude figures, snake-enwreathed, with the stream gushing from the snake's mouth. The sides are filled by the Four Trees of Paradise, the apple of knowledge, the fig of the Fall, the vine of redemption, and the almond of Aaron's rod, of which the miraculous blossoming is a symbol of resurrection. Two more capitals combine, very beautifully, the seasons and the virtues.[1] Prudence is there (Fig. 46) in helm and coat of mail, with the inscription: DAT COGNOSCENDVM PRVDENTIA QVID SIT AGENDVM. Next to Prudence is a veiled woman dressed in a long robe and a floating mantle, holding a casket of perfume. Round her aureole is written: VER PRIMOS FLORES PRIMOS ADUCIT ODORES. She is Spring, and with her come Justice and Summer. On another capital it would seem that Autumn and Winter accompany Fortitude and Temperance. Two other capitals are harder to interpret; their figures, seriously damaged, are merged in the leafage of a Corinthian capital. It is tempting to suppose that they may represent the remaining two of Radulphus Glaber's quaternities, the Elements and the Senses.

The remaining two capitals represent a double quaternity not mentioned by the writer, yet part of the very life of Cluny: the eight chants or tones of the liturgical use. The philosopher Boethius called the harmony of seasons and elements *mundana musica*, the music of the world; and to these Cluny added the celestial harmony of the music of the Church. The first tone is represented by

---

[1] The virtues, alone or trampling on their opposite vices, came into Romanesque iconography through the line-drawings that illustrated the manuscripts of the Psychomachia of Prudentius. They appear on many of the portals of Poitou and Saintonge, and some, notably Concord and Discord, on capitals at Anzy-le-Duc, Saint-Pierre-le-Moûtier, and elsewhere. Certain of the Vices appear on the portal of Saint-Sernin, the capitals of Vézelay, and the porches of Moissac and Charlieu. See Mâle, *Art rel. XIIe siècle,* p. 374.

a man with a lute; the second (Fig. 47) by a woman dancing, the third by a young man with a six-stringed zither, and so on. Each has a metrical Latin inscription that alludes to the particular quality of the chant figured: the rising movement of the third is compared with the Resurrection on the third day, the cadence of the fifth says how low is he fallen that would exalt himself, the sixth pertains to the number six as a symbol of perfection in the active life, the seventh recalls the seven gifts of the Spirit, and the eighth the eight beatitudes. The difficulty that a modern student has in interpreting these inscriptions shows how definitely they were intended for men learned in the lore of their esoteric significance.[1] The four gospels, the remaining quaternity, were represented in the painting of the apse and the sculpture of the tympanum that both showed Christ in majesty with the evangelistic beasts.[2] Only in a community so great and so closely unified as the Order of Cluny was so comprehensive a symbolic intention possible; and only in the Mother House, under the direct influence of a great and learned abbot, could it be put into execution. That abbot, St. Hugh of Semur, added philosophy to ornament and a meaning to beauty.

Suger, the great abbot of Saint-Denis, carried on and completed the work of artistic creation.[3] When he resolved on the rebuilding of his church and the enrichment of its treasury he wrote a Latin account of his work, *Liber de rebus in administratione sua gestis*,[4] which shows him at work. He was a little man of humble birth, thin, weakly, and stunted; his ideas were magnificent. He consciously visualized art as the medium between the human spirit and that intuition of the divine which was the ultimate aim of Benedictine thought: our poor minds may rise through the realities of sense upwards towards the truth. The great doors of gilt bronze, with scenes of the Passion and the Ascension, bore, like much of the work he planned, a Latin verse inscription that made his purpose plain:

> Portarum quisquis attollere quaeris honorem,
> Aurum nec sumptus, operis mirare laborem.
> Nobile claret opus, sed opus quod nobile claret
> Clarificet mentes ut eant per lumina vera
> Ad verum lumen, ubi Christus janua vera.
> Quale sit intus in his determinat aurea porta.
> Mens hebes ad verum per materialia surgit
> Et demersa prius hac visa luce resurgit.[5]

[1] The figures appear to be based on the illustrations of certain Cluniac tropers.

[2] The Benedictine abbey of Saint-Rémi de Reims once had a mosaic of the quaternities of the twelfth century, which combined a scheme not unlike St. Hugh's with the Firmament, the Zodiac, Wisdom, Jacob's Ladder, leading to the Altar, and the Sacrifice of Abraham as a prototype of the sacrifice of the Mass. Mâle, *Art rel. XIIᵉ siècle*, p. 319.

[3] For an admirable account of his iconographical innovations see Mâle, *Art rel. XIIᵉ siècle*, pp. 160–77. Watson, p. 77, denies that Mâle is right in thinking the Saint-Denis Jesse window a prototype.

[4] See E. Panofsky, *Abbot Suger*, Princeton, 1946, for an excellent translation.   [5] Lecoy, p. 155.

He inherited, and used, the Benedictine tradition of iconography: the labours of the months, theme of many monastic voussures, were set in mosaic round the ambulatory; the symbolic mill in which Paul grinds the Mosaic law into the new, that occurs on a capital at Vézelay, adorned a window; the eagle vase he made for the altar owed something to eagle capitals at La Charité and Saint-Révérien. The quaternities of Cluny reappeared in his scheme: the base of the great Cross of the abbey stood on figures of the four evangelists and was adorned with figures of the four elements, earth, air, fire, and water. Symbolism was linked with intrinsic magnificence: the stem of the Cross was enamelled with the life of Christ and its parallels in the Old Testament;[1] the Cross was enriched with all the jewels and pearls that he and his emissaries could collect in ten years; and the workmanship was so perfected that it took a team of goldsmiths from Lorraine two years to complete the figure of the dead Christ.[2]

Suger assembled, indeed, workmen from every part of the country: stone-masons, carpenters, painters, smiths, metal-casters, goldsmiths:[3] and set before them a great scheme with the parallels between Old and New Testaments for its basis. Just as Radulphus Glaber had written of Quaternities, and Abbot Hugh had translated them into art, so Walafrid Strabo had written of these parallels, and Abbot Suger made them visible. Isaac bearing the wood for his own sacrifice prefigured Christ bearing his Cross; Moses with the tablets of the Law prefigured Christ as the bringer of the New Law (Fig. 48); the Passover prefigured the Last Supper, the Brazen Serpent the Crucifixion, the Burning Bush the Ascension. A Christmas play that was performed as early as the end of the eleventh century at Saint-Martial de Limoges and other abbeys[4] had a procession of the prophets who foretold the coming of Christ. So Suger drew the links closer between Old and New Testaments by planning a window with a tree of Jesse and the prophets, and by ordering that statues of the personages of the Ancient Law and of the kings and queens of Judah should stand against the columns of his portal.[5] Again the idea is not wholly new: a magnificent Isaiah (Fig. 49) formed part of the portal of Souillac,[6] a prophet part of the door mullion at Moissac, and a whole series of prophets stood round the chapter-house door of Sainte-Marie-la-Daurade at Toulouse.[7] Suger, however, gave

---

[1] A parallel that goes back to the Early Christians' attempts to prove that they were indeed followers of the Messiah.   [2] Lecoy, p. 194.

[3] *Vita Sugeri* by the monk William, Bk. II.   [4] See Young, ii. 125.

[5] Some of the heads of these statues have recently been recognized at Baltimore. See M. C. Ross in *Journal of the Walters Art Gallery*, iii, 1940, p. 91.

[6] At Conques a console in the tribune has Isaiah with his scroll and St. John Baptist with his book on either side of a carving of the Annunciation. The work, on a small scale, must be roughly contemporary with that at Saint-Denis.

[7] See M. Lafargue, *Les Chapiteaux du cloître de Notre Dame la Daurade*, 1940, p. 87. They must have preceded those at Saint-Denis by some years.

a new importance to the scheme, which in its turn became part of Benedictine tradition.[1] Suger himself set another version of the composition on the portal of Notre-Dame de Corbeil, which he rebuilt (Fig. 50). When Saint-Germain-des-Prés had a new portal about 1160, it was given similar statues; when Saint-Loup-de-Naud was rebuilt about 1165 with the aid of a procession round France of the relics of its patron saint, apostles and prophets were combined in a single scheme.[2] At the Benedictine abbey of Vendôme statue columns of donors were set to guard a cupboard where relics were kept, beneath spandrels carved with the procession of the relics and the story of their reception in the abbey.[3]

On the portal of the abbey of Déols there were figure statues and a voussure with the labours of the months as at Saint-Denis, but the scheme was yet further enriched. The familiar tympanum of Christ in glory was given a new significance in an age of learning. Round it were set the Arts and Sciences that were the glory of Christendom as they had been of Hellenism. At the top of the voussure Philosophy spread her cloak to cover all the other kinds of learning. She handed to Grammar a scroll inscribed:

AVRI GRATIA SONENT SICVT SACRA DICTIO PARTES
PER TE DOCTRINE RELIQVE NOSCANTVR ET ARTES.

Dialectic received another with the legend:

ALTERA QVE DOCVIT SVCCINCTE FILIA MONSTRA
NOTAQVE SINT NOSTRIS PER TE SOPHISMATA VOSTRA.

Below Dialectic came Geometry with her compass, Music with a stringed instrument, and Physics with a globe, and below Grammar was Rhetoric, armed with sword and buckler, Astronomy, looking heavenwards and pointing to a star, and Arithmetic with a measuring-wand.[4]

Suger's abbey was less remote from the world than Cluny had been. It lay within a ride of Paris; when he was collecting jewels for his cross, kings and princes and great men came and stripped the rings from their fingers to add to the treasure. When his new basilica was dedicated on 11 June 1144, it was in the presence of the king, his wife, his mother, four archbishops, thirteen bishops, and innumerable abbots. From the beginning its iconographic scheme was less

[1] See C. de Lasteyrie in *Mon. Piot*, viii, 1902, p. 1.

[2] On the right-hand jamb St. Peter, Solomon, Isaiah, on the left St. Paul, the Queen of Sheba, Jeremiah. In the tympanum the Virgin and Apostles, Christ and the Evangelistic symbols; in the voussures the legend of Saint Loup. Other abbeys and priories which had column statues in the twelfth century are Saint-Ayoul de Provins, Nesle-la-Reposte, Saint-Pierre-au-Parvis at Soissons, Notre-Dame de Châlons, Déols, Saint-Benoît-du-Sault, Issy, Compiègne, Saint-Maur-des-Fossés, Saint-Quentin-lès-Beauvais, Ivry-la-Bataille. Aubert, p. 40.

[3] Willemin, i, pl. 16. The sculptures look as if they were of about 1160.

[4] See *Bull. Mon.* lxxxvi, 1927, p. 49.

esoteric than that of Cluny, and more comprehensible outside the cloister. It found its full development not within the Benedictine Order, but in the great cathedrals. Creation was passing from the Benedictine monasteries. When Abelard established the Paraclete in 1136, he set up a stone group to show in visible form the doctrine of the Trinity that he upheld: three figures in human form, the Father with a royal crown, the Son with a Crown of Thorns, and the Holy Spirit with a crown of flowers.[1] Such an expression of doctrine was, however, becoming rare. Theology was expounded not in art but in the crabbed texts of the Schoolmen; and art was content to portray again and again the story of the Childhood and Passion of our Lord and the parallels between the prophecies of the Old Testament and the gospel of the New. Monks were preoccupied less with the intuition of the Divine, through every human sense, than with the logical apprehension of the Divine through the intellect: the vision dissolved, to give place to the sound of reasoned argument.

5. LIVING-QUARTERS

The colour and emotion of Benedictine life was all concentrated in the church, with the altar as its focus; and with it was concentrated the beauty that the arts could bring inside the monastery. Outside the church monastic life was austere and barren, beautiful only in virtue of bareness. So long as the Benedictine ideal remained high the traditional simplicity of the monks' living-quarters endured. The primitive monasteries, little more than farm buildings, were early reconstructed in stone: both Odilo of Cluny and Gauzlin of Fleury could claim that they had found their abbey of wood and had left it of marble: but these constructions, however dignified in scale and simplicity, had no architectural pretensions. The remains of the eleventh-century conventual buildings at Saint-Bénigne de Dijon are of the plainest kind.[2] Everywhere the dorters were completely unadorned. Such outbuildings as survive, for instance at Cluny, are of a barn-like simplicity. The chapter-house was rarely as richly decorated in Romanesque France as it was in Norman England; a simple arcade to the cloister on either side of the door was usually its chief architectural feature. No infirmary church of the Romanesque period survives; and the lesser oratories in the woods near Saint-Wandrille and Montmajour are interesting only for their trefoil apses. The most common decoration of these monastic buildings was the appropriate one of carved Latin inscriptions. A door at Conques bears the eleventh-century legend:

HAS BENEDIC VALVAS QVI MVNDVM REX BONE SALVAS
ET NOS DE PORTIS SIMVL OMNES ERIPE MORTIS.

---

[1] Mortet, ii. 45.   [2] Cong. arch., 1928, p. 35.

E

Even the schoolroom cupboard had its legend:

ISTE MAGISTRORVM LOCVS EST SIMVL ET PVERORVM
MITTVNT QVANDO VOLVNT HIC RES QVAS PERDERE NOLVNT.

The refectory, the guest-house, and the cloister, the three places where some relaxation of monastic severity was permitted, were the three parts of the monastic buildings, apart from the church, where art had a place. The refectory at Cluny, given before 1093 by Roger de Montgomery, Earl of Shrewsbury,[1] had wall-paintings of founders and benefactors, with at one end a great picture of Christ in glory at the Judgement, with a Latin inscription beneath:

> Ecce dies magnus, quo judex praesidet agnus,
> Sponte vel ingratum cui subditur omne creatum.
> Infelix vere cui non datur ista timere!
> Nam praesens ignis domus est aeterna malignis.
> Deo gratias.

This scene was once reproduced on a smaller scale in the Cluniac refectory at Charlieu, with an arcaded frieze of carved stone with the Annunciation and other biblical scenes set beneath. In the refectory at Lavaudieu the monastic meals were set in relation with heavenly things by a fresco of the Last Supper; at Saint-Bénigne de Dijon a tympanum with the same subject was set above the door by Abbot Peter. At Montmajour, in classical Provence, a figure of Tantalus was set over the refectory door as a symbol of greed.[2]

Few monastic guest-houses have survived; here again it was natural to insist on a lesser austerity. The west cloister walk at Ruffec[3] has on the first floor a great room, lit by five pairs of twin windows looking away from the cloister, and heated by a wide fire-place with sculptured capitals. At Hambye a similar fire-place, carved with the four evangelistic beasts, survives in a room that was either part of the guest-house or a parlour.

The cloister, which linked the monastic buildings with the abbey church, was the place where the monks read for at least an hour a day, where speaking was permitted for half an hour in the morning after the chapter and for a shorter time after sext, when each was free to do his little domestic tasks. The cloisters were work-rooms and living-rooms, filled with light and air and sunshine. The quadrangular scheme would seem to have been derived from the angular wall structures of the East that provided shelter and enclosure, whether for soldiers or travellers or monks. The monastery of Qalaat Seman by the end of the fifth century had its quadrangular cloister fitting into the angle of the cruciform church, and the cloister with marble pillars which Benedict

---

[1] See Dr. Rose Graham in *Archaeologia,* lxxx. 155.
[2] Adhémar, p. 223.   [3] *Bull. Mon.* lxxxviii, 1929, p. 235.

began to build at Aniane in 782 must have followed some such Eastern prototype.

The majority of early Romanesque cloisters seem to have been built of wood, with stone arcades to the chapter-house as their chief architectural feature. At Saint-Aubin d'Angers these arches are prolonged into a richly carved arcade (Fig. 51). The actual doorway to the chapter-house is here of peculiar interest, for it is not only richly adorned with sculpture but also has the actual arch painted with the story of the Magi: a rare surviving instance of an alliance between sculpture and painting that was once common enough.

Odilo before 1049 had rebuilt the cloister at Cluny with columns of marble brought by river from Provence; but the earliest of the few surviving Benedictine cloisters in France is that of Moissac (Fig. 52A), built under Abbot Ansquitil in 1100; even this had its arches reset in the thirteenth century. The columns are alternately single and double, with a united capital for the double ones, a plan followed in other Cluniac cloisters,[1] and in such Benedictine houses as Saint-Benoît near Poitiers. Moissac has solid piers at the middle and end of each walk, with low reliefs of figures of the apostles and of Durandus, abbot from 1048 to 1072.[2] In other cloisters in southern France these piers are treated in higher relief, without arcades, to form statue piers (Fig. 53B): at Chamalières with David and prophets, at Saint-Guilhem-le-Désert and Saint-Étienne de Toulouse with apostles. In central France the sculpture was much less rich; the cloister at Lavaudieu may serve as an example.

All these cloisters, with continuous arcades, were intended to have wooden roofs; the massive piers at the corners provided support for the junction of the cross-beams. As the science of vaulting progressed it came to be applied to cloisters, and the piers were multiplied into a system of bays. At Carennac the pilasters are fluted and the double columns are oddly linked by a curved band. At Montmajour a wide arch to the cloister garth covers three inner arches of the older pattern. Eventually the intermediate columns were dropped out, and the vault rested on a series of massive piers, as at Nieul-sur-l'Autise and Saint-Amand-de-Boixe. The effect is sober and solid; the Benedictine cloisters of the Romanesque period never attained to the poetry and grace attained by those of an age when beauty rather than austerity was sought even within their enclosure.

6. BENEDICTINE GOTHIC

The third abbey church of Cluny, begun as early as 1088, had set a norm for Benedictine building. The influence of the Cluniac order had spread the Burgundian pointed arch from Le Wast in the Boulonnais to Ganagobie in the

[1] Salles, La Daurade, and Saint-Étienne de Toulouse.
[2] Cf. the reliefs of saints and angels at Saint-Sernin de Toulouse, now set round the ambulatory.

Alps; the plan, with a transept and radiating chapels, and an ambulatory in the larger churches, was almost universal for Benedictine churches; and enough stock themes for sculpture had been evolved for there to be no demand for innovations. Saint-Lomer de Blois, begun in 1138 and finished in 1186, is like La Charité in plan and shows little fresh initiative. Saint-Denis still has round-headed doors, and, with its pointed arches, arcaded façade, and false triforium, shows surprisingly little advance on Cluny. Even Fécamp, rebuilt in the first half of the thirteenth century, shows no real cleavage from the tradition that Cluny had established.

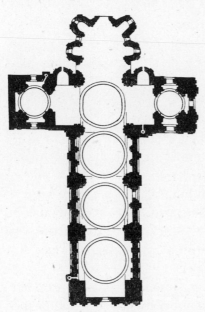

PLAN 4
Cathedral of Angoulême

Yet, for a time at least, it was in the monastic churches that the great experiments in vaulting that were to prove the basis of Gothic architecture were carried on. In a narrow band of country from Cahors by Périgueux and Angoulême to Saintes,[1] a number of churches were being built with a series of cupolas to vault the aisleless naves. The system was a multiplication of the traditional Benedictine cupola at the crossing to cover the wide single naves usual in the south-west. Solignac, consecrated in 1143, Souillac, and Saint-Étienne de Périgueux were among the earliest churches to be vaulted thus, and the plan was followed in some sixty churches,[2] often parish churches in monastic ownership. Such vaulting, however, demanded a particular type of church and a particular kind of stone, and had no more than a local vogue.[3]

The earliest instance in France of a groin vault applied to a nave occurs at Vézelay, revaulted by Abbot Artaud after the fire of 1120. A rib vault, first used for crypts, appears in the four western bays at Vézelay and in the upper story of the last bay of its narthex.[4] The next person to become interested in this system of vaulting seems to have been Hugh, Abbot of Saint-Martin-des-Champs, another Cluniac abbey, between 1130 and 1142. The dependent priory of Notre-Dame d'Airaines was built with rib vaults about 1130, another at Acy-en-Multien about 1140, another at Marolles-en-Brie somewhere between 1130 and 1145. At Saint-Martin itself the east end was rebuilt before 1140 with

[1] See Vallery-Radot, p. 118.   [2] See Lasteyrie, p. 789.
[3] Many architectural histories, assuming it to be a proof of Byzantine influence, have given it undue importance.
[4] I cannot altogether accept M. Oursel's views on its distribution: *L'Art roman de Bourgogne,* p. 99.

a double ambulatory and an elaborate system of rib vaults, with the traditional cul-de-four apse and choir merged into a single whole vaulted with a single system of eight ribs, sustaining gore-shaped cells with rounded sections that fall away from the centre of the vault almost as sharply as would a half-dome.[1]

This scheme in its turn became classical. It provided a model for Suger at Saint-Denis in the choir built between 1140 and 1144. The great Benedictine abbey of Saint-Germer de Fly has a similar but loftier vaulting scheme, and gains much in beauty by retaining the traditional triforium between the ambulatory arcade and the high windows.[2] As late as 1209 the roofing system of the apse with a single roof to cover both ambulatory and chapels was imitated at Mortemer and still later at Saint-Étienne de Caen. Saint-Pierre de Lagny in the thirteenth century still copied the double ambulatory of Saint-Martin, but added a clerestory above the choir arches.

At Cluny flying buttresses were added to the nave after part of its vault collapsed in 1125:[3] the first great range of buttresses to appear boldly above the aisle roofs of the church. At the Cluniac priory of Domont the apse, built soon after 1155, has not only the rib vault of Saint-Martin des Champs and the triforium of Saint-Germer, but also the flying buttresses of the mother house. Thus all the elements which combined to create the Gothic style—pointed arch, rib vault, flying buttresses, and triforium—were early found in Cluniac architecture. No less early were they integrated into a fully developed style. At Saint-Leu-d'Esserent we find true and even mature Gothic soon after 1160, with both quadripartite and sexpartite vaulting, a developed Gothic triforium, and elegant flying buttresses. The yet more advanced choir of Vézelay (Fig. 54), begun in 1170 by Abbot Guillaume de Mello and finished in 1201, has shafted colonette piers, water-leaf crockets, and a double-columned triforium to give it an elegance as accomplished as that of Cluniac Romanesque.[4] The tradition was continued in the town church of Notre-Dame at Cluny and in the apse at Souvigny. Even such lesser priories as Saint-Marcel-lès-Chalon were built in sound, if rather impersonal, Gothic.[5]

The next series of Benedictine buildings in Gothic style, magnificent though they are, derive from no monastic source but from the cathedrals. The bishops had succeeded the abbots as the architectural innovators. The choir of Saint-

[1] See C. Ward, *Medieval Church Vaulting* (Princeton Monographs on Art and Archaeology, V), Princeton, 1915, p. 138, for a detailed analysis.

[2] Another example of the middle of the twelfth century is Saint-Étienne de Beauvais.

[3] See Conant in *Speculum*, iv, 1929, p. 170. They were probably added soon after 1135.

[4] The apse, however, is still experimental. See C. Ward, op. cit., p. 140. Vézelay seems to have inspired the early-thirteenth-century choir of the Abbaye aux Hommes at Caen.

[5] Yet, outside the Île de France, men were slow to understand the rib vault. In the priory of Jazeneuil in Poitou, finished in 1164, and at Luzignan, probably by the same builders, the cul-de-four apses have meaningless ribs that are merely decorative.

Germain-des-Prés, consecrated in 1163, is notably less advanced than the contemporary cathedral of Notre-Dame de Paris. The choir of Saint-Rémi de Reims (Fig. 55), rebuilt by Abbot Pierre de Celles between 1170 and 1190, is peculiarly impressive in the breadth of its vault, the elegance of its arcades, and the coherence of its design;[1] but it is a derivative, with few modifications, of the scheme of the cathedrals of Laon and Noyon. The splendid new nave of Saint-Denis, built between 1231 and 1281, was designed by Pierre de Montereau, essentially a cathedral architect. When in the thirteenth century the monks of Mouzon came to build, they frankly imitated the cathedral of Laon on a smaller scale; when the abbey of Ébreuil in the Allier rebuilt its choir they took Noyon for a model. Sometimes the very masons were the same. When Richard de Saint-Léger, Abbot of Bec, decided to rebuild the abbey church in 1214, he set Enguerrand, who had been *magister operis* of Rouen Cathedral, in charge of the work, though he proved so unsatisfactory that he was dismissed after eighteen months[2] and succeeded by Gautier de Meulan. The crocketed glory of his achievement[3] rivalled any cathedral. Saint-Ouen de Rouen, again, was rebuilt in cathedral fashion by Abbot Jean Roussel in 1318, as a finer and more mature version of the cathedral of Évreux.

The approximation of monastic to secular churches was paralleled by the increasing influence of secular domestic architecture upon the monastic buildings. This is well seen in those of Mont-Saint-Michel, begun in 1203, finished in 1228, and called not without reason *La Merveille*. The exceptional site on a small rocky island made the usual ground-plan impossible. A cellar and almonry were built on the ground floor, with massive rectangular piers and a lofty vaulted roof. Above these was built a large chapter-house,[4] with a central line of slender columns with carved capitals and a high-pitched rib vault. This was finished in 1213. Alongside it the scriptorium of the monastery, built between 1215 and 1220,[5] has two rows of less lofty columns, with leafage capitals worthy of a cathedral. Above the chapter-house is a great refectory, built in 1225 (Fig. 56 B), with arcaded sides, fifty-nine long and narrow windows, and a barrel roof. Over the scriptorium, by a most ingenious plan, is the cloister (Fig. 56 A), with slender shafts and bell capitals, spandrels covered with leafage, and a double arcade set in interlacing fashion with the second row of arches coming in the middle of the first. Originally the capitals and the sculpture were coloured, and the wooden roof glowed with brilliant painting; it must have

---

[1] The plate of Saint-Nicaise de Reims in the *Monasticon Gallicanum* shows it to have been no less splendid and no less cathedral-like.

[2] Swartwout, p. 105. It is noteworthy that he was expected to finish the church within a year and a half.   [3] See an indifferent engraving in the *Monasticon Gallicanum*.

[4] Now called the Salle des Hôtes.

[5] Since the Institution of the Order of Saint Michel by Louis XI in 1469 this has been called the Salle des Chevaliers.

seemed like the page of an illuminated manuscript miraculously turned into a place of meditation upon the summit of a rock in a waste of ocean. The church itself—noble, but less unusual than the monastic buildings—had its topmost pinnacle crowned by a great gilded statue of the Archangel, which turned with the wind, and seemed to defy the elements with its bright outstretched sword.[1] Even *La Merveille* was not built without protest; the *Conte des Vilains de Verson*,[2] written soon after it was finished, reproves the serfs of the abbey for their unwillingness to cart stone for the building and to carry hods for the masons.

> La pierre deivent amener
> Toz les jorz quil est en mestier
> Sanz contredit et sanz dangier . . .
> Il doivent servir les machons
> Et de la pierre et del mortier.

The mature Gothic period did not see the end of Benedictine building. Work of beauty continued to be produced; that much of it perished in the Revolution is no reason why it should be forgotten. The ruins of such abbeys as Hambye and Saint-Wandrille have an architectural beauty that is more enduring than the picturesqueness with which Time has endowed them. The octagon that forms the choir of Saint-Paul de Ferrières may owe its inspiration to an earlier rotunda, but it has a strength and originality of its own. The fine apse of the priory of Évron, built about 1300, has the true elegance of *gothique rayonnant*, with oval columns in the ambulatory, fine window-tracery, and seven radiating chapels. The great window that rose in the fourteenth century between the western towers of Vézelay may seem an anachronism, but in itself it is beautiful. Even in the second half of the fifteenth century a Benedictine church of consistent plan and formal beauty could be achieved. The great church of Celles-sur-Belle, the ambulatory chapel of Saint-Germain d'Auxerre (Fig. 57) bear witness to the sustained vitality of the Order.

Soon, however, a time came when the great abbeys had neither wealth nor inclination to build new churches. La Chaise-Dieu, it is true, was rebuilt between 1344 and 1378, but the new church was the gift of Pope Clement VI who had been a monk of the abbey, and of his nephew, Pope Gregory XI. Of its three architects one at least, Pierre de Cébazat, was primarily a cathedral builder: he finished Clermont. Its pillars, without capitals, and its keystones, with no ornament but the papal arms, show a remarkable lack of iconographic invention. Its chief beauties lie in its stalls (Fig. 58) and its tapestries, both of which are influenced by the art of cathedrals rather than of monasteries.

[1] It was set up at the end of the twelfth century by Abbot Rainulf de Villedieu. A prophecy was made that when it was cast down the abbey would be ruined. It was struck by lightning in 1788, and the prophecy was soon fulfilled.

[2] Delisle, *Étude sur la condition de la classe agricole*, Paris, 1903, p. 83.

7. BENEDICTINE DECLINE

The year 1144, in which Suger's church of Saint-Denis was dedicated, marks the apogee of monastic art. Thereafter, however great the accomplishment, the decline in creation was rapid. In 1146 Louis VII imposed a tax towards the cost of the Second Crusade on the whole country, which bore especially heavily on the old Benedictine foundations. Even rich Fleury had to pawn two great silver candelabra and sell a golden censer outright to meet it;[1] and the tax was but the first of many like impositions. By the middle of the century the monks' influence as educators had passed into the hands of the secular clergy,[2] and with it the hope of many a rich donation and bequest. The Crusades were rivalling and dwarfing other pilgrimages; the Cistercians seemed to have a monopoly of Benedictine fervour. In the thirteenth century secular priests were busy in attacking the monastic saints: Saint Martial was no longer unquestionably accepted as the apostle of the Limousin, and the body of the Magdalene at Vézelay was discredited.[3] The Visitations of Symon, Archbishop of Bourges, between 1281 and 1298 already show many small priories almost devoid of monks, and some deserted and let as farms.[4] It was the glories of the past, rather than splendours that were to come, that inspired most of the abbots who had money enough left to think of building.

Iconographic creation, too, was passing into other hands. The late Romanesque monastic churches of Poitou and Saintonge have a profusion of sculptured ornament, but rarely have any consistent purpose or scheme of decoration. When about 1180 the Abbot of Saint-Denis gave his monks a new washing-fountain, it was adorned with no representation of the Rivers of Paradise, but with some thirty heads of the gods and goddesses of antiquity, without any symbolic connexion or significance.[5] When the Abbot of Montmajour bought a new ciborium for his church (Fig. 59) he got it ready-made from Limoges, and was satisfied with no more symbolic decoration than angels and apostles and a sham Cufic inscription.

About 1200 a new north door was added to the Cluniac church of Saint-Pierre-le-Moûtier. Its design was based on the traditional tympanum subject of Christ in glory, but the scheme was curiously weakened. The Evangelistic Beasts were too strange and irrational to be acceptable to the age; instead, the Evangelists are represented writing at desks,[6] looking like students taking notes

---

[1] Chénesseau, p. 25.

[2] Rashdall, *Universities of Europe in the Middle Ages,* ed. Powicke and Emden, Oxford, 1936, i. 344.

[3] About 1280 it was declared that the true body had been found at Saint-Maximin in Provence.

[4] Coulton, ii. 230.

[5] See Adhémar, p. 265. They included Jupiter, Juno, Neptune, Thetis, Ceres, Bacchus, Pan, Faunus, Flora, Silvanus, the Elements, Paris and Helen, the fable of the Wolf and the Lamb, and Hercules and Geryon. The remains are now at the École des Beaux-Arts at Paris.

[6] The scheme is found in some Carolingian manuscripts.

at a lecture. The beasts' heads, however, still appear in the cusps, and the four angels that traditionally upheld Christ's aureole occupy the voussure. The scheme was reproduced at Fleury, evidently by the same sculptor, with a lintel carved with the translation of the relics of St. Benedict; and again at Donnemarie, with a statue of Christ on the central pier. Yet in the little priory of Parçay-Meslay[1] the old scheme of Christ in Majesty is given a new significance: Christ holds the Gospel in one hand, and in the other the Eucharistic Host.

The scriptoria of the monasteries had ceased to be centres of creation. Even in production they were giving place to the workrooms of professional secular scribes. A life of a saint written and illuminated in the abbey of Saint-Denis in 1250 is a little coarse and distinctly amateurish in execution: no gold was used upon it.[2] The Cartulary of Baignes, of much the same date, is still Romanesque in style.[3] It was, no doubt, this want of an artistic centre in the monastery itself that in some measure caused the decline. The iconography of Benedictine churches after the middle of the thirteenth century is rarely characteristic. The priory of Saint-Mayeul at Veurdre, for example, has late-thirteenth-century wall-paintings with scenes of the three estates at work: nobles, clergy, and labourers: an interesting scheme but one not especially monastic. The glass given to Ambierle by Prior Antoine de Balzac d'Entragues a little before 1491 represents no encyclopedic Benedictine scheme, but a succession of saints under rich canopies. There is his name-saint, Antony; the local saints, Germain, Bonnet, and Haon, and the martyrs of his see of Die, Apollinaria, Achillée, Fortunat, Ferréol, and Julien. The whole scheme, indeed, refers to the donor, and not to the monastery or the universe.

Similarly the later Benedictine wall-paintings lack the force and originality that the Romanesque decorations had derived from their manuscript prototypes. Paintings at Tournus, dating from the middle of the fourteenth century, of the Virgin enthroned beside her Son, with censing angels on either side, and of the Last Judgement, reproduce the central motives of many sculptured tympana.[4] Even when a monastic window establishes a new tradition, as does one from Jumièges[5] with prophets and the articles of the Creed associated with them, it goes back, in fact, to Suger's tradition of parallels between the Old and New Testament. Yet the abbots did what they could to make their workmen feel

---

[1] Indre-et-Loire.

[2] Delisle, *Mélanges,* p. 239. As late as 1317 there was an illuminator at the abbey, Gilles Mauléon, who painted a book of hours for Jeanne de Bourgogne, but he was an exception. Delisle, *Douze livres,* p. 63.

[3] In the Bibliothèque du Grand Séminaire, Angoulême. See *Rev. de l'art chrét.* xxxviii, 1888, p. 324.

[4] Lemoisne, p. 30. The late-fifteenth-century painting of the Virgin and St. Joseph adoring the Child at Lézignan, Aude, seems to be influenced by a contemporary engraving.

[5] Now at La Meilleraye-sur-Seine. J. Lafond, *Les Vitraux de l'ancienne abbaye de Jumièges,* Rouen, 1926. It dates from before 1346.

a real loyalty to the abbey they served, and a real community with the brethren. When Hugh, Abbot of Meaux between 1339 and 1349, ordered a new crucifix for the choir of the lay brethren, he not only provided the sculptor with a naked man as a model, but also agreed that he should carve no beautiful or notable feature save on a Friday, when he had fasted.[1] When in 1402 Abbot William summoned Gautier du Four, a goldsmith of Paris, to Saint-Germain-des-Prés to repair the saint's shrine, he arranged that for two years he and his assistant were to become to all intents and purposes members of the community, though with a much greater ration of food, firewood, and candles.[2]

Few abbeys, however, were rich enough or near enough to an industrial centre thus to re-create a monastic workshop such as Suger had earlier formed at Saint-Denis. The requirements of the sacristy were usually filled from the shops of Limoges or Paris. Even when they were specially ordered they show little originality, and any unusual saints that were represented were portrayed according to a familiar scheme. The chief novelty was the use of a double cross-piece for crosses, a Byzantine form that came to be used particularly by Benedictine abbeys.[3]

By the end of the fourteenth century the design of Benedictine goldwork had nothing characteristic left. Often, too, it was the gift of a layman, and celebrated him as much as the saint it honoured. In 1398 Charles VI gave a reliquary to Saint-Denis representing his patron, Saint Charlemagne; the royal saint, Saint Louis, and kneeling figures of the King, the Queen, and the Dauphin, on the same scale as their heavenly protectors.[4]

The laymen who were excluded from the monastic enclosure in their lifetime invaded it after their death. The abbeys became the mausoleums of the great houses of France:[5] their splendid tombs, that existed to emphasize the importance of the individual, struck a note of worldly glory that formed no part of

[1] Swartwout, pp. 125 and 181.

[2] 'Each working day they shall receive, for two persons, for breakfast one convent loaf and one pint of wine. At the dinner hour, for two persons, two convent loaves, one pint of wine, a piece of beef or mutton and a sufficiency of broth; and at supper, the same as for dinner; and on fast-days, to each person shall be given three eggs or two herrings and broth at dinner and for supper to each person two eggs and a cheese for all the week such as we have; and also we shall give them a sufficiency of firewood to warm them and candles to sup and go to bed by, when necessary. And we agree to provide them with a stout chest, to hold the pieces of the shrine, tools and so on, well and securely and this chest shall have two keys, of which the said goldsmiths shall have one and we the other.' Swartwout, p. 175.

[3] An early one survives in the priory of Les Cars. A fine example from Saint-Vincent de Laon is in the Louvre. It was given by Hugo, abbot from 1174 to 1205. Another from the Abbaye de la Boissière, now in the Chapelle des Incurables at Baugé, Maine-et-Loire, is said to have been brought from Constantinople in the thirteenth century by Jean d'Alleye. It was the origin of the double-cross emblem of the house of Anjou, later adopted by the Dukes of Lorraine.   [4] Courajod, ii. 132.

[5] The royal family at Saint-Denis; the house of Dreux at Saint-Yved-de-Braisne, the house of Auvergne at Le Bouchet, the house of Bourbon at Montet-aux-Moines and Souvigny.

the monastic scale. The monasteries that had ceased to receive laymen as members *ad succurrendum* at their lives' end accepted their dead bodies and the obligation of prayers for their souls. The addition of chantry chapels to abbey churches added another element alien to Benedictine traditions. By the last quarter of the fourteenth century such chantry chapels had grown from little carrels between the buttresses into annexes that were minor churches. Charles V chose the chapel of St. John Baptist at Saint-Denis as a burial-place for himself and his successors, and endowed it with two daily masses and four anniversaries. At Souvigny the original Benedictine plan was modified in 1376 to include a great funerary chapel for Louis II de Bourbon and his wife Anne d'Auvergne, and this was balanced about 1440 by another for Charles I de Bourbon and his wife Agnes of Burgundy. In 1397 Louis d'Orléans founded a chapel at Cluny, enriched it with stained glass and paintings, and endowed a daily mass.[1]

Insensibly the presence of such magnificent monuments influenced their surroundings. The tombs of the abbots, that had once been simple slabs incised only with a crozier or simple decorative reliefs,[2] became more personal.[3] At La Chaise-Dieu the tomb of Abbot Renaud de Montclar, who died in 1346, has ten figures of angels in quatrefoils on the sides. The brass at La Couture du Mans[4] of Abbot Paschal Huguenot, who died in 1399, was as magnificent as any secular brass; indeed, in the fifteenth century the finest brasses were usually those of abbots and bishops, just as the finest incised slabs were usually those of knights. Sculptured tombs were not mere recumbent effigies, but were set within sculptured niches; that of Abbot Jean de Favières, for example, in the abbey of Évron, rested beneath reliefs of the Virgin with the body of Christ, a Crucifixion surrounded by the instruments of the Passion, and an angel with a scroll of prayer.[5]

[1] Laborde, iii. 142. Similar chapels were erected by men not of royal birth: the abbey of Saint-Pierre-de-Fursac has a fine chantry chapel, built in the late fourteenth century as a burial-place for the family of Chabannes, and the priory of Yzeure, near Moulins, has at the end of its north aisle a great chapel founded in 1389 by Jean Saulnier, Chamberlain of Charles V, with an endowment to secure Masses for his soul. Occasionally, too, other links were forged between monastery and feudalism. A reformed Benedictine Order, the Célestins, founded by Pope Celestine V about 1254, before his elevation to the Papacy (Hélyot in Migne, xx, col. 715), derived most of its later wealth from a knightly order, the Ordre de la Couronne, founded by Enguerrand VII de Coucy in 1390 (ibid. xxi, col. 779). Too little remains of any of its twenty-one houses (the most important were Ambert near Orléans, Mont-de-Châtres near Compiègne, Mantes, and Paris) to show if any iconographic or architectural innovations ensued. [2] e.g. the tomb of Peter the Venerable at Cluny.

[3] The sculptured arcaded tomb of Abbot Pierre de Saint-Fontaine, d. 1110, at Airvault may represent an abortive attempt at canonization. A late-twelfth-century tomb of an abbot, sculptured with his effigy in low relief, is in the Museum of Issoudun. The Abbey of Jumièges once had (drawn for Gaignières, Bodleian MS. viii. 36) a long series of floor tombs of the thirteenth century of black, white, and yellow tiles inlaid to form rude effigies, and there were similar tombs at Hambye (remains in the Museum at Avranches).

[4] Gaignières, Bodleian MS. xv. 21. [5] Gaignières, Bodleian MS. xv. 90.

So, too, the figures of lay donors invaded monastic iconography. The portal of the priory of Saint-Thibault, begun in 1297 to receive the relics of a saint who had died only fifty years before, has his statue on the mullion; the death and assumption of the Virgin on the tympanum; and on the jambs statues of the founders and benefactors of the church: Robert II, Duke of Burgundy, and his wife Agnes, his son Hugues V, and Hugues d'Arcy, Bishop of Autun. Gradually this alien splendour invaded other parts of the monastic building. Late Gothic cloisters lack the austerity of those of the great Benedictine age. At Tulle the bays of the cloister have a *voûte angevine*, with liernes and tiercerons in the English manner, and the arcades plate tracery; at Saint-Jean-des-Vignes the tracery has become more elaborate and the external buttresses and cornices more richly decorated (Fig. 60); at Saint-Wandrille the last stages of Gothic are represented in the flowing curvilinear tracery.

A similar course of elaboration may be followed in other parts of the monastic buildings. The early thirteenth-century dorter of Saint-Bénigne de Dijon, some hundred and sixty-three feet long, had rather high-pitched rib vaults resting on slender columns with leafage capitals, with a long row of angular windows, each with an oculus above.[1] The refectory beneath[2] (Fig. 61) is planned like a church, with rib-vaulted nave and aisles. The seventeenth-century plates of the *Monasticon Gallicanum* reveal the existence of a whole series of splendid Gothic refectories that have since been destroyed,[3] lit by traceried windows that would have graced a church. One such building, hardly less fine, still survives at Léhon, near Dinan, with fine Flamboyant windows and a reader's pulpit.

The chapter-house of Saint-Georges-de-Boscherville, built between 1157 and 1211, has a fine rib vault like that of an apse, and capitals carved with the sacrifice of Isaac, Moses with the Tables of the Law, the Passage of the Red Sea, and two monks kneeling and receiving the strokes of a birch from a hooded abbot. At Saint-Pierre-sur-Dives the chapter-house still has its pavement of ornamental encaustic tiles. At Saint-Étienne de Caen[4] even the dormitory had such tiles, on a great rosette scheme, filled in with nineteen coats of arms on a scrolling ground. At Champdieu in the late thirteenth century a series of coats of arms was painted along the refectory wall, to which a figure in armorial garments was added later. Yet the old traditions were not dead, for above the mantelpiece a fine Last Supper was painted, with the prior who gave the picture kneeling below.

[1] *Cong. arch.*, 1928, p. 36.   [2] Now the Musée Archéologique.
[3] At Saint-Germain-des-Prés, an aisleless hall with eight traceried windows on either side, a lofty vault, mosaic floor, rich stained glass, and a reader's pulpit carved with vine leaves; at Saint-Étienne de Caen; at Saint-Évroul; at Corbie, with ten lofty windows and pinnacled buttresses between; at Saint-Martin de Pontoise; and at Saint-Ouen de Rouen.
[4] Now destroyed; painted in Gaignières, Bodleian MS. 18361, p. 2.

Even the monastic kitchens were made more splendid. A group of monasteries in the Loire district[1] each had one made like a circular chapel with hearths in the walls.

While the monastic buildings were being rebuilt, the abbots were acquiring quarters of their own. At Lagrasse the abbot's lodging, built in 1290, has a chapel on two floors like a castle chapel, decorated with frescoes and patterned glazed tiles. In a forest near Boulogne there are still ruins of the country house[2] built in the fourteenth century for the Abbot of Notre-Dame de Boulogne. Jean de Bourbon, Abbot of Cluny, built himself not only a splendid town house at Paris[3] but also a fine palace at Cluny[4] between 1456 and 1485. It has sculptured fire-places that rival those of the palace of the Duke of Burgundy at Dijon. Even this was not splendid enough for his successor Jacques d'Amboise, who built another alongside[5] it of which the façade was almost covered in sculptured decoration.[6] At Clermont, near Laval, the abbot's lodging was painted at the end of the fifteenth century with not only a moral picture of the death of the Just Man, but also with decorative paintings of hunting in a forest and genre figures of an old woman and a pedlar.

This approximation between monastic buildings and castles was increased by the necessity for fortification. The walls of Cluny were strengthened in the middle of the fourteenth century by the erection of a fortified tower that still bears the name of Abbot Hugues Fabry who built it. With its machicolations, arrow-slits, and *chemin de ronde*, it is worthy of any fortress. At La Chaise-Dieu, André de Chanac, abbot between 1378 and 1420, built a great fortified donjon; and in the same century many such abbeys as Uzerche and Saint-Pons-de-Thomières had to have their churches fortified. A common danger drove abbots and feudal lords to employ a common architecture.

[1] See plates in the *Monasticon Gallicanum*. The Trinité de Vendôme; Saint-Pierre de Bourgueil, Saint-Florent de Saumur, Pontlevoy, Saint-Père de Chartres, and Fontevrault. Of all of these only the last survives, in a much-restored condition.

[2] Called Moulin l'Abbé. See plate in *Monasticon Gallicanum*.   [3] Now the Musée de Cluny.

[4] Now the Musée Ochier.   [5] Now the Hôtel de Ville.

[6] At Tournus these splendours were emulated in a lodging built between 1471 and 1496, and at Saint-Ouen in yet more secular style, in a building as rich as a palace.

III

THE CISTERCIANS

1. THE ORDER OF CÎTEAUX

THE abbots of Cluny, by their reform of the Benedictine rule, founded a great Order almost without knowing it. Its *consuetudines* laid down no particular artistic prescriptions, and it was only by virtue of the influence of Cluny and its successive abbey churches that a Cluniac style arose. The next great reform, that of Cîteaux, again created an Order, but one as consciously different from that of Cluny as it was possible to be within the limits of the Benedictine Rule. The Cistercian Rule soon laid down a code of artistic prohibitions to ensure that Cluniac fashions should not be followed. Consequently, while Cluniac art must be considered as a part of Benedictine art, the art of Cîteaux and its daughter houses demands separate consideration.

In 1098 two monks of Molesme, Alberic and Stephen Harding, came to feel that they were pledged by their vows to keep the Benedictine Rule, yet were perjuring themselves by following the lax customs of their monastery. Only outside it could they hope to keep their given word. They worked upon some of their companions, and upon Robert, their abbot, who finally not only gave them leave to migrate but himself went at their head. They persuaded Raymond, Vicomte de Beaune, to give them land in a remote glade in one of his forests, called Cîteaux, where with money given by Eudes, Duke of Burgundy, they built a church and a house of wood. There they instituted a monastery on the Feast of St. Benedict in the spring of 1098, when their black Benedictine robes were changed for white habits as a symbol of new life. The monastery might have remained an isolated experiment, and might have suffered extinction for lack of novices, had not a great man come to join it in 1114: Bernard of Clairvaux, a member of a landed Burgundian family, who came at the head of a band of his friends and relations to bring new life to the little community. He was a born leader of men, but he was born to lead them over stony paths. His faith, narrow and fanatical, gave charity to the naked and the starving, but none to those who followed Christ in another fashion than his own. He himself entered into beauty through the gate not of sight, but of sound; his own gifts as poet and orator gave him no insight into the work of sculptors and artists. He grew skilled in the dialectic and the Latinity of the universities; but any man who used argument in the pursuit of independent thought or Latin as an instrument of humane culture was his avowed enemy. Abelard and his faithful friend Peter the Venerable came to stand for all these enemies, and Peter's Order of Cluny for all that Bernard hated in monasticism.

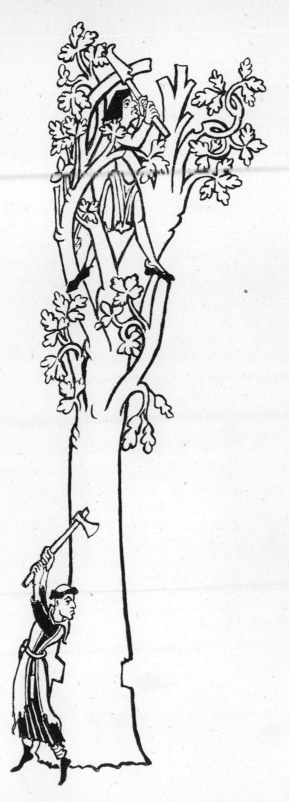

From *Moralia in Job* finished at Cîteaux on Christmas Eve IIII

Hatred and austerity have a force that is not always given to love and toler-ance. St. Bernard's coming made Cîteaux into a living community. Soon, indeed, daughter houses had to be founded to accommodate the brethren who had grown too numerous for Cîteaux herself: La Ferté-sur-Grosne and Pontigny in 1114, Morimond and Clairvaux in 1115, Fontenay in 1119. Bernard himself became abbot of Clairvaux, an abbey endowed by the generosity of Hugh, Count of Troyes, and brought with him the twelve monks prescribed by Bene-dictine tradition for a new house. In the first thirty-seven years of the history of the Order sixty-five abbeys were founded. Fifty years after the foundation of Cîteaux there were five hundred houses in the Order; about 1260 as many as eighteen hundred spread the influence of Cîteaux from Scandinavia to Spain and from Poland to Ireland. Clairvaux itself grew to have as many as seven hundred brethren, including a hundred novices.[1]

These foundations were only made in solitary places. The Benedictines had liked to build on a hill or a spur, and above all to have an open view. The Cistercians demanded water, an enclosed site in a wooded valley or on a plain near a river. The names of their houses in themselves depict the secluded beauty of such sites: l'Abbaye-aux-Bois, le Val-Notre-Dame, Fontfroide, Clairlieu, Clairefontaine, Hort-Dieu, Vauluisant, Clairmarais, Bellaigue, Noirlac, l'Abbaye de l'Eau.[2] Though they were thus situated in rural solitudes, their economic system depended on urban buyers; the Cistercians did not plan their estates, as the Cluniacs had done, merely to supply their own needs, but deliberately farmed on a large scale for the market. Consequently manual labour became of much greater importance, since upon it the prosperity of the abbey depended, and intellectual pursuits took a lesser place than at Cluny. One of the clauses of the Cistercian *Carta Caritatis* was that no Cistercian should compose verse.

Stephen Harding, who had lived at Sherborne, Salisbury, and Paris in cloisters with fine libraries, had a cultivated taste in manuscripts. Those that he chose, or was given, for the library of Cîteaux, and those that were written there under his auspices,[3] are as fine as any contemporary Benedictine books. His Bible,[4] written between 1098 and 1109, has a Queen Esther and a St. James that might figure as column-statues on any façade (Fig. 62); a great page with King David has a fighting scene that is like a fragment of the Bayeux Tapestry. A copy of the *Moralia in Job*, finished at Cîteaux on Christmas Eve, 1111,[5] has all kinds of genre subjects: monks hewing a tree-trunk; a monk harvesting; others busy with the vintage; a group of jongleurs; a man with a flail; cloth-weavers; a

---

[1] Coulton, i. 300.

[2] See J. Laurent in *Saint Bernard et son temps*, p. 168. Other names were devotional: Le Lieu-Dieu, La Bénisson-Dieu, La Grâce-Dieu, La Merci-Dieu, La Clarté-Dieu, L'Oraison-Dieu, La Garde-Dieu.

[3] Since the Revolution the Cîteaux MSS. have been in the city library of Dijon. On them see Oursel, p. 7.

[4] MS. Dijon, 14.   [5] See Oursel, p. 31.

knight starting for the chase; a rider thrown from a horse. I know of no contemporary work with so vivid a sense of the interest of everyday things: the
scribe watched every detail of the life about him with a seeing eye. The legendary of the abbey,[1] written in the second decade of the twelfth century, is
adorned with figures set against panels of ornament, and has a fine page with
Christ and twelve prophets within a border of palmettes, animals, and debased
cufic letters.[2] The most magnificent page is in honour of the Virgin. She
appears, holding the Child, in an aureole, with the legend ΘΕΟΤΟΚΟΣ: Jesse, in
an embroidered mantle, lies below, and round them are symbolic medallions
of Moses and the burning bush, Gideon watching the dew falling upon his
fleece, Daniel in the lions' den, and the Hebrews in the fiery furnace: the symbols
of virginity that had passed into mediaeval religious imagery from Honorius of
Autun's sermon on the Annunciation. Above is the Dove of the Holy Spirit.
The drawing illustrates a sermon in honour of the Virgin by Fulbert of Chartres,
and is at once decorative, literary, and symbolical.

Had Stephen Harding continued to be the leader of the Cistercian movement,
the iconography of the Virgin might have been greatly enriched, for to her the
Order was especially dedicated. But instead Bernard came to dominate it, and
he was a man who despised beauty. He is said to have spent a year in the novices'
room without noticing whether the ceiling was flat or vaulted, and to have
been amazed one day to discover that the apse of the chapel had three windows
and not one. The only art he encouraged was that of music, and that less for
its own sake than as a form of worship. He pruned away all the Cluniac accretions from the bare Benedictine Office, except for the recital of the Office of the
Dead, and strove in like manner to prune away all the accretions of splendour
and beauty from the Benedictine tradition of the abbey church. The Cistercian
documents of his time are full of nothing but prohibitions. The *Carta Caritatis*,
drawn up between 1107 and 1119, forbids crosses of gold or silver,[3] candlesticks,
except of plain iron or copper, vestments of richer stuff than linen or fustian,
altar-cloths of anything but linen, and any curious carving, stained glass, or
paintings in the church. The *Consuetudines* of 1134 specifically forbid illuminated initials in manuscripts: 'Litterae unius coloris fiant et non depictae.' By
the end of the century manuscripts from Vauclerc have uncoloured initials
printed with the aid of metal or wooden dies,[4] and the standard plan for a

---

[1] MS. Dijon, 641.

[2] See J. J. Marquet de Vasselot in *Bull. Soc. Nat. Ants France*, 1925, p. 226.

[3] Precious metal was only permitted for the chalice and paten. Those said to have been used by
St. Bernard were preserved at Clairvaux up to the Revolution. The paten was engraved with an Agnus
Dei, the chalice was quite plain except for a polygonal knop. A drawing of them exists (Bib. de
l'Arsenal, Paris, MS. 5055) and is reproduced in Lavisse, *Histoire de France*, ii. 2, pl. 15. They may,
however, have been funerary, for they bear some likeness to those recently found in the tomb of a
Bishop of Orleans. See *Illustrated London News*, 29 Jan. 1938, p. 161.   [4] Blum, p. 11.

F

Cistercian monastery had ceased to include a scriptorium. Moreover the *Consuetudines* formally excluded from Cistercian churches all figured decoration except a crucifix of painted wood.[1] If any abbot dared to transgress these rules his work was to be destroyed without remission or dispensation.

The early monastic buildings had all been of wood: Cîteaux at the foundation, Notre-Dame-des-Châtelliers in 1121, Morimond in 1124:[2] but for practical reasons they were all rebuilt in stone as soon as funds permitted. It seems likely that the wooden buildings may have been erected by the monks themselves,[3] but those of stone were the work of skilled masons. Just as a sisterhood at its foundation often adopts the plainest possible version of the feminine wear in use at the time, and codifies it into a uniform, so Bernard adopted the plainest possible version of the current Burgundian style as the basis of the architecture of his Order. Such a parish church as Brancion is the starting-point of Cistercian building. Its codification into a Cistercian architecture was no doubt hastened by the remote situation of the abbeys; there could be no question of employing masons from a neighbouring town, and a team of workmen must have gone on from one secluded abbey to another, with little but prohibitions to assist them in their work.

Out of this negative code a style was gradually forged. The only aim of the abbot who directed it was austerity, yet through the skill of the masons beauty would creep in. Nowhere are wide pointed arches of more beautiful line than in Cistercian churches; nowhere is fine masonry better set; nowhere are vaults more honest or better planned.[4] Yet it was a cold and wintry beauty, without warmth or colour. The valley damp might stain the walls, but it was their only adornment; the plane-trees might shadow the windows with green, and their dead leaves star the floor, but it was their only colour. Even our eyes, trained in Puritan standards, find in the Cistercian churches of the Romanesque period an under-water pallor and coldness; and they must have seemed far stranger in their own day, when every other church glowed with colour and gold.

Such ornamental elements as were introduced were dictated not by the fancy of the abbot but by the technical skill of the workmen. A simple rose window was part of the masons' tradition, and they generally used it on all the end walls of the church, façade, apse, and transept. At Silvanès three small rose windows

---

[1] Mortet, ii. 31. These prescriptions were renewed in 1213 and 1251.

[2] Mortet, i. 295.

[3] Ordericus Vitalis (*Hist. eccles.* III. viii in Migne, *Pat. Lat.* clxxxviii) says that the Cistercians built their abbeys with their own hands, but soon after 1133 St. Bernard praises the workmen for their work at Clairvaux.

[4] For this reason the Cistercians unconsciously helped to disseminate vaulting systems; Loc-Dieu and Silvanès brought the cross vault into southern France, as Flaran and Fontfroide near Narbonne did the rib vault. See Mâle, *Art et artistes*, p. 115.

are grouped in a triangle round a larger one to adorn the square apse. Since coloured glass was not permitted, they came to arrange the leading of plain glass in formal patterns.[1] Since figured sculpture was not admitted, and the decorative richness of Cluniac capitals was anathema, a formal capital with a wide plain leaf at each corner was generally used: for the chapter-house and cloister at Fontenay, for example, and for a hundred out of a hundred and thirty capitals at Pontigny.[2] Sculptured portals were not allowed—the tympanum at Pontigny has only the plainest of crosses in low relief—but the façades were sometimes permitted, as there, to have a low arcaded porch across the front.[3] The Benedictine abbeys, often set upon a hill, had demanded towers, spires, and a lofty proportion in every part; the Cistercian houses, lying by the waterside, as naturally sought a comfortable lowness. Towers, portals, great windows, and every form of external adornment were forbidden; from a distance a Cistercian abbey looked more like a great farm than a monastery.

The cruciform Benedictine plan was retained for the church, with the cloister in the usual site between the south wall and the transept. This last was prolonged by a sacristy and chapter-house on the ground floor, and by a dorter above with a stair direct to the church. To the south there were a warming-room, a refectory, generally set with its narrow end to the cloister,[4] and kitchens; to the west a range with storehouses below and a dorter above for the lay brethren who helped with the agricultural work of the abbey. At Clairvaux part of the range was occupied by a dozen or more little cells where the scribes worked, with the library above.[5] Near the refectory entrance the monks' washing-fountain, a wide flat basin with many tubular openings from which the water flowed,[6] was usually sheltered by a kind of canopy.[7] The Rule decreed that, if it were possible, the monastery should be built in such a way as to include within its enclosure water, a mill, a garden, and workshops, so that the monks need never leave it. Fontenay remains as the ideal example of such a site; its abundant streams themselves form the monastic enclosure, and over its gate is written: SPIRITVS DEI FEREBATUR SVPER AQVAS.

The characteristic part of the Cistercian churches, as of all other monastic churches, was the apse. It was nearly always rectangular.[8] In the simplest form[9]

---

[1] Thirteenth-century examples survive at Obazine, Bonlieu, and Pontigny.

[2] The rest, like most of the capitals at Aubazine, are plain.

[3] See Fontaine, p. 84.

[4] e.g. at Savigny, Manche, and Bonport, Eure.

[5] Oursel, p. 11.

[6] Examples of the basins survive at Fontenay, Pontigny, and Bosquen.

[7] A magnificent example of the late twelfth century is at Poblet in Catalonia; the only surviving one I know of in France is at Valmagne, Hérault. At Fontenay the basin was originally in a room with a central column passing through the bowl.

[8] Exceptions are Morimond, Villers, and Chaalis which have round or polygonal apses.

[9] For an excellent account of the development of the scheme see Fontaine, p. 40.

it appeared in the second church at Clairvaux, and was copied at Fontenay (Fig. 63), La Cour-Dieu, and Fontaine-Guérard. In the second church at Cîteaux the rectangular apse was surrounded by angular chapels.

The ascetic influence of St. Bernard served for a time to counterpoise the growing riches of the Order. In 1148 the entire Congregation of Savigny joined the Order, and gradually the tradition of blind austerity was weakened, though not destroyed. As the churches grew yet larger, and the influence of Bernard grew less, a closer approximation to the Benedictine plan was attained. When Pontigny, the second daughter of Cîteaux and the mother of thirty-four dependent houses, was rebuilt in 1150 through the generosity of Thibault the Great of Champagne, it was more splendidly planned than before. It followed the letter of Bernard's prescriptions, but the masons liberated themselves in spirit (Fig. 64). Outside it looks like a great barn; within it has a semicircular apse with an ambulatory and nine radiating chapels. These, however, do not project outside and are nearly square, being formed by party walls in the interior of the church. The elegant piers, the high rib vaults, and the beauty of proportion are as impressive as any much-decorated architecture; the clear glass, the light and shadow on pale stone and on monkish habits no less pale, must once have composed a symphony in white to be the visual counterpart of the impersonal chants of the choir.

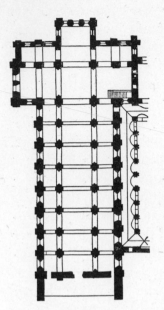

PLAN 5
Cistercian Abbey of Fontenay,
Côte d'Or. Consecrated 1147

A similar scheme with an apse and interior chapels was followed at the third church at Clairvaux in 1172, at Vaucelles, and in the thirteenth-century churches at Savigny, Breuil-Benoît, and Bonport. At the Cistercian house at Paris, built in 1245, the flat apse was beautified outside by flying buttresses which hardly seem to have been structurally needed.

The Cistercian transept, instead of the apsidioles of the Benedictine plan, had small square chapels formed by party walls. The most usual number of these was two[1] in each arm of the transept. At Aubazine, the Abbaye de l'Épau, Clermont near Laval, and Ourscamps there were three; at La Ferté-sur-Grosne four. At Clairvaux and Villers there were such chapels on both the eastern and western sides of the transept, and at Pontigny three to the east, two to the west, and two at the ends. The scheme met the need, always felt in a Benedictine community which included a considerable number of priests, for a multiplicity

[1] At Fontenay, Preuilly, La Bussière, Silvanès, and others. Fontaine, p. 37.

of altars; at Clairvaux there were as many as thirty-two. This plan, however, led to difficulties with the eastward position of the officiating priest; at Pontigny he had, at several of the altars, to stand behind it.

The churches of the Cistercian Order were a deliberate protest against Cluniac magnificence. The monastic buildings, however, were, by an unconscious continuation of this opposition, yet more spacious and well built than those of Cluny. Capitals with figures and grotesques, it is true, are not found, but in every other respect the Cistercian buildings are the finer. The cloisters at Fontenay, with twin bays within a shallow arch and a splendid vault (Fig. 66 A), are as impressive as any of their date; the skilful grouping of the columns and the uniformity of their capitals have a dignity which no more varied ornament could rival. The chapter-house there, with piers of eightfold colonnettes, is in the same style and no less dignified[1] (Fig. 67); the refectory is no less splendid, with a central line of pillars alternately circular and hexagonal, and a bold rib vault.[2] Yet the essential tradition remains unbroken; everything is rectangular, and there is no single apse or curve to mitigate the angularity of the plan. At Bonport, the Cistercian abbey founded by Richard Cœur de Lion in fulfilment of a vow, the refectory (Fig. 66 B), of about 1250, is some ninety feet long and has three small rose windows above three lancets at the end and similar windows along the sides. The later refectory at Royaumont (Fig. 68) is as fine as the hall of a palace. At Vaux-de-Cernay, founded by Simon de Montfort, there is a fine rib-vaulted warming-room with columns down the middle with foliage capitals; above it is a plainer dorter. At Noirlac the whole ensemble remains: warming-room, chapter-house, refectory, and cellar, all nobly built. Most splendid of all is the infirmary at Ourscamps, nearly a hundred feet long (Fig. 69), built about 1230 like a church, with a characteristically Cistercian window scheme and equally characteristic vaulting and capitals.[3] At Vauclerc near Laon the dorter still exists, nearly two hundred and thirty feet long, on two floors vaulted on central columns with an attic above. The many buttresses, arcaded walls, heavy cornice, and graceful fenestration make it one of the most beautiful dorters in existence (Figs. 70, 71).

Even the farm-buildings of the Order were handsomely designed. The great forge of Fontenay and the tanneries of Clairvaux were as fine and as plain as the monastic buildings beside them. The famous vineyard of Clos Vougeot still has a fine building, with a kind of nave and aisles, to hold the four great wine-presses called the *Vendangeoirs de Cîteaux*.

---

[1] The scheme is continued with slight modification as late as the Abbaye de l'Épau, founded by Queen Berengaria in 1230. Another such cloister survives at Notre-Dame du Val near l'Isle-Adam.

[2] Others survive at Notre-Dame du Val, La Clarté-Dieu, c. 1240, and Reigny, near Vermenton.

[3] The fourteenth-century refectory of the Collège des Bernardins still survives at 24 rue de Poissy, Paris; it is aisled and set over a vaulted cellar.

The tradition of austerity in Cistercian church architecture lasted as long as the Romanesque style was used in their building. At the same time as Romanesque gave place to Gothic, Cistercian severity was mitigated by urban influences.

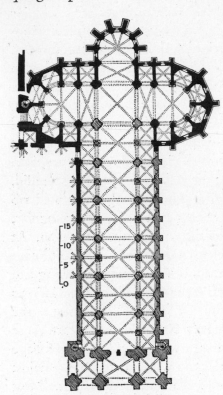

PLAN 6
Cistercian Abbey of Chaalis, Oise.
Consecrated 1219

The foundation of a Cistercian College in Paris, made in 1227 and recognized in 1244, marks the end of the great period of Cistercian history. Luxury was already creeping in. The Cistercian statutes of 1152[1] record various punishments for infractions of the rules of architectural austerity. The Abbot of Longpont had built his dorter in a different form from that prescribed; the church at Vaucelles was unduly magnificent, 'to the great scandal of the many'. Fontfroide had had carpets on the floor, and more than the five lamps that were alone permitted; some abbots had adorned their chapels with coats of arms; some had raised altars without leave; Loroy in Berri had set up images, which must be removed; and the variety of pavements must be stopped and that at Le Gard destroyed. The Abbot of Clairvaux was rebuked for not having corrected these excesses.

In spite of such legislation, with the adoption of the Gothic style Cistercian churches lost their pristine simplicity. The church of Chaalis, begun in 1202 and consecrated in 1219, followed the scheme of the cathedrals of Noyon, Cambrai, and Soissons in having an immense aisled transept with polygonal ends, like two conjoined apses with ambulatories. Its apse, unlike those of the cathedrals, was small and plain, but its nave was as many as eleven bays long and was preceded by a narthex. Longpont, consecrated in 1227, still had the traditional rose windows and the traditional arcaded porch on its façade, but its interior was as fine as the cathedral of Châlons-sur-Marne which seems to have served as its model. Royaumont, founded in 1228 by Saint Louis and built by his architect Pierre de Montreuil, though it had the Cistercian *chevet plat*, was as splendid as any of the secular churches that were due to the munificence of the one and the architectural skill of the other.[2]

---

[1] Mortet, ii. 35.

[2] Conversely the Cistercian square apse was imitated in churches that did not belong to the Order,

Molesme had originally refused to admit outsiders to burial,[1] but forty years after its foundation it accepted the revenues of two parish churches in return for the admission of a bishop to sepulture. By 1152 the Cistercian statutes[2] admitted kings, queens, and bishops to burial within the abbeys of the Order. Their tombs brought a new note of splendour into the churches:[3] at Royaumont, in the middle of the thirteenth century, Saint Louis set up a magnificent series of tombs of his ancestors,[4] while the women of the royal family were often buried at Maubuisson. A great number of tombs of laymen and bishops adorned the church at Noirlac. The Cistercian General Chapter of 1182 had forbidden mass-endowments, but by 1218 Ourscamps was accepting benefactions to endow masses, and by the middle of the thirteenth century these endowments had become so numerous as to create problems of personnel.[5] The consequent wealth enjoyed by Cistercian houses undoubtedly tended to increase the splendour of their churches. The churches had originally been closed to the laity, but they were soon opened to pilgrims. A pilgrimage gradually arose at Cadouin to the relic of the Saint-Suaire, the legendary winding-sheet of Christ, that had been brought back from Antioch after the First Crusade; the chapter of Cîteaux permitted it to be enclosed in a golden reliquary. A new prosperity came to Pontigny when Edmund Rich, Archbishop of Canterbury, who was buried there, was canonized in 1247.[6] Clairvaux had reliquaries given to the abbey by Crusaders from Jerusalem and Constantinople, as well as a precious shrine of the head of St. Mark[7] made for the ninth abbot at the end of the century, and profited from those who came to visit so rich a treasury of relics.

At Aubazine, which became Cistercian within a few years of its foundation, the tomb of its founder Saint Étienne was made a shrine that drew many pilgrims to the lovely wooded hill-side where it still rests (Fig. 72). The tomb is of the gabled shape that befits a saint. On the roof are portrayed all the members of the Order, with Saint Étienne at their head, kneeling before the Virgin: abbots, monks, bearded lay brethren, and finally the shepherds of the abbey farms who lived then, as now, in the chestnut woods by the monastery. On the other side past generations of the Order are represented according to their rank rising from their tombs. The gable ends are filled one with a chestnut-tree with birds in the branches, and the other with an oak, a hawthorn, and an apple-tree. The mouldings are rose and sycamore, and the spandrels are filled with the

e.g. Mennetou-sur-Cher, a priory of Benedictine nuns, Saint-Serge d'Angers, Champeaux, and even a few small Cluniac houses.

[1] Coulton, iii. 51. [2] Mortet, ii. 34.
[3] An impression of the difference they made may still be gained at the Cistercian nunnery of Las Huelgas outside Burgos.
[4] Now for the most part at Saint-Denis. [5] Coulton, iii. 66.
[6] He is still venerated as Saint Edme at Provins, where his relics now are.
[7] See Lalore, p. xviii. Many other relics were added in the thirteenth and fourteenth centuries.

foliage of ivy, willow, hawthorn, maple, oak, blackberry, rose, and strawberry. The sculptures represent a final victory of the beauty of nature over the austerity of the cloister.

Other ornaments began to creep into the churches. In 1240 the Chapter General,[1] hearing that in certain churches the altars were adorned with paintings, ordered their suppression, saying that those who liked painting could paint their altars white. None the less the Abbot of Royaumont dared to have an altar with paintings and sculptures, and columns with angels at the top to hold the curtains round it. The chapter ordered him to destroy them all within the year, or he and his prior general were to be deprived of wine until it was done. Such penalties were not enough; and the abbot could often plead a royal dona- tion in justification of his laxity. Blanche of Castille, for instance, gave to Maubuisson an image of the Virgin and Child of walnut wood, painted and gilt, that opens down the middle to become a triptych, with statuettes of Christ and the Apostles.[2] Even without such justification ornament spread over the churches. At Les Châtelliers[3] the whole church was paved, about 1300, with encaustic tiles in elaborate patterns like rose windows. By the end of the thir- teenth century Fontenay had a similar pavement and a fine sculptured retable, with the Crucifixion in the middle, and figures of the Holy Women and St. John, Church and Synagogue, and on either side a double row of smaller reliefs of the life of Christ.[4] There was even a fine stone statue of the Virgin nearly seven feet high. The priory of Feuchères owned in the fourteenth century a processional cross of silver gilt, with rose-sprays as exquisite as the chestnut at Aubazine; and Clairmarais one no less beautiful.[5]

The riches of the Order might diminish, but not even the Hundred Years War could bring back the old austerity. In 1466 La Bénisson-Dieu had a great bell tower added to its nave. A Virgin of Pity was painted on a wall at Aubazine, and one of the Burgundian priories was enriched with a statue of St. Bernard himself.[6] Thin beneath his heavy habit, he holds a book with the text: 'Omnia tecum habes ante te Deum qui habes.'

The final stage is represented in the retable made for Clairvaux in the fifteenth century.[7] In the middle God the Father upholds His Son upon the Cross. On either side are panels of the Baptism of Christ and of Christ appearing to the Apostles: a scene of which the supernatural quality is shown by His gilded face, feet, and hands. The end panels show St. Bernard holding a model of his abbey, and a mitred abbot. When the Queen of Sicily visited the abbey in 1517 there

---

[1] Arbois de Jubainville, p. 29.   [2] It is now at Saint-Ouen-l'Aumône near Pontoise.
[3] Deux-Sèvres; see Espérandieu in *Bull. Arch.*, 1892, p. 1.
[4] See L. Bégule, *L'Abbaye de Fontenay*, Lyon, 1912, p. 56.
[5] Now in the cathedral of Saint-Omer.
[6] H. David in *Saint Bernard et son temps*, p. 130. For others see David, i. 103 and ii. 101.
[7] Now in the Dijon Museum.

were enough reliquaries for each monk to hold one during Mass, and yet to leave sixteen or seventeen for her to see in the sacristy.[1] The high altar was adorned by a frontal of copper gilt, and behind it were three altars of alabaster, one of which was crowned by an image of St. Bernard under a canopy. There was a bronze candelabrum and a bronze statue of the Virgin nine feet high. A sculptured group of the Resurrection adorned the cloister, and there was a fine library with traceried windows and an elaborately sculptured façade. Men had entered into their inheritance of visible beauty; it had come to form part not only of their daily life but also of their imaginative dreams. The blind austerity of St. Bernard could no longer prevent it from forming a part of their religion.

2. THE ORDER OF THE TEMPLE

The Cistercians, who derived little profit from rural pilgrimages, were more closely connected than the Benedictines with the Palestinian Crusades. It was Bernard who obtained recognition for the Templars, who preached the Crusade in 1147, who was elected in 1148 to lead an expedition to retrieve the failure of the Crusade he had inspired. Yet, since the militant orders, pledged to the defence of the Holy Land, of necessity had their centre in Palestine and Syria, outside the immediate range of Cistercian influence, their architecture developed independently of that austere style.

The Order of the Temple was founded about 1118 when Hugues de Payens and Geoffroy de Saint-Omer went to Jerusalem and obtained permission from Baldwin II to establish a community for the defence of the Holy Sepulchre. At the Council of Troyes ten years later they were given a Rule by Bernard of Clairvaux.[2] Besides the Benedictine vows of chastity, poverty, and obedience, it bound them to perpetual exile and holy war till death. They were never to refuse combat, even if they were outnumbered three to one; they were never to ask quarter or to give ransom. Their white habit was borrowed from the Cistercians, whom their Rule calls 'our brethren and our comrades'. By the time the first Chapter General was held, about 1160, there were three hundred knights in the Order and as many serving brethren, nearly all French.

They inherited their first church at Jerusalem ready built. It was the great mosque of the Dome of the Rock, dating from the end of the seventh century. This is octagonal, with a double aisle round the living rock that rises in the centre. It was covered in mosaics without and within, and these shimmered in the light reflected as from water from the wide stony spaces of the Haram es Sherif. The Templars surrounded the inexorably pagan rock by a magnificent grille of forged iron, and set up an altar to the east of the dome; and in their white cloaks sang their canonical psalms and prayed the prayers St. Bernard

[1] Lalore, p. xviii.   [2] Hélyot in Migne, xxii, col. 612.

had prescribed for them beneath the garlanded mosaics and the fretted capitals of Islam.

Such magnificence they could not equal. It impressed them as greatly as the Church of the Sepulchre impressed other Crusaders. Just as these built miniature Sepulchre churches on their return, so the Templars tried to reproduce the plan of the Dome of the Rock in little, but the resemblance was even slighter than that between such a building as Neuvy-Saint-Sépulcre and the Church of the Sepulchre. In their castle of Château-Pèlerin, on the Palestinian coast, they built a small chapel that in its polygonal plan seems a reminiscence of the great mosque, but its remaining fragments of sculpture are of a current French type. At their French commandery of Laon they built an octagonal chapel in the middle of the twelfth century that is a pathetically poor reproduction of the great scheme. A choir and apse to the east and a porch to the west were added later.[1] The Temple Church at Paris, destroyed at the Revolution, was circular in plan, and may have been inspired by the Church of the Sepulchre at Jerusalem.

Even in the Holy Land the Templars did not always build on a round or polygonal plan; their church at Tortosa is rectangular, as is the chapel built into the donjon at Chastel-Blanc. Their church in Paris,[2] founded in 1211, was originally circular, but was lengthened by rectangular additions later. Their chapel at Beaune,[3] built soon after its foundation in 1220, is an aisleless rectangle with a small choir of the utmost plainness. Their chapel at Pontaubert, near Avallon, follows a local style and plan; it has aisles, a three-sided apse, and its interior resembles Saint-Lazare d'Avallon, in a simpler fashion and on a much smaller scale. The Templars' church at Brébevenez in Brittany is of a simple Benedictine aisled type, with a Gothic vault. Fifty years later the Templars' church at Rampillon followed a similar plan, with a long aisled nave and a five-sided apse. Its sober exterior, depending on proportion and reiteration for its effect, still keeps a reminiscence of Cistercian severity which is carried on in a new form in the plain triforium and rather narrow pointed arches. The sculptured portals are the most striking features of the church. The tympanum of the main door shows Christ, seated as Judge with an angel on either side and the Virgin and St. John beyond, and the Resurrection of the dead on the lintel. The widely splayed jambs have a fine series of Apostles (Fig. 73) under an arcade with a lesser arcade with reliefs of the Labours of the Months below. A statue of Christ adorns the mullion of the door. The side door has a tympanum with the Coronation of the Virgin.[4] The late Templars' church in

[1] A good octagonal Templars' chapel is that of Santa Cruz at Segovia, dating from 1150.
[2] It is shown in an engraving by I. Sylvestre made in 1650.
[3] See C. Aubertin, *Notice sur la Chapelle des Chevaliers du Temple à Beaune*, Beaune, 1886.
[4] Another sculptured tympanum at Pontaubert represents the Adoration of the Magi, and angels bearing a soul to heaven. It is rather clumsy in composition and execution.

the village of Le Temple, Lot-et-Garonne, has a double nave and a flat end in the Dominican manner.

Little remains of the rich interior decoration of their churches. The exceptional survival of a fresco in the Templars' church of Cressac near Barbezieux suggests that they may have had an historical bias in their iconography. It represents the Palestinian victory of Hugues de Lusignan.[1]

The remains of the Templars' living-quarters are even more scanty than those of their churches. A rectangular hall with central pillars, probably their refectory, and the remains of a cloister may be seen by the mosque of El Aqsa at Jerusalem; their other buildings were destroyed by Saladin. At Châtel-Pèlerin the fortifications and donjon remain, and at the end of the promontory is a vaulted room, like a small Cistercian refectory, where they must have lived to the sound of falling breakers. At Tortosa a tower of their fortified enceinte remains in use as a mosque, the city walls and the enormous donjon exist in a ruined state, the great hall is so closely incorporated into modern dwellings that its remains are hard to recognize, and little remains of the chapel but the arched door. The most perfect of their Commanderies is that at Chastel-Blanc, within beacon distance of the Hospitallers at the Krak des Chevaliers. Their buildings here were rebuilt after an earthquake in 1202 and continue to be the perfect expression of militant monachism. Within a double polygonal enceinte, once strengthened by stone ramps and towers, rises a donjon. A well and a vaulted store-room, linked by subterranean passages with the outer defences, are hidden below ground. A few steps above ground-level is a chapel, lit by arrow-slits, some ninety-five feet long and fifty-five feet wide, with a rounded apse between two sacristies, all masked by the thick external wall. Hidden in its thickness a staircase leads to a vaulted hall above, with a central row of columns, lit by arrow-slits in cusped embrasures; it must have served as refectory and chapter-house, and in time of siege as dorter too. The flat top of the tower, with a parapet alternately crenellated and pierced with arrow-slits, must have been all the cloister they had.

In France, as in Palestine, the Commanderies of the Temple were rather castles than monasteries. Their great house in Paris had two square donjons, one built in 1222 and said to be one of the strongest in the kingdom,[2] one with a turret at each corner. The whole of their great estate just outside the city was enclosed by a high wall, that long survived the Order but was destroyed at the Revolution. Their manor at Éterpigny, with a square donjon linked to a great hall on two floors, and a courtyard with wooden arcades, was destroyed by the Germans in the first World War. In the gardens of Montargis are some elegant

---

[1] The church of Maisonnisses, Creuse, contains a fine funeral effigy of a Templar with crossed hands.

[2] Piganiol de la Force, *Desc. hist. de la ville de Paris*, 1765 ed., iv. 345.

windows of the late twelfth century from the Commandery of the Temple at Lorris. They recall those of other town houses of the period.[1]

The justification of the Templars' existence was the defence of the Kingdom of Jerusalem. It fell in 1291, and with it the reason of their being ended. Already the Rule was so far relaxed that the Order stood in ill repute, and its enormous wealth made it an object of royal covetousness. Philippe le Bel arrested all the members of the Order and seized the Temple at Paris on 13 October 1307, and his tool, Pope Clement V, suppressed the Order in 1312. Fifty-nine Templars were burnt for heresy at Paris, and nine more at Senlis. Their possessions passed in law to the Hospitallers and in fact to the king.

[1] A house at Chauvigny (Vienne) ascribed to the Templars has similar, if simpler, windows.

IV

BISHOPS AND CHAPTERS

1. THE ROMANESQUE CATHEDRALS

THE early cathedrals of France were closely modelled on the early monasteries, for it was the monasteries which fanned the fire of life in the Gallican Church. Like the Merovingian abbeys the Merovingian cathedrals usually had several churches: most often a cathedral proper dedicated to the Virgin, a baptistery dedicated to St. John, and a lesser church dedicated to the Protomartyr St. Stephen or to the Apostles. At Bourges, Auxerre, and Sens the three churches lay side by side; at Nantes, Paris, Beauvais, and Rheims they were strung out in line, on a single axis.[1] In Carolingian times these separate churches, like the multiple churches of the monasteries, were most commonly united into a single cathedral.[2]

This age, however, witnessed a deadly rivalry between the bishops and the regular clergy.[3] The feudal and legal rights of both were as yet imperfectly defined; Church and State were linked in a new bureaucracy; and problems of administration played a more important part than ideals of religious unity. From this internecine struggle the bishops emerged the more powerful if the less civilized. The territory of their dioceses was based on the areas dependent on a Roman city; after the ninth century *civitas* meant a see. Consequently there was a place ready made for them in the essentially urban scheme of the Carolingian empire, of which they became in some sense the civic officers. Imperial wealth endowed their treasuries and many of the cathedral churches were rebuilt.

This prosperous state was shattered in the invasions that followed. Chartres was burnt by the Danes in 858; Séez, a cathedral built of wood, in 878;[4] and many of the other cathedrals that lay, unlike the monasteries, in the old cities on the Roman roads by which invaders could travel, were destroyed or damaged or looted in the course of the ninth and tenth centuries.

Yet as soon as order began to be restored to France, not only were the wrecked churches restored but also new churches were built. Clermont Cathedral, consecrated in 946, was rebuilt in the new fashion with an ambulatory and square radiating chapels, and was followed not only by the great monasteries[5] but also by the cathedral of Nantes in 992.[6] Radulphus Glaber,

---

[1] Hubert, p. 39.

[2] Saint-Lizier, however, retained two cathedrals and two rival chapters up to the Revolution. When the churches of Sens were burnt in 968, all three were rebuilt. At Paris the baptistery church of Saint-Jean-le-Rond, rebuilt, continued to exist alongside the cathedral of Notre-Dame.

[3] See Lot, p. 35.   [4] Courajod, i. 34, n. 1.   [5] See p. 22.   [6] Bréhier, p. 144.

writing of the white robe of churches that covered France in 1003, declares: 'Tunc denique episcopalium sedium ecclesias pene universas . . . in meliora quique permutavere fideles.'[1]

As soon as the new cathedrals were built there were benefactors ready to enrich their treasuries. Rheims, that had been given an altar-frontal of precious metal by Archbishop Foulques, who died in 900, was able to have it remodelled and enlarged at the expense of Bishop Hervé and other benefactors at the end of the tenth century.[2] It was divided into three by pilasters: in the centre was Christ in glory, with the two archbishops at his feet; on one side were the Virgin and six donors, on the other Saint Rémi and four more. Besides such portable treasures the cathedral buildings were themselves richly decorated with paintings if not with figured sculpture. In 964 Bishop Guy had the portal of Auxerre painted with the joys of Paradise and the pains of Hell. The Synod of Arras in 1025 could already call the sculptures of the cathedrals the books of the unlettered.

The eleventh century, one of the great ages of monasticism, was less splendid in episcopal history. The great thinkers and writers of the day were all monks. The bishops were still balancing uncertainly between feudalism and religion; Bishop Robert of Coutances, who died in 1048, gave the prebends of his cathedral to his relations, who rendered him homage for them. Simony, feudal war, and a constant struggle against papal encroachments, gave the bishops other things to think about than architecture. The chief stimulus to building, indeed, was still destruction. Most of the cathedrals had wooden roofs over the nave, which made them an easy prey to fire. So Orleans was rebuilt by Bishop Arnoul, between 987 and 1003, after a fire; Chartres by Bishop Fulbert between 1020 and 1028, and Auxerre by Bishop Hugh before 1039, each with an ambulatory and radiating chapels like a Benedictine pilgrimage church. In this century, however, vaulting began to be applied to cathedrals, as it had already been to monastic churches. Before 1030, Hubert, Bishop of Angers, had substituted stone vaults for the wooden ceiling of his church, and glass windows for its wooden shutters.[3]

The only province where cathedral building was prosecuted with enthusiasm was Normandy, that had become Christian once more with the conversion of the Northmen. There at least Norman piety and Norman wealth were building new cathedrals with something of missionary fervour. Rouen, begun before 1037 and dedicated in 1063, seems to have served as a model for Lisieux, dedicated in 1055, Évreux in 1076, Coutances in 1056, and Bayeux, begun before 1050 on the site of a Gallo-Roman temple and dedicated in 1077.[4] This, too,

---

[1] Mortet, i. 4.   [2] Hubert, p. 130.   [3] Mortet, i. 83.
[4] Vallery-Radot, p. 101. A Burgundian element in some of the capitals is doubtless accounted for by the bishop's connexion with Saint-Bénigne de Dijon.

had its ornaments, notably a great hanging chandelier or *corona* with the towers of the Heavenly Jerusalem guarded by the Virtues,[1] with Latin inscriptions to explain the symbolism. At Coutances the bishop laboured night and day at the creation of his cathedral, buying the better half of the city from the duke to get space for it, travelling as far as Apulia to secure gold and gems and vestments from Robert Guiscard and his fellow Normans, and maintaining a little army of workmen from his rents. For nearly forty years he rejoiced in the finished church; and then in 1093 the gilt cock he had set above the tower was struck by lightning and the leaden roof and stonework damaged. He sent to England for Brismet the plumber to make good the damage. The bishop lay on his death-bed; but when news came that the cock was once more bright again and set in its place he sat up in bed and gave thanks to God that it was done; and then, after a little, said: 'I was afraid that if my death came first, never would that cock or one like to it have climbed so high.' So, pronouncing a dreadful curse upon those who should injure his church, he died.[2]

Such curses, if they preserved the cathedrals from spoliation, did nothing to preserve them from beneficent destruction by rebuilding. Except for a few ground-plans and crypts we know very little of French cathedrals before the end of the eleventh century;[3] this little seems to show that they initiated nothing but followed the current models invented for monastic use. The same is broadly true for the ensuing sixty years: that sixty years from 1085 to 1145 which represents the greatest age of monastic art in France. Further, the reform of the cathedral chapters as colleges of Augustinian canons helped to make yet closer the link with monastic art. However much lighter their rule than that of St. Benedict, it implied not only the obligations of a common life but, at the least, a chapter-house and a cloister in which to pursue them; and for these the Benedictine houses provided obvious models.

Yet if creation lay with the monastic houses, construction did not leave the cathedrals. The dreadful necessity of rebuilding after fire continued to be urgent. In the first half of the twelfth century Bayeux Cathedral was burnt in 1101, Laon in 1112, Noyon in 1130, Le Mans in 1134;[4] and besides these other cathedrals were rebuilt on a vaster scale than had been attempted before. The greater number of the surviving Romanesque cathedrals lie in the south, less because more were then built there than because fewer were rebuilt subsequently.[5] Such buildings as the cathedrals of the small sees of Saint-Paul-

---

[1] See Mortet, ii. 17, n. 2; Katzenellenbogen, p. 51, n. 7.

[2] Mortet, i. 75; Haskins, p. 186.

[3] The façade and first bay of Le Mans may date from the time of Bishops Vulgrin and Hoel, 1060–93. They show a survival of Carolingian *petit appareil* decoratively treated.

[4] Lasteyrie, *Arch. rom.*, p. 227.

[5] Romanesque, too, was still in use in the south when the north was using Gothic. A time-lag of fifty years must often be allowed for.

Trois-Châteaux and Vaison are indistinguishable from the churches of the lesser monastic abbeys; they follow the simplest Benedictine plan, without ambulatory or radiating chapels, and differ only in having a shorter choir, since the number of their canons was less than that of the monks in a monastery of average size. The cathedral of Lescar, built about 1125, is equally Benedictine in plan, though with unusual transverse vaults in the aisles and transepts. Its beautiful capitals are closely related to those of Moissac, while the mosaics of the apse, given by Bishop Guy at the time the church was built, recall those in the Cluniac priory church of Ganagobie. The cathedral of Saint-Bertrand-de-Comminges, built about the same date, only retains of this twelfth-century work a door with a tympanum of the Apostles and a picturesque, if battered, cloister that might belong to any Benedictine abbey of the south. Even the cathedral at Arles, rather later and a good deal loftier, offers no particular originality; and its portal is an obvious imitation on a much smaller scale of one of the portals of the Cluniac priory of Saint-Gilles. Its cloister[1] (Fig. 74) is an admirable if late example of the southern version of the Benedictine scheme with square sculptured piers and coupled columns. Here, as on the portal, the iconography is purely Benedictine.

At Le Puy, however, circumstances called for greater originality. It had been a place of small importance, though a bishopric, until the middle of the eleventh century. The cathedral, dedicated to Our Lady, was on the site of a temple of Jupiter on Mont Anis. Then Bishop Adhémar de Monteil (who wrote the *Salve, Regina* and was to die of fever at Antioch on the first Crusade) exploited the legend that the church was on the site of an apparition of the Virgin, and that the dolmen stone within it cured those who slept upon it. His efforts made it one of the great pilgrimage churches of France. Unfortunately additions and restorations have made the plan uncertain, but it seems that when rebuilt early in the twelfth century it was vaulted (like some collegiate and lesser churches) with a series of cupolas on squinches, and that it had two absidioles in the thickness of the wall in each arm of the transept. Its façade, and the much-restored cloister, are built of many-coloured stone in the Auvergnat style. Originally the pilgrim arrived by a vaulted stairway opening on to the floor of the nave, with the threshold inscribed:

NI CAVEAS CRIMEN, CAVEAS CONTINGERE LIMEN,
NAM REGINA POLI VVLT SINE SORDE COLI.

Little remains of the Romanesque decoration of the church but some Corinthian capitals, a great wall-painting of St. Michael, over fifteen feet high, wearing a purely Byzantine stole and girdle, and the sculptured portal with a cusped tympanum and a debased Cufic inscription on the wooden door.

A similar cupola scheme was followed in two other Romanesque cathedrals,

[1] The best account is in A. Gardner, p. 171.

both, like Le Puy, unfortunately over-restored: Angoulême and Cahors. Angoulême, wholly rebuilt by Bishop Girard with financial aid from one of his canons, was begun early in the twelfth century and consecrated (probably in an unfinished state) in 1128. It has three cupolas over the nave, as well as one at the crossing and one at each end of the transept. The apse has no ambulatory but five radiating chapels and an absidiole to either side. The great feature of the church is its sculptured façade, that may be compared with that of Notre-Dame-la-Grande at Poitiers (Fig. 75). It is, however, less original in its imagery: it represents the familiar Beatus scheme of Christ's Second Coming, though by a confusion with the Majesty scheme the evangelistic beasts are also shown. The scale and movement of the whole has a vigour of its own. Cahors, conse-crated in 1119, has two cupolas, and originally had a triple apse. Here the external sculpture, again of the Second Coming, is concentrated in a tympanum, but its loosely grouped scheme is more like that of a façade than of a portal.

The third abbey church of Cluny, begun just before 1090, provided a model and an incentive not only for such abbots as could afford to imitate it, but also for the bishops of central France. The cathedral of Valence, dedicated, like the altars of Cluny, by Pope Urban in 1095, has nothing like the same splendour of scale or design, but visibly belongs to the same school of architecture. The apse, though it has only three radiating chapels, is a simpler version of the Cluniac scheme; the transept piers are in stages, in the Burgundian fashion; the capitals, though by no means so fine, show Burgundian influence; and the great height of the nave, vaulted and supported by cross-vaulted aisles, has a real nobility of proportion.

The most Cluniac of cathedrals, however, is that of Autun, built on a site given by Hugh II of Burgundy. Bishop Étienne de Bagé, its builder, was a close friend of Peter the Venerable's, and ended his days at Cluny. He was ex officio Abbot of Saulieu[1] and his first essay in building had been the re-construction of its abbey church, consecrated in 1119. Therefore it was natural that he should build his cathedral on the ancient Benedictine plan, and in a style of architecture closely based on that of Cluny. Autun, however, was a city that had been continuously important since Augustus made it the capital of the Aedui and still had its Roman gates and theatre and a classical tradition in architecture. So the false triforium at Autun, instead of being graced with Saracenic cuspings like that at Cluny, was based on the Roman Porte d'Arroux, and all the pilasters of the church have Roman flutings. The figured capitals, however, are Benedictine in their iconography.[2] The Adoration of the Magi,

[1] Saint-Andoche de Saulieu was secularized c. 1139.
[2] The Stoning of St. Stephen, the Story of St. Paul, Christ in Majesty, and others, are prefigured in the illuminations of a book of liturgical chants written for the cathedral between 996 and 1024. Paris, Bibl. de l'Arsenal, 1169.

G

Christ washing the Disciples' feet, the Stoning of St. Stephen, are no new subjects, though the sculptor has here succeeded in giving them a new dancing grace. Some scenes—Balaam, the Flight into Egypt, the *Noli me tangere*— had already been used in Bishop Étienne's church at Saulieu. One capital has the Cluniac theme of the Four Seasons: Autumn, with a hunting-spear upon his shoulder; Spring, with a billowing mantle; Summer, lightly clad; and Winter, hooded and with a great cloak to keep him warm.[1]

The great sculptured tympanum of Autun, though rather later in date, is no less Cluniac in inspiration:[2] it is an enormous representation of the Last Judgement, that may be compared with that at Beaulieu, though the central figure of Christ is undoubtedly inspired by that of the great portal of Cluny. The archivolt has the signs of the zodiac and the labours of the months, like that at Vézelay. In true monastic fashion it is completed by inscriptions. Round the aureole of Christ is carved:

OMNIA DISPONO SOLVS, MERITOSQVE CORONO;
QVOS SCELVS EXERCET ME IVDICE POENA COERCET.

On the line that divides the lintel, with figures of the Blest and the Damned, from the actual Judgement scene, are the lines:

QVISQVE RESVRGET ITA QVEM NON TRAHIT IMPIA VITA
ET LVCEBIT EI SINE FINE DIEI
TERREAT HIC TERROR QVOS TERREVS ALLIGAT ERROR
NAM FORE SIC VERVM NOTAT HIC HORROR SPECIERVM.

The capitals of the portal are more original, but show no coherence of plan: Aesop's fable of the wolf and stork is set side by side with St. Eustace and his stag and St. Jerome taking a thorn from his lion's paw.

Autun Cathedral derived all its importance, and much of its wealth, from the fact that it was a place of pilgrimage. It enshrined the body of Lazarus, and this was given a new tomb by a second Étienne, bishop from 1171 to 1189.[3] The resurrection of Lazarus was one of the themes of the drama of the monasteries; it was played at Fleury, and another version was written by Hilarius, a pupil of Abelard.[4] This last was to be played at Matins before the Te Deum or at Vespers before the Magnificat; the characters were Lazarus, his two sisters, Christ and at least six Apostles, and four Jews. It seems clear that this drama inspired the new shrine, which was quite unusual in plan,[5] and was significantly

---

[1] See Terret, *Sculp. bourg.*, pl. xxxix.   [2] It is signed GISLEBERTVS ME FECIT.
[3] See Mortet, ii. 121.   [4] Petit de Julleville, i. 55.
[5] The ensemble was destroyed in 1766, but some statues survive in the Autun Museum and the head of St. Peter in the Louvre. See Gardner, figs. 110 and 111. It was signed by MARTINVS MONACHVS. It may be compared with the tomb of Saint Hilaire from Saint-Hilaire-de-la-Celle at Poitiers, now in the church of the Carmelites. This shows him in his coffin with his disciples Saint Lienne and Saint Just, and six other disciples standing round. An angel strikes the saint's breast and another receives his soul.

carved by a monastic sculptor. It showed the four Jews raising the stone of Lazarus's tomb, with Christ, standing between St. Peter and St. Andrew, directing them. Martha and Mary and Mary Magdalene stood beside the tomb, which was set above a base that held the relics of Lazarus, wrapped in a shroud of embroidered blue silk.[1]

Chalon-sur-Saône must once have had another cathedral in the same Cluniac tradition; the figured capitals that survive have much in common with those of Vézelay. The latest cathedral in the series is that of Langres (Fig. 76), perhaps the most classical of all. It is a remarkable instance of the power of Roman influence that this city, far removed from Provence and the recognized centres of classical style—it lies as far to the north as Orleans and Auxerre—should, in virtue of the remains of the Roman citadel, have been able to maintain so classical a tradition in its architecture in the second half of the twelfth century. Its fluted pilasters and great single pillars, its Corinthian capitals, its acanthus mouldings, and the splendid rinceau round the apse,[2] show that classicism still lived; its triforium is based on the arcade of the surviving Roman gate. Yet the scheme of the great nave is none the less inspired by that of Cluny, though it is much less lofty in proportion.[3] Though the piers are simplified; though there is only a single window above the false triforium, and though there are rib vaults, it is as clearly of Cluniac lineage as are Paray and Autun.

With the middle of the twelfth century the focus of monastic influence over cathedrals passed from Cluny to Saint-Denis. It was after assisting at the consecration of Suger's basilica that Hugues III, Archbishop of Rouen, conceived the idea of rebuilding his own cathedral. This influence, however, was most strongly felt in iconography, since it was in that field that Suger made his chief innovations. The Romanesque cathedral of Bourges has perished, but two of its portals remain. The lunette of one has a Virgin of the cult-statue type, with the Magi and the Annunciation, a variant of the Cluniac tympanum at Donzy-le-Pré. The second has the familiar Majesty; on the lintel are the Apostles under an arcade. The elongated statues on the jambs are true column statues of the Prophets and Precursors of our Lord, and were inspired either by the lost figures at Saint-Bénigne de Dijon or by those that have likewise perished at Saint-Denis.[4] The particularly rich carving that accompanies them is equally characteristic of the finest Benedictine work of the decade from 1130 to 1140.

[1] With beasts and horsemen based on the designs of Eastern brocades; now in the Musée des Tissus historiques of Lyons. The Magdalene no doubt appeared because her shrine was at Vézelay. See Mortet, ii. 121.

[2] It may be compared with that on the lintel of the north door of Bourges.

[3] The radiating chapels of the apse were rebuilt at the end of the fourteenth century; the earlier plan is not known.

[4] Mortet, ii. 63; Acloque, p. 10. The heads of some of the Saint-Denis statues have recently been recognized in the Art Gallery of Baltimore.

Chartres was rebuilt after the fire of 1134 less as an ordinary cathedral than as a pilgrimage church enshrining the precious relic of the Tunic of the Virgin. It may not unfairly be said that it was the deliberate policy of the chapter to develop it as a pilgrimage church; as Jehan le Marchand declares in his *Livre des Miracles*, it was at this time that the series of miracles, beginning with the preservation of the relic of the *Sancta Camisia*, was inaugurated.

> La haute dame glorieuse
> Qui voloit avoir merveilleuse
> Iglise et haute et longue et lée
> Si que sa per ne fu trovée
> Son douz fils pria doucement
> Que miracles apertement
> En s'iglise à Chartres feïst
> Que touz le peuples le veïst
> Si que de toutes pars venissent
> Gens qui offrendes tant feïssent
> Que achevée fust s'iglise
> Qui estoit a feire emprise . . . .

The building proceeded as an act of devotion; lords joined artisans in dragging stone from the quarries, women lent a hand in pulling the loaded wagons through the streets. Banners went before them and when they reached the site torches were lit, prayers said, and canticles sung. A great triple portal was carved for the church, of which one door, dedicated to the Virgin, was given by Richer, Archdeacon of Dunois between 1152 and 1156.[1] The door is obviously linked in its design with that at Bourges; there are the same column statues, taller and more mannered (Fig. 77), the same rich surface decoration of the architecture, and the same Benedictine themes; Christ in Glory in the centre, the Second Coming to the left, the Virgin between Angels to the right. Even the lesser scenes go back to Benedictine prototypes. The Annunciation, Visitation, and Nativity appear below the Virgin, as at Vézelay, and the Presentation in the Temple as at La Charité. Below the Majesty are the Apostles, as at Carennac and Charlieu, and below the Second Coming the usual figures awaiting Christ. The capitals form the customary series of the Life of Christ; the voussures of the central door have the angels and elders, and of the left bay the Labours of the Months and the Zodiac. The Liberal Arts[2] appear over the Virgin's door with renewed appropriateness, since the cathedral school of Chartres under John of Salisbury was, at the time it was made, giving new life to the Benedictine tradition of learning. Each is accompanied, as in

---

[1] Aubert, p. 8. The document that records this states that the Virgin was gilt.
[2] On their representations see Mâle, *Art rel. XIIIᵉ siècle*, p. 123.

Martianus Capella's book, by the figure of a great man:[1] Grammar by Donatus, or perhaps Priscian; Astronomy (who bears a bushel basket in token of the rural work that the seasons regulate) by Ptolemy; Arithmetic by Boëthius, Geometry by Euclid, Dialectic by Aristotle, Rhetoric by Cicero, and Music by Pythagoras.

Chartres, then, was rebuilt as a pilgrimage church, and, indeed, it was in virtue of their relics that the twelfth-century cathedrals grew in importance. The 'fierte' or shrine of Saint Romain at Rouen, originally made by Archbishop Guillaume Bonne-Ame between 1079 and 1110, was stripped of its precious covering to buy bread for the people in a famine; but by 1179 it was restored in all its glory.[2] Every year on Ascension Day the chapter had the right to choose a prisoner from the town prison, who bore the shrine on his shoulders in a procession and then was freed.

The townsmen of Laon destroyed their church in a revolt against their feudal lord the bishop in 1112. But they did not destroy its relics. The canons bore them all over northern France, to Buzançais, Issoudun, Tours, Angers, Le Mans, and Chartres,[3] to collect funds with which the rebuilding was begun. When these funds were exhausted, they travelled to England for more, and by 1114 the church was far enough advanced to be dedicated.[4] The sympathetic interest which the bishops took in the Crusades was rewarded, if not partially actuated, by the acquisition of many relics.

Such relics were naturally enshrined with the utmost splendour. The great shrine of Chartres, made about 1115,[5] included gold reliefs of the four seasons, of the four cardinal and three theological virtues, of the Virgin and of Christ treading a monster under foot; but it had no such integrated scheme as had Suger's treasures, for it was further adorned with parts of a great hunting-horn, cut in two and applied to the shrine.

The embroidered hangings that draped the cathedral sanctuaries on festival days were even more magnificent than the monastic ones. Humbard, Bishop of Auxerre from 1087 to 1114, presented his cathedral with a linen curtain embroidered with kings and emperors, and three great hangings of oriental silk: one green, brocaded with lions in medallions, one with similar medallions of kings riding, and a third with golden lions.[6] One such hanging still survives, the so-called Bayeux Tapestry (Fig. 78): an immensely long strip of linen embroidered in wool with the history of William the Conqueror's invasion of

[1] See Bréhier, p. 216. At Clermont the philosophers take the place of the abstract figures and Aristotle, Cicero, and Pythagoras, sitting in professorial chairs, hold the attributes of Dialectic, Rhetoric, and Arithmetic.
[2] It was destroyed in 1562 by the Huguenots. Havard, *Hist. de l'orfèvrerie française*, p. 129.
[3] The south door at Le Mans closely parallels the central door at Chartres; the voussures contain angels and tiny scenes of the life of Christ.
[4] It was succeeded some forty years later by the existing building.
[5] Mély, p. 18.　　　　[6] Mortet, i. 93; Michel, *Hist. de la soie*, i. 54.

England. It is said to have been made for the Conqueror's half-brother, Odo, Bishop of Bayeux.[1] It was hung on feast days round the nave of the cathedral, and until it went out of use at the Revolution was always called the *toile de Saint-Jean*.

The cathedrals, again, shared with such monasteries as Saint-Denis in the glorious colour of Romanesque stained glass. At some time before 1149 Canon Hugues de Semblençay gave glass to all but three of the windows in the cathedral of Angers. It has been suggested that a surviving window with a seated Virgin may still represent his gift.[2] More certainly of the first half of the century is a window at Le Mans with an Ascension taken straight from a Beatus manuscript; a slightly later version of the same theme exists at Poitiers. So brief an inventory shows how little remains of splendours which even St. Bernard could not censure. It was only to the bishops that he could give licence to use art in churches: 'we know that they, as debtors to the wise and foolish, when they cannot rouse the sense of religion in the carnal multitude by spiritual means, must do so by ornaments that appeal to the senses'.[3]

2. THE GOTHIC CATHEDRALS

Supremacy in creation, that had been the Benedictine prerogative, passed in the second half of the twelfth century to the episcopate. The leadership in learning was passing from the monastic libraries to the cathedral schools of Laon, Tours, Chartres, Orleans, and Paris; prosperity was beginning, with better government and better trade, to be centred in the towns. It is significant that the cathedral cities of Noyon, Soissons, Laon, Rheims, and Amiens were all granted communal charters by the king, generally a little before their cathedrals were rebuilt. Traders joined themselves into guilds that were not merely trade associations but devotional confraternities; those who sold at the stalls before the cathedral on market days began to feel themselves members of the visible Church. At Amiens the people who came in from the villages to sell fruit and vegetables in the market gave a relief to the church, with an inscription recording the donors.[4] At Chartres kings, lords, bishops, and canons gave windows to the cathedral, but so did the nineteen trade confraternities of the town: drapers, goldsmiths, shoemakers, tanners, butchers, bakers, carpenters, masons,

[1] Its date is as hotly debated as that of the *Chanson de Roland*. Professor R. S. Loomis, comparing the armour with that in the Beatus of Saint-Sever, puts it as early as the consecration of the cathedral about 1077; Commandant Lefebvre des Noëttes considers that from the type of harness used it must be about 1130 (*Bull. de la Soc. Nat. des Ants de France*, 1924, p. 118, 1925, p. 287). Others have set it as late as the last third of the twelfth century. Sir Eric Maclagan has summed up the rival theories in the latest publication of the tapestry (*The Bàyeux Tapestry*, London and New York, 1943). Personally I incline to set it about 1120.

[2] Lasteyrie, p. 563; Michel, i. 790.

[3] Apologia to William of Saint-Thierry, written about 1125.   [4] Enlart, i. 88.

stonecutters, and so on, and had themselves represented at their work at the base of the windows. In the thirteenth and fourteenth centuries Sens and Auxerre had *confréries de l'œuvre* for those who were outside the trade guilds. The cathedral not only gave them a proud share in its beauty, not only made them partakers in its constant services, not only baptized and married and churched and buried them, not only led them into ways of salvation in great matters, but also helped in the lesser troubles of life. At Chartres Saint Piat was invoked for fine weather, Saint Taurin for rain, and their shrines were brought down and shown to the faithful according to the season. In every cathedral some venerated image or shrine was there to stimulate devotion and to personify the powers of good; a prayer said, a candle lit, an offering made, and the heart was lightened and the courage confirmed. At Chartres and Amiens, Rheims, Sens, and Bayeux, there were labyrinths of coloured stone let into the pavement of the nave; if a man could not afford to go on pilgrimage to Rome or Compostella, Le Puy or Rocamadour, he could make a spiritual pilgrimage upon his knees.[1] The cathedral was the house not only of God, but also of his people. The bishop on his throne and the canons in their stalls were its accredited ministers; the lord in his armorial coat, the merchant in his cloth robe, and the craftsman in his leather jacket its benefactors; the university teacher and the market woman its frequenters; all had a share in it. Outside its portal the drama of the miracle plays, within the walls the drama of the liturgy, the form and colour of sculpture and windows and tapestry, the 'holy mutter of the Mass' and the chanted psalms of the choir, united in a whole that was not conscious art but living devotion. Feudalism had been re-created as a Christian system that included loyalties as well as rights, duties as well as justice. Even outside the cloister men had freedom and energy to devote to the religious life. The age of the sainted Louis IX, who ruled France from 1226 to 1270, is the age of the great cathedrals.

Churches, that had seemed in the monastic age more than adequate for the needs of their city and diocese, no longer met those needs. Money for their rebuilding was not lacking, for the general prosperity had increased the private fortune and the seigneurial revenues of the bishop, the rents from the pre-bendal estates, and the offerings of those who came to the Church. By the end of the twelfth century Petrus Cantor, precentor of Paris, could complain that the Church was suffering from the *morbus aedificandi*; piety now spent its alms on building and not on the poor.[2]

---

[1] That at Chartres still survives; it is called La Lieue. The verses of the Psalm *Miserere* were engraved on the white stone of the path to be followed. That at Amiens, made between 1220 and 1228, had a long French inscription in the middle commemorating the *maîtres de l'œuvre* of the cathedral; Robert de Luzarches, Thomas de Cormont and his son Renaud (Mortet, ii. 230). Labyrinths were character-istic of the cathedrals of eastern France; exceptionally they were copied in the abbey of Saint-Bertin and the collégiale of Saint-Quentin.   [2] Mortet in *Mélanges Bémond*, p. 116.

A Romanesque abbey can rise from a meadow or a vineyard or a herb garden without loss of proportion or dignity, but a Gothic cathedral is a town product, that needs the narrow streets, sharp gables, and lesser pinnacles of a medieval city to set off its own soaring height. A Romanesque abbey is beautiful within, for it is the centre of an enclosed life; a Gothic cathedral is often more richly adorned without, that it may draw men to itself.

At the beginning of the Gothic period, though the *maître de l'œuvre* of a monastic church was still often a monk, the architectural supervisor of a cathedral was usually a layman. By 1253, for instance, Gautier de Varinfroy, a member of a family of lay architects, was legally installed as *Magister* of the cathedral of Meaux at a retaining fee of ten livres a year and a wage of three sols a day for every day he worked there. The Magister had a *chambre aux traits*, where he drew plans for the masons and templates for the stone-cutters.[1] The post gradually became a profitable one. For instance, Jean d'Ivry, *maître de l'œuvre* at Chartres, where his father or uncle Huguet d'Ivry had filled the post before him, gave up his office in 1382; but he surrendered it to the canons by an act before a notary for a payment of a thousand gold francs. Thereafter the canons had the work done through their own sworn master mason.[2]

The transition from a Romanesque monastic style to a Gothic architecture of cathedrals was gradual. The very foundations of Gothic were no sudden construction, but the work of the whole of the incredibly inventive century that lay between the consecration of the high altar of Cluny in 1095 and the beginning of the new cathedral of Chartres in 1195.

The first great cathedral to merit the name of Gothic—a name which cannot be confined to a pointed arch, a rib vault, or a flying buttress, but must mean their integration into a new style—the first Gothic cathedral known to us is that of Sens.[3] It was begun by Bishop Henri le Sanglier, who occupied the see between 1122 and 1142; it was continued by his successor Hugues de Loucy and consecrated in 1168. The plan was of great simplicity; the transept consisted only in a small side-chapel to either side; the choir was of the same width as the nave; there was an ambulatory but only one radiating chapel behind the high altar. Yet for all its simplicity the plan was a new one, immensely different from that of the almost contemporary monastic churches of Saint-Denis and Saint-Martin-des-Champs. The Benedictine tradition of a cul-de-four apse, ribbed or not, was given up and a true Gothic ribbed chevet was almost for the first time achieved. Further, the vaulting of the rest of the building was sexpartite, each section covering two bays, a scheme involving the use of alternate piers, with the capitals set obliquely, and single columns. The capitals of

---

[1] See Stein, p. 39.
[2] Quoted Morison, p. 130. For a list of masons see Stein, p. 39.
[3] The earlier cathedral, built after a fire in 968, was pulled down, not burnt.

the ambulatory seem to have been equally original in their imagery; one that has survived with men digging and a man pruning a vine while a woman picks up the cuttings, and another with a horseman hunting a bird, suggest that they represented a calendar series. The cathedral of Noyon was built but little later, after a great fire in 1131 (Fig. 79). It is a logical development from Sens. The ambulatory has five radiating chapels; the transept chapels are set with their apses to the north and south at right angles to the axis of the church; an arcade runs above the triforium; but the vaulting and bay systems were originally the same, and above all there is the same unified architectural style. A clear tradition had been established for other cathedrals to follow. Senlis was begun about 1155, when Louis VII permitted the chapter to take the relics in procession round France to collect money for the rebuilding. The choir was finished about 1167, and the whole consecrated in 1191. Its plan is that of Sens on a smaller scale; its apse reproduces Noyon.

The next step was taken at Laon, when it was rebuilt by Gautier de Mortagne, Bishop from 1155 to 1174. The system of alternating piers and columns is here superseded by a uniform series of single columns from which rise alternately light and heavy supports for the vault (Fig. 80). The plan originally comprised a semicircular apse and ambulatory, and an aisled transept with absidioles like that of a Romanesque pilgrimage church. The apse

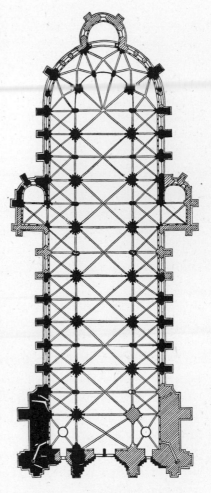

PLAN 7

Cathedral of Sens. Plan in the twelfth century. After Lefèvre Pontalis

was changed at the beginning of the thirteenth century for a much deeper choir with a flat end like that of an English cathedral.[1] Here the great beauty of the external design lay in the towers that were to crown the whole. Seven were planned, two for each façade, north, west, and south, and a central lantern. Only four were built, but these (Fig. 81), in their almost metallic delicacy of line and sureness of plan, make the spectator agree with the medieval architect Villard de Honnecourt: 'j'ai esté en mult de tieres . . .: en aucun liu, onques tel

---

[1] The cathedral of Poitiers, begun by Henry II in 1166, has a flat end in the English style, with an ambulatory in front of the windows, though it has curious Angevin vaults.

tor ne vis come est celle de Laon.'[1]   When a temporary cathedral was being
built in 1112, a wagon laden with stone could not get up the hill to its lofty
site; but suddenly the wagoner saw an ox added to his team which disappeared
as soon as the wagon had safely reached the top.[2]   Sixteen oxen look out from
the upper stories of the towers in commemoration of those which once dragged
the stone uphill.

Laon is composite in its plan; neither its first pilgrimage-church scheme, nor
its second flat chevet, is really characteristic of a French cathedral.   When
Bishop Maurice de Sully decided in 1166 to rebuild Notre-Dame de Paris, of
which the site was still occupied by the twin cathedral churches of Notre-Dame
and Saint-Étienne, the church was planned on the same scheme as that of Sens.
The only changes were the use of rectangular instead of apsidal chapels to form
a small transept, and the introduction of double aisles to give splendour to the
whole.   The single columns are like those of Laon, but the triforium is lighter
and in the choir more elaborate.   Above this the traceried windows are more
lofty; the whole has a new lightness and elegance, but had it not been for Sens
and Laon it could not have been conceived.[3]

Sens and Noyon used alternate columns and piers; Laon, and the churches
that copied it, columns alone.   The great cathedrals of the thirteenth century
exploited instead the other element, and derive their beauty from the use of
complex piers.

Bourges Cathedral (Fig. 82), of which the choir was begun in 1192 and the
nave finished in 1266, is of an extreme simplicity of plan and of an infinite
complexity of elevation.   It has no transept at all; the double aisles are simply
continued round the apse, giving a magnificent homogeneity.   The piers, surrounded by engaged columns, are immensely lofty; the triforum is as light as
that of Paris; and the multiplication of windows—there are a hundred and
eleven windows and thirty roses—gives the whole church an airy luminousness
not seen before.   To some spectators it will always seem not only the most
beautiful but also the most French of cathedrals, for in no other Gothic building
is the pure beauty of line and proportion more apparent.   Its chief rival is the
cathedral of Chartres, begun after a fire in 1194; this, as a pilgrimage church,
retains the old plan of an aisled transept and radiating chapels.   Yet had not
Chartres its exterior sculpture and its glorious windows, few would think that
it surpassed Bourges; the pier is more massive, the scale less lofty, the plan less
simple, and the whole less poetical in conception.   It is externally (Fig. 83) that

---

[1] The towers were copied as far away as Bamberg.
[2] The story is told by the Abbot of Nogent-sous-Coucy. See *Pet. mon.*, p. 58.
[3] The same is true of the cathedral of Soissons, of which the choir was consecrated in 1212.
Here, however, the great triforium of Laon is omitted and the arcade kept, as it is also at Châlons-
sur-Marne.

its chief beauty lies, not only in the great portals but also in the splendid flying buttresses that are almost for the first time an integral and essential part of the design.[1]

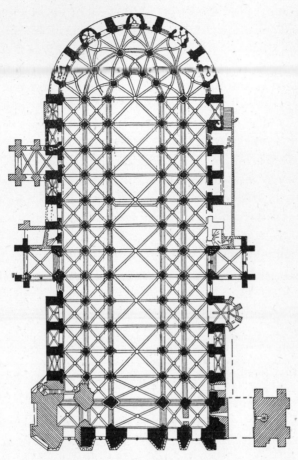

PLAN 8
Cathedral of Bourges. Begun 1192

Notre-Dame de Reims was no less a pilgrimage church than Chartres. The Carolingian cathedral was burnt in 1211, and the first stone of the new cathedral was laid by Archbishop Alberic de Humbert a year later. His architect, Jean d'Orbais, furnished plans for the whole, though its completion was only achieved by several generations of his successors.[2] It retains the ambulatory and radiating chapels of a pilgrimage church, but its choir is wider than

[1] The towers survive from the earlier church; the base of the northern dates from 1134, the southern from 1145.

[2] He probably built most of the choir, 1211–31. It was finished by Jean le Loup in 1241, who also built the transept and began the north door before 1247. Then Gaucher de Reims worked at the great portal, from 1247 to 1255, and Bernard de Soissons built five bays of the nave and the rose of the portal between 1255 and 1290. Robert de Coucy directed work on the great portal until his death in 1311.

the nave and is, in fact, united with the shallow transept. The scheme is a heavier and less lofty version of Bourges; its peculiar beauty lies in the infinite variety of natural leafage with which the capitals are carved, and in the harmony of the whole. Like Chartres, it is even more glorious without than within. The great western portal has windows instead of tympana, but sculptured gables frame them. Sculpture is everywhere; even the pinnacles of the buttresses house angels with outspread wings.

The next stage of creation in Gothic architecture was reached at Amiens, rebuilt by Bishop Évrard de Fouilloy after the cathedral had been struck by lightning in 1218.[1] The nave was built in the sixteen years between 1220 and 1236: the greatest Gothic nave in France. The scale is as lofty as that of Bourges, the piers are derived from those of Bourges, but the plan is based on that of Chartres, with seven instead of three chapels round the apse. The peculiar beauty here lies in the façade (Fig. 84), with the towers even more closely linked than at Rheims and the whole wrought with statues and moulding, crockets and pinnacles, until it is like a shrine.

The choir of Saint-Julien du Mans was rebuilt between 1217 and 1254, with close reminiscences of Bourges in the scheme of the piers and the height of its arcade. Its plan, however, is all its own: the apse has a double ambulatory, and no less than thirteen polygonal chapels round it, the central one much longer than the rest. Inside it is of great beauty; and when the apse is seen from the outside raised high above the old town wall, crowned by a double ridge of flying buttresses, it appears magnificent[2] (Fig. 85).

The northern cathedrals developed a different style, that was based on that multiplication of elements and mouldings which is already a feature of such northern Romanesque churches as Saint-Georges-de-Boscherville. The documents give little information as to the exact date of these cathedrals. Normandy came under the rule of Philip Augustus in 1205, and a fresh wave of architectural influence from the Île-de-France swept in. Yet no one would mistake Coutances for a cathedral of the district of Paris. It is much nearer to Benedictine architecture in its style and plan. The magnificent twin towers of the façade are far closer to the much earlier towers of the Abbaye aux Hommes of Caen than to Amiens or Notre-Dame. The splendid apse (Fig. 86) is much nearer to Saint-Martin-des-Champs than to any purely Gothic chevet. Within, the almost incredible multiplication of colonnettes reminds one of Exeter rather than of any French cathedral. At Rouen (Fig. 87) it is known that an architect named Jean d'Andely was already at work in 1206, though the vaults of the nave were still unfinished in 1234. Nowhere is the Norman multiplicity

[1] His architect was Robert de Luzarches, who built the nave and façade. In 1238 he was succeeded by Thomas and Regnault de Cormont.

[2] The exterior is a logical development from the chevet of Bourges.

more beautiful; the arches of the triforium echo the manifold mouldings of the great arcade. In certain parts such as the south aisle, a definite English influence seems evident, but the use of four stories in the nave is altogether French.[1] The splendid apse shows a considerable development of the window-space, and this development is transferred to the nave in the next cathedral to be built, that of Troyes. In plan it follows Amiens, with a slightly narrower proportion; in style, Rouen, with greater simplification, and the important addition of a glazed triforium below the clerestory.[2] But Troyes seems no more than a faltering experiment when compared with Beauvais (Fig. 88), rebuilt by Bishop Miles de Nanteuil after a fire that destroyed the old cathedral in 1225. The foundations were laid in 1247; had the bishop and his architect been less ambitious, and had the building ever been completed, it would have been the culmination of the French Gothic style. But from the beginning it was ill-starred. The height of every element was raised and the weight of everything, even of the pillars and the flying buttresses, was lightened. The height of the main vault is over a hundred and fifty-seven feet; the cresting of the choir roof nearly two hundred and twenty-four feet from the ground. From the first there was trouble with the vault, which finally fell in 1284. For forty years they toiled at the restoration, setting in fresh columns between the old, revaulting the choir on a sexpartite scheme and strengthening the buttresses.[3] The choir as it remains is a logical development of Amiens, yet its soaring height, its slender proportions, even, perhaps, its unfinished state—for the nave to complete it was never built —give it the sanctity of a temple not made with hands.

The planning of Beauvais in 1247 marks the culmination of cathedral-building, as the consecration of Saint-Denis in 1144 does that of monastic architecture. Thereafter there is a slow but steady decline. Creation was passing to the builders of lesser churches. It was Jehan des Champs, who had made his name as a mason of the Sainte Chapelle, who was in 1248 entrusted with the planning of the cathedral of Clermont. Its choir is a less lofty version of Beauvais, its nave a loftier one of Troyes. Already, however, the first enthusiasm of cathedral-building was losing its impulse; the nave of Clermont was left half-finished in the fourteenth century and was not completed for five hundred years. Jehan des Champs is said also to have designed the cathedrals of Rodez, Albi, and Narbonne. Of these Narbonne is still unfinished, since in the fourteenth century the consuls of the town objected to the threat which its citadel offered to the inhabitants; the builders of Rodez took thirty years to finish the apse and did not reach the nave until the Middle Ages were over;

[1] One was removed later.
[2] An addition also made in the choir of Amiens.
[3] Its troubles were not over. The transept had hurriedly to be built between 1500 and 1510 to protect the choir. The steeple, finished in 1569, fell on Ascension Day, 1573.

only Albi, built as a fortress against the Albigensian heresy, was completed.[1]
Two other cathedrals in the same style were hardly more fortunate. Limoges,
closely modelled on Clermont although it was begun some thirty years later,
about 1271,[2] had only reached one arm of
the transept when the Black Prince sacked
the city in 1370; the rest was only finished in
1876. The rebuilding of Toulouse, another
version of Narbonne,[3] was begun in 1275;
it still had its choir unvaulted and its new
nave unbuilt when it was ravaged by fire in
1609.

The only cathedral churches which
achieved completion were those on a modest
scale. Auxerre, that in the first quarter of
the thirteenth century had been given a
choir influenced by those of Chartres and
Reims, had its nave added in the course of the
fourteenth century in the current style of
gothique rayonnant; Nevers, begun in 1211,
had a still more modest nave added in the
early years of the fourteenth century. Where
something more ambitious was attempted,
it was in the old style; Séez, begun in 1270,
has a most elaborate interlaced triforium
that is the final expression of the Norman
formula of repetition; Évreux has a choir of
the early fourteenth century that is a soberer
version of Beauvais.

PLAN 9

Cathedral of Albi. End of the 14th century

The one great innovation of this time was
the addition of small chapels along each side
of the nave, either enclosed by party walls inside the church or built out between the buttresses. The need for them was a consequence of two things: the
growth of chantry chapels and the formation of innumerable confraternities.
The meeting of such needs involved a certain lessening of the undivided rights

[1] Its plan appears to have been based on the lost Franciscan church at Toulouse.
[2] The bishop, Aimeric de la Serre, devoted the greater part of his private fortune to it. His
successor gave half the revenues of all the vacant livings in the diocese towards the cost; they
would otherwise have been shared between him and the chapter. This lasted from 1290 to 1327,
when indulgences were granted to those who gave. Building was then stopped by the Hundred
Years War.
[3] It has seventeen pentagonal chapels linked by narrow passages. These linked pentagonal chapels
are also found at Clermont, Limoges, and Narbonne.

of the bishop and his chapter over the cathedral church,[1] but the chaplaincies were convenient additions to the prebends. Their number was very considerable. René d'Anjou, for example, not only founded a Low Mass every day at the Altar of St. Maurice in Angers Cathedral, for his Order of the Crescent, but by will established another, and six High Masses a year, at the altar before his tomb.[2] By the end of the fifteenth century there were more than fifty chantry priests at Laon.

Chantry chapels were added to Notre-Dame de Paris as early as 1258, to Laon a little later, to Amiens about 1291,[3] to Sens in 1293, to Coutances in the fourteenth, and to Bourges in the fifteenth century. They became a part of the original plan of cathedrals in the fourteenth century; as at Tours, at Bordeaux, at Carcassonne, and at Saint-Flour when it was rebuilt in 1396. By the end of the fifteenth century they were systematically inserted from Narbonne to Caudebec. In their assertion of individual taste[4] they did nothing to add to the homogeneity of the church; and in their abundant use of heraldic decoration, as for instance in the chapel added to Bourges by Canon Pierre Trousseau in 1404, they introduced a personal element that had no real place in the imagery of the cathedral.[5] Exceptionally even a cathedral might have a larger chapel added to it as an annexe; at Chartres, for instance, the Chapelle Vendôme was built on in 1417. Here, too, the influence of courtly art modified the traditional iconography. The exterior framing of the great window is richly sculptured: Christ stands at the top of the gable; the Virgin and the Archangel of the Annunciation stand in niches on either side of the window itself; and beneath them are set statues on an almost equal scale of Louis de Bourbon-Vendôme and his wife Blanche de Roucy. The chapel of the Bourbons in Lyons Cathedral, founded in 1496 by Cardinal Charles de Bourbon, has its balustrade adorned with the Bourbon winged stag and the motto *Espérance*. Similarly the chapels built or taken over by Orders of Chivalry tended to have a disproportionate amount of heraldry in their decoration. The Order of the Knights of the Fetter, who had to wear a prisoner's iron hanging by a chain from their left leg on Sundays, was founded by Jean de Bourbon in 1414.[6] Their chapel in Notre-Dame de Paris, endowed for the celebration of a daily Mass, was enriched by the members of the Order with a picture of Our Lady with their arms. If any of their number

[1] Such chapels were, however, sometimes endowed by the bishop himself. At Albi, Bishop Béraud de Fargis founded six chapels by 1334 and Bishop Pictavin de Montesquiou six more in 1347.

[2] Quatrebarbes, i. 84.

[3] One of the early ones there was erected by the bishop, who had been chaplain to Louis IX, in his honour after his canonization in 1297.

[4] A fourteenth-century chapel at Coutances is a welter of cusped arcades of different shapes and sizes.

[5] Cf. the heraldic decoration of the sacristy given to Bourges Cathedral by Jacques Cœur in 1447 to take the place of the old sacristy pulled down to make room for his chantry chapel.

[6] Hélyot in Migne, xxi, col. 263. The Order did not last long.

should be victorious in combat, his picture was to be set up, with his arms and the arms of the man he had vanquished. The Order of the Crescent adorned its chapel in Angers Cathedral with a fine altar and image of St. Maurice, patron of Chivalry, and a series of pictures some four feet high with the arms, crests, and mottoes of each of the knights and squires of the Order. Even a single tournament might receive commemoration in a cathedral. In 1449 the *Pas de la Fontaine aux Pleurs* was held at the end of the bridge near Chalon-sur-Saône. A picture was set up in a pavilion by the bridge, representing the Virgin and Child. At their feet was a lady weeping. Her tears fell into a fountain, beside which was a unicorn holding three shields: white, for the combat with the axe, violet for the sword, and black for the lance, all sprinkled with blue tears. When the tournament was over the picture was dedicated and set up in the Duke's Chapel in the cathedral of Boulogne.

Not all men could afford a chantry chapel,[1] but many could afford to endow a Mass. Consequently in certain churches the high altar was so arranged that the altar behind it, where Obits and Masses for the dead were said, was visible above the high altar.[2] The *Autel des Ardens* in Notre-Dame de Paris was set in this fashion, and so was one in the cathedral of Troyes.

3. CATHEDRAL ICONOGRAPHY

It is not easy to determine the part played by the bishops and their chapters in the design of the Gothic cathedrals. Presumably they suggested a ground-plan and a model, or chose from alternative plans submitted to them by the *maître de l'œuvre*. Their part in the choice of subjects for the sculptured decoration is much clearer: they chose them, just as the abbots had chosen them earlier. The bishop, or a canon delegated with the office, drew up the iconographic scheme. There was little or no direct recourse to illuminated manuscripts to find a model; the cathedrals had no scriptoria and the *maître de l'œuvre* had by now his own repertory of designs, and was capable of producing fresh ones to meet the canons' needs. He had probably worked on other Gothic cathedrals, and had certainly visited them and made drawings of any work that was especially striking. It has been pointed out[3] that the designer of the Rheims sculptures evidently had sketches of the Job tympanum at Chartres, and of details of the Judgement at Paris, and of the Resurrection of the Dead at Amiens.[4] The note-book of Villard de Honnecourt[5] survives to show us the

---

[1] O. de la Marche, *Mem.,* chap. xxi.

[2] As the High Chantry of Henry V is above the altar at Westminster. E. Bishop, *Liturg. Hist.,* p. 32.　　　　　　　　　[3] Lefrançois-Pillion, *Sculpteurs de Reims,* p. 19.

[4] Copies are rare, but Rouen has an almost exact copy of the Coronation of the Virgin at Rheims, and Meaux another of the St. Stephen's door at Paris.

[5] Bibl. Nat. français 19093. Villard de Honnecourt may have been a pupil of the *Maître des figures antiques* who carved the Annunciation group at Rheims (Fig. 97). See Adhémar, p. 278.

kind of drawings that served for the purpose (Fig. 89) and the formulae which such men employed to dash off a quick sketch as it was required. The sketch, once made and accepted, served both as a basis for the contract and as a model for the stone-carvers who worked under the master. The contract between the Chapter of Rodez and the stone-cutter Jacques Maurel, drawn up in 1448, for the sculptures of the south door, states that the hundred and eight statues are all to be according to the *patrons* or sketch designs presented by him to the chapter, approved by them, and handed over before a notary to the sculptor.[1]

As a consequence of this system there is less constructive originality in Gothic than in Romanesque imagery. It was addressed to an unlearned public and could not be so esoteric in its symbolism as monastic art had been before. Honorius of Autun could write of the art of cathedrals: 'Ob tres causas fit pictura: primo, quia est laicorum litteratura; secundo, ut domus tali decore ornetur; tertio, ut priorum vita in memoriam revocetur';[2] and indeed a didactic, decorative, or commemorative purpose will be found to underlie all the imagery of the great cathedrals.

Its development tended to be on the didactic and ethical side. It is in such details as the representation of the Virtues that innovations are made. At Notre-Dame they are a new assembly and have new attributes: Humility a dove, Prudence a snake, Chastity the bird Charistia, that hovers unharmed above a burning mountain; Charity a lamb, that gives its own wool; Hope a banner; Faith, a cross and chalice; Fortitude, armour and a lion; Patience an ox, Meekness a thong, Concord an olive-branch, Obedience a camel, and Perseverance a crown of life.[3] At the great door of Amiens they appear as seated maidens, bearing such emblems as these upon a shield; at Chartres again they are as at Paris, bearing banners with their symbols.

It is an interesting contrast with the derivation of Romanesque iconography that these new series and new types appear to have had no literary source. The culture of the cathedral was not the humanism of the monastery.[4] The new dialectical and theological writings of the cathedral schools and the universities lacked the qualities that could inspire an iconography. Gothic imagery is perfectly consistent with the thought and knowledge of the time, but it is not directly based on any of its literature. It is by an exception that Philosophy is represented at Laon with her head in the clouds, and a ladder upon her breast rising from Π, Practical Philosophy, to Θ, Theoretical Philosophy; some canon had been reading his Boëthius and imposed his learning upon the stone-carver. In the same place a side-door represents the prefigurations of the Virgin Birth—the Burning Bush, Aaron's rod, Gideon's fleece, the closed door of Ezekiel's

---

[1] Mortet in *Bull. Mon.*, 1902.   [2] Mortet, ii. 14.
[3] See Katzenellenbogen, p. 76.   [4] See Adhémar, p. 270.

H

Vision, the Hebrews in the furnace, and Daniel in the lion's den, according to Honorius of Autun: the canons may have understood them, but it is doubtful if many of their flock were familiar with such symbols.

The connexion with illuminated manuscripts is not much closer than with the literary texts. Such books may serve to our generation to interpret a subject in sculpture that might otherwise remain obscure,[1] but they hardly ever served as models in their own day.[2] The production of such manuscripts was passing into lay workshops that produced them chiefly for a lay public. The secular workshops were centres less of intellectual creation than of technical dexterity; they received their religious concepts at second hand and gave them exquisite expression, but they did not out of their own learning create a new iconography. Colour, however, remained to link sculpture with painting. At Notre-Dame, for instance, the triple portal, its voussures and tympana, were entirely painted; the gallery of Kings was painted and gilt; and the two great arcades above this were painted and the central rose gilt.[3] Before 1914 a little door in the north transept at Rheims showed a mixture of coloured sculpture and painting on the flat, while the north and south doors at Rouen originally had paintings on the walls above the tympana.

On the other hand, drama, the third great influence on early medieval iconography, continued to operate, if through different forms. Mystery plays, intended to be acted on stages outside the church, at least provided parallels with sculpture. When the *Mystère de la Résurrection* was played in the late twelfth century, with its 'mansions' and its representations of Hell and Heaven,[4] it must have offered many analogies with a Judgement tympanum; when in the *Mystère d'Adam* devils came to attend the death of Adam and Eve and to chain and manacle them and drag them to Hell, the scene must have looked like a lintel carved with the Damned; when in the Christmas Play at Laon[5] the Procession of Prophets appeared—Isaiah and Jeremiah bearded, wearing dalmatics, Daniel, young and splendidly dressed, Moses, vested and bearing the tables of the Law, David in kingly raiment, and Habakkuk, bald and bent—it must have looked as if the statues of the porch had stepped down from their places. At a later date the parallel between sculpture and the wordless mimes of state pageantry must have been no less striking. In 1313, for instance, Philippe le Bel entertained the King of England. Among other spectacles he was shown a mime of the life of Christ, with the Adoration of the Magi and of Paradise with ninety

---

[1] See, for instance, E. M. Paillard, *Portail de Reims,* in which certain Champenois manuscripts are used for the detailed interpretation of the iconography.

[2] Exceptionally the sculptures of the base of the façade of Auxerre seem to be in relation with an illustrated Genesis.

[3] The upper work was uncoloured. Viollet-le-Duc, *Dict. rais. de l'arch.* vii. 109.

[4] Petit de Julleville, i. 92; Cohen et Réau, p. 420.

[5] Young, ii. 145.

angels.[1] Such wordless mimes continued in use alongside spoken drama well into the fifteenth century. One was played at the entry of Charles VI and Henry V into Paris after the Treaty of Troyes in 1420: 'un moult piteux mystère de la Passion de Nostre Seigneur au vif, selon que elle est figurée autour du cuer de Nostre Dame de Paris'.[2] Four years later the Duke of Bedford entered Paris in his turn, to be entertained before the Châtelet by a representation of the parallels between the Old and New Testaments, 'fait sans parler ne sans signer comme se ce feussent ymages enlevez contre ung mur'.[3]

The Gothic cathedrals were no less richly adorned with sculpture than the Romanesque abbeys, but it was differently placed. The capitals were no longer the focus of sculpture, for the new vaulting systems made them smaller and less important. Their imagery was no longer of scenes that it needed a monastic education to interpret, but of foliage that grew closer and closer to Nature[4] as the city crowding round the cathedrals drove her farther away. It had no particular symbolic significance; all that Bishop Guillaume Durand could find to say about it in the *Rationale* he wrote in 1284 is that 'sometimes they add flowers and trees with their fruit, to represent the fruits of good works, that grow from the roots of virtue'.[5]

The use of such foliage changed the traditional Corinthian capital into something new and strange. At Lisieux, though full of life, the leaves are still acanthus; at Laon, though they are still formal, they are no longer classical. The use of such capitals was geographically extremely limited. None of the cathedrals where they are to be found are very far from Paris: Lisieux, Rouen, Rheims, Laon, and Notre-Dame itself.[6] The introduction of great piers of grouped columns with a single frieze-like capital, as at Rheims, meant the complete renunciation of the classical tradition. Their leafage was drawn from every kind of plant and tree—oak, maple, pear, fig, ash, poplar, holly, elm, ivy, chestnut, vine, laurel, olive, wild rose, water-lily, bracken, raspberry, and mulberry.[7] These, like Romanesque capitals, were usually painted. About a century ago a capital of the nave of Évreux still had the upper wreath, of maple-leaves, painted olive green, edged with black, and with the back of the leaf dark purple; the lower wreath, of ivy, was white, edged and ribbed in black, again with purple backs. The astragal below was vermilion.[8] It was not long before foliage sculpture was extended to every decorated part of the structure: friezes,

[1] Petit de Julleville, ii. 187.
[2] *Journal d'un bourgeois de Paris,* quoted Petit de Julleville, ii. 189.
[3] Ibid. ii. 665.
[4] I have traced the development in some detail in *Nature in Design,* pp. 58 et seqq.
[5] Bk. I, ch. xxi, ed. Barthélemy, i. 51.
[6] See D. Jalabert in *G.B.A.,* 6th series, v, 1931, p. 283.
[7] See Lambin, *La Flore des grandes cathédrales de la France,* 1897.
[8] Viollet-le-Duc, *Dict. rais. de l'arch.* ii. 533, s.v. Chapiteau. The colour has now disappeared.

mouldings, spandrels, finials, crockets,[1] and panels. Each architectural feature was transmuted into the appropriate vegetable form. By the beginning of the thirteenth century the transept portals of Chartres have leaves that are recognizably those of hepatica, ivy, holly, hawthorn, fig, and rose, and at Noyon there are sprays of maple, gooseberry, and vine. On the west door of Notre-Dame de Paris there is a frieze of watercress and another of celandine, crockets of snapdragon flowers and copings of hepatica leaves. At Rheims (Fig. 90 B) some of the interior walls are panelled with reliefs of plants that might serve as illustrations to a herbal.

If figure sculpture was thus banished from the capitals, it was by no means exiled from the cathedral. Inside, it is true, there was less of it, though the builders of Rheims found a new field for it by covering the entire west wall with sculpture: a dado of drapery below, and seven rows of statues in arcaded niches with panels of foliage to fill the wall. The chief field for sculpture in the Gothic cathedrals[2] was on the great portals of the façades and on the gables above them: a field that had already been exploited in such Romanesque cathedrals as Angoulême. In all but the south-west, however, the fashion had been for a single great portal, and this was continued in the earliest Gothic cathedrals. At Senlis, dedicated in 1191, the door was designed in honour of the Virgin, the patron of the church. The scheme is entirely derived from the imagery of the great Benedictine abbeys. On either side are column statues of the Prophets and Forerunners,[3] as at Saint-Denis.[4] The tympanum is filled with a beautiful composition in honour of Our Lady: a panel —now much damaged—sculptured with her death, her resurrection on the lintel, and her Assumption, seated in glory beside her Son, in the lunette with angels on either side. The scheme is again Benedictine; a version of it, much cruder than that at Senlis, appears in an eleventh-century sacramentary from Saint-Bertin.[5] Yet the sculptor of Senlis might claim to have added beauty to the whole; the angels that come with a flurry of wings to bear the Virgin to Heaven are unforgettable (Fig. 91).

The success of the scheme was attested by its many imitations. The cathedrals that imitated it, however, did so as part of a larger plan.[6] The west door at Chartres, with its triple portals with scenes of the Second Coming, Christ in Majesty, and a Virgin door, had set a fashion that with variations on the theme was followed by nearly all the subsequent cathedrals. Just as Christ in

[1] On these see Mademoiselle Jalabert in *Bull. Mon.* xci, 1932, p. 217.
[2] An admirable series of photographs of these sculptures will be found in A. Gardner, *French Mediaeval Sculpture.* [3] Badly damaged and ill restored.
[4] M. Mâle has pointed out that Bishop Thibault, the builder of Senlis, was a friend of Suger.
[5] Bib. Nat. lat. 819, fol. 97ᵛ. The scene is also represented on the tympanum of the collegiate church of Saint-Pierre-Puellier at Orleans. See Mâle, *Art rel. XIIᵉ siècle*, p. 435. It is now in the Museum of Bourges.
[6] In the abbey of Longpont it was imitated as a single door.

Majesty with the evangelistic beasts is the most characteristic Romanesque tympanum, so is the Virgin seated beside her Son that most typical of the Gothic Age.

The first of these, in date as in magnificence, is that of the north transept at Chartres, which must have been begun soon after the fire of 1194. Here the central tympanum is closely based on that of Senlis. The whole, however, is given a new splendour. Against the mullion of the door stands a great figure of St. Anne, of whom the church contained a famous relic, holding the baby Virgin. To one side stand the precursors of Christ, a splendid retinue: Melchizedek, Abraham, Moses, Samuel, David; and to the other the prophets who foretold His coming: Isaiah, Jeremiah, Simeon; St. John, who baptized Him, and Peter, the first head of His church. The voussures are filled with the Virgin's genealogy.

The portal to the right has a new theme: the patriarchs of the Old Testament.[1] They do not figure there in their own right, but again as prototypes and precursors of Christ and the Virgin Birth. Job, who endured a Passion, and Solomon, who built a Temple, appear on the tympanum; Samson and Judith, who overcame evil, Tobit, who brought sight to the blind, Gideon, whose fleece was wet with dew, appear on the voussures; Balaam, who had Faith, Solomon, who had Wisdom, the Queen of Sheba, who had Reverence, stand on one side; Jesus, the son of Sirach, and Joseph, who overcame evil by speech, on the other.

The portal to the left is a Nativity door. The tympanum has the Magi, the Nativity, and the Shepherds in a scheme familiar in such Romanesque work as the side-door at Vézelay. In the voussures, again according to a Romanesque scheme, are the Wise and Foolish Virgins and the Virtues and Vices. Beyond these are twelve women. On one side one is washing wool and another carding it, one pounding hemp and another carding it, one spinning and the other winding the thread: they represent the *vita activa*. On the other side are six veiled women, reading, meditating, praying, and in ecstasy: the *vita contemplativa*.[2] The standing figures represent the Annunciation, accompanied by Isaiah, and the Visitation, accompanied by Daniel, another prophet of the Virgin Birth.

The central door at Laon has its tympanum on the same scheme; there are two angels on either side, one with a censer and one with a candlestick. The voussure has first a line of Angels, then another of Virtues, then a third of the symbols of virginity according to Honorius of Autun.[3] The Virgin's door at Notre-Dame de Paris, almost contemporary with that at Chartres, represents the next phase. The scheme is more clearly divided into three zones, of which the Prophets and Precursors, reduced to three of each separated by the ark

---

[1] Cf. Adam of St. Victor, Sequences XXIII–XXVI.
[2] See Mâle, *Art rel. XIIIᵉ siècle*, p. 159.   [3] See p. 65.

of the Covenant, occupy the lowest. It follows in essentials that of Senlis, although the scenes of the apostles round the Virgin's bed and of the angels lifting her up are fused. This scheme is used again on the Virgin's door at Amiens, though here the recumbent Virgin is represented twice, once in death and once in resurrection; again at Poitiers, though without the Prophets and Precursors; and again later at Auxerre, on a less noble scale.

The southern porch at Chartres (Fig. 92) has the traditional subject of the Last Judgement as the theme of its central door, with Christ trampling on the asp and the basilisk against the mullion. The treatment of the Judgement Scene is altogether new (Fig. 93). Christ appears as no apocalyptic figure, but as the Son of Man, who holds up His hands that men may see the wounds of their salvation. The figure is no greater and no more royal than those of the Virgin and of St. John seated on either side as the advocates of humanity. The angels do not bear the censers or candles of worship, but the instruments of the Passion. Here is not only a new scheme, but a new vision. On the lintel beneath are the Blessed and the Damned, but there is a new quietness. Both are too much awed by the vision above them to show fear at the gate of Hell or joy at the sight of Paradise.

Here the right-hand portal is that of the confessors. St. Martin and St. Nicholas fill the tympanum, and the great saints of the church stand on either side. The left is that of the Martyrs, with St. Stephen in the tympanum, and the Martyrs whose relics were venerated at Chartres in the jambs.

These side-portals are special to Chartres, but the great theme of the central door was widely imitated. At Paris[1] the actors change places, and the angels stand next to Christ; the Virgin and St. John kneel, but the great central figure remains the same. At Bourges the angels are doubled, and in the friezes below the Blessed and the Damned go to their fate with beatific smiles (Fig. 94) and horrible anguish.[2] On the door of the north transept at Rheims the whole field is occupied by a series of friezes, each stressed by a conventional line of clouds or a trail of foliage. The dead rise from their tombs with every variety of sentiment and action. Some, a little dazed from their long sleep, sit on the edge of their tombs; some rise from the jars of primitive burial; some, classically draped, majestically raise the lids of their sarcophagi; others leap joyfully back to life. Below them the Elect are separated from the Damned, and on the lowest frieze a chain-gang of sinners, including king, bishop, and monk, go to the flames, and angels respectfully bear the souls of the righteous to rest in Abraham's bosom.

At Bordeaux, carved after 1308, the balance is shifted, and Christ, the angels, the Virgin, and St. John occupy the central zone of the tympanum, with the dead rising from their coffins below. Even at Auxerre, nearly two

---

[1] Much restored.   [2] This was imitated as far away as Ambronay in the Ain.

hundred years after Chartres, the central figure of the tympanum is little changed.

The great central tympana of the transept porches at Chartres established two great schemes, the Coronation and Assumption of the Virgin and the Last Judgement, which appear on nearly all the great portals of the Gothic cathedrals. These usually had three portals, and the subject of the third door, and of any subsidiary portals, varied considerably. At Laon the third door is dedicated to the childhood of Jesus, like the left-hand portal of the north transept at Chartres. At Paris an older tympanum was reset to form another such portal, again combined with a Last Judgement and a Virgin's door, with another Virgin's door and a St. Stephen's door for the transepts. At Amiens the Last Judgement and the Virgin's door appear combined with a portal in honour of Saint Firmin, with a wholly new scene of the finding of his tomb; with its crowd of clerks and laymen, devout and curious, with mothers holding their babies and fathers lifting the children to see the relic, it is a fitting entry to the place wherein just such people entered to visit the saint's shrine. At Bourges the three doors were increased to five: a Last Judgement in the centre, with a Virgin's door and a St. William's door to the right, and a St. Stephen's and a St. Ursin's to the left. At Rheims the tympana were replaced by glass, but in the gables there are the familiar Judgement and Coronation, here exceptionally accompanied by a Crucifixion. At Rouen the portals were divided between façade and transept; their subjects are the Last Judgement, the Passion,[1] and the lives of St. John Baptist and St. John the Divine. At Poitiers the usual Judgement and Virgin's door are completed by one dedicated to St. Peter, with scenes of his Mission and of the veneration of his shrine.

The theme, or rather the dedication, of the portal usually dictated the subject of the statue that stood against the mullion of the door.[2] Three magnificent Virgin statues still survive from her doors at Paris, Rheims, and Amiens (Fig. 95), showing an increasing elegance and a gradual transition from the Mother to the Queen. The Judgement Portals usually have a statue of Christ, as at Chartres, where He appears as the teacher without a halo, Amiens, and Bourges. There are three St. Stephens: an early one at Sens (Fig. 96) and later examples at Meaux and Bourges. At Chartres there is a St. Anne, at Amiens a Saint Firmin, and at Rheims a Saint Sixte to commemorate saints who were especially honoured in the church.

At Chartres the triple portals of the transepts were extended soon after their erection by porches set in front of them, with richly sculptured decoration of their own. At Laon such porches were envisaged from the first. On the other great cathedrals the sculptured decoration of the portals was extended to cover

[1] These two subjects reappear at Bayeux.
[2] As in Romanesque sculpture, e.g. the narthex of Vézelay.

most of the façade. As a consequence of the use of multiple portals the statue-columns were extended to form a great range of figures across the front of the church. At Notre-Dame de Paris the statues[1] still stand in front of a meaningless row of close-set columns; at Rheims (Fig. 97) the pillars are both more structural and more independent of the figures; at Amiens the colonnade has disappeared altogether and canopies take its place.   There was a like extension in the subjects of the statues: at Chartres the Confessors and Martyrs; at Amiens the Apostles, the Annunciation and Visitation, and a great line of sixteen prophets and of local saints; at Rheims, besides the Precursors and Prophets of the old tradition, another series of local saints, another file of Apostles and Evangelists, the Annunciation, Visitation, and Presentation. These statues came to be surrounded by a wealth of minor sculpture, of which a satisfactory study can only be made on the spot: by brackets beneath at Chartres; by arcades and medallions with reliefs at Paris; by exquisite quatrefoils of the zodiac, the labours of the months, the Virtues and the prophecies of the Prophets above them at Amiens; by sculptured drapery at Rheims; by an arcade with spandrels sculptured with scenes from the Old Testament at Bourges; and by an elaborate diaper like an embroidery at Auxerre, with rich arcading in the actual jambs of the portals. Besides these lesser adornments, the inner faces of the door mullions and, indeed, every free surface was sculptured with reliefs: the Labours of the Months, the Ages of Man, the Virtues and Vices at Paris; the seasons and a hundred other subjects at Rheims; grotesques in medallions at Rouen[2] and Lyons; sculptures as lively and as varied as the decorations of an illuminated psalter.

Above the level of the actual portal, the tide of sculpture gradually rose up the façade. At Paris a great line of twenty-eight statues stretches across the front of the church: the crowned kings of Judah who figure there as ancestors of the Virgin. At Amiens the porches have gables and pinnacles of their own, then there is a traceried arcade, and then, just below the first stage of the towers, another *galerie des rois*. At Rheims the gables are more richly sculptured, the great rose and the twin windows on either side of it rise higher than the arcade of Amiens, and the kings, surmounted by a canopied and pinnacled arcade, crown the façade. But at Rheims every part of the church as it reaches heavenward has its population of statues. In the niches of the buttresses of the façade are Resurrection scenes: Mary Magdalene brings news of the Resurrection to St. Peter; Christ appears to the apostles and to the incredulous St. Thomas, and, wayworn and wearing a pilgrim's hat, to the disciples journeying to Emmaus.

---

[1] Restored.

[2] A centaur; the doctor who is half a goose; the pig-headed philosopher; the cock-bodied musician; the calf-headed lady; the dog-man and bird-woman. The Portail de la Calende has, under the Apostles, little panels with the stories of Jacob and Joseph, the lives of Saint Romain and Saint Ouen, Dives, and the *Lai d'Aristote*.

Above the arch David hurls his stone against Goliath, and on either side of it are scenes from the lives of David and Solomon, who, as anointed of God, are especially fit for honour in a Coronation church. At the very top is the Baptism of Clovis, the first Christian King of France, and on either side the statues of kings continue on three sides of all six towers. Who shall say whether they are kings of France or of Judah? They are kings by divine right, crowning the building where the kings of France were anointed with the Holy Oil, and fit symbols of Sovereignty. Finally, a heavenly host of angels stands as guardians in the supports of the flying buttresses round the whole church.

Rheims, indeed, marks the zenith of sculptured decoration applied to an architectural whole. Yet other cathedrals, with a less abundant wealth of sculpture, gained the utmost effect from them by skilful placing. At Sens the Wise and Foolish Virgins are carved in low relief on either side of the tympanum, climbing towards two doors on either side of its gable. One is open to show the Spouse awaiting the Wise; the other is shut in the face of the Foolish. At Chartres the apse had an immense angel on the roof that turned to follow the sun and seemed to hallow the passing of the hours.[1]

Yet by the beginning of the fourteenth century the coherent iconography of the Gothic portals was beginning to break up. The great door of the cathedral of Bordeaux, given by Pope Clement V about 1314, has a composite tympanum: on the lowest frieze the Last Supper, on the next the Ascension, and at the top Christ in Judgement. The great statues of the jambs represent six sainted bishops, the voussures angels and saints, and by a singular inappropriateness, the statue of the mullion Pope Clement V himself. At Limoges, at the end of the fourteenth century, the Martyrdom of St. Stephen was represented to the left of the façade. The saint kneels and his murderers stone him; but all force has left the composition, since each figure rests on a separate sculptured bracket and is sheltered by a separate arcaded canopy.

4. STAINED GLASS

One of the greatest glories of the cathedrals of France is their stained glass, that in many buildings still preserves to our use the glorious mediaeval colour that is elsewhere dimmed or effaced. Any one who has seen the heavenly blue, the flame and ruby and green, of Le Mans, the illumination colours of Chartres, or the sunset glory of Auxerre has shared in a part of mediaeval beauty that is still unchanged.

The windows of the cathedrals were commonly given by the faithful of the diocese or by devotees of the shrine, according to their piety and their degree. At Chartres the Kings of France and Castille, the Counts of Champagne,

---

[1] It was destroyed in the fire of 1836. Villard de Honnecourt describes how it worked.

Boulogne, Chartres, and Dreux, and such great lords as those of Montfort and Courtenay gave the high lancet windows with single figures. The great roses of the transept were given by Louis IX and his mother and the Duke of Brittany and his wife. The windows with medallions of the saints were given by the guilds of traders and artisans, most of whom were represented at their work at the bottom of them. St. Charlemagne has the draper, measuring cloth with his yardstick; St. Antony, the fish-merchants, selling from a barrow and in a little shop; St. John the Evangelist, the armourers at their anvil; St. Theodore, the weavers at their looms. The St. Vincent window has Pierre Baillart, a canon of the cathedral, kneeling at its foot. At Beauvais windows were given in the thirteenth century by the skinners and the bowmakers.

The scheme was doubtless worked out by a cleric and offered for execution to the workmen. A contract of 1408 between the Dean of Troyes and Guiot Brisetour, glazier, is for roundels of the evangelists 'as the canons shall direct'.[1] Teams of glassworkers moved on from one cathedral to the next; the Paris windows are of the same school as those of Chartres. This city, indeed, became a recognized centre of the art; a thirteenth-century window at Rouen, with medallions of the history of Joseph, is signed CLEMENS VITRARIVS CARNOTENSIS.

The development of glass-painting was later than that of sculpture; yet it was at Suger's abbey of Saint-Denis that it first played as important a part as stone-carving not only in the decoration of the building but also in its iconographic scheme. Its traditional schemes are therefore Benedictine in origin: Bourges, Chartres, Le Mans, Tours, Lyons, Rouen, all have great windows with the parallels between the Old and New Testaments such as Hrabanus Maurus and Honorius of Autun expounded and Suger made the scheme of his imagery. In all of them there are central medallions of the Life of Christ, either of the whole or of the Passion, and lesser medallions or other decorative compartments with the Old Testament parallels.[2] The east window in the cathedral of Poitiers given by Eleanor of Guienne and Henry II of England about 1180, recalls the themes of Romanesque manuscripts and Romanesque sculpture in its composition (Fig. 98). The bottom medallion, the crucifixion of St. Peter, recalls the dedication of the cathedral. Above it a small frieze depicts the Holy Maries coming to the Sepulchre and the angel by the tomb. Then comes the chief theme, the Crucifixion, much as it is represented in any Sacramentary of about 1130. Finally, the Ascension occupies the top of the window; two angels lift the mandorla, as in the illustrations to Beatus's commentary on the Apocalypse,

---

[1] Fagniez, ii. 192.

[2] See Mâle, *Art rel. XIIIe siècle*, p. 171. He suggests that as Hrabanus' and Honorius' works were used as preachers' manuals, the parallels may have been familiar even to a lay congregation. Some of these windows are in close relation, both in subject and in the arrangement of the medallions, with such thirteenth-century *Bibles moralisées* as Bib. Nat. lat. 11560.

and below are the angels and apostles as they appear on many sculptured lintels of about that date.[1]

The Apocalypse, indeed, as represented in rather later manuscripts than those of Beatus's Commentary, continued to inspire the glass-painter; a fine fifteenth-century window at Auxerre shows St. John the Divine and his visions in a scheme that is clearly in close relation with such a manuscript.

The other great source of inspiration, the drama, likewise had its influence; the *Miracle de Théophile*, one of the plays in honour of the Virgin that used to be acted in front of the cathedrals, is represented in the glass at Beauvais, Chartres, Laon, Troyes, and Le Mans.

After the great iconographic schemes of the façades had been worked out, their sculptures inspired the design of glass. A thirteenth-century window at Rouen has a Judgement, and Lyons a Coronation of the Virgin, such as might appear on any tympanum; Chartres has a Virgin that might serve as a mullion figure. The Liberal Arts appear in glass at Auxerre, Chartres, and Laon as they do on the sculptures of the cathedrals; and the Virtues in the foliated borders of the Magi window at Lyons just as they do in the voussures of the portals. The local saints are congregated in windows at Bourges and Chartres exactly as they are as statues on the façade of Amiens. Exceptionally a whole scheme was worked out on similar lines to those of a great cathedral façade. Chartres has a great rose window in the end wall of each arm of the transept. That to the north, given by Saint Louis and his mother between 1223 and 1226, has the Incarnation and its prophecy for its theme. The Virgin and Child in Majesty occupy the centre, surrounded by angels, by the ancestor kings, and by the prophets of the Messiah. The lancets below have in the centre St. Anne and the child Mary, such as they appear on the mullion of the portal, on either side David and Solomon, Melchizedek and Aaron, with their opposites, Pharaoh, Jeroboam and the Golden Calf, Saul and Nebuchadnezzar, much as they might appear on the jambs of a portal. The southern rose, given by Peter Mauclerc, Duke of Brittany, and his wife between 1217 and 1221, has the Second Coming for its theme. Christ is enthroned in the centre, bearing a chalice. Round Him wheel the evangelistic beasts, eight censing angels, and the twenty-four Elders of the Apocalypse. The lancets have a new theme; the four major Prophets bearing the four Evangelists upon their shoulders.[2] The unusual scheme may well have been inspired by a saying of Bernard Sylvestris, the great Chartres philosopher of the twelfth century: 'He stood upon the shoulders of the giants of antiquity, and thanks to them he could see farther than they.'

Just as one door of a cathedral was normally dedicated to a saint held in particular honour in that place, so the altar dedication of a chapel, and the relics consequently exhibited there on feast days, commonly dictated the subject of

---

[1] Cf. the Ascension window at Le Mans.   [2] See Bréhier, p. 308.

its windows. In the chapels of the apse at Chartres the subjects of the glass exactly correspond with the old dedications: St. Julian, St. Stephen and the Martyrs, the Apostles and the Confessors.[1] The other saints who most often appear are those of the great pilgrimages: St. James of Compostella, St. Martin of Tours, and St. Nicholas of Bari.[2] These were doubtless given by confraternities or by pilgrims; indeed one of the windows at Chartres dedicated to St. James shows six pilgrims as donors, led by Robert de Bérou, chancellor of the church.[3] Chartres has four of St. James, Tours two; Auxerre and Bourges two of St. Nicholas; Tours, Bourges, and Le Mans two of St. Martin.

With the end of the century new themes came in. The fourteenth-century windows of the Lady Chapel of Rouen shows the twenty-four archbishops of the province who are honoured as saints; the Chapelle Sainte-Croix in the cathedral of Carcassonne has a window interpreting the mystical poem *Lignum vitae* ascribed to St. Bonaventura; one in the left arm of the transept at Angers has the signs that predict the end of the world, oddly coupled with the labours of the months. Such innovations, however, are usually for single windows and are not repeated. For gradually the ordered schemes were beginning to break up. A window of about 1300 at the east end of Dol cathedral, with the Last Judgement above, has the most varied subjects in the lancets below: the stories of St. Margaret and of Abraham, the Childhood and Passion of Christ, the stories of St. Samson and St. Catherine of Alexandria, and the first six bishops of Rennes with the bishops of Léon, Quimper, Tréguier, Saint-Brieuc, Aleth, and Vannes.

The whole scheme of window design was changing, in obvious sympathy with the changing style of manuscript illuminations. Canopy work of the richest design was coming into fashion in every form of art, and was especially appropriate to stained glass, for it linked the glass with the architectural setting. The painted canopies of windows in the Lady Chapel at Rouen, of the end of the fourteenth century (Fig. 99 A), show what a wealth of ornamental detail they could be made to comprise. As a consequence medallion schemes went completely out of fashion, and designs based on single figures under a canopy everywhere took their place. The donors were no longer represented in some obscure bottom corner of the design, but instead appeared on an equal footing with the Virgin or the saint they had honoured. They were represented, too, in portraits, with every detail of their dress and jewels (Fig. 99 B). The scheme of canopied figures, admirably adapted to windows of moderate size, was even used for such immense windows as that in the north transept of Le Mans, dating from about 1440. The wheel at the top represents, rather awkwardly, the

[1] See Mâle, *Art rel. XIIIᵉ siècle*, p. 362. It will be remembered that the Martyrs and Confessors each have a door of the south porch.

[2] See ibid., p. 368.   [3] Ibid., p. 371.

Coronation of the Virgin and Christ in glory. The lower window is filled with the Apostles, two sainted bishops of Le Mans, and Saint Louis, arranged in two rows under canopies, while the donors of each light—two canons, a bishop, two lords and their ladies, and the king—kneel at the foot.

Great figured windows of stained glass hardly ever occupied all the windows of a cathedral. In the thirteenth century the rest were usually filled with *grisaille* windows painted in graceful formal patterns. Later, however, the influence of secular windows was more strongly felt; such windows as those in the Lady Chapel at Rouen, with borders of birds and leafage, diapers and scrolls or roses, and occasional coats of arms, could be set as fitly in a castle hall as in a chapel of the Virgin.

5. CATHEDRAL ART

The sculptures of the portals and façades and the windows of stained glass comprised the organized scheme of imagery in a cathedral; it likewise held much that was no less significant, though more disparate. The canons' choir was separated from the rest by a *Jubé* or screen; no part of the fabric has endured more damage than these, at the hands of eighteenth-century canons as well as of Huguenots and revolutionaries, and few remain.

They seem often, and appropriately, to have been the gift of the canons themselves. A contract for the choir screen of Troyes Cathedral, drawn up between the chapter and the master mason in 1382, is specifically for the structure; 'senz les ymaiges les quelles Messeigneurs feront faire à leur plaisir et à leurs propres couz et despens'. Mathieu des Champs, Bishop of Chartres from 1247 to 1259, had a screen made for his cathedral with the outer side sculptured all round with reliefs of the Magi, the Shepherds and other Nativity scenes, and the Evangelists. The fragments that remain[1] show how fine was the sculpture of the whole. About 1300 Bourges had such a screen, given a strange brilliance by a background inlaid with squares of glass, like the diapered background of an illuminated manuscript. The screen at Paris[2] still exists to show a complete scheme of imagery: the apparitions of Christ after death, whether recorded in gospel or in legend, in the exact order in which they appear in the *Legenda Aurea*.[3] It is signed: 'C'est maistre Jehan Ravy qui fust masson de Notre Dame de Paris par l'espace de xxvj ans et commenca ces nouvelles histoires et maistre Jehan le Bouteiller son nepveu les a parfaictes en l'an mccccli.'

Inside the screen the stalls themselves were of richly sculptured wood. The earliest that survive are those of Poitiers Cathedral, of the middle of the thirteenth century. The spandrels of these are carved with an infinite diversity of

[1] In the crypt of Chartres and in the Louvre.   [2] Much restored.
[3] See Mâle, *Art rel. XIIIᵉ siècle*, p. 264.

subjects, religious and grotesque: the Virgin and Child; angels holding crowns; a cock, a bat, a cat, monstrous birds and a phoenix, griffin and centaur. The arcade at the back, added some fifty years later, has a series of secular subjects: wrestlers, a pork butcher, a man picking fruit, and an architect with his level, T-square, and compasses. The stalls at Rouen, carved between 1457 and 1469, represent many of the trades, callings, and professions of the period, and may have been given by those who followed them.

For festivals hangings of silk or of tapestry were affixed high above the stalls. In 1428 Charles VII gave the cathedral of Angers four pieces of tapestry to hang in the choir, with the history of the world from the Creation to the Judgement in a great number of medallions like those of a window. In return prayers were to be said for him daily, and Masses sung after his death.[1] Another set of the Life of St. Maurice for the back of the stalls on feast days was given by Canon Hugues Fresnan in 1459.[2] He paid two hundred crowns for them to Jean Despaing, weaver, of Paris, who wove them specially. The cartoons for them, painted on linen, were hung in their place on ordinary days. The design of such tapestries was, indeed, a pursuit for the learned men of the period: Jean Germain, Bishop of Chalon, in 1457 wrote a moral work, *Deux Pans de la tapisserie chrétienne*, a *patron ou figure* for tapestry with pictures which might serve as cartoons.[3] The standard subject, however, was the life of the patron saint of the cathedral: thus a fine set of the life of St. Peter was given to Beauvais in 1460 and still hangs there. Other benefactors gave paintings to the church. Towards the end of the thirteenth century Guillaume le Jeu, canon and precentor of Clermont, gave a wall-painting of the Virgin with himself kneeling in his white surplice before her. At Le Mans the vaults of the Lady Chapel are painted with lovely angels, given by Bishop Gonthier de Baigneux at the end of the fourteenth century. A little later panel-paintings took the place of wall decorations. Of these a picture of the Nativity, given by Cardinal Jean Rolin, Bishop of Autun, to his cathedral before his death in 1483, may serve as an example (Fig. 100). The bishop kneels like a fine courtier, three paces behind the Virgin, with his fat old dog, which has grown rather like him with the years, sitting on the skirts of his robe. Joseph might appear unnoticed at any Burgundian market; the background is the familiar Morvan country; the Child has the bowed legs and helpless arms of extreme youth. The whole is set in a pastoral key; not even the Virgin has a halo, and the wings of the two angels are unseen. Yet thanks to the pensive face of the Virgin and her exquisite hands

[1] Farcy, p. 3. The subjects were the Fall of the Angels, the Creation, the Fall of Man, Cain's Murder, the Flood, the Sacrifice of Isaac, the giving the Tables of the Law, and their setting up, the Passover Sacrifice, the Circumcision of the Jews, Prophets foretelling Christ, the Annunciation, the Marriage of Our Lady, the Suspicion of Joseph, the Nativity, the Star, the Entry into Jerusalem, the Last Supper, the Passion, the Descent into Hell, the Resurrection, and others.

[2] Ibid., p. 4.   [3] Doutrepont, p. 252.

the picture is at once deeply religious and deeply poetical. The painter, the anonymous Maître de Moulins, served his patron well.

Within the enclosure of the choir rose the high altar, which in its turn received fitting adornment. That of Chartres may serve as an example. Here the canons seem to have concentrated their benefactions first upon the fabric, and to have given portable ornaments only when the cathedral and its porches were built. By 1259 the goldsmiths were working on the great altar and the shrine of the chief relic, the Virgin's robe; a contract exists in which the bishop makes an agreement with them about the food they are to receive while engaged on the work.[1] In 1306 a canon of the cathedral who became Precentor of Paris gave Our Lady of Chartres a silver-gilt ciborium to hang above the high altar. The bowl and cover each had five panels of scenes of the life of Christ; it was signed on the base *Johan Mereuin me fecit*.[2] We may imagine it to have been a more elaborate version of the 'Sainte Coupe' which still exists at Sens (Fig. 101). A century later the Duc de Berry gave a splendid retable for the high altar, thirteen feet long and eight feet high, embroidered with the Coronation of the Virgin, a great number of angels and saints, and King Jean and his sons, with their patron saints St. John Baptist, St. Charlemagne, and St. Louis of Toulouse, kneeling below on one side, and his Queen, her two daughters, and St. Catherine and St. Louis of France on the other.[3] In 1457 the altar had bronze columns added at each corner, joined by rods from which curtains were hung. Alexandre de Vannes, metal-founder, of Paris, cast four angels of bronze, each holding a candlestick, to surmount the columns.[4] Besides such major ornaments, the inventories show a great number of lesser but precious objects, for the most part given by the bishops of Chartres and their canons in the fourteenth and fifteenth centuries.[5]

Each bishop had his own accredited list of purveyors: in Paris and certain other cities these were exempt from royal justice and under episcopal jurisdiction. They usually included a goldsmith.[6] A contract drawn up in 1228 between the Bishop of Beauvais and his goldsmith, Master Yvon,[7] sets out that the man holds the fief of Les Meigneus and gives annually a piece of gold for it, and must mend the bishop's mazers with silver wire, if need be. The bishop gives him two measures of corn a year, and in return the goldsmith must mend his saucepans up to six a year, and his basins, and make two new plain ones annually if they are required; he must mend the cups and jugs, make three new feet to mazers and three new bands round knives, and mend the bishop's rings and make six new rings a year if wanted, and generally keep the metal and crystal of the chapel in order, all with gold and silver provided by the bishop. For

[1] Fagniez, i. 199.   [2] Mély, p. 95.   [3] Ibid., p. 93.   [4] Ibid., p. 109.
[5] Ibid., pp. 7 et seqq.   [6] e.g. the Bishop of Paris's list in 1222. Fagniez, i. 134.
[7] Ibid. 139.

another measure of wheat he is to mend the censers of the cathedral and make new chains for them when needed; and mend the crosses and gospel-books, the reliquaries that hang before the altar, and the gold ciborium and morses, again with the bishop's gold and silver. New pieces of gold work, however, were generally bought from some eminent smith in Paris, or some other centre. Such enamelled crosiers as one found recently in a bishop's tomb at Orleans, such reliquaries as that of St. Thomas Becket at Sens, were probably made at Limoges, while the delicate chasing of a second Orleans crosier and of the Sens ciborium suggests Paris work.

Besides the gifts of their own clergy, votive offerings came from kings and nobles to enrich the treasuries of the cathedrals. After Philippe le Hardi had beaten the Flemings at Rosebecq he gave a silver Virgin to Chartres that weighed thirty marks. It used to stand before the choir screen; there was an endowment for the oil of a silver lamp burning perpetually before it. After the Treaty of Troyes Henry V gave Chartres a portable altar of marble on a base of chased silver gilt, which is still the property of the cathedral; and in 1342 the English gave a reliquary of the Virgin's milk.[1] Others gave gifts that served as deeds to secure an annual donation to the abbey, such as a golden 'tableau' given to Chartres by Louis de Vendôme in 1404 to secure an ounce of gold yearly from the revenues of his county.[2] No single treasury now contains even a modicum of what all must once have held; a chalice (Fig. 103) and some reliquaries at Rheims (Fig. 102), a reliquary at Soissons, a ciborium and a reliquary at Sens, a few objects scattered in public and private collections,[3] a painted cupboard at Noyon, a few old chests of vestments, are all that remain to shadow forth for us the glories of a medieval cathedral sacristy. Such treasures, indeed, demanded rooms to themselves: Bayeux Cathedral still has a thirteenth-century annexe on two floors, the lower a sacristy and the upper a treasure-house; while the treasury of Laon, in the upper part of the south transept, with doors to the triforium and the tower, a winding stair to the sacristy and a little door to the chapter-house, is a vaulted building as fine and more light than a church, with an apse with two rows of windows and a rose window at the side. At Senlis the fifteenth-century sacristy has a capital carved with a nun playing the organ and another blowing its bellows, a man carrying a great roll of hangings and another folding vestments: the habitual occupations of the room it adorned.

The naves and ambulatories of the cathedrals came to be almost as rich in works of art as the choir. The centre of the nave was often inlaid with a maze in stone of different colours. The rest of the floor came in time to be paved with the tomb slabs of those *venerables et discrettes personnes* the canons; the

[1] Mély, p. 11.   [2] Ibid., p. 34.
[3] Among these may be mentioned a fine French jewelled cross of the fourteenth century in the Vatican Gallery (no. 48).

collection of drawings made by Gaignières contains a large number of those in Notre-Dame de Paris, either of engraved stone or brass, with the figure surrounded by a canopy with little figures of saints portrayed in its niches. Bishops generally had tombs raised above the floor, as befitted their feudal dignity.[1] At Lisieux there is a bishop's tomb of the late twelfth century with a niche behind it carved with a frieze of six angel musicians playing celestial duets. Two more angels bear the soul to Heaven in the niche above.[2] The sculpture of a similar niche has been transferred to the small door of the north transept of Rheims: the arch is carved with a choir of angels, and a little group carrying the soul forms the keystone. On either side at the base are priests reading the funeral service from books held by their acolytes.[3] At Carcassonne the niche above the tomb of Bishop Ralph, who died in 1266, is filled by his standing effigy, with the *Manus Dei* above.[4]

In the thirteenth century these niches were occupied by recumbent effigies in the round. Two magnificent examples survive at Amiens: the bronze tombs, each resting on six lions with a winged dragon at the foot, of Bishops Évrard de Fouilloy, who died in 1222, and Geoffroi d'Eu, who died in 1236, and between them rebuilt the cathedral. In the middle of the century Aymeric Arips, Archbishop of Lyons, and Gerald, Bishop of Cahors, both had tombs all of Limoges enamel, which have been destroyed. At Limoges, however, Cardinal Raynaud de la Porte, who was bishop from 1294 to 1316, had a stone tomb, on which he is represented behind curtains held back by censing angels.[5] Below the great stone effigy are statuettes and bas-reliefs of the stories of the three saints chiefly honoured at Limoges: Valérie, Stephen, and Martial.

In France it was chiefly the princes of the Church who favoured the tomb with a sculptured canopy over it, which is familiar to us in England: those of Aycelin de Montaigu, Archbishop of Narbonne,[6] who died in 1318, of Pope John XXII at Avignon, made by Jean Lavenier of Paris in 1345,[7] and the tomb of Pope Clement VI, erected before his death in 1352, at La Chaise-Dieu, may serve as examples.

Such elaborate tombs were commonly ordered in the lifetime of the men they commemorated. Thierry d'Hireçon, for instance, ordered his tomb in 1327 from Jean Aloul, 'marbrier' of Tournai. A few months later Thierry was made Bishop of Arras, and had to commission the sculptor once more to change the

---

[1] Exceptions are the incised tomb-slabs recorded by Gaignières of Pierre de Corbeil, Bishop of Sens, d. 1222, and Barthélemy, Bishop of Paris, d. 1229.   [2] Gardner, fig. 232.

[3] Gardner, fig. 233. The niche, probably originally painted, is now filled by a Virgin and Child.

[4] Gardner, fig. 353.

[5] The type is Italianate; he died as Cardinal Archbishop of Ostia. Style and tomb, however, are entirely French.

[6] At Saint-Cerneuf de Billom. It is rather in the manner of the tomb of Aymer de Valence at Westminster.   [7] Lasteyrie, *Arch. rel. ép. goth.* ii. 571.

I

effigy from priest to bishop at a cost of twenty-three livres.[1] The fashion for weepers or *pleurants* added to their magnificence: Bernard Brun, who succeeded his uncle Raynaud de la Porte as bishop of Limoges and died in 1350, had reliefs of such mourners placed round his tomb, and Denis du Moulin, a bishop of Paris who died in 1447, had a bronze statue resting on a bronze tomb with forty-seven such figures in niches round it.[2]

A considerable number of bishops, however, contented themselves with slab tombs only. Henri de Poitiers, Bishop of Troyes, had a brass bought from Jean de Moyère, *ouvrier de lames ou tombes de laiton* at Ghent, through a merchant of Paris;[3] and a similar tomb, engraved with an extravagantly rich canopy with forty-one little figures in the niches, sufficed for a bishop of Le Mans who died in 1339.[4]

Occasionally the munificence of a bishop or a canon extended beyond the offering of a single object or the erection of a personal memorial to the building of a new altar or even a new chapel. Bishop Pierre de Roquefort, who rebuilt the choir of Saint-Nazaire de Carcassonne between 1300 and 1325, set up no less than twenty-two statues within and without it: the Apostles, the Virgin, Saint Nazaire, Saint Joachim, Saint Celse, Saint Gimer, St. Helena, St. Paul, Christ, and an angel bearing the instruments of the Passion. At Lisieux Bishop Pierre Cauchon, the judge of Joan of Arc, gave a whole Lady Chapel between 1432 and 1442.

Votive statues of one sort or another were often set up in the cathedral nave. In 1328 Philippe VI dedicated his horse, arms, and armour to Notre-Dame de Paris as he fought the battle of Mont Cassel. The horse was sold for the benefit of the chapter, and the housings and armour were set up against a pillar of the nave on a stiff wooden horse, where they remained until the Revolution.[5] In the same cathedral was a great wooden St. Christopher *de merveilleuse haulteur et noble ouvrage* given by Antoine des Essarts in 1413.[6]

Finally, the great bells of the cathedral were often individual gifts, and like a portal or a window were dedicated to a saint. On them alone the Latin verses of the Romanesque period continued in use. A bell of 1408 at Laon is inscribed:

> Horis nocturnis pulsum donoque diurnis;
> In sacris dego; sum Julianus ego;
> Ut plebs vocetur ad que bona quisque tenetur.
> Laudes reddo Deo, qui me levavit ab ymo,
> Anno milleno quadringentesimo quinto
> Ipse ter juncto, maii vicesimo quinto.
> Gilet de Montigny me fist.[7]

[1] Richard, p. 311.   [2] Courajod, ii. 429.   [3] Koechlin and Marquet de Vasselot, p. 7, note 2.
[4] Gaignières, Bodleian MS. 18360, fol. 21.   [5] Montfaucon, i. 286.
[6] Le Roux and Tisserand, p. 153; it is described by Guillebert de Metz.   [7] *Pet. mon.*, p. 111.

At Le Puy another was inscribed:

> Jhesus,
> Sit procul a nobis et corruat omne malignum
> Dum canimus laudes intactae Virginis almae.
> Maria vocor. Anno M.CCCC.LXXX.

6. THE CATHEDRAL CLOSE

A cathedral, with its bishops and chapter, necessarily had a close of buildings for their use. The canons lived like the Augustinians they were, with separate houses and a chapter-house, refectory, and cloister. At Paris the canons had a city to themselves in the rue des Chantres, with thirty-seven houses, their conventual buildings and the cathedral schools. Hugues de Fouilloi, himself a canon, advised them to live in houses away from secular habitations; houses simple, humble, dignified, and unostentatious; of stone if they would, but not carved, nor with painted walls.[1] These houses were normally grouped near the cathedral, and were cathedral property; in 1275 the chapter of Notre-Dame de Paris decided that there should be an annual visitation of canons' houses by the dean, two canons, and the architect and carpenter of the cathedral, to assess the dilapidations.[2] Few survive in their entirety. The *Maison du Chapitre* at Le Puy has a fine hooded chimney-piece of stone; some canons' houses at Chartres have graceful foliage sculptures over their doors; a few stone doorways and mullioned windows survive in other cathedral cities to bear witness to what the canons' houses were like. At Meaux, as in certain Augustinian houses, some of the canons lived in collegiate fashion; their house remains to the north of the apse with a turret corbelled out at each corner and a wooden outside staircase. There is nowhere an ensemble to compare with that at Wells. The houses were simply furnished. The furniture of Guillaume as Feives, once Canon of Meaux,[3] comprised in 1302 a few coverlets, three chests, four benches, four trestle tables, four chairs, one stool, and a cupboard. He had copper cooking pots and pans, pewter plates, two mazers, six silver plates and nine spoons, and seven or eight books.[4] Pierre Cardonnel, Canon of Paris and Archdeacon of Auge, was more luxurious.[5] At his death in 1438 his parlour was hung with red hangings powdered with roses and adorned with a picture of the Annunciation. He had a private chapel handsomely furnished with a dark-blue carpet powdered with red roses, an alabaster statuette, five Limoges candlesticks, and some thirty

---

[1] Mortet in *Mel. Bémont,* i. 113.   [2] Mortet, ii. 301.

[3] Stein in *Bull. Soc. hist. Paris,* x, 1883, p. 45.

[4] The inventory of Jean de Saffres, Canon of Langres, made after his death in 1365, indicates a larger library: nearly 40 books of romances, a number of chronicles, a few lives of saints, and some legal and philosophical works, as well as service-books; but he seems to have had private means. *Bull. arch.* iv, 1847–8, p. 329.   [5] E. Bishop, *Liturg. hist.,* p. 425.

books. In 1419 Nicholas de Baye, Canon of Paris, had two tapestries, one of the Passion and Ascension and one of *l'istoire de Beatrix fille du Roy de Tyr*.[1]

The other chapter buildings have been less drastically rebuilt than the houses. A many-windowed refectory is still visible near the cathedral at Autun; a few chapter-houses and cloisters survive; at Noyon there is a chapter-house, cloister, and library to give some idea of the ensemble. The chapter-houses are for the most part[2] plain and rectangular, deriving their dignity from the rib vaults of the roof. At Noyon the pointed window and the door into the cloister are edged with a double row of bud moulding; at Bayeux the end wall has a triple arcade; at Troyes the room was paved with quite secular tiles with grotesque subjects.[3] The most splendid of the chapter-houses is that at Sens,[4] built like a great hall with a wide single span of vault rising from leaf capitals. It has six magnificent windows. The external buttresses each end in pinnacles with a statue greater than life-size: St. Stephen, patron of the cathedral; Saint Potentien and Saint Savinien, the sainted bishops of the place; Louis IX of France and Archbishop Gillon Cornu who built the chapter-house about 1250.

France is now less rich than England in cathedral cloisters of the Middle Ages; time, fashion, and revolution have dealt hardly with them. The choir school of Lyons has some remains of an early Romanesque cloister and Le Puy one of the twelfth century so much restored that it has little historical value. The Gothic period is better represented. The cloister at Laon is vaulted; the twin arcade is surmounted by a large oculus. At Noyon and Rouen[5] arcade and oculus are merged in a splendid traceried window. At Langres the inner wall is finely arcaded. Finally at Cahors, about 1500, a cloister was built (Fig. 104) that with its liernes and tiercerons and original doorway forms a worthy close to the series.

7. THE BISHOP'S PALACE

From the beginning of the Middle Ages the bishop seems to have had a separate residence, which was not of a monastic but of a feudal type. His status was that of a baron, taking the oath of fealty to the king and receiving the liege homage of his dean, precentor, chancellor, and other officers, and he lived accordingly. His house, however, was in a town, and was therefore protected by the town walls and not fortified.[6] It was one of the grievances against

---

[1] Guiffrey, p. 25.

[2] That at Tulle has a central column and is like a Benedictine chapter-house.

[3] The remains are now in the Musée diocésain de l'Aube; they date from the early fourteenth century.

[4] The 'Officialité'; now used as a cathedral museum.

[5] Tragically damaged in the recent war.

[6] An exception is the palace at Beauvais which was built on the city wall and forms part of its fortifications.

Hugues de Noyers, Bishop of Auxerre from 1183 to 1206, a warrior bishop who fought against the neighbouring nobles and even against the king, that he had his house surrounded by a moat, defended by palisades, and fortified by a donjon with turrets, ramparts, and a drawbridge.[1] Generally if a bishop built a castle it was on one of his country estates, and followed the current feudal style. Jacques de Bazoches, Bishop of Soissons, when he built the castle of Septmonts in 1223, built it as an enormous corbelled donjon. Mauzun, a castle of the Bishops of Clermont destroyed in 1750, had three enceintes and nineteen towers to defend it; the castle of the Bishop of Nevers at Bordes had a square machicolated entrance tower linked by curtain walls to strong round towers; and as late as the end of the fifteenth century the della Rovere bishops of Agen built the castle of Hautefage as a single hexagonal tower, with the size of its windows increasing as they rose out of reach of attack.

Normally, however, the bishop's residence was *palatium* rather than *castellum*. That at Angers, built between 1098 and 1148, is a T-shaped building adjoining the transept of the cathedral. On the ground floor is a long gallery divided into two groin-vaulted aisles by six columns. At right angles to it is a second presumably servants' hall, of similar shape. The capitals are carved with heads of monsters trying to swallow the column. Out of the gallery is a small library. On the first floor is a great hall more than sixty-five feet long and nearly thirty-three feet wide, with a second room at right angles divided from it by a triple arcade. Each room is lighted by fifteen windows. Against the south wall is a washing-place like the lavatory of a medieval cloister, inscribed in truly feudal spirit:

CLERICVS ET MILES PERGANT, AD CETERA VILES,
NAM LOCVS HOS PRIMVS DECET, ILLOS VILIS ET IMVS.

On the second floor is a room with a fifteenth-century machicolated chimney-piece with the arms of Hardouin de Bueil, and three other rooms for the bishop to live in. The bishop's palace at Auxerre has been modified inside but still retains the arcaded *logie*, as they were then called, built by Hugues de Montaigu, bishop from 1116 to 1136.[2] At Meaux the lower hall remains, built in the middle of the twelfth century with rib vaults rising from square piers on square bases, with engaged colonnettes at each angle and composite square capitals, and a simple rectangular hall with an apse-like end above.

Such houses make one realize why Hugues de Fouilloi in 1153 inveighed against the luxury of bishops' palaces. 'The bishops have painted walls and embroidered hangings,' he declared, 'while the poor go naked; they have walls painted with Trojans clad in purple and gold, and deny an old rag to Christians. Their courts are full of columns and their gates bristle with fortifications, to

[1] He built his castles according to the precepts of Vegetius, *De re militari*. Mortet, i. 96.
[2] See Mortet, i. 95.

keep out, not to welcome in, the poor.'[1] When thirty years later the Bishop of
Paris, Maurice de Sully, a man of peasant birth, built a new and more splendid
palace with a two-storied chapel like that of a castle, his subordinate Petrus
Cantor declared that such houses were now too magnificent, and the donjons
and ramparts useless.[2] Fortifications, indeed, became less useful; great halls, it
may be, less magnificent; at all events the chief glory of the Gothic bishops'
palaces was their chapels. These followed the scheme of castle chapels, being
on two floors: the lower for the servants' devotions, the upper for their masters'.
The bishop's chapel at Laon, built by Gautier de Mortagne, bishop from 1155
to 1174, is on this plan; it has a pentagonal apse. The archbishop's chapel at
Rheims, a lesser version of the Sainte-Chapelle, has a beautiful tympanum with
the Adoration of the Magi.

By the end of the fourteenth century the standard of luxury had definitely
diminished; the inventory of the archbishop's palace at Rheims, made after the
death of Richard Picque in 1389,[3] reveals no great store of tapestries such as a
castle would have had: only some painted cloths, some red hangings with coats
of arms and some others with unicorns. Only in the great papal palace at
Avignon was the old standard of magnificence maintained, in a style that may
be of the south but is not of Italy.   Rebuilt after 1334, under the supervision of
Pierre Poisson and Pierre Obreri, and finished under Jean de Loubières and his
successors some forty years later, it would have represented the bishop's palace
in excelsis, had not its use for more than a century as a barracks and a prison
completed a ruin that time had begun, and had not modern restorers restored
it all too completely. Yet even now certain rooms remain to give an idea of
how the greatest of bishops lived in the middle of the fourteenth century: the
aisleless chapel, the superbly calm great hall (Fig. 105) once adorned with
frescoes of the Crucifixion and the Last Judgement, and the little room in a
tower decorated with paintings of rural scenes (Fig. 106) that still bring a sense
of coolness on the hottest Provençal day.[4] The palace was originally defended
from attack by battlements and by seven towers, and kept its secrets by having
only one open staircase, all the others being hidden in the thickness of the walls.

Towards the end of the fifteenth century the bestowal of rich abbatiates on
bishops *in commendam* and the rise of great prelates of the royal house brought
new wealth into episcopal palaces. That at Beauvais was rebuilt by Bishop Jean
de Villiers; that at Évreux in 1481 by Bishop Raoul du Fou; that at Noyon
in the reign of Louis XII. Jean de Bourbon, Abbot of Cluny and Bishop of
Le Puy, may stand as a type of the noble pluralist of the time: we know his
splendid tastes not only by the abbot's house he built at Cluny, with fireplaces

---

[1] Mortet, ii. 91.   [2] Mortet in *Melanges Bémond*, p. 116.   [3] Sartor, p. 21.
[4] They are influenced by treatises on hunting and show the different kinds of chase: *chasse à la
pipée,* with birds in their nests, *chasse au cerf, chasse au furet, chasse au faucon.* Van Marle, p. 266.

as splendid as those of his cousin the Duke of Burgundy in his castle at Dijon, but also from a magnificent chest carved with his arms and flamboyant arcades against a background of fleurs-de-lis.[1]

The chief expression of the wealth of such bishops was, like that of their royal kinsmen, in tapestry and gold work. An altar frontal and retable of tapestry remain to measure the standard of magnificence. They were made for the chapel of Cardinal Charles de Bourbon, Archbishop of Lyons;[2] the altar frontal is bordered with his devices. It represents in colours as gorgeous as those of an illumination the Adoration of the Magi. The retable carries further the theme of Adoration. In the centre is the Coronation of the Virgin, surrounded by a circle of Cherubim in the Bourbon colours of red and blue. On either side are queens of the Old Testament: to the right, Bathsheba, crowned by her son, Solomon; to the left Esther interceding with King Ahasuerus for the lives of her people: fit prototypes of the Virgin's Coronation by her Son and her intercession for us.

Towards the end of the Middle Ages bishops, like abbots, began to build themselves country houses where they might escape for a time from the press of business. Simon Bonnet, Bishop of Senlis from 1448 to 1490, built himself such a pleasure house at Mont-l'Évêque: a square manor with turrets and high dormers. Jean de Bernard, Archbishop of Tours between 1455 and 1464, enlarged an older country house at Vernou near Tours and enriched the chapel with a retable painted with a *Pietà* and figures of himself and one of his nephews.

Pierre d'Amboise, Bishop of Poitiers from 1481 to 1505, built a pretentious residence at Dissay, three miles from the city: it is protected by a moat and its entrance between two great towers is as strong as the gate of a town. The inner courtyard has a polygonal stair-turret and two lesser turrets on corbels. The eastern tower holds the bishop's chapel, with wall-paintings of David and the Crucifixion. It shows the closest approximation with a seigneurial house of the time, and fitly epitomizes an age when bishops ranked as men of letters, statesmen, and courtiers rather than as men of God and princes of His Church.

[1] Now in the Musée Crozatier at Le Puy.
[2] They were given to the cathedral of Sens, where they still are, by Cardinal Louis de Bourbon, Archbishop of Sens from 1536 to 1557.

AUGUSTINIAN CANONS

1. COLLEGIATE CHURCHES

THE system by which the clergy of a cathedral church lived as a community with a common Rule was often extended to other large churches. At the end of the eighth century Chrodegang, Bishop of Metz, modified the Rule in accordance with Benedictine principles. The discipline came to be known as the *vita canonica*, and the priests who followed it took the name of canons. They had two functions to perform: they were responsible for the offices of public prayer in their church, and for the administration under their bishop or provost of its revenues. The Rule imposed the use of a common refectory and a common dormitory, but any canon who desired it could have a room of his own within the cloister. In 1049 the canons of Saint-Barnard de Romans were allowed by their archbishop to build two cloisters, one next the church, *ubi communiter et legaliter vivant*, and another *ad proprias mansiones edificandas*.[1] Each canon retained the right of private property, and took a prebend from the revenues of his church.

This position, half-way between monk and priest, could not remain undefined for long. The Lateran Synod of 1059 recommended that it should be regularized, and by the end of the eleventh century a Rule based on the advice given to a community of nuns by St. Augustine was generally adopted. For a century or more it was subject to various reforms: by the Blessed Yves, Bishop of Chartres, in 1078; by Étienne de Muret, about 1080; by Robert d'Arbrissel, about 1100; by St. Norbert in 1119. These last three reforms established Orders within the Augustinian framework, much as the Cluniac reforms had founded one within the Benedictine Rule.

Étienne de Muret established the Order of Grandmont as a kind of compromise between the Augustinian and Benedictine Rules, but its members were called clerks and not monks and wore the Augustinian surplice and square cap in choir. Its Rule imposed great stretches of silence, but did not include any teaching, preaching, or almsgiving; Grandmont, indeed, was a contemplative Order. Its history was stormy. When its code was finally fixed soon after 1140 it owned more than sixty houses in western France,[2] which were reduced in the fourteenth century to thirty-nine priories with an average of sixteen brethren. The Blessed Robert d'Arbrissel, who founded Fontevrault about 1100, was a poor man who had made his way as a Doctor of the University of Paris. When

---

[1] Mortet, i. 142.

[2] See Hélyot in Migne, xxi, col. 412. The lesser houses were commonly called cells, and the public gave the members the name of Bonshommes.

he retired to lead an anchoretic life many followed him, both men and women, and there gradually grew up a 'double' monastery which accepted a version of the Augustinian Rule. It comprised the 'Grand Moustier', or convent of the nuns, a hospital dedicated to St. Lazarus, a hospice for penitent women, and the monastery of Saint-Jean-de-l'Hort for the male canons. The third reformer, St. Norbert, having failed to introduce his codification of the Augustinian Rule into the collegiate church of Saint-Martin de Laon, founded a new house at Prémontré in Champagne in 1119. Thanks to the benefactions of the Counts of Champagne there were by 1150 nearly a hundred Premonstratensian communities.

By the thirteenth century the Augustinian Rule was followed in communities of three categories: in the chapters of the great cathedrals, in the lesser churches served by colleges of canons,[1] and in communities such as the Trinitarians or Mathurins which were primarily charitable, with the monastic Orders of Grandmont, Fontevrault, Prémontré to link them with Benedictinism.

The enclosed world of the Benedictine cloister with its peculiar culture and its peculiar limitations was bound to create an art of its own. The existence of monastic scriptoria, monastic libraries, and the liturgical dramas of the monasteries as inevitably led to the creation of a characteristic iconography. The Augustinians, on the contrary, for all their vows lived in the world. Their religious duties lay in the recognized services of the Church, not in their extension by the additional offices of the Cluniacs. They had no scriptoria, and their libraries were personal, not the basis of a common culture.

The fact that they had adopted the Augustinian Rule because it offered a reasonable way of life to men vowed to the service of religion yet primarily occupied in practical work seems to have deprived the colleges of canons of that atmosphere of religious enthusiasm which gave fire and spirit to those who followed a sterner Rule. The canons in their surplices and fur capes, muttering psalms and prayers in a choir islanded in an empty church, might indeed be meeting the spiritual needs of an absent congregation, their advice and help might be of real aid to their fellow citizens; but *surtout point de zèle* might often have been their chosen motto. Peter, Precentor of Notre-Dame de Paris about 1190, is bitterly eloquent on the part money played in their lives. Where the chapter deducts a certain sum for the canons' non-attendance at service, you may see them running up at the last moment 'like old women after a greased pig; some bent forward, others leaping over the bar to enter, others pressing in disorderly fashion through the open door'.

It may be in consequence of this want of enthusiasm that the Augustinians,

---

[1] A college of canons, even in a small parish, might be installed anywhere: Henri le Libéral of Champagne, for instance, on Crusade in 1148, vowed in a moment of danger at sea to found three canonries in the church of Pougy, and did so on his return.

for all their wealth and leisure, cannot be said to have produced a characteristic art, as did the Benedictines and Cistercians. Rather, they followed the fashion set by whatever was the dominant influence at the time, in the finest style of which local masons and artists were capable. Two things, however, served to characterize their churches. Since their endowments freed them from the necessity of attracting congregations by festal processions, the aisles of their churches have rarely as important a development as in those of other communities; and since their particular privilege was the holding of private property, their churches were inordinately full of small and disparate works of art, for each individual canon was free to give what he would.

The greater number of the collegiate churches of the eleventh and twelfth centuries are aisleless: Mehun-sur-Yèvre, built about 1040, Saint-Hilaire de Poitiers, a few years later, Notre-Dame de Loches, about 1160, Saint-Front de Périgueux, Saint-Frambourg de Senlis, and Châtellerault, dating from the end of the twelfth century, may serve as examples.[1] Bénévent-l'Abbaye and Le Dorat, built in the middle of this century, have exceptionally narrow aisles. Apart from this Augustinian churches tend to follow in plan whatever architectural fashion was dominant at the time they were built. The Collégiale of Mehun-sur-Yèvre, for example, follows a simple version of the Benedictine pilgrimage plan, with an ambulatory and three radiating chapels. There is neither transept nor aisles; the nave originally had a wooden roof. Saint-Hilaire de Poitiers, when it was rebuilt just before 1049,[2] was planned with a single large apse and a long transept.[3] In the second half of the eleventh century the Benedictine plan with side apses linked to a central apse was in fashion for collegiate churches. It is followed at Plaimpied, founded in 1080, in the contemporary church of Saint-Outrille-lès-Graçay, with a magnificent exterior apse, and as late as 1136 at Sablonceaux, an Augustinian house founded by William X of Aquitaine. The extension of this plan by the multiplication of parallel apses also influenced Augustinian churches. The Benedictine abbey of Saint-Genès at Château-Meillant has seven parallel apses; the Augustinian Église du Chapitre there imitated it with five. Les Aix-d'Angillon, a collegiate church later united to the chapter of Bourges, has likewise five such apses, with a very long choir with a cusped triforium like that of Cluny, and a certain nobility of scale that also recalls Cluniac architecture (Fig. 107). The Benedictine plan with

---

[1] Other aisleless collegiate churches are Saint-Martin-aux-Bois, Saint-Barnard de Romans, Écouis, Mézières-en-Brenne, Saint-Émilion. Sainte-Radegonde de Poitiers was so rebuilt late in the thirteenth century, and the Augustins of Toulouse between 1460 and 1504.

[2] The vaulting—a succession of domes on squinches—the aisles, and the radiating chapels were added later.

[3] Its master-mason was Walter Coorland, an Englishman who had settled at Civray in Poitou. Mortet, i. 140. It recalls Beaulieu-lès-Loches in style. The same plan was followed about 1120 for the collegiate church of Blanzac, near Angoulême, with a very long choir.

an ambulatory and radiating chapels is imitated on a noble scale at Saint-Julien de Brioude, and at Notre-Dame-du-Port at Clermont, and with a yet closer approximation to Cluniac style at Notre Dame de Beaune.

In the twelfth century collegiate churches tended to exploit the local style of architecture to its utmost, at a time when Cluniac influence was making Benedictine architecture more homogeneous. Bénévent-l'Abbaye in the Limousin (Fig. 108) remains a magnificent example of this tendency. The college was founded in 1028 by a canon of Limoges and was rebuilt in 1080 with a church and six canons' houses. The church was again rebuilt in the middle of the twelfth century, with an ambulatory, three chapels round the apse, and a transept with absidioles, all polygonal.[1] There is no real aisle, but heavy arcades down the walls pierced by a narrow passage. The nave has a splendid vault, the crossing a cupola on pendentives. The whole is a magnificent experiment in pure architecture, a theorem in stone. This same attitude to architecture, differing alike from Cistercian austerity and Cluniac love of decoration, is equally evident in the church of Le Dorat, begun about 1130 but finished rather later. This has a stereotyped plan with three radiating chapels and a transept with absidioles; but the ambulatory is modified to form a square tower, and though the aisles are wider the whole scheme recalls Bénévent. The entrance is defended by a massive tower, half fortress and half belfry, that finds a parallel at the Collégiales of Saint-Yrieix and Saint-Junien (Fig. 109).

Notre-Dame-la-Grande at Poitiers is an equally remarkable example of local style. Its magnificent façade is like the illustrated frontispiece to a book, that sums up what is taught within; and the curiously lofty proportions of its interior are as impressive as those of Le Dorat. The collegiate church of Notre-Dame de Loches,[2] built before 1168 to hold a relic of the Virgin's belt brought from the Holy Land, has a triple apse, unusually massive towers over the entrance porch and the crossing, and a unique system of vaults. Each of the two bays of the nave is covered by an eight-sided stone pyramid.[3] The aisles have only narrow arches to join them to the nave. The Collégiale of Saint-Martin d'Étampes, begun about 1140 but slow in building, has the particularity of having an ambulatory with three deep radiating chapels and no transept, with a particularly complicated and experimental system of rib vaulting. The arcade of the ambulatory is borne cloister-fashion alternately by heavy single columns which take the vaults, and by twin columns of lighter proportion with a common capital. Fontevrault in its turn has one of the finest examples of a cupola vault in France (Fig. 110): a succession of four domes on pendentives,

[1] A similar apse, without an ambulatory, was used for the collegiate church of Saint-Jean-de-Côle, founded in 1086 but finished later. The nave has been destroyed.

[2] Now Saint-Ours.

[3] See Mortet, ii. 117, for a contemporary account of them.

with another at the crossing before the apse. A similar plan, and a similar vault, has made the collegiate church of Saint-Front de Périgueux one of the most famous in France.[1] As late as 1200 three domes were used to roof the nave of the Augustinian church of Notre-Dame de Châtres in the Charentais, which has a fine arcaded façade in local style.

These variations on a Benedictine theme were modified about the middle of the twelfth century by a wave of Cistercian influence. When its canons began to rebuild Saint-Martin de Laon in 1132[2] they adopted a purely Cistercian plan, with a square east end and three chapels in each arm of the transept, though they followed an Augustinian habit in having no aisles. Benedictine influence is visible, however, in the twin towers at the angle of the transept and the nave, and in the sculpture that adorns the church. On the gable there is a bas-relief of the Charity of St. Martin; the portal was later adorned with sculptures of the martyrdom of St. John and St. Laurence and with statues.

Cistercian influence was at this time often directly exerted upon canonical communities. It was under the personal influence of St. Bernard[3] that the canons of Saint-Vorles de Châtillon tried in 1138 to make their Rule stricter and more monastic. They built the church of Saint-Pierre for such of the canons as were willing to follow this Rule, with a plain cross vault, pointed arches, a flat-ended choir, three square chapels in each transept, and a total absence of sculpture: a purely Cistercian church with many resemblances to Fontenay. A Premonstratensian church near Avranches, with the lovely name of La-Lucerne-d'Outremer, has a similar square east end, with a system of arches to form chapels in the transept.[4] Sablonceaux, when it was altered in 1189, had its apse rebuilt with a flat end, as did La Couronne, near Angoulême, rebuilt between 1171 and 1201.[5] This has a row of columns along the transept with party walls to form two chapels in each arm, in Cistercian fashion. It is, however, richly ornamented in the local style.[6]

This simple square-apsed plan was not the only Cistercian scheme to be

[1] It is grossly over-restored. The domes date from after 1123 and before 1182. The church became a cathedral soon after 1577. Similar domes were added to the collegiate church of Sablonceaux (Charente-Inférieure) in 1189.

[2] It became Premonstratensian very soon afterwards.

[3] See *Cong. arch.*, 1928, p. 205.

[4] It was built in 1164 and is aisled. The aqueduct of its water-supply is interesting.

[5] Mortet, ii. 125. Notre-Dame-de-Châtres was altered to a *chevet plat* as late as the fourteenth century. Other collegiate churches with flat ends are Montréal, Saint-Junien, Notre-Dame des Andelys, and Saint-Martin de Champeaux, near Melun.

[6] Its dependency, Saint-Michel d'Entraigues, built in 1137, is quite exceptional in plan. It is octagonal with an absidiole in each side, and can only be compared with the chapel of the Sepulchre of the Collégiale of Saint-Léonard in the Limousin, which is a twelfth-century rotunda with four shallow absidioles. I have sometimes wondered whether the building at Fontevrault restored as a kitchen was not originally a chapel of this kind. It is octagonal, with an absidiole on each of the eight sides.

copied by Augustinian churches. The plan of Pontigny with radiating chapels hidden in the wall of a rounded apse was copied between 1153 and 1163 in the Premonstratensian church of Dommartin near Abbeville, one of the first Gothic churches in the district. The slightly later canons' church at Meung-sur-Loire, likewise in early Gothic style, followed the plan of Chaalis, with apsidal ends to the transepts. Saint-Quiriace de Provins, begun in 1180, has an extraordinary compromise: the long choir has a semicircular end, but beyond it lies a rectangular apse divided into three square chapels. An apse with an ambulatory and square radiating chapels, such as the Cistercians used at Savigny,[1] Breuil-Benoît, and Bonport in the early thirteenth century, was copied a little later by the canons at Le-Plessis-Grimoult.

The Premonstratensians had at one time authorized the Cistercians to make visitation on their houses, and this supervision doubtless strengthened Cistercian influence over their architecture. The very strictness of the supervision, however, helped to bring the influence to an end. The Prémontrés of Vicogne, near Valenciennes, rebuilt their chapter-house and church just before 1212. The Cistercian visitors, coming soon after it was complete, ordered the wall-paintings to be removed. The Premonstratensians refused, and the visitations came to an end. The rebels celebrated this victory over austerity by buying two great bells and one lesser one, a hanging candelabrum of gilt metal, two silver candlesticks, a new censer and vestments, and a large copper pot for beer, *ad honorem domus Dei*.[2]

The congregation of Grandmont remained a little longer under Cistercian influence. As late as 1240 their statutes decreed: 'Omnis pictura et omnis sculptura inutilis et superflua a nostris penitus absit aedificiis. Voutae quidem ecclesiarum sint tantum planae, et simplicitati nostrae religionis congruae.'[3] Their churches continued to be plain and aisleless with a semicircular or polygonal apse.[4]

Outside this congregation, the strictest connected with the Augustinians, the influence of the Cistercians gave way in the thirteenth century before that of the cathedrals. Even at the very beginning of the century the Collégiale of Notre-Dame de Mantes dared to imitate the cathedral of Notre-Dame de Paris, with magnificent sexpartite vaults, and an ambulatory with five polygonal chapels round it. It differs from its prototype only in size, in the absence of a transept, and in the alternation of cylindrical columns and complicated piers. The Collégiale of Eu, dedicated to St. Laurence O'Toole, Archbishop of

---

[1] Dept. Manche. There are at least five monastic houses of this name in France of different Orders.
[2] Mortet, ii. 214.
[3] Mortet, ii. 265.
[4] e.g Grandmont (destroyed at the Revolution); Sauvigny-les-Bois, Yonne; Saint-Jean-des-Bonshommes between Avallon and Montréal. The plan may have influenced that of the Collégiale of Saint-Yrieix.

Dublin, originally followed the plan of Notre-Dame, though its elevation is nearer to that of the cathedral of Rouen.[1] The Collégiale of Saint-Quentin, rebuilt in the middle of the century, was designed in the style of Rheims.[2] At Saint-Urbain de Troyes, founded in 1262 by Pope Urban IV, son of a shoe-maker, on the site of his father's shop, the west door, of the very end of the century, is modelled on that of the cathedral of Sens.[3]

Saint-Urbain is famed for the lightness and elegance of its fenestration; this may be paralleled in the magnificent apse of the Collégiale of Saint-Martin-aux-Bois. Here, in what, but for its collegiate endowments, would be a small country church, the influence of the great cathedrals has transformed a simple building into a work of great architecture. Without aisles or transept, all the force of the design lies in soaring height and luminous windows. Even as far south as Romans the Collégiale of Saint-Barnard was rebuilt like a Gothic cathedral, though without aisles. Even later than the thirteenth century the collegiate church of Saint-Lô dared to imitate a cathedral, with a triple portal of sculptured stone and two great steepled towers to crown the façade.[4]

Certain new foundations of the fourteenth century retained and beautified the old simple collegiate plan. The Collégiale of Écouis, consecrated in 1313, is aisleless. Its choir, longer than the nave, ends in a five-sided apse. It contains sculpture more beautiful than any of its date in France; and the gable has an angel for finial, bearing a shield with the arms of the founder.[5] The church of Tour-en-Bessin, again, is of remarkable elegance. It has a flat chevet, but the corners are truncated and separately vaulted, giving a triple apse within (Fig. 111). The refinement of tracery, vaulting, and arcading, and the vigour of the carvings of the Labours of the Months over the stalls, give the whole an unusual charm. No one could mistake it either for an ordinary parish church or for the church of a Benedictine monastery.

In the fifteenth century the architecture of the collegiate churches was influenced by that of the Preaching Friars. The Collégiale of Dammartin-en-Goële, built in 1487,[6] has the Dominican double nave with a line of fourteen pillars down the middle. At Saint-Lô and Guérande outside pulpits of Dominican type, elegantly sculptured, were likewise added.

[1] It was built between 1186 and 1280.

[2] It may possibly have had Villard de Honnecourt for architect.

[3] Notre-Dame de Semur-en-Auxois, another collegiate church, was rebuilt in the thirteenth century. It is more original, especially in the disposition of the apse, but its general lines and sculptured portals are strongly influenced by cathedral architecture. The same is true of the collegiate church of Saint-Jean-des-Vignes at Soissons.

[4] All reduced to rubble in the campaign of 1944.

[5] The Collégiale of Mézières-en-Brenne, founded in 1339, has a similar plan with a three-sided apse. A transept was added later.

[6] It was founded by Antoine de Chabannes la Palice, seigneur de Dammartin and one of the comrades of Joan of Arc. He is buried in the choir.

The collegiate churches thus reflect the dominant style of the age in which they were built: Benedictine and Cistercian influences pale before those of the great cathedrals, and these in their turn give way before Dominican influences. There are great achievements, but few innovations; and the negative feature of the absence or unimportance of the aisles is one of the few marked characteristics.

2. LIVING-QUARTERS

The canons' living-quarters attached to the collegiate churches were much less rigid in plan than the monastic buildings of the Benedictines. They seem usually to have included a cloister, with a refectory, chapter-house, and other rooms used in common, and a close with canons' houses, but by the nineteenth century France had no single example of such buildings complete. The canons' houses, in particular, were nearly all rebuilt in the seventeenth and eighteenth centuries. They seem to have differed in little from ordinary town houses; the fifteenth-century Maison du Doyenné at Moulins and the house of the Blessed Appeleine, a canon of Prémery who died in 1466, remain as typical examples. At Montpezat, however, the dean and the fourteen canons lived in a large single house with wooden galleries to link the rooms.

The cloisters of the Augustinians, since they did not, like those of the Benedictines, comprise a little world, tended to be simpler and lower than those of monastic houses. The cloisters at Sablonceaux were extremely plain with a wooden ceiling. The finest surviving are those at Toulouse (Fig. 112) which retain the twin columns of the earlier tradition but have graceful cusped arches and a wooden roof. They were built late in the fourteenth century by Jean Maurin, stonemason, with various subcontractors for the woodwork.[1] They are set, like those of Saint-Géniez and Sablonceaux, to the south of the nave. The chapter-houses opened out of the cloister and were usually simpler versions of the Benedictine type.[2] In the Order of Grandmont, however, they were still plainer, with no columns down the middle and a wooden roof.

The prebends of the canons were for the most part derived from agricultural land, and like the Cistercians they went in for handsome farm buildings. The tithe-barn of Saint-Quiriace at Provins is a magnificent building of the late twelfth century, on three floors. The ground floor (Fig. 113) is occupied by a great vaulted room with two rows of columns with capitals sculptured with leafage. It once had round-headed openings all down one side on to the street, alternately doors and windows with stone benches in the embrasures. At Clermont-les-Fermes, again, seven farms of Saint-Martin de Laon were protected by a common wall.

[1] *Cong. arch.*, 1929, p. 125.
[2] e.g. Notre-Dame-de-la-Roche, Seine-et-Oise.

3. COLLEGIATE ART

The Augustinians did not create an iconography of their own, but were content to follow in the Benedictine tradition. The tomb of Saint Front at Périgueux, which was round, like the Holy Sepulchre, and carved all over with figures, monsters and beasts, was made for the canons about 1080 by Guina-mond, monk of the Benedictine abbey of La Chaise-Dieu, one of the rare monkish sculptors of whom we have certain knowledge. The tomb of Saint Junien was a version in stone of such a metal tomb as that of Saint Gilles, with Christ in Glory between the evangelistic beasts, the Virgin and Child, and the Elders, holding lute and phial, under arcades. The twelfth-century stucco portal of Saint-Julien de Brioude represents the Ascension according to the familiar Benedictine Beatus scheme.

The capitals of the Augustinian churches show no striking originalities. Those of Notre-Dame-la-Grande at Poitiers come from the usual repertory of the mason doing monastic work: knotwork, birds, palmettes, and anthemia of a manuscript type, debased Corinthian foliage, and Christ in an aureole upheld by angels. At Saint-Caprais d'Agen there are capitals of the end of the eleventh century with the story of Saint Caprais; every figure is carefully labelled. At Notre-Dame-du-Port at Clermont the capitals seem to be by the same sculptors as those of the abbey of Saint-Nectaire; there is one, derived from the *Psychomachia* of Prudentius, on which Largitas and Caritas in coats of mail pierce with their lances the Vices beneath their feet (Fig. 114). Miseri-cordia and Avaricia prepare to engage in hand-to-hand conflict, and Anger kills herself with her own sword, since Patience will not give battle. On another, Adam, driven out of Paradise, revenges himself by pulling Eve along by the hair.[1] The remaining side resembles the votive capital at the priory of Volvic (Fig. 6 B). It shows a man in citizen's dress holding a capital. In front of him an angel holds a book inscribed IN ONORE S. MARIAE STEFANVS ME FIERI IVSSIT. Two of the few sculptural originalities in an Augustinian church are the treat-ment of a rose window as a Wheel of Fortune at Saint-Étienne de Beauvais[2] (Fig. 115) and the decoration round the key-stones of the vault erected at Notre-Dame d'Étampes when the choir was enlarged in the second half of the twelfth century. One has four kings and one eight angels, set wheel-wise. Soon after 1262 Saint-Urbain de Troyes was enriched with a piscina of quite remarkable beauty. At the top is a rich battlemented canopy, with tiny archers shooting from the battlements as they sometimes do in contemporary manuscripts. Underneath, the Coronation of the Virgin is fitted into the central spandrel, while on either side the donors, Urban IV and Cardinal Ancher, hold models

---

[1] Cf. the *Jeu d'Adam,* l. 534; Bréhier, p. 212.
[2] Saint-Étienne de Beauvais became collegiate in 1072.

of the windows and towers they have given to Saint Urbain and his church. The whole is more in the style of lay illumination than of that found in churches. The portal, like one of the doors of the cathedral of Sens, is conceived as a stained-glass window with its tracery and its storied glass turned into stone (Fig. 116). Christ sits in judgement in the upper quatrefoil, with a strange little group of Elders below Him. The Virgin and St. John kneel in supplication in medallions beneath, and at the bottom the arcaded lights are carved with Abraham holding souls in his bosom, the company of the Blest, and devils carrying off the Damned to hell. On the lintel the dead are rising from their graves. Again the note of elegance and decoration is struck; again the spirit is that of a psalter painted for lay use rather than of a monastic manuscript. If a monastic manuscript served as a model, it was sometimes one of considerable antiquity. When in 1269 two windows were set up in the collegiate church of Sainte-Radegonde de Poitiers, representing the unusual subject of episodes from her life, they were based on manuscript illuminations painted two centuries before.[1]

Exceptionally, the sculptured exterior decoration of the Romanesque collegiate churches is more original. That of Saint-Barnard de Romans, it is true, is like a segment from Saint Gilles, but the door from the cloister to the church of Notre-Dame-du-Port has real originality. The gable-shaped lintel is filled to the left with the Adoration of the Magi, and to the right with the Presentation in the Temple and the Baptism of Christ. Simeon's altar, under a ciborium, makes a centre to the composition. In the lunette above Christ sits enthroned between two six-winged seraphs, according to the Vision of Isaiah.[2] Isaiah himself and John the Baptist appear on reliefs above the door. It lacks the originality of the Virgin's door at La Charité, but it is an evident attempt at integrated composition with the two themes of the Virginity of Our Lady and the Baptism of Our Lord. Latin inscriptions on the edge of the lintel describe the subjects without offering any symbolic interpretation.

The finest example of sculptural decoration on a collegiate church is that on the façade of Notre-Dame-la-Grande at Poitiers (Fig. 117). At first sight it seems a mere confusion of grotesque ornament and gesticulating figures; yet when it is examined in detail it proves to be an expression in stone of the sermon ascribed to St. Augustine that is read at Matins on Christmas Day. On the spandrels Adam and Eve, Nebuchadnezzar, the four prophets who announce the coming of Christ, the Annunciation, the Tree of Jesse, the Visitation, the

---

[1] Mâle, *Art rel. du XIIe siècle*, p. 238. The manuscript is now in the Poitiers municipal library. There is too little evidence available for it to be certain whether wall-paintings also tended to be behind the times. At Saint-Hilaire de Poitiers a series of hieratic standing saints can be traced, and at Notre-Dame-la-Grande there is a late twelfth-century Virgin and Child. Saint-Junien had thirteenth-century paintings of St. Christopher and St. Martin. (See *Bull. Mon.*, 1932, p. 121.)

[2] On manuscript versions of this theme see Mâle, *Art rel. XIIe siècle*, p. 25.

K

Nativity and Baptism of Christ lead up to the reconciliation of Old and New Testaments, just as they do in the sermon, with inscriptions that are further proof of their derivation from this source.[1] Above, under arcades, are statues of St. Hilary of Poitiers, St. Martin of Tours, and the twelve Apostles, and over all Christ and the evangelistic beasts.

With the Gothic period such rich decoration went out of fashion, and the collegiate churches contented themselves with portals that were versions on a small scale of those of the great cathedrals. That at Étampes, now much battered, has column statues like the earliest at Chartres, and a tympanum with the Ascension. By a kind of reminiscence of such sculptured façades as that of Poitiers the spandrels on either side are filled by figures of floating angels. The tympanum of the Collégiale at Mantes is yet more old-fashioned in subject: like Notre-Dame-du-Port it has the Vision of Isaiah for its theme, while on the lintel are the Holy Women coming to the empty Tomb. At the end of the thirteenth century the collegiate church at Villeneuve-l'Archevêque (Fig. 118) was graced with a portal with statues of saints under canopies on the splayed-out jambs, and a tympanum with the Coronation of the Virgin under an arch with figures of saints and angels. At Sillé-le-Guillaume a contemporary tympanum of the Last Judgement, with donors beneath, attempts to reproduce a classic cathedral theme on a smaller scale.

The particular riches of the collegiate churches lay in the tombs of their canons and in their treasuries filled with the individual gifts of the members of the community. No rule of humility prevented Augustinian canons from having decorated tombs, and collegiate churches, like cathedrals, had their floors paved and their walls encrusted with the memorials of the dead.[2]

The treasures of the collegiate churches were full of reliquaries and sacred vessels of one sort and another; these, however, were less individual in design than those of the richer monastic houses. The canons of the collegiate churches must have been among the chief patrons of the enamellers of Limoges and the more commercial goldsmiths of Paris and the provincial towns. Saint-Sernin de Toulouse, which by the thirteenth century had become Augustinian, has a typical Limoges reliquary[3] made to contain a relic of the Cross brought back

[1] See J. Durand.

[2] Very few survive; the most numerous are at Champeaux. Examples that will suffice to illustrate their variety are a wall-slab to a canon named Stephen at Plaimpied, of the second half of the twelfth century, carved with a figure of Abraham receiving the soul of the dead man into his bosom, and an incised thirteenth-century slab at Les Andelys to Richard de Saint-Laurent, abbot of the Collégiale. He is represented kneeling beneath a figure of the Virgin; the inscription records that he wrote a book in her praise. In the Collégiale of Saint-Quentin a series of sculptures, painted and gilt, of the life of the saint are surmounted by the obituary inscription of the donor, who died in 1351. A series of later and more stereotyped Augustinian tombs will be found in Gaignières. Exceptionally a funerary chapel might be attached to a collegiate church, as the Chapelle de Navarre was to that of Mantes.

[3] *Cong. arch.*, 1929, p. 49.

from the Holy Land by Raimond Botardel, a notary of Toulouse who had gone there on pilgrimage in the middle of the thirteenth century. The cover has stock designs: Christ in Glory between angels, the Annunciation, the Holy Women at the Tomb. The base was made specially, and is enamelled with the story of the relic. On one side is the Invention of the Cross by St. Helena. On the front, before a wall labelled IERVSALEM, the Abbot of Notre-Dame-de-Josaphat hands a reliquary to the pilgrim: ADDAS DE IOSAFA DE CRVCE DAT RAIMVNDO BOTARDELLI. Then Botardel is depicted getting into a ship, with sail set and a rower at the oar: HIC INTRAT MARE. On the further side he gives the relic to the Abbot of Saint-Sernin, Pons de Montpezat, and two of his canons: HIC DAT ABBATI PONCIO. At the back the abbot and his canons offer it to Saint Sernin, with a background of fortified wall labelled TOLOSA and the legend: CANONICI CVM ABBATE OFFERVNT CRVCEM SATVRNINO. Saint-Yrieix still has a dove-shaped pyx for the host, of Limoges work, to hang over the altar, as well as a silver bust reliquary of the saint and a shrine of copper gilt that both look as if they had been made locally. Grandmont had a particularly copious treasury.[1] Henry II and Richard Cœur de Lion gave it a great altar frontal of copper gilt and enamelled, with Christ and the evangelistic beasts surrounded by figures of apostles and saints, and scenes from the Old and New Testaments and from the life of Saint Étienne de Muret. His life was again represented upon his shrine of copper gilt. These were destroyed at the Revolution, but a certain number of pieces from Grandmont still survive. In 1226 the canons of Saint-Sernin gave it a reliquary with relics of the thirty-seven saints represented in their own treasury.[2] Another typical shrine[3] of Limoges enamel held relics of the Theban Legion (Fig. 120). Besides these there was a statuette of the founder, Saint Étienne de Muret, in gilt copper[4] (Fig. 119), a bust reliquary of his head,[5] and the dalmatic given to him by Matilda, wife of the Emperor Henry V.[6] A reliquary of St. Julian and an angel reliquary in crystal and copper gilt, with cloisonné and champlevé enamels[7] and an arm reliquary are also, like most of the rest, of the thirteenth century.

The collegiate churches were also patrons of another form of industrial art, English alabaster retables of the fifteenth century; fine examples still survive at Saint-Léonard in the Limousin and at Montréal near Avallon, which also has an admirable fifteenth-century lectern evidently made by the local joiner, with flamboyant tracery like that carved on contemporary chests. Nowhere, indeed, can the current productions of ordinary workshops be better studied than in such collegiate churches.[8] The Collégiale of the charming but always unimportant

[1] See L. Guibert, *L'École monastique d'orfèvrerie de Grandmont*, Limoges, 1888.
[2] Now at Châteauponsac.
[3] Now at Ambazac.
[4] Now at Les Billanges.
[5] Now at Saint-Sylvestre, Creuse.
[6] At Ambazac.
[7] At Saint-Sulpice-les-Feuilles.
[8] e.g. Notre-Dame des Andelys: fine fourteenth-century glass, tombs, wooden cross, statue of

town of Montpezat-de-Quercy, founded by Cardinal des Prés in 1334—an aisleless church—has the fine sculptured tombs of the founder, of his nephew the Bishop of Castres, and of others of his family; the original stalls and an elaborate font; admirable late Gothic tapestries with scenes of the life of St. Martin of Tours, patron of the church; a stone statue of Our Lady of Pity; an alabaster Virgin and Child, with the Child holding a bird's nest; some hand-some carved chests; and a treasury that still has three typical reliquaries and a bag embroidered with figures of the Months. A charming diptych, that may once have graced a canon's own oratory before he bequeathed it to his church (Fig. 121), shows on one leaf a Crucifixion, and on the other a Christ of Pity to whom Our Lady presents a kneeling Augustinian in his surplice and fur cape. Its decorative quality suggests that it must have come from a good Paris workshop.

The Collégiale of Écouis, founded by Enguerrand de Marigny in 1310, con-tains one of the finest series of detached works of sculpture left in any church in France: a Virgin and Child, an Annunciation group, a St. Anne, a Saint Nicaise, a Saint Denis, a Saint Laurent, a St. Cecilia, and, most beautiful of all, a St. Veronica (Fig. 122). These, however, are probably due rather to the munificence of the founder than to the personal gifts of the canons, for they have exactly that aristocratic quality in which the ordinary furnishings of a collegiate church are lacking.

Sometimes, too, the canons agreed that their gifts should form a definite iconographic scheme. The canons of the collegiate church of Saint-Martin at Champeaux-en-Brie in the late fifteenth century gave a set of windows of the life of St. Martin, but it is significant that the series is broken by a St. Michael given by Canon Michel Paien and a St. Nicholas by Canon Nicolas Sauvaige.[1] It is only exceptionally that an iconographic scheme was specially planned and fully carried out. The classic instance is the tapestries made for the canons of Saint-Urbain de Troyes in the middle of the fifteenth century.[2] They decided that they should portray the legends of St. Valerian and St. Cecilia. A canon hunted up the literary sources, largely in Vincent de Beauvais, and drew up a scheme for the painters making the cartoon. Everything was decided for them.

'Sera faict et pourtraict ung lieu et tabernacle comme à manière d'une belle chambre dedans laquelle sera ladicte saincte Cecile humblement prosternée à deux genoux et les mains joinctes faisant manière de prier Dieu. Et auprès d'elle sera le dict Valerian

St. Anne, and fifteenth-century Sepulchre and stalls. Notre-Dame-de-la-Roche, near Dampierre, has late thirteenth-century choir stalls that are, with those of Poitiers, the earliest in France, as well as a series of fine tombs.   [1] See *Bull. arch.*, 1896, p. 105.
  [2] Guiffrey, p. 46; Mâle, *Art rel. XIIIe siècle*, p. 437. The collegiate churches were rich in tapestries: two from a set of six from Saint-Martin d'Angers and two more from Saint-Jean d'Angers are now in the cathedral. Both depict the story of the patron saint.

faisant grande admiration et regardant un ange, lequel estant dessus leurs chiefs tiendra deux couronnes faictes et pourtraictes de lys et de roses desquelles il fera manière de asseoir et poser l'une sur le chef de saincte Cecile et l'aultre sur le chef du dict Valerian son époux; et de la bouche d'icelluy ange sortira un grand rosleau, auquel sera escript, si possible est, ou partye: Istas coronas mundo corde et corpore custodite quia de paradiso Dei ad vos eas attuli, nec unquam marcescent, nec odorem amittent.'

There can be no more manifest example of the influence exercised by the medieval patron upon the artist who worked to his orders.

4. THE ORDER OF HOSPITALLERS

It remains to consider an Order of Augustinian canons who combined the duties of fighting for the Holy Land and tending the sick with the obligations of a regular life. The Order of the Hospitallers of St. John of Jerusalem came almost spontaneously into being to meet a want. The pilgrims of the Western Church who reached Jerusalem, often ill and worn out by the fatigues and perils of the journey, needed friendly hands to tend them. In 1113 a congregation was founded by a Provençal knight, Pierre Gérard, to meet this need, with a chapel dedicated to St. John Baptist at Jerusalem. Its Rule, confirmed in 1120, was based on the Augustinian Rule. The brethren were vowed to poverty, chastity, and obedience, but like the Augustinian canons, though living in common, they were not enclosed. The brethren might leave the cloister, but never alone, and only to beg. Their peculiar duties were those of defending the Holy Sepulchre and caring for the pilgrims who came to visit it. About 1118 the Hospitallers were reorganized on a militant basis to defend the Christian Kingdom of Jerusalem and were divided into three classes: one of nobles, to fight; one of chaplains, to say Mass and to pray; and one of serving brothers. By 1130 they were organized as a knightly order.[1] Gérard's successor, Raymond of Provence, had the hospice and chapel transferred to finer buildings near the Church of the Sepulchre. Another Order, the Knights of St. Lazarus, was closely associated with them, and was devoted to the care of lepers.[2]

The larger of the surviving Hospitallers' churches in the Holy Land[3] show the Augustinian scheme a little modified to meet the needs of congregations of pilgrims. Both the church of Qariat el Enab near Jerusalem and that of St. John, now the Great Mosque, of Beyrouth, have aisles and rounded apses. The former, lying out in the country, is a fortress church with few and high-set windows; the latter, a city church, would not seem incongruous in any French town.

---

[1] Hélyot in Migne, xxi, col. 820.

[2] Hélyot, ibid., col. 145. He gives the houses in France surviving just before the Revolution as the Commanderie de Boigny, La-Lande-Daron, and Saint-Thomas de Fontenay.

[3] Santa Maria Latina has been rebuilt as a Lutheran church.

Their cross-vaults of fine stone, their square piers, enriched at Beyrouth by engaged columns to take the dosserets of the vault, and their lofty proportion all indicate that they were built by French workmen.

The capture of Jerusalem by Saladin in 1187 drove the Hospitallers to the coast at Acre and to various strongholds in the north. The chapels in the fortresses of the Krak des Chevaliers and Marqab are of an extreme simplicity. They combine the round cul-de-four apse of the larger churches with the typical aisleless nave of a collegiate church. The comparatively unimportant place they take in the piled-up fortifications of the citadels shows how preponderant were the military duties of the Order at the time that they were built.[1]

The first Grand Priory of St. John of Jerusalem founded in Europe was established at the town of Saint-Gilles by Raymond IV of Toulouse at the beginning of the twelfth century. Nothing remains of it. The Order established several houses in Languedoc, of which a little more is known.[2] Even there the fortress tradition of the Holy Land continued for a time to influence the plan of the Hospitallers' convents. At Saint-Gilles de Toulouse the walls of the enclosure were crenellated, in mark of seigneurial domination, and a square donjon dominated the whole. This apart, the house conformed to the usual plan, with a church, cloister, living-quarters, and in addition a hospital for the poor and infirm.[3] Nothing remains but the inscription once set above the lintel of the church:

HIC DEVS ORATVR DOMVS EIVS ET ISTA VOCATVR
HVC ERGO VENIAT QVEM CONSCIA CVLPA FATIGAT.

Their commandery in Paris seems to have approximated more closely to the Palestinian plan: it comprised a church, with an aisleless nave and high-set windows, a dwelling for the commander, and a fortified tower of four stories for the knights.

By the thirteenth century the militant role of the Hospitallers was played out, and their buildings seem to have approximated to those of any small collegiate house. The Commanderie de l'Hôpiteau near Coulommiers still has a thirteenth-century chapel, simple, yet notably elegant in its proportions. Its portal had a tympanum with the Coronation of the Virgin and statues of prophets;[4] they show no particularities in scheme or style, nor do the fifteenth-century living-quarters. Very few Hospitallers' houses have survived; there is nothing

---

[1] After Acre and Marqab fell in 1291 the Hospitallers made Cyprus their base. In 1310 they withdrew to Rhodes and in 1522 to Malta. The centre of the Knights of Malta is now on the Aventine at Rome. The English Order of St. John is a modern foundation with no real historical connexion with the ancient order.

[2] Mention should also be made of the twelfth-century ruins at Ribiers and the church of Lardiers, Hautes-Alpes, then outside France.   [3] See Rey, *Cat. Augustins,* Toulouse, 1912, p. 221.

[4] Now in the Musée archéologique at Troyes.

at Lurol, nothing at Corbeil, nothing at Beaune, nothing of Saint-Jean de Latran at Paris, nothing earlier than the eighteenth century at Pézenas or La Rochelle. The rich flamboyant chapel at Keramanac'h in Brittany almost alone remains;[1] there is not enough evidence left to show the history of the architecture of the Order in France.

[1] I know of no medieval French pictures connected with the Order except for a picture in the cathedral of Apt of St. John wearing the mantle of the Order.

VI

THE MENDICANT ORDERS

I. THE FRANCISCANS

THE Benedictines served the whole world by their prayers, but their material charity began at the abbey door and ended with the boundary of the abbey lands. As society grew more complex, and abbeys more feudal, need arose for men devoted to the ministry of God who were free to leave the cloister and to work in the service of all Christians without thought of territory or enclosure. 'Non sibi vivere sed et aliis proficere' was the motto of the new age. The need was met by two men, St. Francis and St. Dominic, in the foundation of two Orders alike in aim and strangely different in spirit. If the earlier centuries are those of the Benedictines, and the century between 1150 and 1260 that of the Bishops and Canons, the next epoch belongs to the Friars. In France, however, great though their influence was upon the ways of religion, their influence on art was in no wise so powerful as it was in Italy.

The Franciscan Order had its beginnings, like most new orders, in a brotherhood that formed itself spontaneously among the friends of the founder. Recognition by the Church was achieved in 1217, with an organization into the provinces of Spain, Portugal, France, Germany, Hungary, England, Italy, and Syria. The Benedictine vows of chastity, poverty, and obedience were maintained, but a new emphasis was laid on poverty, which was extended from the individual to the Order. This ban on corporate property, which was to become a source of endless dissension in the Order of Friars Minor, naturally precluded any fine architecture for so long as it was observed. The first Franciscan buildings were of wattle and daub, and this in an age when the Benedictines had long been building in fine stone. The difference serves to emphasize the fact that in many ways the Order founded by St. Francis was the antithesis of that founded by St. Benedict.

In 1217 Brother Pacificus and Brother Agnellus set out to establish the Order in France; two years later a house was established in Paris, and by 1233 the Province of France was flourishing. The second Franciscan Order, the nuns of the Order of St. Clare, came to France with the foundation of their house at Rheims in 1229; it soon had daughter houses at Montpellier, Cahors, and Bordeaux.[1]

Every friar was a missionary to his province, and, like a missionary, he was a

---

[1] Hélyot in Migne, xx, col. 968. A mitigated form of their rule was followed by the nuns of the Ordre de l'Humilité de Notre Dame, later called Urbanistes, founded by Innocent IV in 1264. Their chief houses were at Longchamps, Provins, Saint-Marcel near Paris, Moncel, Nogent-l'Artaud, Argentan, Laval, and Fougères. Hélyot in Migne, xxiii, col. 748.

nomad. Settled establishments with fine buildings were no part of the Franciscan scheme; the early generations of French Franciscans did as little for Gothic architecture as the Salvation Army did for the architecture of the Victorian age. Since friars were frequently moved from one community to another their houses lacked that continuity of habitation which is a necessary basis of architectural development. The Franciscans were not, like the Benedictines, attached to a place, and consequently had not the natural desire, stronger than any restrictive regulations, to make that place beautiful. There is a colourless and uninterested quality about their early architecture far removed even from the negative strength of Cistercian building. Their churches had no characteristic plan; they merely followed the most barnlike version of a local type. The chronicle of Jacques de Guise on the building of the convent of Friars Minor at Valenciennes[1] shows that architects were consulted chiefly on the choice or site. When the plans were to be made the designers were warned by the officials of the Order not to design the church too grandly or their scheme would not be accepted. Finally it was built in six bays with aisles, with four altars and a tower. In Italy, it is true, the canonization of St. Francis in 1228 was immediately followed by the erection of a great pilgrimage church at Assisi to hold his relics; but such architectural splendour found no parallel elsewhere. It was, indeed, only exceptionally that one of the earlier Franciscan churches in France was a place of pilgrimage. That at Montferrand, consecrated in 1229, held some of the relics of St. Thomas Becket, to whom it was dedicated, and had the windows over the high altar filled with the story of his life in stained glass, given by the nobles of the district.[2]

In 1260 the Statutes of the Order were regulating its buildings in a spirit of austerity.[3] They were only to be erected under licence from the Provincial and according to his plan. They were to show no excess of *curiositas* in their design; they were not to be vaulted, except over the high altar. They were to have no stained glass except in the window behind it, and in this only representations of the Crucifixion with the Virgin and St. John, St. Francis and St. Antony,[4] were to be permitted. Like the Cistercians they were forbidden to have bell-towers, vestments embroidered with silk or gold, or silver crosses or censers. The prohibitions were renewed in 1292;[5] by then the Order was richer, and golden censers and crosses had also to be forbidden. By 1316 the veto had to be extended to golden candlesticks.

The subsequent riches of the Order which made its members hated, and the fact that their churches were in or near prosperous towns, later caused the destruction of a surprising number of French Franciscan churches; consequently

<hr>

[1] Mortet, ii. 235.   [2] Fodéré, p. 332.   [3] Mortet, ii. 285.

[4] St. Antony of Padua, who was half-French, founded a Franciscan convent at Brive in 1226 and lived there for a time.   [5] Coulton, i. 275.

our knowledge of them is far from complete. The extreme simplicity of their
earlier buildings is exemplified in the church of the Cordeliers at Châteauroux:
a plain rectangle with a wooden roof. The thirteenth-century church at
Parthenay is likewise rectangular; its nave, however, is vaulted, though the
long narrow windows that light it are of a Cistercian austerity.[1]

Soon, however, even the Franciscans permitted themselves aisled churches.
Their church at Provins, built in 1284 and now destroyed, added aisles to the
traditional long rectangle with a wooden roof, and completed it with a pentagonal apse; the early church at Paris, which is said to have been the longest
church in the city, seems to have followed the same plan. The good aisled
ogival nave at Lavaur extends for eight bays, though some of these were added
later; and the late Gothic church of Saint-Bonaventure at Lyons has both aisles
and side-chapels. The final development was the transition from a modest bell-
tower to a fine brick *clocher*, as at the fourteenth-century Chapelle de Rieux at
Toulouse,[2] and its later imitation at Pamiers. At Angoulême,[3] built in 1260,
the nave is simply vaulted, the choir more elaborately; the windows have rose
tracery in their heads, and there is an octagonal tower and steeple to the side of
the church. At Clermont-Ferrand the church,[4] begun in 1273 and consecrated
in 1284, has tall windows with the same rose tracery in the head to light the
first three bays of the aisleless nave.[5] Here, too, there was a small octagonal
bell-tower to the side.

The church at Assisi, consecrated in 1252, had a single nave ending in a polygonal apse. The scheme was followed on a small scale in the church at Agen,
with the traditional wooden roof to the nave. In the Franciscan church of
Toulouse, built about ten years later, the scheme was enriched by a multiplicity
of small chapels: eleven each side of the nave, and five in the polygonal apse.
A second chapel beyond had four chapels each side, and another polygonal
apse. The style of the building was austerely architectural; the façade was simple
almost to meanness.[6]

Already, however, the patronage of the Royal House was beginning to
modify Franciscan austerity. Saint Louis himself and members of his family were
probably tertiaries of the Order. The king left by will a part of his library and
a large sum of money to the Paris house. Royal gifts caused the early fourteenth-

---

[1] Cf. the remains of the Franciscan church at Angers. The destroyed church at Blois had no apse,
but a flat end on the Cistercian model.   [2] Rue du Collège de Foix.

[3] Now the chapel of the Hôtel-Dieu.

[4] Now used for the Archives Départementales. Part of another thirteenth-century church at Parthenay survives as shops, and the church at Souillac (1278) remains with a restored tower. At Brive the
very simple façade of the nuns of St. Clare survives at the corner of the rue Blaise Raynal and the rue
du Docteur Massénat.

[5] This appears to have had sexpartite vaults rising from sculptured capitals.

[6] Rey, *Art gothique du Midi,* p. 86. It was burnt in 1871.

century Franciscan church at Hyères, dedicated to the royal saint, to be more solidly built than usual: though plain, it has barrel vaults over the aisles, and ogival vaults over the nave, apse, and absidioles. Plainness was forgotten in the royal foundations near Paris, which were many. St. Isabel, sister of Saint Louis, began in 1255 the work of foundation of the monastery of the Humility of the Blessed Virgin at Longchamps, from which sprang a branch of the Order of St. Clare of somewhat mitigated austerity. She was buried in the convent church when she died in 1270, and the miracles wrought at her grave made it a place of pilgrimage. Another house, the Cordelières of Lourcine, was founded by her sister-in-law, the wife of Saint Louis; a third, the Abbaye du Moncel, by his grandson, Philippe le Bel. This last, founded in 1309, just outside Pont-Sainte-Maxence, was finished in 1328. Its buildings are among the best monastic architecture of the time in France: a fine refectory, with a reader's pulpit; a columned library; a muniment room with a central column and an eight-ribbed vault; great dorters with magnificent wooden roofs, and the usual kitchens and chapter-house. After the canonization of Saint Louis, his daughter Blanche had the cloister of the Clares of Lourcine painted with scenes of his life, based on the book of Guillaume de Saint-Pathus, and probably copied from an illustrated manuscript, such as she might be expected to have owned. Mahaut d'Artois, again, when she founded a house of Clares at Saint-Omer, graced its portals with painted statues of the Count and Countess of Artois, the Queen of France their daughter, their Councillor Thierry d'Hireçon, and the nuns of the convent, grouped round a Crucifixion. The cloister was adorned with twelve statues of the Apostles and the church with a sculptured rood and a retable of wood, painted, gilt, and inlaid with coloured glass, framing a Crucifixion, with paintings of the Seven Canonical Hours below, and a predella with the Coronation of the Virgin and the four Evangelists.[1]

The glories of the Franciscan Order in France were intensified in the fourteenth century. From 1329 to 1358 the whole Order was governed by Generals of French birth, who naturally took an especial interest in the houses of their own Province. The reform of the Observance—*stricta observantia regularis*—instituted in the cloister of Mirabeau about 1380, which spread through central France, brought new vigour to its houses. The letter of Franciscan law was kept, yet beauty crept in. The vaulted chapter-house of the Cordeliers of Auch still survives. When the Franciscans of Saint-Émilion rebuilt their convent, soon after 1383, they planned the church as simply as ever, aisleless, with a wooden roof, and a stone vault only over the sanctuary;[2] but they rebuilt

---

[1] Richard, pp. 309 and 351. The retable was painted by Eloy le Clokemacre of Saint-Omer.

[2] Even in 1454 the convent of Franciscans founded by Philippe le Bon at Dijon had its buildings all of wood, Pinchart, 1st series, ii. 53. The Franciscan convent at Montluçon, built in 1453, was not vaulted but ceiled in wood. F. Clandon, *Les Cordeliers du Bourbonnais,* Moulins, 1901, p. 47.

their cloister as an imitation of that in the canons' church hard by. Handsome
cloisters, indeed, continued to be a mark of the later Franciscan houses in
France; those at Lyons and Clermont were painted with scenes from the life of
St. Francis.[1] They had a certain character of their own: low-pitched, wooden-
ceiled, with a multiplicity of slender colonnettes to support the rafters. A fine
example is that at Charlieu, built about 1390, chiefly at the expense of Honoré
d'Urfé de Châteaumorand. Trapezoidal in shape because of the limitations of
its site, it has an arcade with double capitals carved with grotesques and foliage,
and gargoyles; *curiositas* has crept in after all.[2] Later examples of the same type
are the cloister of the Clares at Provins (Fig. 123), with a fifteenth-century
arcaded east side with alternate slender and heavy piers, and a colonnaded west
side some fifty years later in date; that at Dinan[3] and that of Saint-Projet-le-
Désert in the Cantal, built in 1489.

The Franciscans exercised a considerable influence over the development of
iconography in Italy; it has been claimed that the particular religious sensibility
which they fostered was no less influential in the development of French art.[4]
It would rather seem that their function in Italy was to be a conduit of French
influence. The influence of the religious drama of France over iconography
was disseminated through them in Italy; but in France itself it is hard to find an
innovation of their making. Their breviaries were extremely plain and had no
pictures.[5] What remains or is recorded of works of art made for their own use
is not remarkable for originality. The Franciscans had no tradition of learning;
their founder, indeed, had declared: 'Books are a temptation; the brethren
who cannot read shall not seek to learn.' Consequently they had no such great
common culture as that which made the creation of Benedictine symbolism
possible. Art, if not altogether proscribed, was not encouraged in the houses
of those who had wedded our Lady Poverty; there was no such abundance of
painting and statuary, painting and gold work, tapestry and embroidery, as
was natural in the well-endowed collegiate churches. The Franciscans, indeed,
are represented in the art of the cathedrals before ever they had any art of their
own: they appear at the head of the Elect in the sculptures of the Last Judgement
at Amiens in 1225, as well as at Le Mans and Bourges. It is even uncertain
whether a reliquary of St. Francis, of Limoges work, now in the Louvre (Fig.
124), was made for a Franciscan house; it represents him receiving the stigmata,
standing between two trees that in their natural beauty provide a fit setting for
the saint who preached to the birds. More certainly authenticated works of
Franciscan art are less characteristic, and seem generally to reflect the taste of

---

[1] Fodéré, pp. 354 and 510.   [2] Compare that of the Cordeliers of Châtellerault.
[3] Now incorporated in the College.   [4] Mâle, *Art rel. fin*, p. 177.
[5] e.g. Bib. Nat. lat. 1280–2. The only ornamented ones were made for lay owners and later
given to the Franciscans, e.g. Bib. Nat. lat. 1046–8.

their donors rather than any peculiarly Franciscan spirit. Jean Tissandier, Bishop of Rieux, who had been a Franciscan, built between 1324 and 1348 a funerary chapel for himself attached to the Franciscan convent of Toulouse. It was decorated with a statue of Christ blessing while He holds a globe, seventeen statues of saints and apostles (Fig. 125), painted with gilt, originally set under carved stone canopies painted red and green,[1] and a statue representing Jean Tissandier himself, in Franciscan habit and mitred, kneeling to offer a model of his church. The middle of the chapel was occupied by a great tomb sculptured with his effigy: a symbol that episcopal pride had conquered Franciscan humility.[2]

2. THE DOMINICANS

St. Dominic unconsciously began the foundation of his Order when as a Premonstratensian canon of Osma in Spain, who had come to France with his bishop on a diplomatic mission, he undertook to preach to the heretics of Languedoc. Gradually a confraternity grew out of his work, with a Rule that received papal confirmation in 1216. It was Augustinian and Premonstratensian in its inspiration, and at first the Dominicans wore the habit of the canons regular. From the beginning it was intended to be primarily a preaching Order. Humbert de Romans, one of the greatest of the Dominican Ministers General, pointed out that 'Christ once only heard Mass; there is no evidence of his having confessed; but he laid great stress on prayer and preaching, especially preaching'.[3] The Dominicans cultivated learning and practised austerity as earnestly as had the monks in the great Benedictine age; but they did not do so to create a microcosm of holiness within the cloister, but to bring sanctity into the life of the world outside the convent walls.

The first foundation of the Order was the nunnery of Prouille, established in 1206 for ladies who might otherwise have been married to Albigensians. Eleven nuns, of whom nine were converted Albigensians, were there trained to teach village children the ways of good housewifery and the tenets of true religion.[4] This foundation was followed in 1215 by that of a men's convent near the Porte de Narbonne at Toulouse, in the family house of two of Dominic's disciples. It was soon transferred to the existing church of Saint-Romain. A convent was founded in Paris in 1218[5] as a house for students, and was followed by foundations

[1] Fifteen of the statues are in the Musée des Augustins at Toulouse, two in the Musée Bonnat, Bayonne, and two on the façade of the Église du Taur, Toulouse.

[2] Cf. a picture in the Museum of Aix-en-Provence (no. 186) given by Count Robert of Provence and his wife Queen Sancha to the local convent of Franciscan nuns in 1340. It represents Saint Louis of Toulouse (Robert's brother), wearing a cope over his Franciscan habit, with angels setting a mitre on his head. The donors kneel at his feet.

[3] Coulton, i. 124.

[4] Hélyot in Migne, xxi, col. 74. The nuns had to spin the wool and linen for their own habits.

[5] It was in the rue Saint-Jacques, whence the Dominicans derived their popular name of Jacobins.

at Lyons in the same year, at Rheims, Limoges, Orleans, and Clermont in 1219, at Poitiers in 1220, at Montpellier in 1221, and in the years to follow by many more, especially in southern France.[1] It was characteristic of the Order that its houses were founded in great cities.

> Bernardus valles, montes Benedictus amabat,
> Oppida Franciscus, celebres Dominicus urbes.

It was the urban Franciscans and Dominicans who instituted a third Order of laymen in their communities, that find a parallel in the city confraternities of the Middle Ages.

The Dominicans, like the Franciscans, began by avoiding architectural splendour.[2] Legend declares that the first plan of a Dominican church was revealed to the founder in a dream. He saw snow falling and forming a plan on the ground as it fell; and an angel revealed to him that it was to be the plan of his church: a T-shaped plan, with chapels in the arms, like a Cistercian church bereft of its choir. Whether this plan was followed at any of the early houses is uncertain. The statutes of 1228[3] prescribe *mediocres domos et humiles*; the church is to be only thirty feet long and is not to be vaulted, except possibly in the choir and sanctuary. One of the earliest French Dominican churches of which anything is known is that of Angers, built about 1236: it had a single flat-ended nave, with a wooden roof.[4] The church at Auxerre, begun soon after 1240, was very long and narrow; its massive choir screen made it seem like two churches set end to end. The exterior had a flat end, which concealed a shallow apse inside. At Périgueux, however, the Dominicans, who were given the priory of Saint-Martin on their arrival in 1241, rebuilt its semicircular apse as a flat chevet. Clermont-Ferrand, built in 1246,[5] was still of the primitive type, with a wooden roof over the nave and a vaulted choir with a flat end pierced by three plain narrow windows with three oculi above. The type continued in use, indeed, for lesser houses down to the end of the Middle Ages,[6] sometimes with the

The original buildings were destroyed in the Hundred Years War. In 1362 Charles V gave the Order the Hôtel de Bourgogne, which was rebuilt for their use.

[1] For a complete list see Rohault de Fleury, *Gallia Dominicana,* which is also the prime source of information for Dominican architecture.

[2] Like the Franciscans, the Black Friars were at first committed not only to individual but also to corporate poverty, but the difficulty was early evaded by the legal fiction that their property was held by the nunneries of the Order which were exempt.

[3] Mortet, ii. 246.

[4] Some chapels were added later. Three capitals of the church are now in the Musée Saint-Jean.

[5] Now Sainte-Marie-de-la-Visitation.

[6] Le Mans, middle of the thirteenth century; Tours, 1260; Limoges (Sainte-Marie); Bourges; Caen (Saint-Jacques); and with added chapels at Marciac, Gers, founded 1321; Argentan, rebuilt in the fifteenth century; and Saintes, rebuilt 1424–60, with a fine window in the English curvilinear style in the flat chevet.

modification of a round[1] or polygonal apse,[2] sometimes with an added transept.[3] Occasionally aisles were added to the single nave.[4]

The Dominican devotion of the Rosary, which legend declared had been revealed to St. Dominic by the Blessed Virgin herself, and its importance in their work among the laity, led to the building of Chapels of the Rosary which rivalled the main church in importance. Sometimes, as at Langres and Chartres, both of about 1275, the two were joined on a single axis; more often they were set side by side.[5] Generally the church had a round or polygonal apse, and the chapel of the rosary a flat end. It is difficult to say how much this scheme had to do with the adoption of the most characteristic plan of the Order: the double-naved church.

Unlike the Franciscans, the Dominicans were ardent in the pursuit of learning; they were the leaders of the intellectual life of Europe from the middle of the thirteenth century until the Renaissance. This noble vocation, once assumed, entailed a new scale in architecture: dignity had to take the place of humility, and the dissemination of learning to dictate a new plan. For the first time in monastic history the true focus of the church was not the high altar but the pulpit. The change is first evident in the Dominican house at Paris, of which the plans are said to have been drawn up by St. Dominic himself about 1220. It had a plain square apse and a double nave, which enabled a large congregation to see and hear the preacher with the minimum of interference by the columns.[6] The plan was repeated in the middle of the century at Agen, with lancet windows with two lights and a rose in the head. There was a campanile near the door curiously corbelled out from the wall.

The next stage in the development of this Dominican plan was reached at Toulouse, which was rebuilt[7] in the middle of the thirteenth century. Plans were drawn up about 1245,[8] when Pope Innocent VI granted a hundred days'

---

[1] Mâcon, soon after 1255; Compiègne, 1258; Albi, c. 1300.

[2] Chartres (now Saint-Paul), begun 1277; Nevers, 1305; Saint-Girons, 1309; Clermont-l'Hérault (with side-chapels), begun 1321; Blois (with side-chapels), mid-fourteenth century; Évreux, c. 1380; Saint-Flour (with side-chapels), early fifteenth century.

[3] Montargis, 1245; Cahors, soon after 1304 (with flat end: a Cistercian plan); Rouen, 1261; Langres, thirteenth century.

[4] Notre Dame de Confort, Lyons, consecrated 1251; Dijon, mid-thirteenth century; Le-Port-Sainte-Marie, Lot-et-Garonne, mid-thirteenth century; Bordeaux, 1263; Provins, c. 1270; Rheims, finished 1280.

[5] At Tours, built in 1251; Châlons-sur-Marne; Agen, begun in 1254 and finished in 1281; Angoulême and Amiens, finished in 1446.

[6] An alternative plan was to have a separate hall for preaching: this was followed at Laval, Beauvais, and Sens.

[7] The original house, dedicated to Saint Romain and in use about 1216, was extremely modest.

[8] See Cong. arch., 1929, p. 87.

indulgence to all who gave to the work.[1] The actual building does not seem to have begun before 1260; the first Mass was celebrated in the church on Candlemas Day, 1292, and it was not altogether finished until 1304 (Fig. 126). It was not planned like a basilica with nave and aisles but like a refectory with a line of seven pillars down the centre.

Sapientiae aedificavit sibi domum, excidit columnas septem.[2]

It is no *mediocris domus et humilis*: the columns soar over seventy-two feet upwards. The height is prolonged by a lofty vault; the nave was lit by tall windows in two lights filled with stained glass.[3] The apse was originally planned as a shallow rectangle, but was soon altered to form a semi-circle with five low radiating chapels, the outer polygonal and the central chapel of the Rosary rectangular. The apsidal vault boldly continues the system of the double nave: the apse, some sixty-three feet across, is spanned by a single vault divided into triangular segments by eleven ribs rising from the last pillar of the nave, each segment reinforced by a lierne and two tiercerons. The University of Toulouse had been founded as a school of orthodoxy to combat the Albigensian heresy, by a clause of the treaty between Saint Louis and the defeated Count Raymond, signed on Maundy Thursday, 1229–30. By that treaty the theological faculty was entrusted to the Dominicans, and therefore their church came to serve as a University Church, with the community sitting in one aisle and the rest of the congregation in the other. For this reason it had a second pulpit above the entrance, from which University Acts could be promulgated. The whole is

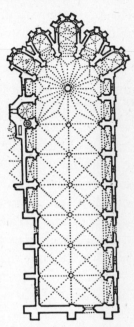

PLAN 10
Dominican church,
Toulouse. Begun 1260

logical, austere, and dignified as the Dominicans themselves: an expression of the 'clarity in a right proportion' which Aquinas declared to be the quality of art. It was worthy to receive his body, brought here in 1308 and venerated here until the Revolution. The exterior is extremely plain. The great portal originally had statues of the first two protectors of the Order, Bishops Foulques and Raymond du Falgard. The magnificent bell-tower, of pure Toulousain style, became the prototype of endless local variations.[4]

---

[1] Much was given by Brother Pierre Guillaume de Godivo, who became a cardinal and was buried there. A statue was set up over the door to the cloister which showed him offering a model of the church to the Virgin, and his arms appeared in several parts of the building.   [2] Proverbs ix. 1.

[3] The only surviving glass from the church—one window—is now in the cathedral of Saint-Étienne at Toulouse.

[4] It was itself derived from the tower of Saint-Sernin. It was copied at Beaumont-de-Lomagne,

The two-naved plan became classic in the Order.[1] It was followed at Fontenay-le-Comte in 1317, at Saint-Émilion in 1378, at Nantes and Bagnères-de-Bigorre and Beauvais in the fifteenth century, and doubtless in many other churches of which we now know nothing. That it was not widely copied outside the Order was an indirect tribute to its appropriateness to the Dominicans' own particular work of preaching and to no other use.[2]

The nuns of the Order, however, were cloistered and led a life of contemplative devotion which demanded a different scheme. The nuns' church at Prouille, finished in 1285, had square chapels in the transept and a polygonal apse. Their great church at Poissy, founded in 1304 by Philippe le Bel in honour of Saint Louis and finished in 1330, was planned like a Benedictine church, with aisles, a narrow transept, and a great choir across the whole width with seven radiating chapels, shut off from the rest of the church by a screen with statues of Saint Louis and his wife.[3]

The Dominican Convent at Toulouse still has its monastic buildings,[4] which serve to show what was customary in the Order at the height of its fame. The chapter-house, built in 1301, is finely vaulted and is divided into two by a pair of slender columns. It has a small raised apse to the east with an altar, since the Dominicans celebrated the Mass before chapter meeting in the chapter-house itself, and not, like the Benedictines, in the main church. The refectory, finished in 1303, is comparatively simple; the cloister, built between 1308 and 1310, is notable for the beauty of the naturalistic carving of its capitals, which are adorned with birds and beasts and leaves. The church-like sacristy had, like the chapter-house, a polygonal apse. In 1341 the chapel of Saint-Antonin was added to serve as a funerary chapel, to hold the twenty-four graves of the members of the house most recently dead. It was built with a benefaction from the Bishop of Pamiers, himself a Dominican. Saint Antonin was especially venerated at Pamiers; he appears on one of the vaulting bosses, and his story was depicted with an accompanying Latin text on the frieze. The vault was painted with Christ holding the Lamb, surrounded by the twenty-four Elders.

Grenade, Rieux, Lombez, Saint-Jacques de Moieux, the cathedral of Pamiers, Montrecoux, and elsewhere. See Rey, *Art gothique du Midi de la France*, p. 73. A charming fifteenth-century Dominican tower, hexagonal, with three stories of light arcading and heraldic decoration, still exists at Bagnères-de-Bigorre.

[1] It even influenced the Franciscan churches at Pontoise and Salins.

[2] At the same time certain Dominican churches in southern France with the normal two aisles should be noted: Avignon, early fourteenth century; Barcelonette, *c.* 1316; Le Puy (Saint-Laurent), fourteenth century; and Saint-Maximin, finished 1404.

[3] A few Dominican churches offer complex plans caused by the exigencies of the site or successive building campaigns: Montauban, begun in 1278; Langres, thirteenth century; Rodez, 1283; and Auch, end of the fourteenth century.

[4] Reference should also be made to the very simple façade of the mediaeval living-quarters, with tiny lancet windows, at Marciac, Gers.

L

On one wall there was a long painted inscription asking for God's mercy on the dead of the Order, and over the entrance were painted Saint Antonin, St. Dominic, and St. Peter of Verona. A sham window, painted in to balance a real one, has four lovely angels grouped round it. The paintings seem to be inspired by a manuscript of the Paris school of illumination.[1] The great Crucifix of the choir screen (Fig. 127) was painted in 1385.

By the fourteenth century enough of Dominican austerity had gone for it to be possible for members of the Order to be represented on their tombs. Cardinal de Fréauville, once a Dominican of the Rouen house, left orders that his heart should be buried there, and he erected in his lifetime a great kneeling statue of himself in his cardinal's robes.[2] Marie de Bourbon, sister-in-law of Charles V, who became a Dominican nun at Poissy in 1351 and prioress in 1380, had a royal tomb made in her lifetime in which, according to the contemporary fashion of the court, she is represented with remorseless naturalism, plain, kind, and stupid as in real life. Far more true to the Dominicans in spirit were some thirteenth-century tombs of their benefactors, which were in gratitude permitted within Dominican churches. At Châlons-sur-Marne, for instance, the simple tomb of Jean de Dommartin and his wife, 'qui furent especialement bienfaiteurs des freres preschers', showed him in a plain gown and her in travelling-dress under simple canopies,[3] and that of Jeannette de Chaubriant, who died in 1313, was incised with her effigy between those of her sister and her mother, with the six Dominicans and the altar they had helped to endow below.[4]

Most beautiful of all is the tomb of the heart of Thibault de Champagne, once set up in the house of Dominicans he endowed at Provins[5] (Fig. 128). It does not represent him at all, but round it are carved seated figures of the Dominicans who were able to study and preach through his endowments. They sit in their black and white habits, under coloured arcades, against panels alternately green and blue, in perpetual remembrance of his generosity.[6]

It might have been expected that the French Dominicans, like their brethren in Italy, would have created an iconography of their own.[7] That they did not may partly have been due to the ascetic tradition expressed in the statutes of 1298.[8] 'Inhibemus quod, in conventibus nostris, in picturis vel sculpturis seu in quibuscumque aliis similibus nulle curiositates notabiles fiant.' Such manuscripts as survive that were written for Dominican use have comparatively little

---

[1] Lemoisne, p. 32. A similar sham-window scheme may be seen in a chapel of the cathedral of Limoges.　　　　　　　　　[2] Gaignières, Bodleian MS. vii. 91. He died in 1314.

[3] Ibid. x. 31.　　　　　[4] Ibid. 48.　　　　　[5] Now in the Hôpital Général, Provins.

[6] The original colours, still traceable twenty years ago, are shown in their brilliance in Gaignières, Bodleian MS. x. 55.

[7] For their Italian contribution see e.g. the tomb of St. Peter Martyr, in Sant' Eustorgio at Milan, and the work of their member Fra Angelico.　　　　　　　[8] Mortet, ii. 246.

ornamentation: a small Bible,[1] for instance, probably written about 1256 for their convent at Clermont, has only a marvellously minute Tree of Jesse and miniature initials. Such of their houses as had scriptoria, notably that at Paris, seem chiefly to have devoted them to the copying of service-books. When Mahaut d'Artois founded a house of Dominican nuns at La Thieulloye in 1324 she ordered the choir books from the scriptorium of the Paris house.[2]

The Dominican church at Avignon, rebuilt between 1330 and 1397 and now destroyed, had a tympanum sculptured with the Virgin and Child between St. Dominic and St. Peter Martyr; the same saints were represented over the door of the Dominican church at Paris. The capitals of the Avignon cloister[3] were carved with such subjects from the Old Testament as Rebecca at the Well and Jacob's Dream, but the only originalities consisted in a few simple representations of the life of St. Dominic. He appeared again in a painting in the cloister at Clermont, that showed him kneeling before the Pope to receive the confirmation of his Order. At Angers a chapel was painted with the story of St. Catherine of Siena.[4] The chief contribution of the Dominicans to Christian imagery was not made until the fifteenth century, when their Brother Alain de la Roche preached the cult of the rosary up and down France. As a result of his preaching many confraternities of the Rosary were founded soon after 1470.[5] Their devotional pictures usually represent a legend that by then had become current in the Order. St. Dominic was said to have gone to Heaven, and to have been amazed and sorrowful that he saw none of his brethren there. Then the Virgin opened her cloak, and they were all sheltering beneath its folds.[6] Then, as lay confraternities grew up under Dominican auspices, their members came to be represented in like fashion. The picture was the more widely disseminated because it formed part of the illustrations of the *Speculum humanae salvationis*, the Dominican manual of devotion that was widely distributed both in manuscript and in print at the end of the Middle Ages.[7] A picture at Saint-Céneri is the earliest that survives; it dates from between 1362 and 1372[8] and is clearly based on an illustration to the *Speculum*. Another, painted some fifty years later, at Le Puy, has St. Sebastian and St. Roch, the saints who protected from plague, added to the picture: two saints, both Dominican nuns, uphold the Virgin's mantle. Sometimes such pictures

---

[1] B.M. Add. MS. 35085. Cf. the Dominican breviary, Bib. Nat. lat. 1305.

[2] Richard, p. 193.   [3] Some are in the Musée Calvet, Avignon.

[4] An exceptional historical painting was that on the walls of the refectory at Agen, which depicted the restitution of the Agenais to the King of England.

[5] M. Perdrizet considers that the cult is ultimately Cistercian in origin.

[6] Antonius de Siena, *Vita Patrum Ordinis S. Dominici,* p. 46, and Thomas de Cantimpré, *Bonum universale.*

[7] See p. 273. The subject occurs in the Lamoignon Hours, *c.* 1438–42.

[8] Mâle, *Art rel. fin*, p. 208.

were votive offerings, not from a confraternity but from an individual, like the beautiful Virgin of Mercy (Fig. 129) ordered from Enguerrand Charonton and Pierre Villatte in 1452 by Pierre Cadart, seigneur of le Thor, and his wife.[1]

By the end of the Middle Ages, Dominican influence was most widely exercised through the indirect channels of books written by the members of the Order, which printing had brought to the knowledge of a great public. Not only was the *Summa* of St. Thomas Aquinas the foundation of learned thought, but the *Legenda aurea* and the *Speculum humanae salvationis* were the bases of popular iconography. All three were of Dominican origin, and through them Dominican thought insensibly influenced the age: and influenced it, as Dominic would have wished, in the outside world rather than in the cloister.

3. THE CARMELITES

The third Mendicant Order that was at all widely diffused in France was that of the Carmelites.[2] Just as the Dominicans were linked with the Augustinians in organization, so were the Carmelites linked with the Carthusians in spiritual life. In its origin their Order was purely contemplative. It was founded towards the end of the twelfth century, by a crusader who established a hermitage for himself and ten companions on Mount Carmel. Their first rule was given them by the Latin Patriarch of Jerusalem in 1205 and received papal confirmation in 1224. After Frederick II made peace with the Saracens in 1229 their position became untenable, and led by the Breton General of the Order they migrated first to Cyprus and then to Sicily, France, and England.

Their rule decreed that, like the Carthusians, the Brethren were to have separate cells and to spend most of their time there; an oratory in the middle of the cells was to serve for Mass, a library for study, and a refectory for the common meals. The prior was to have a cell near the gate.[3] Manual labour, rather than writing, was prescribed, and as a consequence the Carmelites were less literary in their culture than the Carthusians. The reform of the Order by St. Simon Stock in 1245 established the Carmelites as a Mendicant Order. Little remains of the mediaeval buildings of the Order; the rule decreed that no great or sumptuous work was to be undertaken without the consent of the Prior General or Provincial. It is not hard to guess that royal patronage gradually transformed their pristine simplicity. The first house, apart from those on the coast of Provence, was that founded by Saint Louis at Charenton, the second in the Place Maubert at Paris. A picture there showed the Virgin

[1] Lemoisne, p. 84.   [2] See Hélyot in Migne, xx, col. 667.
[3] See B. Zimmermann, *Monumenta historica carmelitana*, Les Lérins, 1905, i. 13.

appearing to him as he knelt at the head of a group of Carmelite monks.[1] This was rebuilt between 1349 and 1353 through the generosity of Jeanne d'Évreux, who sold her jewels to provide the money. She had the cloister walls adorned with paintings. On one wall were scenes of Saint Louis visiting Mount Carmel, returning by sea from the Holy Land, and arriving at Marseilles. On the others were the stories of Elijah and Elisha, prototypes of the anchoretic life, and scenes from the history of the Order with explanatory verses in French.[2] The cloister was notable for a rich ceiling supported by more than eighty little figures of apostles and saints. It contained a pulpit, set high in the wall, a bronze Crucifixion,[3] and a sculptured entombment. Statues of the Virgin, Saint Louis, and St. Elisabeth of Hungary were set above a door. We know little of the church, except that a great Lady Chapel rose behind the altar; it is not hard to imagine that it shared in the Valois tradition of magnificence. Such patronage continued to the end of the Middle Ages; Françoise d'Amboise, Duchess of Brittany, who founded a convent of Poor Clares at Nantes and was a bene-factress of the Dominican house in that city, crowned her patronage of the Mendicants by founding a convent of Carmelites at Vannes and entering it. After her election as prioress she transferred the house to larger buildings at Nantes, of which nothing remains.[4] Three fifteenth-century buildings, how-ever, remain to give us an idea of Carmelite style. Their church at Tours[5] was built by Louis IX in 1473. It is aisled, with a wooden roof to the nave, enriched with carved rafters, a flat east end lighted by a great window with fine flam-boyant tracery, and good stalls and stained glass. The picture is completed by the fifteenth-century chapter-house at Loudun and the contemporary cloister at La Rochefoucauld (Fig. 130), which is close to Franciscan style in its sloping wooden roof and cusped arches above a continuous base. The processional cross of the Grands-Carmes of Paris, however (Fig. 131), with its flamboyant tracery and base delightfully designed like a walled city, has nothing of Fran-ciscan simplicity about it.

[1] Stein, *État des objets d'art placés dans les monuments religieux de Paris au début de la Révolution française,* 1890, p. 105. Other mediaeval pictures in the monastery in 1790 included St. Anne and the Virgin, and a Virgin and Child.

[2] Piganiol de la Force, *Description historique de la Ville de Paris,* v, 1765 ed., p. 160.

[3] Stein, op. cit., p. 105.

[4] For a manuscript from it with miniatures of historical personages see M. R. James, *A Descriptive Catalogue of the MSS. in the Collection of Henry Yates Thompson,* 1898, p. 190.

[5] Now called Saint-Saturnin.

VII

THE CARTHUSIANS

THE duty of the Benedictine was to labour and to pray; the calling of the canon was to say Mass; the vocation of the friar was to preach. Yet another aspect of the religious life, perhaps, indeed, the religious life *par excellence*, was that of contemplation. The fulfilment of the contemplative life early became the prime intention of certain communities, who, if they lived altogether outside the world, none the less came to influence it by other means besides their prayers.

The first great contemplative Order of Europe was that of the Carthusians, founded in 1086[1] at the Grande Chartreuse. St. Bruno, the founder, had served as a canon of St. Cunibert at Cologne, and as a teacher at Rheims and Paris before in 1082 he entered the Benedictine monastery of Molesme, that focus of monastic creation whence the Cistercians were to issue a few years later. He yearned, however, for more solitude than its cloister afforded; and Abbot Robert gave him a piece of land, not far off, where he retired with five or six like-minded companions to found a community of hermits.

St. Bruno followed another path than that of St. Benedict; his aim was to re-create the anchoretic life devoted to contemplation, such as had once sanctified the deserts of Egypt and the hills of Syria. From Sèche-Fontaine the community soon migrated to the Dauphiné, where under the protection and encouragement of Bishop Hugh of Grenoble they established their community at a place called the Chartreuse. It was set in wild and remote mountain country, different alike from the civilized beauty of Benedictine sites and from the well-watered valleys that were to be the characteristic home of Cistercian houses.

The first buildings, rude erections of wood, followed the Augustinian scheme with which Bruno had grown familiar at St. Cunibert's. Twelve little cells, each detached from the next, opened on to a common cloister that likewise contained a refectory and a chapter-house. With no cathedral or great church to serve, the buildings must, to medieval eyes, have recalled a leper-house. Within the cells his brethren were to work, sleep, and eat, drawing their water from a conduit which ran all round the cloister. They left their cells only three times a day, for Matins, High Mass, and Vespers. Only on feast-days did they say the Hours together in the choir and eat together, in silence, in the refectory.

In 1132 these primitive buildings were swept away by an avalanche, and the Chartreuse was rebuilt by Prior Guigues at a slightly lower level. The cells

---

[1] Hélyot in Migne, xx, col. 843.

were cottages, each containing three rooms; they opened out of three sides of a quadrangular cloister. On the fourth side were the church, refectory, chapter-house, kitchen, and store-rooms. The whole was surrounded by a wall. The few windows by day, and the fewer candles by night, did nothing to encourage any elaborate ornament within the church. At the beginning the most austere standards were imposed upon the Carthusians: there were to be no gold or silver ornaments or vessels in the church except for a single silver chalice and *calamus*, no hangings or carpets; their only luxury was to be the books in the library.[1] The statutes drawn up by Prior Guigues between 1116 and 1132[2] decree that if, as might exceptionally happen, a brother should be received who was a craftsman, he might be allowed to have the instruments of his craft and to practise it; and that every brother who could learn should be taught to write. Every Carthusian, indeed, was in the early days a potential scribe; the comparative fewness and smallness of their houses and the simplicity of decoration prescribed, alone prevented them from having as great an influence on the art of manuscript as had the Benedictines before them.[3] They lacked, too, the inevitable stimulus of growth and change. The Order can boast that it has never needed reformation. Even to this day the Carthusians maintain in their offices and in their chants something of the archaic simplicity of the church of Lyons in the eleventh century. Their part is not to initiate change, but to contemplate eternity.

The plan of small cells strung out round a cloister remained obligatory in the Order; but even by 1135 the Prior General had to write to the Carthusians of Mont-Dieu to tell them to maintain in their buildings the simplicity and austerity that the rule prescribed.[4] What remains of the earlier charterhouses of France—at Le Liget, founded in 1176 by Henry II of England; at Bellary, founded in 1209 in the woods between Clamecy and Cosne; at Glandier in the Limousin, in a wild and remote valley among forests of chestnut; at Port-Sainte-Marie in Auvergne, founded in 1219—is all of the utmost simplicity and austerity. The plan alone is characteristic; the architecture might be that of any poor monastic house.[5]

A good instance is the charterhouse of Sainte-Croix, founded in 1280, where a great parallelogram of cells is held between the confines of two brooks. But a new scale was being introduced by the generosity of wealthy patrons of the Order; Saint Louis's own gift of his Château de Vauvert must have been a landmark in this development, which was continued by his successors and by

[1] Mortet, i. 265. [2] Ibid. 358.
[3] A Carthusian Breviary written in 1182 (Bib. Nat. lat. 10477) has only a few rough and simple floriated initials in red and black ink. [4] Mortet, ii. 39.
[5] I have not been able to get any information about the charterhouses of Notre-Dame de l'Épau near Donzy, of La Rose near Rouen, or of Saix in the department of the Tarn.

the Avignon Popes. The Chartreuse of Villeneuve-lès-Avignon, founded by Pope Innocent VI in 1356 under the name of Val-de-Bénédiction, has a great cloister, with little houses all round it, and a lesser cloister with the chapter-house, the refectory for feast days, and the entrance to the church. The same plan is followed at the Chartreuse of Champmol, outside Dijon, founded in 1383 by Philippe le Hardi, for twenty-five monks, five lay brethren, and the prior.[1] The church, dedicated on Trinity Sunday, 1388, was like an unusually large college chapel, aisleless, with fifteen windows on each side over the stalls and a rose window to the west. The choir held a statue of the Trinity, to whom the church was dedicated. The bronze lectern was mounted on a phoenix, with figures of evangelistic beasts to support the book; there was very rich silver-gilt altar plate, and a great gilt cross. Three chapels were attached to the nave, with a ducal oratory set like a castle chapel above that nearest to the east end.

The classic plan with two cloisters was also followed at Villefranche-de-Rouergue, founded in 1456 under the will of a rich merchant of the town, Vésian Valette. The smaller cloister (Fig. 132) has its arcades divided window-fashion by mullions, and contains a little chapel for meditation (Fig. 133). The washing-fountain remains, in a niche near the refectory door, with a relief of Christ washing the disciples' feet, and the refectory still has its pulpit from which a *lecture pieuse* was read during the meals on feast days. The aisleless church has a pentagonal apse with an austerely beautiful vault; the chief decoration lies in the very rich stalls, begun in 1462, which took seventeen years to complete[2] (Fig. 134).

So long as charterhouses were founded only in remote and solitary places, their cloisters could defend themselves by austerity and prayer, but as they came to be established nearer to the highways and towns they inevitably needed to be protected from plunder and invasion. Several charterhouses, notably Sainte-Croix and Basseville, have fortified gateways with circular turrets at the corners to defend the peace within.

The Chartreuse du Liget, founded in 1176, still retains some remains of its original frescoes[3] (Fig. 135). They include a remarkably complete cycle of the Life of the Virgin, with a beautiful scene of her death, a picture of her holding the Child, and the Tree of Jesse with seven doves nestling in its branches. The whole series, even in its present damaged state, breathes the serene beauty of monastic contemplation. Yet even such art was not wholly approved: the

---

[1] It was a 'double' charterhouse, the normal number of monks being twelve. The architect was Drouet de Dammartin, who had already made his reputation at Paris.

[2] The master masons were Conrad Rogier and Jean Coupiac; the sculptor Pierre Viguier, *lapicider* of Salles-d'Albigeois. The door of the church is carved with figures of monks holding shields of the founder's arms.　　　　　　　　　　　　　　[3] See *Bull. mon.* ci, 1943, p. 195.

statutes of 1261 decree 'picturae curiosae de ecclesiis et hospitiis deleantur'. The spirit rather than the letter of this rule was followed, and very gradually the Order purified its art from mundane and personal things. The fourteenth century brought many benefactors to the Order, and with them a wave of that donors' art which is made to the taste of the giver. At Sainte-Croix, for instance, fourteenth-century paintings represent the death and funeral of Thibaud de Vassalieu, who died in 1327; at Paris the great cloister, which contained fourteen cells given by Jeanne de Châtillon, Comtesse d'Alençon, was adorned with a bas-relief which showed her presenting the fourteen Carthusians to the Virgin and Child and her patron saint, St. John the Baptist.[1]

Gradually the Order acquired legends and an iconography of its own. In the fourteenth century the story of St. Bruno and the canon of Paris was established as a legend.

According to this,[2] St. Bruno was drawn from the world of intellectual Paris by a terrible event that he witnessed. A canon of Notre-Dame died. The Nocturns for the dead were being sung round his open coffin. As the priest began to read the lesson *Responde mihi*, the dead man raised his head and answered in agony, 'I am justly accused before the tribunal of God', and fell back once more into the coffin. The next day the ceremonies proceeded, and as they carried him to the church the dead man once more raised his head and spoke: 'I am justly judged by the tribunal of God.' On the third day, as a great concourse of people followed the coffin to the graveyard, the dead man spoke once more: 'I am justly condemned by the tribunal of God.' The horrified people cast the body into the gutter; and Bruno determined to leave the world for the cloister.

The story is not found before the fourteenth century, but by the middle of the century it was represented in a wall-painting in the refectory of the charterhouse of Villeneuve-lès-Avignon. The Italian paintings of its chapel, however, are less characteristic, being devoted to the story of its patron saint, St. John the Baptist, with the Apostles and the Crucifixion in the apse.[3]

[1] Piganiol de la Force, vii. 240. A scroll issuing from the countess's mouth was inscribed:

'Vierge Mère et Pucelle, à ton cher Fieus présente quatorze Frères qui prient pour moy',

to which Christ's reply was

'Ma fille, je prens le don que tu me fais,
Et te rens tous tes mesfaits.'

In another walk of the cloister a similar tablet showed Pierre de Navarre with the four Carthusians whose cells he endowed in 1396 (Gaignières, Bodleian MS. i. 2). He was buried in the church and the four monks were represented on his tomb on either side of Abraham receiving his soul. Sometimes the votive picture and the tomb were combined; the king's painter, Girart d'Orléans, who died in 1361, was buried in the little cloister of the Paris charterhouse under a picture of the Virgin which he had painted. Poëte, p. 33. [2] See E. Baumann, *Les Chartreux*, 1928, p. 5.

[3] See E. Muntz, 'Fresques inédites du XIVe siècle à la Chartreuse de Villeneuve, Gard', in *Gazette archéologique*, xii, 1886, p. 298, and 1888, p. 21.

Even in the fifteenth century, indeed, Carthusian art was to some extent overwhelmed by alien influences. The works given to Champmol by Philippe le Hardi reflect Burgundian rather than Carthusian taste, and Flemish rather than French art. The great retable,[1] with painted panels by Melchior Broder-lam and carved ones by Jacques de Baerze, shows scenes of the Childhood of Christ; it was a version of one that the duke had admired in the Flemish monastery of Ternemonde,[2] and not specifically Carthusian. The two lesser gilt wood retables are also of Flemish origin. Similarly the ducal chapel contained a Van Eyck Annunciation[3] and a Flemish picture of the Presentation in the Temple,[4] as well as a lost picture of the Virgin with St. John the Baptist and St. Antony.[5] Such pictures, however, sealed the inclusion of art within the charterhouse. Most significantly the duke also ordered Jean de Beaumetz (who had already painted a Virgin and Child for the Chartreuse de Ligny) to paint a picture for each of the twenty monks' cells.[6] It is possible that some surviving panels,[7] sometimes thought to be part of a polyptych, are a part of these: they represent the Nativity, St. Christopher, the Baptism of Christ, the Crucifixion, the Resurrection: they are competent rather than distinguished works of art.

The noblest of his gifts still survives (Fig. 136): a roundel of the Trinity, to whom the Chartreuse of Champmol was dedicated. God the Father upholds the dead body of the Son; a tiny bird, pecking at the Crown of Thorns, represents the Holy Spirit. The Virgin tries to embrace her Son, and St. John mourns beside her. The whole is elegiac in its restrained grief; a fit subject for a life-time of contemplation.[8] Another picture at Champmol, given by a member of the family of Juvénal des Ursins, was Simone Martini's painting of Christ's March to Calvary.[9]

Other pictures were given to Champmol by men who themselves entered the Order. One (Fig. 137), probably by Henri Bellechose, has a curious scheme: it combines into one composition the Crucifixion, with the accompanying figures of the Holy Maries and St. John, and scenes from the life of St. George,

---

[1] Two panels are now in the Dijon Museum; others are scattered. See J. Dupont, loc. cit.

[2] See Dehaisnes, *Histoire de l'art dans la Flandre, l'Artois et le Hainaut*, Lille, 1886, p. 498.

[3] Now in the Mellon Collection, National Gallery, Washington.

[4] See S. Reinach in *Burlington Magazine*, 1927, p. 237, and J. Dupont in *Bull. de la soc. de l'hist. de l'art français*, 1937, p. 155.   [5] Prost, ii. 3652–7.

[6] One of these may possibly survive: the triptych (No. 1688) in the Deutsches Museum, Berlin, with a representation of the Trinity with four angels in the centre, and the Evangelists at desks in the side-wings. See Dupont, p. 15.

[7] Two in the Mayer van de Bergh Museum at Antwerp, and four in the Walters Art Gallery, Baltimore. See Dupont, p. 18; Sterling, p. 28.

[8] A noble Christ of Pity, by the same hand, perhaps also from Champmol, survives in a battered state in the Museum of Troyes. See Sterling, fig. 49.

[9] Now in the Louvre. See Reinach, loc. cit.

perhaps the patron of the giver. Its Carthusian donor kneels at the foot of the Cross; from his mouth runs a scroll with *Miserere Mei Deus*: the *Miserere* that recurs like a refrain through the Carthusian day. A second, also perhaps by Henri Bellechose, shows the Last Communion and Martyrdom of Saint Denis.[1] A third[2] represents the Crucifixion with a kneeling Carthusian donor.

The influence of donors upon the pictures in Carthusian houses is well illustrated by the *Coronation of Our Lady* given by Jean de Montagnac to the Chartreuse of Villeneuve (Fig. 138). For this the contract exists[3] signed by him and Enguerrand Charonton the painter on 14 April 1453. 'Firstly there shall be the Paradise and in the Paradise there shall be a Holy Trinity with no difference between the Father and the Son, and the Holy Ghost in the shape of a dove, and Our Lady in front according as it shall seem fit to the said Master Enguerrand, and the Holy Trinity shall place the crown upon the head of Our Lady . . .' and so on, in all the details of an elaborate composition. Yet in the lovely and essential calm of the picture something of Carthusian contemplation seems to have inspired the whole.

Lay influence is likewise evident in most of the sculptures from Champmol: the tombs of the Dukes of Burgundy and the portal with its ducal statues may fairly be considered courtly rather than monastic. One great piece of sculpture there, however, more fitly expresses Carthusian feeling. A cross was their symbol; STAT CRUX DUM VOLVITUR ORBIS their motto. A great crucifix was set above the well in the monks' graveyard, on a high base of sculptured stone.[4] Of the central group of the Crucifixion, the Holy Maries, and St. John, nothing survives but part of the figure of Christ (Fig. 139): a magnificent piece of sculpture, a little exaggerated in treatment, since it was to be seen from below at a considerable distance.[5] The base (Fig. 140), however, remains in place and untouched; there are even traces of its original colouring. The prophets of the Atonement—Isaiah, David, Zechariah, Jeremiah, Moses, and Daniel—continue the tradition of the Mystery Plays, which had earlier influenced the iconography of the cathedrals,[6] but they are here treated with an extraordinary

[1] Louvre: it is dated 1416.
[2] See *Revue de l'art*, 1937; Sterling, fig. 55; in a private collection.   [3] Lemoisne, p. 85.
[4] The architectural base was begun in 1395, the actual sculptures in 1397, by Claus Sluter, his nephew Nicholas de Werve, and his workmen Jean Prindale and Jean Hust. The angels at the base and the Maries at the foot of the Cross were carved between 1399 and 1402; by this year most of the prophets were completed. When they were set in place Jean Malouel and Hermann of Cologne coloured them. The foliage *culs-de-lampe* were by Pierre Beauneveu, a relative of the painter André Beauneveu.
[5] With an incongruity characteristic of the time, shields of arms of Burgundy and Flanders were hung from the extremities of the cross-piece.
[6] See p. 98. M. Mâle, *Art rel. fin*, p. 57, considers that they are directly influenced by the *Jugement de Jésus*, as the texts of the scrolls the prophets bear are identical with those in the play. That of Moses has: 'Immolabit eum universa multitudo filiorum Israel ad vesperum'; David's: 'Foderunt manus meas

dramatic sense and power of characterization. The strong hands of David are strangely different from the narrow thinker's hands of Jeremiah; the very angels are of different orders of spiritual life. This must have been all the more vivid when the colours applied by Jean Malouel, the painter, and the gold set on by Hermann of Cologne, the gilder, were still bright. The pedestals were green; the prophets' mantles golden; their tunics red and blue with golden stars. Isaiah, however, was altogether dressed in cloth of gold. Jeremiah once wore a pair of spectacles of gilded brass over eyes screwed up in weary short-sighted intensity.

A similar strain of northern influence is evident in the fragments of a great altar-piece from the Carthusian monastery of Thuison near Amiens.[1] This has scenes of the Last Supper (of which the scheme is borrowed from a Dutch engraving), the Ascension, and Pentecost, with a Carthusian monk in the background. The outside wings had figures which, perhaps because they were more individually linked with the spiritual life of the monastery, seem to breathe a nobler air. A beautiful Virgin and Child (Fig. 141) is balanced by standing figures of St. John Baptist, the patron of the eremitic life, Saint Honoré, Bishop of Amiens, under whose patronage the charterhouse at Thuison had been founded, and St. Hugh of Lincoln (Fig. 142), the Carthusian saint whose relics were preserved at Thuison, wearing the Carthusian habit beneath his cloak and accompanied by his swan. The same true contemplative beauty is to be found in the contemporary *Pietà* of the Dijon school from the charterhouse of Villeneuve-lès-Avignon (Fig. 143): one of the noblest pictorial compositions that the Middle Ages have bequeathed to us. Its pedimental scheme and strong contrasts of colour, skilful though they are, increase the spontaneous and heart-felt emotion which makes the desolate calm of the Virgin praying over the rigid body of her Son most deeply moving. If this quality were dictated by the Carthusian donor, the contemplative life has rarely been better justified in art.

Even in the late fifteenth century the springs of Carthusian energy were not exhausted. The windows of the chapter-house of Villefranche-de-Rouergue have a figure of the Virgin and Child, with branches from which heads of Carthusian saints in their white hoods rise like flowers. There are St. Basil, the founder of western monasticism; Bishop Goswin of Iceland; Cardinal Nicholas Albergati; St. Guigo, Prior of the Grande Chartreuse; Stephen, Bishop of Die, and William van Absel of Breda: a notably international congregation that

et pedes meos, dinumeraverunt omnia ossa mea'; Jeremiah's: 'O vos omnes qui transitis per viam, attendite et videte si est dolor sicut dolor meus': while Isaiah, Daniel, and Zechariah all announce the death of our Lord. A certain parallel is afforded by the description of a silver-gilt crucifix in the inventory of Louis d'Anjou. Our Lady and St. John stood at the foot of the Cross, and the base had figures of the four evangelists and the four major prophets. Moranvillé, p. 141.

[1] Now in the Art Institute of Chicago, to whose officers I am indebted for photographs and other information.

serves to show how wide was the scope of the Order. The chapter-house has another window on which angels and shepherds sing the *Gloria in Excelsis*; underneath, the arms of the donors are upheld by Carthusians. The great triptych of 1485 from Le Liget[1] is far less particular in its iconography; but its noble panorama of the Bearing of the Cross, the Crucifixion, and the Deposition has the true Carthusian quality of contemplative grandeur.

By this time, indeed, the Carthusians had come to realize that to those who followed the contemplative life the contemplation of paintings and sculpture of religious subjects was a legitimate if early stage of the Mystic Way. One of the great mystics of the Order, Denys de Ryckel, who died in 1471, even wrote a treatise entitled *De venustate mundi et pulchritudine Dei*.[2] Naturally he sets the *increata pulchritudo* of God above all things, but yet he admits beauty in all things, since all things have form and are created by God. There are, he maintains, two kinds of created beauty: essential and intrinsic on the one hand, and accidental and adventitious on the other. The second completes the first, which without the action of the mind cannot be perfected. He finds beauty in flowers, plants, metals, stars, the greatness of mountains, and the space of wide views; and though he makes no mention of man-created beauty yet evidently the Carthusian, gazing upon the painting that beautified his cell, could say with Augustine, 'Tu, Domine, fecisti ea pulchra.'

The *vita contemplativa* had its own standards of beauty, and the works of art produced for the Carthusians had a quality of their own. They might be symbolical, but it was with no recondite literary symbolism; they might be narrative, but narration was not their true intention. Theirs was a new purpose: the expression of religious emotion in so profound and penetrating a form that it would remain eternally moving. This was only achieved comparatively late in the Order's history, when the Order had grown conscious of what it wanted in art, and when lay painters had become skilled in the expression of emotion.

---

[1] It was given by a Carthusian whose initials were F. I. B. Now in Saint-Antoine de Loches; Sterling, fig. 88.

[2] See D. A. Mougel, *Denys le Chartreux*, Montreuil-sur-Mer, 1896, p. 32. Text in *D. Dionysii Cartusiani Opera Omnia*, Opera Minora II (XXXIV of the whole collection), Tournai, 1907, p. 227.

VIII

KING AND COURT

1. THE CASTLE

ALL the art hitherto considered has been Church art, created to the order of clerics for the service and beauty of the Christian religion. That it is, as known to us, the most important part of the art of mediaeval France, is largely owing to the historical accident that less of it has been destroyed, and less altered out of recognition, than of the art made to the order of lay patrons. At the same time the religious art of mediaeval France covers a wider stretch of time than does the civil. The Church, and in particular the monastic houses, secured the wealth and security without which art cannot flourish, at a time when the aristocracy of France was still preoccupied by the ceaseless devastation of feudal war. The *Pax Dei*, established in 969, had anathematized those who in the course of private warfare broke into churches or destroyed clerical property; the *Truga Dei*, first proclaimed in 1027, declared certain seasons to be immune, in virtue of their holiness, from private war, but did nothing to protect private property and little to stamp war out altogether. The royal power had to be extended and confirmed by continual campaigns against recalcitrant vassals before internecine feudal warfare vanished, and even then the kings themselves had sometimes to wage it against the rulers of the Angevin provinces and Flanders, Brittany, and Burgundy, when they refused to acknowledge the obligations of their vassalage.

Only when Church and King had brought a measure of peace to feudalism was it possible for the civil arts to flourish. Just as the earliest known secular epics are some two centuries later than the earliest religious verse in French, so is castle architecture later than that of churches. Long after the monasteries and cathedrals had been building for beauty's sake, castles remained fortresses of which the design was dictated only by safety.

There was a less continuous tradition of fine architecture in civil than in religious buildings. The greatest Carolingian palaces had lain outside France; those at Attigny in the Ardennes and Quierzy on the Aisne were only on the frontier and of lesser importance than those of the Rhine provinces. A great number of the old fortified manors of Gaul had been destroyed by various invaders; and those that had been rebuilt in obedience to an edict of 853 had been reconstructed as defensive posts with little reminiscence of the Gallo-Roman tradition of the country house. Often, indeed, they had become no more than a palisaded enclosure with a wooden keep in the middle where a small permanent garrison could live.

Gradually the castle became a symbol of the feudal system. The suzerain had the right to occupy it in time of war; his vassal had the right to live there always, and both owed their rights to the duty of defence. The castle had to combine habitation and fortress. It is hard to estimate the number that existed in France in the early Middle Ages; the evidence seems to show that it was considerable.[1] The census of the fiefs of Champagne made at Troyes in 1213 includes 2,200 knightly fiefs, and the existence of most of these implied a castle. Such fortresses might consist of little more than a wall and a donjon, but they were cores round which greater castles would be built in the future.

As men came to build with dressed stone in city and monastery, its use was extended to castle keeps. The Carolingian *petit appareil* was of little use for a fortress, but Romanesque ashlar kept out fire and arrows and withstood battering-rams as nothing else could. At the end of the tenth century one Lanfroi, a layman, had already made a name for himself as an architect of such stone castles.[2]

The earliest known French donjon of stone was that built for Foulques Nerra at Langeais about 990; all that remains shows it to have been a plain keep. The keeps were normally divided into three or four stories by floors and ceilings of wood. All were lit by arrow-slits in the lower floors and by small windows above. All seem originally to have had gabled roofs of moderate pitch. The buildings have the dignity of age and massiveness, but art had no part in their making.

In the next stage the keep was maintained as a general shelter in time of attack, and alongside it, within the same enceinte, a second fortified building, a castle, was erected for the habitation of the lord. At Castelnau de Bretenoux, for example, the square donjon and the triangular castle, with great round towers at the angles and others engaged in the sides, all of a lovely russet stone, are defended by fosses forty feet wide and over twenty deep.

At the same time the defensive power of keeps and castles was increased by the development of the wooden superstructure as a place from which the beleaguered could attack their enemies.[3] At the end of the twelfth century there was a passing fashion for *bossage* on the walls; a lumpy kind of rustication intended to break the ricochet of arrows. Every architectural development, indeed, had its justification in defence; the great fortress of Château-Gaillard, begun in 1196, may stand as the fully developed type of castle which is essentially a fortress, with every detail of its architecture dictated by defence.

[1] Between 994 and about 1140 Foulques Nerra and his son, and the vassals under their orders, are known to have built Langeais, Montrichard, Montbazon, Montboyau, Montreuil-Bellay, Montrésor, Sainte-Maure, Mirebeau, Faye-la-Vineuse, Moncontour, Passavant, Maulévrier, Montrevault, Montfaucon, Saint-Florent-le-Vieil, Château-Gontier, Baugé, Mateflon, Durtal, Briollay, Beaupréau, Montjean, and Chemillé: and it is hardly likely that the list is complete. Halphen, p. 153.
[2] Mortet, i. 276. He built the castle of Ivry near Évreux for Aubrée, Countess of Bayeux.
[3] See A. Mersier, 'Hourds et mâchicoulis', in *Bull. mon.* lxxxii, 1923, p. 117.

The next stage was reached when in 1214 the Battle of Bouvines assured the position of the French monarchy. The castles might still be needed as centres of defence, but they were also to become centres of a bureaucratic system that was gradually to transform feudalism. After the time of Philip Augustus the keep was no longer the central fortress; it might form part of the enclosing wall, it might be right outside it, or, exceptionally, it might be absent altogether.[1] Normally, however, it was there, but in a subsidiary place. In compensation the enceinte became more complex; its light outer defences, fosses and scarps, were increased, its towers were multiplied, and its entrance was defended by a barbican.

Coucy, begun about 1230, remained until its destruction by the Germans in the First World War the finest example of such a castle. Its enceinte, which extended to protect most of the little town which depended on it, was defended by twenty-eight towers. The Porte de Laon, covering the one weak spot in the defences, had a barbican defended by two strong towers and a 'dog's leg' entrance.[2] Within this a second enceinte delimited the *basse-cour* where goods and cattle could be kept in time of siege: an irregular hexagon, divided from the larger enclosure by a drawbridge with a gate at either end. Here was the castle well and the church: an aisleless building with a triple apse. The castle proper, on the end of a natural spur, was composed of a quadrangular building with four angle towers. To the east stood the great circular donjon, the largest in the world, with walls nearly twenty-five feet thick, in which spiral staircases to the upper floors were hidden.

Here for the first time the architecture included some decorative elements. In the main tower the hexagonal room on the ground floor had a vault with six ribs rising from capitals carved with foliage, and a sculptured keystone. The first floor had an equally elaborate vault and niches in the walls. The donjon door had a tympanum carved with a knight, armed with sword and shield, fighting a lion single-handed; the voussures were carved with figures of the Virtues. Outside the door there was a stone structure like an altar on which the vassals of the Lord of Coucy swore faith and homage and paid certain dues. It was formed of a slab resting on statues of three lions, one devouring a child, and another a dog, with a fourth couchant upon it.[3]

Much the same amount of architectural decoration may be seen in the remains of the great hall of Lucheux, only a few years later in date. It is lit by a series of twin windows framed in a heavily moulded arcade, with cloister-like piers between to take the vaults of the roof. The capitals are plain leaf capitals of a Cistercian type.

---

[1] e.g. at Boulogne-sur-Mer.　　　　　　　　[2] A similar scheme exists at Marqab in Syria.

[3] It was drawn by Androuet du Cerceau in 1576 and some fragments survive. See Lefèvre-Pontalis, *Coucy* (Pet. Mon.), p. 61. A similar table was set up in the great hall of the palace at Paris.

The development of the cross-bow and of 'machines' of attack made a stronger defence needful, and the wooden 'hourds', of little use against the fire-missiles that had come into use from the East, were gradually replaced by machicolations of stone, with crenellations above that provided a breastwork to protect the defenders, and holes through which missiles could be launched downwards. With these improvements the castle, the donjon, and the inner enceinte were sometimes combined into a single system; at Chalmazel, for instance, built soon after 1231 by Armand de Marcilly, three round towers and a square donjon were linked by machicolated curtain walls. The development of fortification continued to bring architectural enrichment in its train. Before long the corbels of the machicolations became more complex; the arrow-slits were developed cross-wise; and the crenellations were edged with bold concave mouldings to deflect arrows that might strike near their edges.

The end of the thirteenth century witnessed new developments, that heralded an age in which art should make her habitation within the castle. Peace with England, victory over the Flemings, a dependent papacy at Avignon, gave France a feeling of security that she had never enjoyed before. The consequent prosperity, and such illicit gains as the confiscated estates of the Templars, brought new wealth to the royal treasury. With the accession of the dynasty of Valois in 1328 this wealth began to be spent on display and luxury.

Already, especially in the south, some men of the seigneurial class had built houses in the towns that were larger than those of ordinary citizens and carried to a higher level the modest comforts of an ordinary citizen's house. At Saint-Antonin the town house built by Archambaud de Saint-Antonin between 1120 and 1125 (Fig. 145) shows a considerable degree of ornament. The lower story is an arcade leading to storehouses beneath; the *piano nobile* on the first floor has a line of sculptured pillars separated by piers carved with figures like the angle-piers of a cloister; and the floor above has cusped twin windows under an arcade. The chief difference from an ordinary town house lies in the tower alongside, a mark of seigneurial rank. It was from such houses, of which the finest were in Paris, that ornament flooded into the architecture of castles.

The era of luxury in France begins in the opening years of the fourteenth century. Courajod says[1] that the fourteenth century was 'un siècle d'argent, de jouissance positive et immédiate'. The 'Grand' Salle du Palais' of Paris, begun in 1299,[2] had statues of the Kings of France from Pharamond down, set over every capital of the wall consoles and of the eight central columns. Its traceried windows were filled with stained glass; its splendid wooden roofs were painted in blue and gold.

[1] Leçons, ii. 48.   [2] Known to us from an engraving by Ducerceau.

M

Not even the beginning of the Hundred Years War in 1337 could check the blossoming of a courtly civilization that had no equal at its time and has had few rivals since. Crécy and Poitiers might be lost, King John imprisoned, Paris in revolt; but wise statesmanship and skilful diplomacy restored hope, and the campaigns of du Guesclin brought victory and prosperity. By 1380 England held only Calais, Cherbourg, Bordeaux, and Bayonne and by 1382 the citizens of Ghent had been defeated at Roosebek. Charles V, whom Christine de Pisan calls 'sage artiste, vrai architecteur, deviseur certain, prudent ordeneur', was a great builder materially as a part of his effort to rebuild his country spiritually. He rebuilt, or added to, the castles of the Louvre, Saint-Germain-en-Laye, Creil, Melun, and Montargis, and built his town house at Paris, the Hôtel Saint-Pol, and his pleasure-house at Beauté-sur-Marne, as well as the fortresses of the Bastille and Vincennes.

In the reign of Charles VI war was renewed, and with war, defeat; but the tradition of luxury had been established. The king lived as the centre of an enormous household. 'Hanter les cours des princes et des roys' had become one of the marks of a good knight, a duty on a level with courage, generosity, and the defence of the weak. To read the accounts of such a monarch as Philip of Valois is to see the great ghostly army of his retainers go by to get their money: clerks and scriveners, chaplains and doctors, falconers and bowmen, valets and cooks, artists and workmen, the whole army of butlers and pantrymen, washerwomen and nurses, armourers and tailors, all the hangers-on who brought and took messages or came with a vague recommendation from some royal cousin or the abbot of some great monastic house: and with them the Masters of the Mint, the treasurers of war, the tax-gatherers and stewards and exchequer officers, who made their existence possible. With these men of the household, with faces as expressionless as eggs, walked a very different band of men of war: guards and mercenaries, officers drawn from the younger sons of good families, *condottieri* from Genoa or the south, men skilled in the machines of war from Picardy and Artois. The dukes of the royal house maintained a lesser but similar household, as did the greater feudal lords; and their example was imitated on a yet smaller scale by men of lesser estate.

As a consequence a new conception of a castle came to be held; it might still be a refuge and stronghold in time of danger, but its normal purpose was to house the family and the retainers of a wealthy man. Consequently new castles were built with more rooms, more decoration, more windows, and a greater approximation to town houses; similar additions were made to the formless masses of older strongholds; and machicolated towers and a separate donjon, often of older date, sufficed to give reassurance in time of peace and defence in time of war. Even the use of cannon, first employed in Flanders in 1341 and first used in France in 1346, modified the height and disposition of the fortifications of the enceinte but did nothing to check the increasing luxury of the castle itself.

That luxury soon represented a new balance in seigneurial expenditure. The careless generosity of the wanderer who has few possessions began to give place to a more settled economy; it has been noted that in the course of the fourteenth century the virtue of 'largesse' disappears from the conventional portrait of a hero of romance. A noble's money came to be spent not in general hospitality and general almsgiving but in private festival and in the purchase of luxuries to provide a background for a life of cultivated ease.

It is hard to re-create this background. Because the fourteenth-century castles were not built primarily for defence, they suffered more during long centuries of warfare than did the older fortified keeps; and because their *raison d'être* was pleasure they were modified later to meet the prevailing fashion as the fortress donjons never were. Little remains, for instance, of the Château de Beauté, the favourite residence of Charles V between 1370 and his death: the castle where he kept his famous Flemish organ, his best Paris tapestries, his great clock, his aviaries of nightingales, and his flocks of white doves.

At the same time as the new castles were being built, new luxuries were being introduced into their actual fabric. Painted glass began to be used for the windows. As early as 1299 Maître Othon, the glazier of Arras, furnished glass *peinte d'imagerie* for the castle of Hesdin.[1] The Hôtel de Conflans was between 1316 and 1319 equipped with glass not only in its chapel but also in its living-rooms. Their *voirre vigneté* came from the same man, Jean de Séez, who furnished the glass with *imagerie à tabernacles* for the chapel.[2] Armorial windows were used at the royal castles of Mantes and Vincennes soon after the middle of the century, and other houses had glass painted with birds and fantastic figures.[3] Sculpture, too, was used in decoration. In 1365 Charles V added a splendid staircase to the Louvre, of which Raymond du Temple was the architect.[4] The projecting turret that contained it was carved with statues under canopies, by a team of sculptors headed by Jean de Saint-Romain. The first floor was guarded by two statues of sergeants-at-arms. On the floor above were statues of the king and queen and their four sons; at the top stood figures of the Virgin and St. John. We may gain an idea of these sculptures from statues of Charles V (Fig. 146) and his wife, that still survive: works of impressive vitality and realism.[5]

The royal castle of Vincennes was rebuilt between 1336 and 1373. The donjon, the first part to be built, is square in plan, with round turrets at the angles.

---

[1] Richard, p. 298. It was sold by the square foot at twice the price of plain glass.   [2] Ibid., p. 303.

[3] Some fourteenth-century domestic glass of this kind has been reused in the windows of Saint-Père de Chartres.   [4] Sauval, ii. 23.

[5] These well-known statues, now in the Louvre, are generally said to come from the church of the Célestins. They are in fact from the portal of the chapel of the Quinze-Vingts.

The ground floor is occupied by kitchens. The great entrance is on the first floor: it leads to a central hall vaulted from a central pillar with round turret-rooms off it. The two upper floors are similar in plan; all have sculptured consoles and chimney-hoods with carved mouldings. The gate before the don-jon has its cornice adorned with similar mouldings, and has niches for statues over the door.

Sculpture soon began to spread all over the upper works and inner faces of the buildings, even if the lower floors of the outside walls remained plain in the interests of defence. King Charles VI and his brothers the Dukes of Berry and Orleans all built or rebuilt castles, which are known to us from surviving remains and from the exact pictures of them in their pristine beauty, which adorn the Calendar of the *Très Riches Heures* of the Duc de Berry.

The Louvre (Fig. 147) is depicted as seen from a window of the Hôtel de Nesle, Jean de Berry's favourite residence in Paris. It stands four-square behind its crenellated enceinte, with corner turrets and two engaged turrets in the centre of each wall. The plan is in the main defensive, but the sculptured cornice and the multiplicity of sloping roofs and little dormers and wind-vanes that crown it give a more modern air. Mehun-sur-Yèvre, built by Jean de Berry between 1367 and 1390 on an island, was far more richly decorated (Fig. 148). Its entrance was surmounted by the soaring edifice of the castle chapel, and its four solid towers were each topped by a hexagonal room as richly sculptured and traceried as a palace in a fairy tale. Only enough of the building remains, and that sadly decayed, to show that Pol de Limbourg, who illuminated the manuscript, was an exact artist. Saumur, a fortress of the older fashion, was lightened by crenellations crested with fleurs-de-lis and crocketed dormers. The ducal palace at Poitiers built by Jean de Berry on old foundations between 1386 and 1395 is represented in the manuscript as a simpler version of Mehun-sur-Yèvre, with a charming line of ornamental windows giving on to the courtyard. These have disappeared, but the great hall and the Tour Mau-bergeon remain. The hall, partly rebuilt under the supervision of Guy de Dammartin between 1384 and 1386, is chiefly remarkable for its end wall (Fig. 149). This combines into a single convincing whole a great triple fire-place surmounted by coats of arms held by angels, a balustraded gallery with spiral staircases at either end, and an extremely rich scheme of traceried windows. When it held its original colour, and served as background to the high table where the duke and his family were served with great pomp and circumstance, the effect must have been magnificent.

We can only see it in imagination. From the distant door of the great hall the dais and all upon it are a moving pattern of light and colour. The night sky turns the windows above the chimney-piece into a dun-coloured arabesque against a ground of deep and luminous blue. Screens shut out the three fires beneath from the back of the duke who sits at the high table; the rosy glow from them is answered by the yellower light of the torches that are held by men in striped liveries standing below the dais. The gold plate, so splendid in detail, is no more than a glitter for us; the abundant food, so delicately prepared, no more than a spicy smell. We do not understand the hierarchy of ministrants, men in parti-coloured livery, in stiff brocade, in furred cloth, with napkins over their shoulders or wands in their hands, ceremonially bearing cups or dishes or great golden knives; or the functions of the attendant clerics, two canons, a Dominican friar, and a Cistercian abbot, who wait with crossed hands till the lord shall deign to speak with them. But we can see the order and rhythm with which they circle, like planets round a sun, round a single focus; the long plain face, sallow and elegant under a fur cap, of the duke seated at the table; the man whose ancestry and inheritance has made him the cause and reason of this strange patch of wealth, abundance, and elaboration in a world of poverty and simpleness.

As it now stands, grey and empty, one of the most interesting features of the great hall at Poitiers is the beauty of the statues of Charles V and his wife Jeanne de Bourbon, and of Jean de Berry and his wife Jeanne d'Armagnac, that stand between the gables of the tracery, at a height at which they are hardly visible (Fig. 151). These are admirable examples of the current production of the court school of sculpture: elegant and accomplished in drapery, subtle in modelling, at once realistic and dignified in style. They draw inspiration from the same air as the lovers of the lyrics of courtoisie, and remain perfect examples of how exquisite an art a court can produce.[1]

The Tour Maubergeon at Poitiers, built between 1386 and 1395, is a further example of the courtly enrichment of feudal style. Its exterior still keeps a fortified air, though it has no defensive value; but it was crowned by twenty statues, representing its builder the Duke of Berry and his wife, and the Nine Preux and Nine Preuses of romantic chivalry.[2] The rooms within remain perfect examples of the royal private apartments of the time. The larger rooms in the central part (Fig. 152), with simply traceried windows and vaulted roofs, are intended as the frame for decorative hangings that have departed. They were once brightened by tiled floors brilliant with the arms and devices of the duke in green and gold on a white ground. Their interest lies in their simple elegance of proportion and in such details as the avoidance of shadow

[1] The fire-place was so much approved that Jean de Berry ordered Guy de Dammartin to build another of the same kind in the great hall of his palace at Bourges. In 1456 King René ordered for a building at Angers a chimney 'a trois jambages, en la forme de la cheminée d'un palais'. Another was built in the hall at Coucy.

[2] The nine worthies—three pagans, three Jews, and three Christians—are first found in Jacques de Longuyon's Les Vœux du Paon at the beginning of the fourteenth century. See Huizinga, p. 61.

by the skilled bevelling of jambs and mullions. The little hexagonal tower rooms that lead from them have their vaults resting on consoles carved with grotesques and figures of prophets.

The castle built by Louis, Duc d'Orléans at La Ferté-Milon between 1392 and 1407 (Fig. 153) shows a more defensive combination of fortification and ornament, since it was more dangerously situated. The rectangular donjon is defended by an outer building with three almond-shaped towers[1] joined by a curtain wall, with a monumental entrance from the drawbridge. There were originally eight towers, each having a statue of one of the Preuses in a niche. Over the gateway is a relief (Fig. 154) of the Assumption of the Virgin, that in the elegance of its draperies and in the heraldic and foliage decoration of its frame is characteristic of the court school of sculpture.[2] Here, too, the pictorial quality in the composition must have been greatly enhanced by its original colouring. Another castle of the duke's at Angoulême had sculptured consoles like those in his brother's castle at Poitiers; one of the rooms had them carved with comical musicians.[3] Pierrefonds, which he rebuilt between 1392 and his death in 1407, had eight towers each called after the Preux whose statue it bore,[4] like those at La Ferté-Milon.

Such decoration spread very gradually to the castles of the lesser men, whose estates did not lie in the comparative security of the royal domain and its apanages. The castle of Coucy had two halls added to it about 1387: a *Salle des neuf Preux* to the west and a *Salle des Preuses* to the north. Lavardin, rebuilt at the end of the century as a fortress with a triple enceinte forming three terraces, yet had its habitable rooms adorned with sculpture, chiefly heraldic in subject. Yet though a few small and elegant rooms might be built, perched like a nest on the formless trunk of some earlier castle, the chief consideration outside a few privileged castles was still defence. Even royalty could not forget it; the castle of the Duke of Burgundy at Nuits-sous-Ravières, built during the English invasion of 1359, was remarkable for its four great octagonal towers, each as strong as a donjon.

Lesser lords in their turn tried to combine the claims of defence, comfort, and beauty in a just proportion. Vitré in Brittany, for instance, has five towers and a fortified *châtelet* at the gateway. The entrance-door has corbels carved

[1] The almond-shaped plan was defensive, and is found as early as the thirteenth century at Château-Gaillard and La Roche-Guyon. The towers of the enceinte of Loches are also almond-shaped, as is the tower at Bonneval, Haute-Vienne.

[2] It may be compared with Cluny Museum, No. 247, a relief of the Coronation of the Virgin from the convent of Argenteuil, and with the relief from the Abbaye du Trésor now in the church of Écouis. A door of the Louvre was carved *c.* 1360–70 with the Virgin and nine Angels, by Jean de Saint-Romain; he may have been the sculptor employed at La Ferté-Milon.

[3] A bagpiper and a flautist survive.

[4] These were described by Antoine Astesan in 1451; Leroux de Lincy and Tisserand, p. 560.

with lions and the machicolations are elegantly cusped. Combourg (Fig. 155) included an earlier tower in an impressive quadrangular fortress that reserved decoration for the inner quadrangle.[1] The great donjon of Polignac, rebuilt by Randon Armand X, Vicomte de Polignac between 1385 and 1421, has arcaded machicolations, pointed trilobed windows, and a decorated staircase, and fine chimneys on all three floors. Exceptionally such castles had a chimney-piece as delicately sculptured as that at Poitiers. The museum of Graville-le-Havre preserves a statue of the early fifteenth century that probably comes from one. It merits comparison with those of Poitiers (Fig. 156): a lady lovely yet strongly characterized, she gains a ghostly realism from the traces of colour that remain in the golden hair, flesh-coloured face, red dress, and blue-green surcoat.

Even in a house that was also a fortress life could be at once agreeable and luxurious. The standard-bearer of Pero Niño, a Spanish knight who paid a visit in 1405 to Renaud de Trie, Admiral of France, at his castle of Sérifontaine in Normandy, has left an account of the daily round there that gives life to the crumbling ruins of to-day.[2] The Admiral

'dwelt in a house, plain and strong, arranged and equipped as if it had been in the city of Paris. He had there with him his squires and his servants for every kind of office, as befits such a lord. In this house was a very fair chapel, where Mass was said every day; and minstrels and trumpeters who sounded their instruments marvellously. A river flowed before the house, on the banks of which were orchards and gracious gardens. . . . This knight had for wife the most beautiful lady then in France. . . . She had her own noble dwelling apart from that of the Admiral: a drawbridge crossed from one to the other and both were within the rampart. The furnishings of this dwelling were so many and of so outlandish a sort, that it would be long to tell them. . . .

'I will recount to you the order and rule that the lady followed. In the morning, after she had risen, the lady went with her damsels to a grove, which was near there, each with her Book of Hours and her rosary. They seated themselves each apart from the other and said their Hours, and spoke not until they had finished prayers. There-after, picking flowers and violets as they went, they came back to the Castle and went to the Chapel where they heard a Low Mass. Coming out thence, they took a plate of silver on which were chickens, larks, and other birds roasted and ate, and left as much as they would, and then they were given wine. . . . That done, Madam rode with her ladies on the best harnessed and finest hackneys that could be found, and with her rode any knights and gentlemen who might happen to be there; and they rode for some time in the country, making chaplets of flowers. . . . In like manner they came back to the Castle at the hour of dinner, dismounted and came into the hall, where they found the table laid. The Admiral and my Lady . . . took their

[1] Now much changed. The castle was finished c. 1420.
[2] See Gutierre Diaz de Gamez, *The Unconquered Knight*, trans. Joan Evans, 1928, p. 135.

places at the high table, and the steward presided over the other table and caused
a knight or squire to sit beside each lady. . . . During the repast there were players,
making pleasant music upon divers instruments. Grace said, and the tables removed,
the minstrels came in, and my Lady danced with Pero Niño, and each of his gentlemen with a lady. This dance lasted for an hour. When it was ended . . . they brought
in spices, served wine, and everyone went to his siesta. The captain Pero Niño withdrew to his chamber in my Lady's house, which was most fairly furnished and called
the tower room. After the siesta they mounted their horses and the pages came up
with the falcons. . . . When they had finished beating the valley, my Lady and all
the people with her dismounted in a meadow; there fowls, cold partridges and fruit
were brought to them and all ate and drank and made chaplets of greenery; then
singing most delightful songs, they went back to the castle. . . . They ate late and afterwards my Lady went to seek distraction afoot in the country and they played bowls
until night fell, and thereafter went back to the hall by torch-light; and then came
the minstrels. They danced far into the night; then, after fruits and wine had been
served, they took their leave and went to bed.'

Such was life in a castle in 1405, with a constant refrain, 'then came the
minstrels'. But then, instead of minstrels, came the armies of England, and what
the chronicler calls 'dear delights and abundance in all things' came to an end.
In 1433 Jean Juvenal des Ursins wrote 'toute la beauté de France s'en est alée
et partie, et sont fais les princes aussi esbahis comme moustons qui ne trouvent
point de pasture'.[1]

Such castles as were built, or rebuilt after the English had destroyed them,
spoke of war. Charles VII claimed control of all castles; none could be repaired
or built without his leave, and his intention was necessarily to fortify his
diminished frontiers. Vaillac, with its six machicolated towers; Saint-Saturnin,
with its quadrangular crenellated donjon; Roquetaillade, with its rectangular
castle defended by six highly fortified towers; Murols, with its fortified enceinte, may stand as types of defensive castles built after the disasters of Agin-
court and the Treaty of Troyes: Montbrun, with its ancient donjon newly
crenellated and defended by four great towers linked by curtain walls, for those
fortified anew.

Even after the final French victory in 1453, which left the English holding
nothing but Calais and the Channel Islands, such severity was only gradually
mitigated. Ternay, a quadrilateral defended by towers at the angles, has elegant
gables on to the courtyard; Flaghac, with a moat, towers at each angle, and a
chemin de ronde behind its machicolations, has a sculptured doorway; Château-
neuf, begun by Philippe Pot in 1457, has an elegant lodging for its master
and a little pleasure-pavilion within its machicolated walls; Lassay, rebuilt in
the same year, is yet more of a fortress with its eight towers linked by a

[1] Denifle, 1511.

machicolated wall and a barbican on its weakest side. The second castle at
Langeais, built by Jean Bourré about 1460, is entirely defensive except for
ornamental turrets and wider windows in the inner courtyard.

Already, however, the tradition of the town house had been revived
and enriched. We know comparatively little of the royal Hôtel Saint-Pol
at Paris, begun about 1364, but it seems to have been a town house built
round a courtyard in an irregular fashion.[1] It may have served as a model
for the most famous house of the fifteenth century, the Hôtel Jacques Cœur
at Bourges.

The most powerful man at the Court of Charles VII was no great noble, but
a merchant, Jacques Cœur by name, the son of a fur-seller of Bourges. In 1432
he was a modest merchant of the Frankish Khan at Aleppo: a crusader of commerce who had gone to the Levant to try to gain some of the Eastern trade that
had become a monopoly of the Venetians and the Genoese. In little more than
ten years he became a great trader with his 'galées fleurdelysées dans les mers
estranges'. He was one of the great financial forces in France: as a merchant,
owning mines and dye-works and paper-works, exporting French wine and
importing all the treasures of the East, and as the financier of the king, enabling
him once more to establish his realm upon a sound footing.

He began to build himself a house in Bourges in 1443; when René d'Anjou
visited the city in 1453 the house was finished.[2] It remains as a perfect example
of the mansion of a rich man in the middle of the fifteenth century. It is, in fact,
a town castle; the exterior walls, based on the Gallo-Roman city walls, are plain
and defensible, and include a strong hexagonal donjon. The entrance, on the
street side away from the city wall, is by a great door under a canopy that
once held a statue of Charles VII, between two sham windows from which a
sculptured man and woman look out to see what is passing in the street. The
façade is adorned with hearts and shells, in allusion to Jacques Cœur's name
and to his patron St. James, and with his device: A VAILLANS COEURS RIENS
IMPOSSIBLE.

Within the courtyard (Fig. 157) we have stepped into a new age. The shallow
building that protects the courtyard from the street has a gallery on the ground
floor, a kind of secular cloister, with a frieze sculptured like the border of a
manuscript with foliage, lizards, snails, and dogs. The chief features of the
courtyard are three polygonal staircase turrets. That in the centre, leading to
the living-rooms of the house, is sculptured with emblems of the interests of its
master. The double doorway is inscribed DE MA ♥♥ JOIE and FAIRE. DIRE.
TAIRE. Above the doors are two panels, each carved with three trees: one with

---

[1] See F. M. Graves, p. 6.

[2] The architects are unknown; the work was directed by two burgesses of Bourges, and a factor
of Jacques Cœur's. Cong. arch., 1931, p. 56.

the palm, the date, and the orange of the East,[1] the other with trees of the temperate North. Between them grow the herbs of Cœur's dye-works. On the upper stages of the tower figures are carved in quatrefoils: a peasant and a lord, men beating hemp with clubs, men fulling cloth, and women spinning: symbols of the riches of Berri and of the man who profited by them. The tower is crowned by an elegant arcade and a balustrade of hearts and shells.

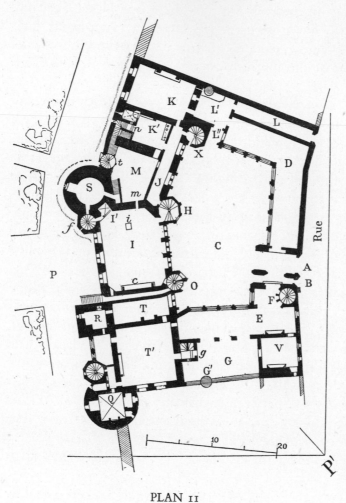

The right-hand turret leads to the kitchen and offices, and is plainer than the others. The one to the left (Fig. 158) leads to the chapel. The staircase is entered by a kind of inner porch, with elegant arcading. One door has its tympanum carved with such figures as might be found at the entrance of a church: a beggar, a bell-ringer, and a priest with an aspergil. The door that leads to the sacristy has a man making ready an altar for Mass, another unfolding a maniple, and a third with a rosary. The third door, leading directly to the stairs, has three ladies going to service attended by their page. These half-secular subjects are fittingly reserved for the entry: the chapel door itself is sculptured with the Annunciation.

PLAN II

Hôtel Jaques Cœur, Bourges. Begun 1443

The rooms of the house are, by medieval standards, surprisingly numerous. The palace of Jean de Berry at Bourges had only five large rooms: Jacques

---

[1] It is worth noting that these three trees are the only trace of oriental influence on the decoration of the house, though Jacques Cœur had lived for some time in the East and always traded with it.

Cœur's has fourteen.[1] The duke's rooms were very large—the largest was a hundred and sixty-four feet by nearly fifty-six—and led out of each other; Jacques Cœur's were much smaller—the largest barely fifty-one feet long—and were linked by stairs and passages.

This room, the long gallery, has a keeled roof,[2] walls left plain for tapestries, and two fire-places: one is carved like a window,[3] with four women looking out and a castle battlement above, with soldiers drawing cross-bows and arbalests behind the crenellations, while the other is carved to represent three windows, each of which frames a man and woman, probably portrait statues; one pair play chess,[4] the others take fruit from a basket. Above these windows is a series of grotesques: peasants jousting on donkeys, blowing trumpets, beating one another, and setting out on a journey. One of the windows had the arms of Jacques Cœur—azure on a fess or three cockle-shells sable between three hearts gules—set in a wreath of orange-flowers and fruit, encircled by a border of his hearts and of his master's badge of feathers. Above was a figure with donkey's ears and the motto 'Taire', and another with a padlocked mouth and the inscription: 'En bouche close n'entre mouche.'[5] The dining-hall originally had windows with figures of the twelve peers of France, the nine Preux, and the nine Preuses.[6] Another room is decorated with representations of Jacques Cœur's famous galleys (Fig. 159). One is carved over the chimney-piece, another over the door, and another, with carved guard-rails and a great single sail, a pennon of his device, and a cargo of bales, was painted on the window, ploughing through a stormy sea to an Eastern port.[7]

The donjon, with no less than six floors, contains the strong room of the merchant, with a fortified door and an immense lock. Its vault has a console most delicately carved with a scene from the romance of Tristan and Yseult, with King Mark watching them reflected in the fountain.

The pride of Jacques Cœur went before a fall: betrayed by his friends, condemned by his master, he was sent into exile after three years' imprisonment. The Pope alone would receive him, and he died fighting at the head of the papal fleet against the infidels of Chios. Yet he left a permanent mark not only on the financial system of France but also on its domestic architecture.

Jacques Cœur's house, indeed, as the archetype of a rich man's house of which the prime intention was habitation rather than defence, influenced not only the

[1] The town house at Rouen of Pierre Sureau, Receveur-Général of Normandy, who died in 1435, had as many as nineteen rooms, large and small.

[2] Cf. the even finer keel-shaped roof of the same date at the Château de Sully, Loiret.

[3] Cf. a chimney-piece in the Salle des Gardes of the Ducal Palace at Dijon.

[4] Cf. the couple playing chess on a window of 1430–40 from the Hôtel de la Basée at Villefranche-sur-Saône, now at the Château de Sassangy.

[5] Palliser, *Historical Devices, Badges and War-cries*, p. 72.

[6] *Cong. arch.*, 1931, p. 75.   [7] Now in the Bourges Museum.

other fine town houses of the period but also the castles of the country-side. The castle of Dunois the Bastard of Orleans at Châteaudun has a staircase as rich as that at Bourges; with an open arcade below, a magnificent clerestory on the first floor, and high crocketed gables enriched with sculpture above. Inside the turret, the angles formed by the spiral staircase are filled by stone benches with pierced stone brackets with lanterns above them to give light at night. At Lavardin a similar staircase, built by Jean VIII de Bourbon, has a similar lantern crowned by three masks through whose open mouths the lamp-smoke could escape. Such staircases in decorated turrets continued to be the chief ornamental feature in fine French houses. Luynes, for example, still has its outer walls purely defensive, but about 1465 the inner courtyard was rebuilt with decoration in brick and stone, mullioned windows, elaborate crocketed dormers, and a hexagonal stair-turret in the new style.

Decorative sculpture spread into every corner of the building. When Jean Gendrot, an architect who had worked for René of Anjou, designed the castle of Le Lude in 1468 for Jean de Daillon, Chamberlain of Louis XI, he set a lovely angel (Fig. 160) on the highest point to serve as a wind-vane. The figure can never have been closely seen, yet the head is as subtle in its modelling as the statues of the chimney-piece at Poitiers.

The next stage in the development of French domestic architecture was the creation of the manor-house. Brunetto Latino declared in his *Livre dou Trésor* that the French loved 'maisons grandes et planières et paintes, et chambres lées, pour avoir joie et délit sans noise et sans guerre'. For long years the fear of enemies had confined them within narrow walls. Now parts of France gradually became peaceful enough to make another way of living possible.

The cautious and crafty diplomacy of Louis XI might bring war on the frontiers, but it brought peace to central France. When the king built a house for himself at Plessis-lez-Tours after he bought the estate in 1463, the actual house was built with all its sides as elegantly decorated in stone and brick as an inner courtyard customarily was, and all its windows mullioned. A house of this type, whatever its exterior enceinte might be, was generally characterized by the height of its proportions and the compactness of its plan. The scheme of a donjon and towers, linked by walls, was given up in favour of a single building. This single building naturally retained some elements of fortification, but they were integrated into the plan. At Chevenon, for example, the façade is machicolated, there are towers at the angles and lesser turrets on either side the gateway; but the whole, tall and small, follows the type of the manor rather than of the castle. Jumilhac-le-Grand is another such manor-castle, curiously romantic in its height and in the variety of the turrets and dormers of its skyline. Cherveux (Fig. 161) has a fortified entrance that is half a donjon, but the rest of the building is rather manor than castle. The manor of Courtangis in the

Perche (Fig. 162) combines the corbelled corner turrets called *échauguettes*
with crocketed gables and a polygonal stair-turret.[1]

The tradition of the castle, however, continued for greater buildings and for
those in situations where defence was still a pressing need. At Frazé the gate-
house built by Florentin Girard, Seigneur de Brantôme, about 1486 (Fig. 163)
is in the old tradition, with drawbridge, portcullis, machicolations, and crenellations; only the three-mullioned windows over the entrance are an innovation.
Le Plessis-Bourré, built between 1468 and 1473 by Jean Bourré, Secrétaire des
Finances of Louis XI, is defended by wide moats of running water crossed by
a bridge seven arches long. The building is on the old plan of a great quadrilateral, with massive towers at the angles and machicolations and a *chemin de
ronde* all round the outside. The courtyard is rather less severe, but the whole is
definitely a place of defence. Other officials of Louis XI built castles that were
equally defensive in plan. Fougères-sur-Bièvre, built by his treasurer Pierre de
Refuge, has an entrance over a drawbridge between two turrets, and machicolated towers at the angles. The doors of the courtyard, however, are beautifully carved with St. Michael and angels in honour of his membership of the
Ordre de St. Michel. The castle of Isle-sur-Arnon, built by Jean Dumas,
Louis XI's counsellor and chamberlain, is a great quadrilateral with a fortified
tower at the entrance.

Elsewhere the defensive tradition is yet more evident. At Oudon an octagonal
donjon was built late in the fifteenth century, of schist with a framing of white
stone, as a rectangle with the angles cut off, with windows only in these angles;
while Bonaguil in the Agenais was rebuilt as late as 1488 as a fortress, with the
only windows of any size on an inner courtyard.

Yet the future lay with the house rather than the castle, and very gradually
the domestic tradition became dominant. Martainville (Fig. 164), built by the
Rouen bourgeois Le Pelletier, may stand for the new tradition. Though it still
has towers at the angles, three of them are windowed; only one remains as a
place of defence in emergency.[2] The fosses with brick walls and low towers
that divide it from the garden are as much decorative as defensive. The main
building is elegant with mullioned windows and sculptured dormers; and over
the great door a graceful oriel juts out. Le Clos-Lucé, near Amboise, built about
1490 by Étienne de Loup, maître d'hôtel to Louis XI, is equally cheerful and
domestic. Like Martainville it is built of stone and brick; its graceful staircase-
turret, small chapel, and pointed dormers are less pretentious than the towers
and oriel of Martainville, but no less delightful. Gradually a compromise was

---

[1] Other manor-houses in the district—e.g. Courboyer and La Lubinière—show the same characteristics.

[2] Cf. Saragosse, Cher, which has corbelled turrets at three corners and a heavy round tower at
the fourth.

reached by which even a great castle could share in this gaiety. The Château du Moulin[1] built between 1480 and 1502 by Philippe du Moulin, on the plans of Jacques de Persigny, is a manor built of brick in lozenge patterns of black and red, with stone framing;[2] but it is approached by a drawbridge, is defended by wide moats, and is guarded by a fortified gateway that seems disproportionately heavy for the building it guards. At Argy a vast square donjon and a thirteenth-century round tower already existed when at the end of the fifteenth century Charles de Brilhac began to build new domestic quarters. The elegant arcaded galleries that surround the courtyard are wholly French in detail and in line, but the idea is a southern one. The long tradition of French castle-building was far from being exhausted, but in its artistic aspect it was beginning to be influenced by Italy. Yet between 1490 and 1505 the court façade of Josselin could be built (Fig. 165) in pure Flamboyant style; its elaborate dormers, its sculptured balustrades and gargoyles, its ogival doorways, and its heraldic decoration combine to make it a perfect type of French domestic architecture of the end of the fifteenth century.

2. FEUDAL ICONOGRAPHY

Feudal society had to create its own literature, its own iconography, and its own civilization. At the beginning of the eleventh century literature was still confined to the cloister: by the end, in the heroic years round 1100, the new genre of the *Chanson de Geste* was in process of creation: epic poems to be sung by minstrels in the crowded halls of castles, lauding the feudal virtues of courage and loyalty, and full of battles for the delight of those whose main business was fighting. Some slight reflection of these songs may be found in ecclesiastical imagery; none as yet in the donjons and halls of the knights.

Then the ladies' chamber above the hall or in one of the lesser towers became a centre of living. There a new civilization was created, personal, romantic, decorative, and secular, such as had not been witnessed in France since the barbarians invaded the villas of Roman Gaul. For the first time for centuries there grew up within the framework of a Christian civilization a lay culture not primarily concerned with religion, owning enough wealth, leisure, and freedom from care to create a decorative framework for its way of living. Its influence on both literature and art is incalculable, for with it traditions that still endure had their beginning. The lyrics, novels, and biographies of modern times, the adornment of our houses, the flowers of our gardens, our whole conception of humane living, owe their existence to the courtly life of thirteenth-century France.

[1] Half-way between Blois and Romorantin.
[2] Cf. the castle of Glin built by Anne de Beaujeu in 1494. A rather similar plan occurs at Bienassis with a *corps de logis* flanked by two small towers and a larger for defence, all surrounded by a crenellated wall and a wide moat.

It was for the ladies' chamber that the characteristic literary genres that appeared in the second half of the twelfth century were created: *chansons de toile*, *pastourelles*, courtly lyrics and romances. The first famous troubadour was Count Guillaume IX of Poitiers, a feudal noble;[1] his granddaughter Eleanor of Aquitaine, her daughters Marie, Countess of Champagne, and Alix, Countess of Blois, led the train of noble ladies who gave the poets their protection and fostered the cult of courtly love.

Even when the matter of a romance was classical, feminine influence helped to turn it into something altogether of the Middle Ages. Subjects from such romances figure in medieval art, but not for some generations after the romances were written. At first, indeed, they only appeared in odd conjunction with subjects drawn from ecclesiastical imagery. Baudri de Bourgueil says that he saw in the rooms of Adela, wife of Stephen of Blois, a great tapestry on which scenes from the Bible were set side by side with Jupiter and Saturn, episodes of the Trojan Wars, and scenes from the *Metamorphoses*.

In the late twelfth and early thirteenth centuries it was the knights and ladies, the troubadours and minstrels, who were represented in art, rather than the subject of their lays. A secular coffer of wood,[2] covered with parchment painted rather in the style of Limoges enamels, is adorned with figures of a dancer and a fiddler, a knight in his tent, another who has descended from his horse to greet a lady; and minstrels and dancers appear on some of the little basins of gilt and enamelled copper that knights used as finger-bowls. Similar subjects may be found on jewels at a rather later date (Fig. 166 A). Exceptionally the actual songs were used in decoration. Adenez himself, in the romance of *Cléomadès* that he presented to Mahaut d'Artois, describes a bed-tester:

> De soie est ouvrez par maistrie
> D'uevre cointe, noble et jolie,
> Par tout avoit chançons escrites,
> Les meillours et les plus eslites.

Yet outside the ladies' bower the castle was the abode of men. The chief inspiration of the thirteenth-century secular decoration was heraldic. About 1180 a closed helm was adopted for battle, making it impossible to recognize the wearer; consequently a distinguishing token on the shield, that had already been adopted by some lords, became a general necessity. From the shield the use of this personal device spread everywhere: by 1230 to clothes, both for men and women, lords and their servants; to hangings, and to every field of decoration. Even as late as the middle of the fourteenth century hangings powdered with heraldic devices were common in every castle. King John between 1350

---

[1] Lambert d'Ardres says that Baudouin II, Comte de Guines (1169–1206), was so good a poet that he might have rivalled the most famous minstrels both in *chansons de geste* and *romans d'aventure*. Langlois, *La Vie en France*, Romans, p. xiv.   [2] Now in the treasury of Vannes Cathedral.

and 1364 acquired more than two hundred such tapestries, as well as a set of hangings of blue velvet embroidered with 8,544 fleurs-de-lis;[1] and Girart d'Orléans, his painter, had in 1352 to devote much time to painting the velvet seats of chairs with the royal fleurs-de-lis.[2]

Besides such conventional patterns, heraldry inspired even in the thirteenth century many designs of a more interesting kind. The craftsman soon paints, weaves,

> forge et entaille
> Chevaliers armés en bataille,
> Sur beaux destriers trestous couverts
> D'armes indes, jaunes ou verts. . . .[3]

A pricket candlestick of about 1270 is enamelled with four knights bearing shields mounted on horses, with housings embroidered with the arms of Charles d'Anjou, King of Sicily and lord of Dammartin, Dreux-Bretagne, and Burgundy, and two men on foot each wearing an armorial tunic and holding two banners with the arms of the knights. The small enamelled hand-basins used by lords at table often had similar themes of decoration; one described in the inventory of the Dauphin's plate in 1347 had shields of the Order of St. John of Jerusalem and figures of two mounted knights, one bearing the same shield and the other one charged with a scorpion.[4] Sometimes a number of heraldic shields were combined into a diaper. A Limoges casket, probably made for William of Valence, Earl of Pembroke, between 1290 and 1296 (Fig. 166 B), has a diaper of the arms of Valence, England, Dreux, Angoulême, Brabant, and Lacy, with which his family was allied; the 'cassette de Saint Louis', given with the hair-cloths of the sainted king, at the time of his canonization in 1297, to the abbey of Notre-Dame-du-Lys by Philippe le Bel,[5] has shields of no less than twenty-three bearings, combined with eight medallions of animals in relief. It may be compared with a casket of about 1300 enamelled with the arms of France and England and grotesque figures, which in the rest of its decoration reflects the spirit of the *roman courtois*. On the lid are two pairs of lovers: a young man with a falcon on his wrist lays his arm across the shoulders of a girl, and another gives his sweetheart a ring. Round the rim is the inscription:

> Dosse Dame ie vous aym léalmant
> Por dié vos prie que ne n'obblie mie.
> Vet si mon cors a vos comandemens
> Sans mauvesté et sans nulle folie.[6]

---

[1] Guiffrey, p. 16.

[2] Laborde, 199. The hangings were often worked by men; the accounts of Mahaut d'Artois give the name of Jean de Savoie, bourgeois de Paris, as 'ouvrier d'armoierie, de broudure et de keute pointerie'. Richard, p. 211.   [3] *Roman de la Rose*, before 1318, l. 1705.

[4] Laborde, *Glossaire*, p. 151, s.v. 'bacins à laver'.   [5] See Viollet-le-Duc, p. 81, s.v. 'coffret'.

[6] Cf. a purse that once belonged to Thibaut de Champagne, now in the treasury of Troyes Cathedral.

Such scanty remains are all that we have from which to reconstruct the decoration of castles in the thirteenth century. Yet the manufacture of their furnishings was already organized on a scale that showed its growing importance. The carvers and painters of Paris were already organized into guilds, demanding from eight to ten years' apprenticeship when Étienne Boileau codified the statutes in 1268. The *Livre de la Taille* shows a very considerable number of craftsmen paying taxes in Paris in 1292: twenty-four scribes, thirteen illuminators, twenty-five carvers of images, thirty-three painters, five brooch-makers, five enamellers, fourteen makers of rosaries, two metal-founders, twenty-four tapestry-makers, and a hundred and sixteen goldsmiths, as well as more than two hundred weavers. The age of luxury was approaching when a new wealth of ornament was to invade the castles of France.

3. MANUSCRIPT ILLUMINATION

We know most of the castles of the Middle Ages as roofless ruins; the few that survive intact are grey as ghosts; and it is harder to endue them in our minds with their pristine colour and their original abundance of hangings and wall-paintings than it is to restore a mediaeval cathedral to its ancient splendour. The walls, flat and bare for some nine or ten feet from the ground, give an impression of austerity; not until we have painted them with brilliant colours or hung them with no less brilliant tapestries can we see the rooms as they were meant to be.

The development of this secular wall-painting was conditioned and paralleled by the development of a school of lay illuminators, for it had the same dependence on illuminated manuscripts as monastic art had had round about 1100. Before the thirteenth century it is hard to find a single illuminated manuscript that can certainly be attributed to a lay workshop; after that date the preponderance of such workshops is so great that the monastic scriptoria are altogether overshadowed.[1] It was in these workshops that the foundations of feudal art were laid.

The shift from monastic to lay ateliers was accompanied, and to some extent caused, by a like shift in literature. The romances, *fabliaus*, *chansons de geste*, chronicles, and encyclopaedias belonged to the castles as naturally as the earlier Latin works had pertained to the monasteries. As a consequence of the creation of this new literature, fresh subjects had to be illustrated and a secular

It is embroidered with Love, figured in angelic guise, looking at a sleeping girl, and with two ladies working with a saw upon a heart set upon an altar.

[1] The earliest signature of a lay painter known occurs in Bibl. Nat. franç. 412, a manuscript of 1285:

> Henris ot non l'enlumineur
> Dex le gardie de deshonneur
> Si fu fais l'an M.C.C.IIII^{xx}et V.

N

iconography created. The head of a workroom often wrote in indications to the illuminator, when the subject was not a traditional one, either very lightly so that his instructions could be erased, or right at the bottom of the page so that the binder would cut them away. Some have been preserved that show the process.[1] Such instructions were naturally more frequent when the book was unfamiliar. When Thomas de Maubeuge, who lived in the rue neuve Notre-Dame, copied the Chronicles of France in 1318[2] he had to give such directions to the painter as: 'Comment .j. roys est en biere et grant luminaire entour et grant plenté de dames et de chevalier et de clergie' and leave it to him to make a clear and harmonious composition. The original manuscript of Gilles li Muisis[3] has such brief pencilled instructions to the illuminator as '.i. pape .i. abé par devant'. Elsewhere the instructions were long and minute. A manuscript of *La Dame à la Licorne* of the middle of the fourteenth century[4] tells the illuminator: 'Chi endroit faites une dame tenant .j. miroir seant et une licorne derriere li et .j. chevalier seant devant la dame, escrisant sur son genouil. Asiete li chevaliers sur une mote de terre. Et y ait plusieurs arbres et plusieurs oiseles sur les arbres et une fontaine yssant de la mote de terre.' Sometimes the head of the atelier would himself design a scheme. A manuscript of the *Pèlerinage de la vie humaine*[5] copied in the workshop of Oudin de Carvanay in 1393 has in one place the instruction to Pierre Remiet the illuminator: 'Remiet ne faites rien cy car je y ferai une figure qui y doit estre.'

At first the style of such illuminators was influenced by other arts. In the time of Saint Louis a scheme of circular medallions like those used in stained glass was in fashion, until it was superseded towards the end of his reign by a wave of architectural influence. Tabernacles, pinnacles, pierced balustrades, and tracery appear as the background even to scenes that take place out of doors. Then as the lay illuminators of manuscripts became more highly skilled their art became more independent, and followed that way of realism[6] that must always be a primrose path to a painter in water-colours: a realism that showed itself not only in the naturalistic grotesques that make the charm of such manuscripts as the poems of Robert de Blois[7] and the *Romance of Alexander*[8] but also in a new richness of colour, in the introduction of landscape backgrounds and the expression of a new depth of sentiment.

In the early Middle Ages, in a literature and an art that was religious and symbolical, men had sought eternal and unchanging verities. In the fourteenth

[1] See H. Martin, 'Les Esquisses des miniatures', in *Rev. arch.*, 4th ser., iv, 1904, p. 17.
[2] Bibl. Nat. franç. 10132; Berger et Durrieu, p. 16.   [3] Dyson Perrins MS. 36, fol. 110b.
[4] Bibl. Nat. franç. 12562; Berger et Durrieu, p. 22.   [5] Bibl. Nat. franç. 823; ibid., p. 26.
[6] Comte Durrieu has suggested that Charles V had a positive and personal taste for realistic art. Michel, iii. 112. The change is most marked in the reign of Charles VI, 1380–1416.
[7] Arsenal 5201, end thirteenth century. H. Martin, *Min. franç.*, fig. xxix.
[8] Bodleian 264. The illuminator Jehans de Grise finished his work in April 1344.

century men were conscious, instead, of the beauty of change. They were peculiarly sensitive to things that were lovely because they were not lasting: to flowers that fade, and to moments that cannot endure. They responded to the charm of spring mornings and summer evenings and autumn sunsets, to moments of heightened physical sensibility, when the hound leaps on the quarry and the falcon is loosed from the wrist, when lovers ride together through the woods or read poetry to one another in the orchard. At times they even attempted, in art as in literature, to perpetuate the moments when the exquisite ordinariness of things—the passers-by in the street and the women selling fruit in the market—seem to have a transcendental significance that makes them subjects for eternal art. It is this poetic naturalism expressed first in poetry, then in the manuscript illuminations to poems, and then in the manifold decorations of castles, that sets the note for the imagery of ornament in the later Middle Ages.

The romantic note in literature was loudly struck at the Court of René of Anjou, and in the illustrations of certain of his manuscripts it received visible expression. In particular a manuscript of his romance of *Le Cœur d'Amour épris*[1] (Fig. 167), in the stress it lays on passing effects of light, in the use it makes of subtle colours far removed from the heraldic tinctures of the mediaeval palette, in the choice of composition and of scene, may stand as the beginning of a truly modern art.

4. WALL-PAINTINGS

Already in the thirteenth century the walls of castles were being painted in a style like that of their owners' books. At first, indeed, the imitation was so close as to include the text as well as the illustration. In 1235 the poet Thibaut de Champagne had the songs which he had made with Gaston Brulé painted on the walls of his halls at Provins and Troyes,[2] and early in the fourteenth century all the words and some illustrations of *Le Jeu de Robin and Marion*, written by a *trouvère* patronized by the house of Artois, were painted in the 'Salle aux chansons' of their castle of Hesdin.[3]

Painting, however, was already beginning to be a lay art apart from the illustrations of books. The Paris tax-book for 1292[4] records the existence of a colony of four painters in the rue Bertin Porée and of twenty-nine in other

[1] Imperial Library, Vienna, MS. 474. E. Pognon, in his edition of René d'Anjou's 'Traité de la forme et devis d'un tournoi', *Verve, Revue historique et littéraire*, iv, 1946, says that the sketches for this (B.N. franç. 2695) are by the same artist.

[2] Laborde, *Glossaire,* p. 347, s.v. 'inscriptions décoratives'. Occasionally verses were used even to decorate dresses; in 1379 Louis d'Anjou had a belt of gold woven with a virelay (Moranvillé, p. 585) beginning 'Se par fausse trayson', and in 1404 Charles d'Orléans had a dress with the sleeves sewn with pearls with the words and music of the song 'Madame je suis plus joyeux'. Laborde, iii. 267.

[3] Richard, p. 324. This, the earliest light opera, was first performed for the French Court at Naples at Christmas, 1283.   [4] *Livre de la Taille,* Renaux, p. 25.

parts of the city,[1] apart from thirteen illuminators of books. Six years later Philippe le Bel sent his painter Étienne d'Auxerre to Rome, and by 1304 had three Italian painters in his service.[2] Their work, however, seems to have had little influence on the current style of painting, which remained as French as that of illumination.

The subjects of the paintings on the walls of castles were often in direct relation with chronicles[3] and other books in lordly libraries. The Palais du Séjour at Étampes has a wall-painting of the beginning of the fourteenth century representing the donation of the barony of Étampes to Louis d'Évreux by Philippe le Bel in 1307,[4] that must surely have been based on an illustration in a family chronicle. In 1349 the Duke of Normandy wrote to his treasurer: 'Envoiez nous tantost a Lery le meilleur peintre de Paris et III ou IIII paintres avecques li, garniz de coleurs pour ouvrer à destrampe, quar nous voulons fair paindre hastivement chambre en nostre chastel du Val de Ruel.' Jean Coste was sent and did the work, taking his main subjects from a book the duke lent him of the Life of Caesar. Lesser rooms were painted with scenes of the chase, probably derived from a hunting-treatise.[5]

Charles V had a fine library in one of the towers of the Louvre that, besides law and theology, science and history, included innumerable romances. It must have been from this source that his painters drew inspiration for the 'Chambre de Charlemagne', 'Chambre de Matabrune', and 'Salle de Thésée' in his Hôtel Saint-Pol. The long gallery, painted in 1335, reflected in its turn the love of woods and forests, orchards and gardens, that was a natural part of feudal life. It represented a great wood, interspersed with apple, pear, cherry, and plum trees, with lilies and roses and other flowers growing beneath.

Such work has no exact parallel in manuscript decoration, though it is in obvious relation with the wooded backgrounds of the later fourteenth-century book illustrations. Already artists were capable of independent creation. Sometimes they worked straight on the wall. At Landes[6] is a figure of an archer, doubtless part of a picture of the legend of St. Hubert or St. Giles. Time has lightened the background to show two preliminary attempts before the complicated foreshortening of the attitude finally represented was achieved.

The accounts of Mahaut, Comtesse d'Artois, show all the kinds of painting used in castles of the early fourteenth century. The ceilings were painted blue or green and stuck with metal stars, usually gilt or silvered; the vaulting-ribs,

---

[1] Géraux, p. 506.   [2] Poëte, p. 6.

[3] For an interesting instance of the application of such a theme to a hospital given by a layman see P. Lauer, 'Un Projet de décoration murale inspiré du *Credo* de Joinville', in *Mon. Piot*, xvi. 61. The drawings there published are interesting as showing the kind of sketch that formed the transitional stage between manuscript illumination and wall-painting.   [4] Lemoisne, p. 13.

[5] Or from the decorative borders of such a manuscript as Bodleian Douce 336, a *Mireur du Monde* decorated with all the stages of a stag-hunt.   [6] Charente-Maritime.

rafters, and wainscot were painted in varied and brilliant hues. The walls were often painted with sham stonework, sham curtains, or a simple powdering, ready to be hung with tapestry[1] when the lord and his baggage-wagons arrived. When they were pictorially treated the subjects were usually literary in origin, like the Wheel of Fortune that Laurent de Boulogne painted in 1334 in the castle of Hesdin.[2] Then came the wars; just after Crécy in 1346 the accounts show all the Countess of Artois's painters and some of her carpenters leaving their work to become soldiers under the captain of her castle.[3] Work only began again after Calais had been taken, and it was some time before anything on a grand scale was attempted. Then she ordered Pierre de Bruxelles, a Paris artist, to paint the gallery of her castle of Conflans with the feats of her father, like an illustrated chronicle. The contract makes clear the commemorative intention of the Countess, and her consequent wish for historical accuracy.

'Et sera l'image du conte d'Artois en tous lieuz là ou il sera, armoiez des armes dudit conte; et les autres ymages des chevaliers nuez de plusieurs couleurs, et leurs escuz, en lieu ou il apperront, seront armoiez de leurs armes, et enquerra l'en queles armes ils portoient ou temps qu'ils vivoient, et les galies, nez et vessiaus de mer, armees de genz d'armes, et les diz vessiaux faiz selon ce qu'il sont en mer, en la meilleur maniere que il pourront estre faites en painture. . . . Et dessus les diz ymages aura lettres qui deviseront par brieve compilacion le fait de l'estoire . . . et fera tant d'ymages et d'estoires ès dites galeries comme il est contenu en un roole qui est pour droit dudit Pierre.'[4]

Such battle-paintings remained a stock subject for the decoration of halls and galleries all through the Middle Ages, for they were peculiarly congenial to feudal society. 'Les chevaliers de nostre temps', says the *Songe du Vergier*, 'font en leurs sales paindre batailles à pié et à cheval, affin que par manière de vision ilz preignent aulcune délectation en batailles ymaginatives.'

5. TAPESTRIES AND HANGINGS

The aristocrats of the fourteenth century, though they might always inhabit a settled castle, led a nomadic life. Mahaut, Comtesse d'Artois, for instance, visited Artois regularly twice a year from Paris, and often made a progress through all the province, stopping a day or a week in her various towns and castles. She went rather less often into Burgundy, to visit her estates and to pray at her husband's tomb. Besides these visits to her own lands she went regularly to the royal castles and abbeys near Paris: Fontainebleau, Vincennes, Conflans, Pontoise, and Maubuisson.[5] Her life was typical; the great lords and ladies of France needed not the furniture of a permanent abode, but furnishings that could be moved from one castle to another in the baggage-wagon.

[1] Richard, p. 323. [2] Ibid., p. 341. [3] Ibid., p. 342. [4] Ibid., p. 356. [5] Ibid., p. 55.

Wall-paintings might grow faded and damp-stained in empty castles; tapestries and embroidered hangings came to be preferred, since they could be varied at will and carried from one castle to another. They had the further advantage of bringing warmth and quiet to a room of cold and echoing stone. In 1292 there were twenty-four tapestry-makers in Paris, but we know nothing of their work; tapestry-weaving, as known to us, is essentially one of the arts of luxury of the fourteenth and fifteenth centuries, when it was fairly evenly divided between Paris and Arras.[1] The embroidered hangings were also worked by men; the *Livre de la Taille* and the accounts of Mahaut d'Artois give about a dozen names, of whom Gautier de Poligny was the one employed for the finest work. The enormous number of both tapestries and hangings in medieval French inventories is accounted for by their being periodically changed. Just as the Court had new dresses at the great feasts, so the rooms had fresh hangings. The accounts of King John in 1352 and the succeeding years[2] record sets 'de Pâques', de la Toussaint', and 'de Noël'. The Easter set for the king's room consisted of six green wall-tapestries, with the arms of France in the corners; the counterpane, dorsal, tester, and curtains of the bed, and a bedside mat, all of green cendal lined with blue linen and embroidered with silver stars; chair cushions of blue velvet and green cendal, and green serge window curtains.

The design of such wall-hangings naturally followed at first the same lines as that of contemporary wall-paintings. Such inventory items as 'ung tappiz de gallerie ancien, où il y a batailles'[3] show how exactly such paintings as those of the feats of arms of Mahaut d'Artois's father could be translated into tapestry. Sometimes the hangings represented scenes from the *Chanson de Roland* (Fig. 168) or other subjects of the epic cycles.[4]

During the Hundred Years War some were woven of new historical events; the Duke of Burgundy by 1404 had tapestries of Pontvallain and Cocherel, the great victories of du Guesclin,[5] and others are recorded later with 'les haults fais d'armes de la Pucelle d'Orléans'.[6] In 1420 Philippe le Bon had tapestries of the Battle of Liége and the Battle of Roosebek.[7] The other stock subjects of feudal iconography, the Twelve Peers of France, the Nine Worthies and their female counterparts, were also represented.[8] Part of a set of the Neuf Preux, made at Aubusson in 1495, is at the Château de Lapalisse, and Penthesilea survives out of a set of the Preuses at Angers.

[1] Weavers from Paris used often to set up their looms in the castle of their patron. Guiffrey, p. 47.
[2] Douet d'Arcq, *Argenterie*, p. li.   [3] Inventory of the Duke of Orleans, 1454. Laborde, iii. 350.
[4] The perspectiveless, yet crowded, composition may be compared with that in contemporary illuminated manuscripts: e.g., Bible de Raoul de Presles, Bibl. Nat. franç. 20065.   [5] Guiffrey, p. 26.
[6] e.g. inventory of Philippe le Bon, 1420. Laborde, ii. 269. A rather more elaborate scheme was used on some tapestries bought by the Duke of Burgundy in 1454: 'trois saiges, trois puissans et trois fors.' Laborde, i. 166.   [7] Laborde, ii. 269.
[8] *Mém. de la Soc. des Ants de France,* 3rd series, x, 1868, p. 38.

The men of the Court were great readers of romances; in 1378 the Duc de Berry bought special flat candlesticks of ivory 'pour tenir chandelle de bougie à lire romans',[1] and the accounts of the Burgundian library show that the romances had to be more often rebound than other books. It was not long before the tapestry-weavers, working at Paris and no doubt in close touch with the illuminators of manuscripts, embarked upon romantic themes.

The classical subjects of such books as the *Roman de Thèbes* and *Roman de Troie* were depicted at the end of the fourteenth century, when a Petrarchan influence once more made classicism the mode:[2] the Trojan War by 1376, Paris and the three Goddesses by 1385, the 'Dieu d'Amour' in 1404, and Hercules in 1422.[3] The personifications of such compositions as the *Roman de la Rose* were even more popular. Philippe le Hardi owned a manuscript of the poem, and in 1386, 1387, and 1393 bought tapestries portraying some of its episodes.[4] His wife had one with 'Demoiselles qui défendent le châtel' from the same cycle. Philippe le Bon had a hanging with the 'Chastel de Franchise' and a 'Chambre de la Plaiderie d'amours', the Duke of Anjou, 'le tapis d'Humilité et Orgueil', and Jeanne d'Évreux 'Amis et Amies, Bonté et Beaulté'.[5] Charles V owned tapestries with the Fountain of Youth, and Charles VI one with the 'Verger de Jeunesse',[6] while others were woven with the 'Cité de Dames' of Christine de Pisan.[7] The classic *pastourelle*—a genre which describes a knight riding out on a fine spring morning and making love to a shepherdess—inspired tapestries 'du chevalier qui prie d'amour une bergère'.[8] The literary glorification of a shepherd's life, sung by such poets as Eustache Deschamps and amplified by such prose-writers as Jean de Brie, was yet more fertile in its inspiration. In 1403 the Duke of Orleans had a set of green hangings 'a bergiers et bergeres faisant contenance de mengier noiz et cerises',[9] and Philip le Bon in 1420 another set of red velvet embroidered with shepherds and sheep.[10] It was a complete set: four small and ten large wall-hangings, tester, ceiling, and bedspread, three curtains and four cushions. Sometimes a text now lost is recorded, like that which formed the subject of a tapestry bought by the Duke of Burgundy in 1386: 'L'istoire d'un roy qui s'en ala chacier et perdi en un bois ses gens et ses chevaux

[1] Koechlin, i. 13.

[2] A small but influential côterie in Paris led by Gontier Col, protégé of the Duc de Berry and Secretary of Charles VI, Jean de Montreuil, another royal secretary, and Nicolas de Clamanges began to read Horace, Virgil, Ovid, and Cicero with their Italian friends about 1380, but war brought their studies to an end.   [3] Adhémar, p. 293.

[4] Guiffrey, p. 40; Doutrepont, p. 329. Doutrepont, p. 117, notes the parallels between the romances in the Duke of Burgundy's Library and on his tapestries. Another tapestry with the *Roman de la Rose* belonged to Jean de Berry in 1416. Guiffrey, ii. 208.

[5] Guiffrey, p. 41. Cf. Philippe le Bon's 'Personnages d'honneur, de noblesse, largesse, simplesse et autres'. Laborde, ii. 267.   [6] Guiffrey, p. 40.

[7] E. Muntz, 'La Tapisserie à l'époque de Louis XII', in *Les Lettres et les Arts,* 1886, p. 213. Inventory in the archives of Milan.   [8] Guiffrey, p. 39.   [9] Laborde, iii. 206.   [10] Ibid., ii. 267.

et y trouva une merveilleuse aventure de fées qui le jugerent devenir cerf.'[1] The literary derivation of such pieces was generally stressed by verse inscriptions. The 1420 inventory of Charles VI indicate a tapestry with a cavalcade and an inscription beginning: 'Véez cy jeunesse . . .'; a verdure with people walking and 'Droit cy à l'erbette jolie' and other 'tapisseries à écritaux'.[2]

Such tapestries as had no literary source for their imagery commonly represented one of the occupations of the Court: pastimes often designated in the inventories as *esbatemens* or *donoiemens*.

Hunting-scenes were a common subject. A fourteenth-century embroidery[3] shows the departure for the chase and the return from it against a delicate background of oak-leaves. Philippe le Hardi had in 1388 a tapestry of 'Dames partant pour la chasse' and another 'à ymages de chasse'.[4] In 1416 Jean sans Peur gave to the Emperor's ambassador a tapestry with knights and ladies hawking,[5] and Philippe le Bon had nine large ones with flights of plover and partridge and figures of Jean sans Peur and his wife on foot and mounted. Sometimes such a theme was turned rather to the celebration of the joys of country life: such joys as Philippe de Vitré, the friend of Petrarch, had celebrated in *Le Dit de Franc Gontier*. In 1422 the English sold the tapestries of Charles VI that they had captured.[6] Among them was 'ung tappiz, bel et riche, sur champ vermeil, nommé la Haquenée . . . et y a quatre personnages, c'est assavoir: ung chevalier et une dame qui s'en vont au boys jouer, et deux varlez, dont l'un tient les chevaux, et y a une volerie d'oyseaulx de riviere'. Sometimes other scenes of court life were represented, like the ball with men and women dressed as hairy wild folk of the forest on a tapestry at Saumur[7] that recalls the disastrous *bal des Ardents* of 1393 when flames consumed the dancers. From such scenes it was an easy transition to conversation pieces with portraits. Three tapestries survive[8] (Fig. 169) with figures of men and women, obviously portraits, against a background of green and white, the personal colours of Charles VII, and the trails of the rose-sprays he sometimes used as a device.[9] Another exists with portraits of the Duke of Orleans and his wife Valentine de Milan, in a pavilion[10] (Fig. 170).

The chief interest of the Court and the dominant influence on decoration was the pageantry of chivalry. The idea of vassalship had been commonly expressed as early as the time of Saint Louis by a man wearing a dress of his lord's colours, and by the end of the fourteenth century such livery was enriched

---

[1] Dehaisnes, p. 346.   [2] Guiffrey, p. 68.
[3] In the Musée historique des tissus, Lyons.   [4] Guiffrey, p. 17.   [5] Pinchart, p. 19.
[6] See Guiffrey in *Bib. de l'École des Chartes XLV*, iii, 1887, p. 106.
[7] Now in the church of Notre-Dame de Nantilly.
[8] See S. Rubinstein in *Amer. Journ. Arch.*, 2nd series, xxii, 1918, p. 166.
[9] They correspond closely with some bought by Philippe le Bon in 1428: 'palée de coulleurs de vert et de blanc, semée de roseaux et à plusieurs ymages.' Pinchart, p. 25.
[10] Musée des arts décoratifs, Paris. The identification is assured by her badge of the chantepleure.

with the lord's devices. In 1387, for instance, the king and the Duke of Touraine appeared on May Morning in mantles of green cloth embroidered with sprays of broom, the royal device, and gave twenty-five similar mantles to gentlemen of the Court.[1] On May Day, 1393, the Duke of Orleans gave *houppelandes* of black frieze with a band of his six colours and a wolf upon the sleeve;[2] in 1408 the Duke of Guienne had a similar cloak with the peacock feathers and broom of the king's badges, mixed with hawthorn branches in honour of May, and sewn with the king's four colours, white, green, red, and black.[3] In 1411 the Duke of Burgundy gave devices of silver *rabots* to his gentlemen, the joiner's plane that he took as his badge when the Duke of Orleans adopted a knotty branch to show his firmness of purpose;[4] and no less than forty-two dresses powdered with these *rabots* appear in his inventories.[5]

From this use of a livery and a badge for a royal household it was an easy transition to the foundation of Orders of Chivalry, intended to give new strength to the institution of knighthood itself. The Order of the Star, inspired by the Arthurian romances, was founded for five hundred knights by Jean II in 1351. It fell into desuetude after many of its knights were slain in battle against the English. In 1369 Louis II, Duke of Bourbon, on his return from imprisonment in England, founded the order of the Golden Shield[6] with *Espérance* as its motto. Then in 1378 Charles V founded the *Ordre du Cosse de Genêt*, with white and green for its colours, broom for its device, and *Jamais* for its motto: devices represented not only in the borders of his manuscripts[7] but also in his tapestries.[8] A succession of Orders followed: the Ermine of John of Brittany, the *Camail* of Louis d'Orléans, the *Écu*, the *Chardon*, the *Fer d'Argent*, until they were all eclipsed by the Golden Fleece founded by Philip the Good of Burgundy in 1429.[9] Nineteen years later he ordered from Tournai eight immense and magnificent tapestries, famous even in their day, 'de l'Histoire de Gédéon ou de la Toison d'Or'.[10] These were primarily intended to be hung at the assemblies of the Order, but were also used at such festivals as the coronation of Louis XI and the wedding of Charles the Bold. Finally, in 1469, Louis XI founded the Order of St. Michael; but he was a founder too thrifty to celebrate his foundation in the furnishings of his castle.

These personal orders were accompanied by the use of yet more personal

---

[1] Douet d'Arcq, *Nouveau recueil*, p. 194.

[2] Laborde, iii. 70. In 1396 his little son, aged two, had a green cloth robe with the six colours for May. Champion, p. 8.   [3] L. Pannier in *Rev. arch.* xxvi, 1873, p. 219.   [4] Laborde, i. 28.

[5] In 1416 he gave forty embroidered with *rabots* to his household, as well as 420 plainer robes. Laborde, i. 123.   [6] Ibid., xxi, col. 138.   [7] e.g. Bibl. Nat. franç. 2705.

[8] 1422 Inventory. Tapestry 'de la devise du Roy notre sire, c'est a savoir grans fleurs de liz d'or et dyaprure de branches de genestre, semé parmi du mot du Roy, ou il y a *jamais*'. Guiffrey, p. 26.

[9] See Hélyot in Migne, xxii, col. 679.

[10] Doutrepont, p. 156. Four years were allowed for their making.

devices. Charles V, for instance, put himself under the patronage of two saints, Charlemagne (canonized in 1165) and James. His sceptre has three medallions on the knop. On one St. James, habited as a pilgrim, appears to Charlemagne. On the second Charlemagne kneels at the head of his peers before the vision of the saint; and on the third the death of the emperor is represented. Above the knop Charlemagne sits enthroned; on the base of the throne is the inscription: KAROLVS MAGNVS: ITALIA: ROMA: GERMANIA.[1] The royal treasury likewise contained two flasks with Charlemagne and St. James.[2] Charles VI, in his turn, had a tapestry representing himself sitting enthroned among his peers.[3] Charles VI, however, also took a flying stag with a golden collar and the motto *Caesar haec mihi donavit* as his device, after he had seen them in a dream,[4] and Charles VII continued the use of his father's badge. He owned a tapestry[5] with his arms supported by winged stags standing in a flowery mead, and another (Fig. 171) with three winged stags within a wattled enclosure. Two are gorged with a royal crown from which hangs a shield of France; the third bears the royal banner. The shield-bearers each have banderoles, one inscribed:

> Armes porte très glorieuses
> Et sur toutes victorieuses—

and the other:

> Si nobles n'a dessoubz les cieux
> Je ne pourraye porter mieux.

Over the standard is another banderole:

> Cest estendart est une enseigne
> Qui a loial françois enseigne
> De jamais ne labandonner
> S'il ne veut son honneur donner.

   Such fanciful and literary devices, in their turn, were paralleled in the pageantry of tournaments. By the fourteenth century the old conception of a tournament as a mimic battle that afforded a training in warfare had given place to the picturesque and romantic idea of a chivalrous combat with honour for its prize. This idea in its turn was gradually modified by the development of jousting as a formal pageant with a code of etiquette rather than an ideal to govern its manifestations: a modification largely carried out in the fifteenth century at the Court of Burgundy, the refuge both of feudalism and of chivalry. The Burgundian knights did not even pretend that they were warriors; they were courtiers, and courtiers of a court hag-ridden by etiquette and finding its only release in pageantry.

[1] The sceptre is described in the inventory of 1380. The lily was then enamelled white.
[2] In 1406. Lacroix, *Histoire de l'orfèvrerie et de la joaillerie*, Paris, 1850, p. 77.
[3] Guiffrey, p. 28.   [4] Froissart, bk. ii, chap. 104.
[5] Gaignières, Bib. Nat. Estampes, pc. 18, fol. 1.

The reign of Charles VI was the great age of tournaments at the Court of France. He had three sets of tapestries commemorating the three most important. The first represented the 'Combat des Trente', the tourney between thirty English and thirty Breton knights held at Ploermel in 1351.[1] The second portrayed the 'Joutes de Saint Inglevert', held in 1390;[2] it was bought some six years later. The third, the 'Joutes de Saint Denis', was ordered at the time of the tournament, which was held in 1397 to celebrate the knighting of Charles d'Orléans and Louis d'Anjou. It portrayed not only the combat but the pageantry of the lists; one panel showed an armed man led by a lady, with two other ladies watching from a gallery, and a clump of golden oak-trees against which the standards of the knights were displayed, held by their squires.

The most famous Burgundian tournaments were the *Pas de l'Arbre Charlemagne*[3] held at Dijon in 1443, a reflection of the royal devotion to the Emperor; the *Pas de la Belle Pèlerine* held at Saint-Omer in 1449, with Lancelot, Palamedes, and Tristan as protagonists; and the *Fontaine aux Pleurs* held at Chalon-sur-Saône in 1499.[4] A fountain was built, and beside it a pavilion raised to shelter the effigy of a lady, which remained there a year, holding a unicorn by the horn and bearing three shields. On the first day of each month the knights came to touch the shield and thus to pledge themselves to the combat. It is impossible not to compare this scheme with that of one of the tapestries (Fig. 172) of the set known as *La Dame à la Licorne*; there may be no direct connexion, but the pavilion, sprinkled with tears, the lady, the unicorn, and the banners of the tourney are common elements. Similarly the fanciful supporters of banners in the lists were represented in tapestry; Charles V, for example, had in 1369 nine tapestries with a selvage man holding his helm in the middle,[5] and another with four beasts holding banners in the corners.[6] Indeed, all the details of the lists, mottoes and pavilions, pennons and supporters, shields of peace hung from trees, and the rest, appeared in art.[7] The besetting sin of the later Middle Ages was pride, and these devices remain as emblems of its domination.

6. FURNITURE AND PLATE

The furnishings of mediaeval castles were such as could be bundled into a baggage-wagon: neither fixed, fragile, nor bulky. Any great lord's belongings must have spent weeks in the year in being bumped about over bad roads from one castle to another. When Galeran set out from Brittany for Lorraine he

[1] Guiffrey, p. 28. It was bought about 1383.
[2] A fine illustration of this tournament is in the Froissart manuscript, B.M. Harl. MS. 4379, f. 23b.
[3] Monstrelet, vi. 68.
[4] O. de la Marche, *Mém.*, chap. xxi. The later jousts of the *Chevalier au Cygne*, Lille, 1454, *Dame Inconnue*, Brussels, 1403, *Perron fée*, Bruges, 1463, and *Arbre d'Or*, Bruges, 1468, were all held outside France. Doutrepont, p. 105.   [5] Labarte, *Inv. de Ch. V*, p. 280.   [6] Ibid., p. 379.
[7] I have treated the subject in more detail in *Pattern*, chap. iii.

travelled with thirty sumpter mules laden with hangings, dishes, cups, spoons, clothes, and arms. Because it forms no fixed picture it is peculiarly hard to envisage mediaeval furniture clearly; this is perhaps the measure of its unimportance. It is significant that Joinville, who could paint a picture in words and loved the details of apparel, never describes a room. The early inventories are all ecclesiastical, and do nothing to help us. Even such inventories as those of the castle of Sommières in 1260 and Gimel in 1269 enumerate little besides stores, military equipment, and chapel furniture.

If the hangings of a mediaeval room were rich and abundant, its actual furniture was, by modern standards, plain and scanty. The simple and massive tables owed all their beauty to the cloths with which they were spread, and the chairs and stools most of their decoration to the cushions with which they were strewn. Each room usually held two beds, a small day bed and a larger bed to sleep in, that were covered and curtained to match the hangings of the room. The dressers were mere shelves for the display of gold and silver plate.

The heavy chests were more richly carved, but remained strong and simple enough to be used as travelling chests at need. The inventories record a certain amount of inlay work in ivory and dark wood, but mediaeval furniture as it is known to us is nearly all of massive oak. The commonest decoration of such furniture was carved tracery like that of windows; decoration carried right across the front of the chest in a continuous arcade (Fig. 173 A) until at the beginning of the fifteenth century a series of panels of similar ornament took its place. Exceptionally such chests were carved with figure subjects : one has a tournament scene (Fig. 173 B) and another the coronation of Louis XI.[1] Such furniture was made not by specially skilled cabinet-makers but by carpenters, and carved by the *tailleurs de coutel*. Such accounts as those of Mahaut d'Artois shows these carvers working indifferently at the angels of a chapel ceiling, the window-frames of a hall, a machine for bending cross-bows, and instruments for the countess's astrologer, as well as upon her chests and chairs.[2]

If furniture, as we conceive it, thus took a second place, the lesser things of personal use were of major importance. They were usually of precious material, gold, silver, or ivory, and wrought by highly skilled men who had undergone a long apprenticeship to gain admission to a privileged guild. The ivory-carvers in particular were infinitely more skilled than the workmen in wood. Their subjects were entirely derived from the miniature-painters and imagers,[3] but use made certain subjects of the romantic cycle peculiarly their own. Ladies' mirror-cases and jewel-caskets were appropriate fields for such subjects as scenes from the *Châtelaine de Vergi*, *Perceval*, *Le Chevalier au Cygne*, *Tristan et Yseult*[4]—

[1] Musée historique, Orléans.   [2] Richard, p. 306.   [3] Koechlin, i. iii.
[4] See, e.g., Economos Collection. S. de Ricci, *Exposition à l'ancien hôtel de Sagan*, mai–juin 1913, no. xliv.

lovers seated in a garden, riding, or playing chess together; for romantic allegories like the Castle of Love (Fig. 174), and for carvings in which ladies look down from a gallery at the knights jousting in their honour.[1]

Work in ivory, however, was of small importance compared with work in gold and silver. The mediaeval abundance of such precious things cannot be paralleled even in the royal inventories of the eighteenth century. For a great lord to eat off mere silver enamelled with designs in black—*vaisselle de Carême*—was a Lenten penance. Louis of Anjou had the very pot-hook-stand of his kitchen of silver, decorated at the top with a seated figure of the chef in a long gown and a high cap, holding a sausage. Beneath him stood a figure of the turnspit in a short coat holding a spit with a goose upon it; a cook's boy with two partridges, and, on the other side, the porter carrying in the carcass of a sheep and an under-cook with a roast sucking-pig. The lord himself normally ate off gold. Charles the Bold, for example, had a complete service for his high table in this metal.[2] It comprised a dish for sweetmeats borne by the jewelled figures of seven women, with seven more on the cover, and seven archers on the base; fourteen covered cups and thirty-six goblets decorated with coats of arms and other devices; twelve ewers and another jug; sixteen salt-cellars, and a dozen or so single pieces, all of solid gold. Besides these he had uncountable quantities of similar vessels in silver gilt.

The chief ornaments of any royal table were the nef (Fig. 176), which held the master's knife, spoon, fork, napkin, and touchpiece against poison[3]—a vessel to which all who passed the table bowed, even when the table was empty—and the fountain, which held his wine. These were sometimes made *en suite*. Louis d'Anjou, for example, had in 1379 a nef and a fountain that each represented the Fountain of Youth. The nef[4] was adorned with fifty-four figures in the round, some coming in litters or walking on crutches or riding on mules to the magical fountain, some making ready and casting off their shoes, and others bathing in its waters. The body of the vessel was decorated with people crying their wares as they might in the streets of Paris,[5] and with dances of men and women. The fountain[6] had at the top, within fortifications guarded by a watchman, a flowery garden with trees of gold and walks and seats, where men and women sat and rested, and in the middle another Fountain of Youth with a man and two women bathing in it. The base was decorated with grotesques like the margin of a manuscript: animals 'les unes seans à table, les autres dansans et les

---

[1] See Koechlin, i. 360–75 for a detailed analysis.   [2] Laborde, ii. 31.

[3] e.g. 1380 Inventory of Charles V: 'La navette d'or goderonnée et y met on dedans quand le Roy est à table son essay, sa cuiller, son coutelet et sa fourcette.' Laborde, p. 403. The vessel first came into use *c.* 1180 and became important in the fourteenth century. Its use continued at the French Court on formal occasions until 1782. Laborde, p. 403.   [4] Moranvillé, p. 251.

[5] Cf. the 'Dits' of the end of the fourteenth century: Dit des forgerons, des Boulangers, des cris de Paris, &c.   [6] Moranvillé, p. 227.

autres chantans messe et faisans autres esbas'. The inventory of King John in 1353[1] includes eight nefs and five fountains; that of Charles V, of 1380, includes five nefs of gold and twenty-one of silver gilt.

Every great inventory of the time starts with such pieces and continues through an infinity of *drageoirs*, cups, pots, flasks, goblets, ewers, salts, dishes, basins, trenchers, and plates: first in gold, then in silver gilt, finally, in enormous quantities, in silver for the lower tables.

These plainer pieces might be decorated only with their owner's arms. The finer pieces, however, nearly all bore figured ornament drawn from the same literary sources as the imagery of wall-paintings and tapestries. A few derived their subjects from religious and didactic books. The inventory made after the death of Queen Jeanne d'Évreux in 1372 includes a cup with cover and stand *de l'histoire de Saint Loys*,[2] and a golden cup still survives[3] (Fig. 175), enamelled with the story of St. Agnes, that originally belonged to the Duc de Berry, and then to Charles VI.[4] In 1410 Charles d'Orléans sold a nef with figures of the twelve apostles in high relief round it, and a castle at each end with Our Lady in one and an angel in the other. The vessel was shaped like a ship; its mast was a cross upheld by the four evangelists and the four major prophets, with a crucifix at the mast-head. The sails were enamelled with fleurs-de-lis. In the body of the ship were Adam and Eve, a king, an emperor, and other figures.[5] It recalls one of the few nefs that have survived: once belonging to Anne of Brittany, later given by Henri III from his ancestral treasury to serve as a reliquary in the cathedral of Rheims, where it still is[6] (Fig. 176). The figures represent St. Ursula and her Virgins. Louis d'Anjou owned a silver-gilt flagon on which the virtues and vices were given a feudal twist: the virtues had as the central figure *Liberalitas*, and the vices *Vana gloria*.[7]

Lay literature was naturally a much more fertile source of imagery. Louis d'Anjou had four pieces of plate, including a most elaborate fountain and nef, with the nine worthies,[8] and Charles VI a drageoir with its cover adorned with them and with the figure of Du Guesclin.[9] Louis d'Anjou had several pieces of gold plate decorated with scenes from the story of Tristram and Yseult: King Mark watching the lovers from a tree, on the stem of a great salt-cellar, with

[1] Douet d'Arcq, *Argenterie,* p. 304.

[2] Leber, *Coll. meilleurs dissertations,* 1838, xix. 134. Cf. a nef with a similar theme, Guiffrey, ii. 103, dating from 1402.

[3] In the British Museum. Its original stand, with winged-dragon feet, the cresting of the rim, and the knob set with sapphires, rubies, and pearls, are lost.

[4] Charles V was born on St. Agnes's Day and owned thirteen objects in precious metal with her figure. See Delisle in *Journal des Savants,* May 1906, p. 238. The cup may have been made for a birthday present in the year of his death, and never given.   [5] Laborde, iii. 252.

[6] The Renaissance figure surmounting the mast has been blotted out on the plate.

[7] Moranvillé, p. lxx.

[8] Ibid., p. lxix.   [9] Laborde, p. 256.

his head reflected in a stream enamelled on the foot; the same scene, and Tristram and Yseult playing at chess, on a pair of enamelled basins; and Tristram playing his harp to Yseult while King Mark hunted, on a flagon of enamelled silver gilt.[1] The 'chevaliers et dames anciens' of the cycle of Troy adorned a dish in his collection[2] with a companion piece with figures from the Breton romances. Scenes such as those described in the *Roman de la Rose* and the *Cité des Dames* appeared on several pieces, notably a pair of goblets with 'un chastel que deux hommes assaillent de fleurs et de rosettes et trois dames le defendent'.[3] Scenes such as adorned the manuscripts of poems on courtly love adorned several pieces of the plate of Louis d'Anjou: a drageoir set with enamels of pairs of lovers talking ('et font l'un à l'autre plusieurs signes d'amour'), with the God of Love shooting at a knight and a lady in the middle;[4] and two basins with enamels of knights and ladies talking,[5] in company with the ladies' lap-dogs *à oreilles pendans*. Some represented the pastoral fashion, found alike in literature and in art. Louis d'Anjou had a pair of flagons enamelled with wood-cutters and other country workmen[6] and a crystal cup on a stand enamelled with grazing sheep and three shepherdesses 'jouans de la cornemuse, emmantelées de petis manteaux . . . et sont enchapelées de trois chapeaux differens en façon et chascune tient son chien à une corde de fil d'argent'.[7] Others, like certain tapestries already mentioned, set portrait figures against a woodland background. Louis d'Anjou owned a goblet of finely chased and enamelled gold, with a meadow enamelled on the base, on which rabbits were playing. From this rose varied shrubs and taller trees that covered the body of the goblet, with deer among them, *fais sur le vif*. The basin that went with it was likewise enamelled with a green meadow, on which was a throne. On this Louis d'Anjou was represented seated, in a violet robe and a blue hat, and his duchess in a blue surcoat and a horned head-dress with a crown. Their son stood between them at his father's knee. Pierre d'Avoir, Sire de Châteaufromont, the friend and chamberlain of the duke, was represented kneeling before them in a lavender gown, with the napkin that was the badge of his service over his shoulder, offering a dish of spices to his master.[8] A drawing of a covered cup of the same date[9] (Fig. 177) shows a knight and a lady walking in a meadow by a river, with a lady-in-waiting to bear the long train of her mistress, and a man and woman

[1] Moranvillé, p. lxiii.

[2] Ibid., p. 481. He also had a flagon with Paris, Hercules, Ulysses, Troilus, Hector, and Achilles. Ibid., p. 446.   [3] Ibid., p. 343.

[4] Ibid., p. 470.   [5] Ibid., p. 498.   [6] Ibid., p. 451.

[7] Ibid., p. 35. Other pieces of plate with shepherds and shepherdesses are described in the inventories of Valentine de Milan and the Duc de Guienne.

[8] Ibid., p. 85. A similar scene was represented on a great bottle. Ibid., p. 463.

[9] Bodleian Gaignières MS. 1836, fol. 63. In the seventeenth century the cup belonged to Monsieur de Caumartin.

hawking. A goblet and ewer owned by Charles V, with a woodland scene, was enamelled like the background of a calendar scene of the *Très Riches Heures* with his favourite castle of Vincennes.[1]

Heraldic subjects were particularly well fitted to the decoration of plate. Besides the endless shields and diapers that served at once as ornaments and marks of ownership, more elaborate schemes of heraldic decoration were also used. The goblet of Philip the Good remains[2] to show how elegantly initials and a badge—in this case the flint and steel of Burgundy—could be used in gold work. All the devices of the lists appeared in turn. Queen Jeanne d'Évreux at the time of her death in 1372 owned a nef from which rose two banners of her arms held by wild men of the woods standing on castles;[3] Louis d'Anjou a few years later had a mother-of-pearl salt-cellar set with enamels of knights riding with shields of their arms, and on the cover the God of Love shooting arrows at a knight and a lady;[4] and a fountain with the knights of the *Pas Saladin*, and the inscription:

> Loyaument vueil estre demenez
> Car de loyauté est on honnorez,
> Qui loyaux est toute sa vie
> Honnorez est sans villenie.[5]

Others represented the more romantic aspects of the tournament: such as the lady helming the knight who kneels before her, on a goblet and a basin and a drageoir belonging to Louis d'Anjou.[6] The mottoes borne by knights appear in equal profusion. Charles the Bold, for example, owned in 1467 a gold cup inscribed with his own motto *La plus du monde*; a chalcedony salt-cellar with Louis de Bourbon's *Esperance* and other pieces of plate inscribed *Tant plus y pense, j'ay obey*, and *Moien*.[7]

Only two forms of ornament are found on plate and not (so far as we now know) on tapestry, probably because they are both appropriate to work on a small scale. One of these, animal grotesques, had ultimately a literary source in such books as the *Roman de Renart*. In *Renart* the hero goes into a monastery and sings Matins with great effect; in his study at the Hôtel Saint-Pol, Charles V had an ebony fox *en guise de cordelier*.[8] In art, however, monkeys played a more important part than they did in literature. Louis d'Anjou had pieces of plate decorated with monkeys, mitred and holding a crosier, giving a benediction to a fox, preaching to geese, playing the bagpipes, riding on a donkey, and fishing for barbel.[9] Besides these a certain number, but not many, of the hideous composite monsters of the manuscript borders were translated into precious metal.[10]

---

[1] Labarte, *Inv. de Ch. V*, p. 72. [2] In the Kunsthistorisches Museum, Vienna.
[3] Leber, *Coll. meilleurs dissertations*, 1838, xix. 142. [4] Moranvillé, p. 281.
[5] Ibid., p. lxix. [6] Ibid., p. lxv. [7] Laborde, ii. 34.
[8] Labarte, *Inv. de Ch. V*, p. 244. [9] Moranvillé, pp. lvi and lvii.
[10] e.g. Comptes royaux, 1352 : 'Une aiguière d'un homme séant sur un demi coq, à une teste

The other fresh type of ornament was oriental in origin. Saracenic silks and glass had been imported into France in the thirteenth century, and in the fourteenth and still more in the fifteenth century, luxury expressed itself in an abundance of silks of rich colour and oriental design.[1] Many of these, like Saracen glass- and metal-work, had inscriptions in Cufic characters, and these inscriptions were soon imitated, especially in gold and silver. *Lettres de damas* or *lettres moresques* or *lettres sarrasines* occur on a hundred and sixteen pieces of plate belonging to Louis d'Anjou,[2] mixed with heraldic and naturalistic decoration. No such plate survives, but the style may be represented by a bowl carved in the mazer wood that was used for receptacles for new wine which might have been tainted by metal[3] (Fig. 178).

Besides this extravagant abundance of table plate every other personal possession that could be of precious material was made of the richest available. The inventory of Louis d'Anjou, though incomplete, contains over 3,600 items.[4] Even the *hernois de guerre* was garnished with gold, pearls, diamonds, and enamels; even the steel gauntlets were inlaid with gold. As Martial d'Auvergne says, *on s'harnachoit d'orfaverie*.

Finally, the cult of naturalism brought in another manifestation of luxury: the portrait. Its development in sculpture, in the tomb and the donor-statue, continued in the donor-figures in painting and was further developed in the portraits in the genre scenes of tapestries.[5] Yet this development, in painting particularly, happened in a very short space of time. The manuscript of *Dina et Kalila*[6] illustrated in 1313 has a purely formal picture of the royal family; the translation of Durandus's *Rationale* painted in 1374[7] depicts them characterized as individuals. It is the age of the Valois, from 1328 to 1498, that is the age of realism in France, and that age witnessed the development of the portrait under the patronage of the Valois dynasty. The earliest French panel portrait now in existence is that of Jean le Bon (Fig. 179), painted on canvas over wood about 1359, probably by his painter Girart d'Orléans. The inventories of Charles V and of the Duc de Berry mention four panels folding together with portraits *faits au vif* of King John, Charles V, Edward III of England, and the Emperor Charles IV, and it is just possible that the surviving portrait formed

d'évesque, qui tient une crosse', 1363, Duc de Normandie: 'Un oisel qui a visage d'ome ou cul et le chevauche une fame.' Laborde, *Glossaire*, p. 503.

[1] e.g. Brussels Bib. Roy. MS. 9027 has a picture of a Chapter of the Golden Fleece held at Bruges in May 1468, with the table covered by a brocade with birds in Perso-Chinese style.

[2] Moranvillé, p. xxi.

[3] See Evans in *Burlington Magazine*, xxviii, 1928, p. 32.

[4] It is a curious commentary on the mutability of such riches that only one item—an antique cameo vase now in the Walters Art Gallery at Baltimore—has been identified. See Marvin Chauncey Ross, 'The Rubens Vase', in *Journal of the Walters Art Gallery*, vi, 1943, p. 9.

[5] e.g. tapestry with portraits of Jean le Bon and his wife. Laborde, ii. 267.

[6] Bib. Nat. lat. 8504, fol. 1.   [7] Bib. Nat. franç. 437.

O

part of this ensemble.[1] Other folding portraits of the kind were produced by
the Burgundian Court school; one depicts Philip and Margaret of Burgundy
against a background powdered with the coats of arms of their seigneuries.
Other portraits were rather in the nature of illustrations drawn on paper. That
of Louis d'Anjou—the owner of all the plate—shows his fine profile under a
fantastic turban; it is a perfect expression of the age of the Valois (Fig. 180).
Finally, in the pictures of the time of Jean Fouquet (Fig. 181) the portraiture of
character achieves accomplishment.

7. SAINTES CHAPELLES

The knight was a knight in virtue of his Christianity. The Church blessed
his sword and gave it to him naked, with the words: 'Receive this sword, in the
name of the Father, the Son and the Holy Ghost, and use it to defend yourself
and the Holy Church of God, and to bring to confusion the enemies of the cross
of Jesus Christ . . . and, in so far as the frailty of human nature will allow, wound
no man with it unjustly.'[2] The Church in the eleventh century regulated the
fury of feudal war, and in the twelfth brought knightly warfare under a religious rule in the Militant Orders. By the thirteenth century every true knight
set religious duty as part of the framework not only of his life but also of his
working day. He began it, before he rose, with a paternoster and an Ave; once
he was up, one of his first duties was to hear Mass said by a priest of his household. Consequently a chapel was an essential part of a feudal castle.

In the early centuries of the Middle Ages it was almost as simple in its architecture as the defensive parts of the building. From the earliest days such chapels
were divided into two parts, one for the retainers and one for the lord and his
family.[3] The castle of Montmoreau near Angoulême still retains a chapel of the
middle of the twelfth century, small in size, elegant in proportion, and once
richly adorned with frescoes. It is preceded by two short bays, forming a kind
of narthex, and presumably intended for the retainers.[4] The church itself is a
rotunda under a cupola, with three small apsidal chapels[5] radiating from it: a
scheme that permitted of three altars in a building small enough to be a private
oratory. Soon, however, the castle chapels were made an integral part of the
main building, a necessary adjunct of the great hall. Since this was normally
raised above a servants' hall, the chapel was similarly built with the retainers'

[1] Michel, iii. 107. The 1471 inventory of René d'Anjou includes an eightfold panel picture with
portraits *tirés de plompt* of him and his wife and other friends and relatives.

[2] Pontifical of Guillaume Durand.

[3] This division is found at the dawn of the twelfth century in the private chapel of the abbot of
Cluny at the abbey grange of Berzé-la-Ville.

[4] Cf. the chapel of Villebois-Lavalette, Charente-Inférieure.

[5] It may be a miniature version of the Sepulchre plan: cf. the castle chapel at Ludlow, Salop, and
the church of Ozleworth, Glos., in its original form.

oratory below and the lord's above, each on the same level as their refectory. An early example is the chapel of the Counts of Champagne at Provins, dating from the end of the twelfth century.[1]

The true development of castle chapels in France dates from the reign of Saint Louis: the first king to make the practice of religion the core of his waking hours and the proof of his royal policy. He used to rise at midnight and dress to be present at Matins, and return to bed half-dressed until awakened for prime. After prime he would hear two Masses, and in the course of the day terce, sext, nones, vespers, and compline; he lived, in fact, half as king and half as religious. The chapel he built at Saint-Germain-en-Laye is a perfect expression of his religion in the forms of Gothic architecture: in slender columns, lofty vaults, and luminous windows that once glowed with colour. Yet it was not the final achievement of his idea of a king's chapel.

In 1239 Saint Louis bought from the Emperor of Constantinople for an enormous sum the precious relic of the Crown of Thorns. To house it he rebuilt the old chapel of St. Nicholas in his palace at Paris as a *Sainte Chapelle*, in which all the splendour that he denied himself in other things was employed to the glory of his Master.[2] Soon after it was finished, in 1249, he acquired from Constantinople additional relics of the Cross and the Lance. He endowed his foundation as a collegiate church, with canons to serve it,[3] but it remained a private royal chapel. Saint Louis reserved to himself and his successors the absolute property of all the jewels in its treasure.[4] It was built, like most castle chapels, on two floors: the lower, dedicated to the Virgin, to serve as a place of worship for the lesser retainers of the royal household, the upper to be at once the shrine of the Crown of Thorns and the oratory of the king. The upper chapel, long and aisleless, is a casket of light. The walls, above a rich arcade, are of great lanceolated windows only divided by the slender shafts that support the vaulting; the west end is half-filled by a great rose; and the apsidal sanctuary (Fig. 182) continues the scheme of the nave. The windows, in a medallion scheme,[5] are like the illustrations of a magnificent royal Bible of the time,[6]

---

[1] Other twelfth-century buildings of the kind were the chapels in the bishop's palaces of Angers, Laon, and Meaux.

[2] Guillaume de Saint-Pathus says that the building cost more than 40,000 *livres tournois,* and the shrines 100,000. Mortet, ii. 241. On it see H. Stein, *Le Palais de Justice et la Sainte Chapelle de Paris,* 1912.

[3] They acted as guardians of the great library which he established a little later, which was kept in an adjacent building.   [4] The right continued to the Revolution.

[5] Some windows from the Sainte Chapelle were for over a century in the church of Twycross, Lincolnshire, but are now happily returned to the chapel for which they were made.

[6] Little Bibles for lay use came into fashion in the first half of the thirteenth century. Saint Louis owned one. Others were translations into French. Their illustrations influenced larger manuscripts, for example, the marginal illuminations of the Bible of the Sainte Chapelle, Bibl. Nat. lat. 1732b, and the MSS. of the *Bible moralisée* and the *Bible historiée,* almost all of which were made at Paris for the king and the members of his court.

illustrative rather than symbolic. One tells the story of Moses in a hundred and twenty-one medallions; another, in as many, the chronicle of the Books of Kings; another devotes 120 medallions to the Book of Esther. Even Judith has forty medallions to tell her history. No Bible, however rich, was illustrated on this scale: here is creation in narrative imagery. To the Biblical cycle is added the story of the finding of the Cross by Saint Helena and its history down to the consecration of the chapel. This copious illustration, however, was intended for the delight of laymen, and there is little, if any, symbolism either in the scheme or in the detail.

Below the windows runs a rich arcade like that of a triforium, carved with censing angels on the spandrels; like all the stone-work, it was once brightly painted.[1] Against each of the vaulting piers is set a statue of an apostle that by a new and beautiful scheme bears one of the twelve consecration crosses of the church.[2]

The chapel built by Saint Louis at Paris remains the Sainte Chapelle *par excellence*, but it had several rivals. The king and his successors occasionally gave away fragments of the precious Crown, and each was housed in worthy fashion. One was early given to the Benedictine abbey of Saint-Germer; instead of a chapel of a more monastic form, a Sainte Chapelle closely based on that of Paris, and evidently by the same architect, was appended to the abbey church.[3] Its glass is less complete than that at Paris, but some of its foliage capitals retain their delicate colouring of yellow and blue-green.

It was not long before the pure flame of religion kept burning by Saint Louis was tinged with a grosser fire. His own canonization in 1297 was in itself a matter of glory for the royal house; and after his exhumation in 1298 the greater part of his body and the bones of his head were added to the relics in the treasury of the Sainte Chapelle, and in 1306 enshrined in two reliquaries of the utmost splendour.[4] As a consequence an element of ancestor-worship entered the chapel and, since lesser relics of the sainted king were owned by most of the royal family,[5] it likewise invaded the Saintes Chapelles which they built, for their devotion to their own saint was strong and natural. Mahaut d'Artois, for

---

[1] The painting was renewed by Viollet-le-Duc.

[2] The fashion of setting such statues against piers spread in the fourteenth century, e.g. at Saint-Nazaire de Carcassonne; Chapelle des Rieux, Toulouse; Saint-Étienne de Troyes; Saint-Jacques-des-Pèlerins at Paris. See Courajod, ii. 46. They may be compared with the statues of the Preux and the Preuses similarly set in great halls.

[3] The Sainte Chapelle is said also to have furnished the model for the Lady Chapel of Saint-Germain-des-Prés. Sauval, i. 341.

[4] A lay jeweller, Raoul, made the shrine and was ennobled for his pains; the head-reliquary was made by Guillaume Julien, another of the king's jewellers. See Enlart in *Mon. Piot*.

[5] The Empress and the Comte de Saint-Pol and the brethren of the Val des Écoliers were each given a finger-joint, the Dominicans of Paris and the abbey of the Lily a bone of the hand, the abbey of Pontoise and Notre-Dame de Paris a rib, and the abbey of Royaumont a fragment of the shoulder.

example, a great-niece alive at the time of the canonization of Saint Louis, had a magnificent reliquary with some of his bones; she kept his feast day with almsgiving and minstrels; she founded a chapel in his honour at his mother's abbey of Maubuisson; she had his statue carved for her oratory, and his figure painted on the walls of her chapels of Hesdin and Rihoult; and she used in her orisons a book *des offices Monseigneur Saint Louis* that her father had given her.[1] Thenceforward the French royal house had its own saint, and worshipped him reverently, for by his sanctity their own prestige was increased.

The next great Sainte Chapelle was that added to the castle of Vincennes between 1379 and 1382;[2] this was planned as a collegiate church for its fifteen canons, on one floor. Time has dealt hardly with it, but the delicate naturalistic sculptures of its mouldings, with roses and maple, snails and caterpillars, betray the influence of the realism of secular art.

In 1372 Charles V gave to the Duc de Berri a fragment of a relic of the True Cross Saint Louis had acquired soon after he began to build the Sainte Chapelle. Some years later Jean de Berri began to build a Sainte Chapelle at Bourges that was to house it and to serve as his mausoleum.[3] The time was past when a king would build a chapel to the sole glory of his Master; the Sainte Chapelle at Bourges celebrated its builder no less than his relic. Its windows[4] represent the prophets, standing under most elaborate gabled canopies; below them are angels holding roundels enclosing not consecration crosses but shields of arms. Among the statues were some of members of the duke's family (Fig. 183 B).

Jean de Berri built a second Sainte Chapelle at Riom, under the direction of his architect Guy de Dammartin. This survives; it retains the traditional plan, with the addition of two small side-chapels. The windows, a little later in date than the building, show in their turn how the portrait of the individual had invaded the iconography of the church; they represent Jean de Berri, his son-in-law Louis de Châtillon, and Jeanne d'Armagnac presented to the Virgin by St. John, St. Louis, and St. Margaret. His third Sainte Chapelle, at Mehun-sur-Nièvre, was adorned with statues of the apostles like its prototype at Paris.[5]

The next Sainte Chapelle to be built was that at Châteaudun begun by the great Dunois, Bastard of Orleans, in 1451. It was dedicated to his patron, St. John, to the Virgin, patroness of his wife, and to the Holy Angels. Its apse is three-sided; a small oratory branches off on each side of it. Here the old two-storied plan is reversed: the great chapel is on the ground floor, and the lesser

[1] Richard, p. 377.
[2] Work went slowly on until about 1400, when war stopped it. The chapel was altered and completed by Charles VI and Francis I.
[3] It is possible that this is the Sainte Chapelle, with statues of the Apostles and a magnificent shrine above the altar, which forms the background to the Annunciation in the Hours of Étienne Chevalier.
[4] Some are now in the crypt of Bourges Cathedral.
[5] The head of one of these is in the Louvre.

servants' chapel in an attic. The chief decoration consists in its numerous statues
of female saints: St. Elisabeth of Hungary, St. Agatha, St. Barbara, St. Catherine,
St. Agnes, St. Mary Magdalene, Sainte Geneviève, Sainte Radegonde, St. Mary
of Egypt, and St. Margaret. Besides these there are statues of the Virgin and the
two St. Johns, the patron saints of the Church, of St. Francis, and of Dunois
himself (Fig. 183 A). These, all of painted stone, are set against the engaged
columns of the vault. A little later Louis I de Bourbon, Comte de Montpensier,
built a Sainte Chapelle at Aigueperse. It was dedicated to his ancestor Saint
Louis, and was destined to serve as his mausoleum. It has two fine statues of
the Virgin and its patron saint. Of the fine Sainte Chapelle built by Anne,
Duchess of Bourbon and daughter of Louis XI, at Bourbon-l'Archambault,
nothing now remains but a few fragments of its glass.[1]

Nowhere in the world is the mature Gothic that makes the walls of a building
a succession of splendid windows of fairy lightness better exemplified than in
the Saintes Chapelles. Their devotional inspiration, the wealth and pride of
their founders, and the skill of their builders, working at a time when the architectural style was at its perfect moment of ripeness, achieved buildings of which
each was a masterpiece.

8. CASTLE CHAPELS

A Sainte Chapelle was a royal oratory, enshrining a relic, however minute,
of the Passion of Our Lord. It had an architectural tradition of its own, which
even the royal chapels which did not contain such relics hardly aspired to follow.
These, indeed, like castle halls, depended upon wall-painting for their chief
adornment. A contract made between the king and the painter Jehan Coste[2]
in 1356 lays down the scheme for the chapel of the castle of Vaudreuil in Normandy. It is to have sham marble painted below the existing frescoes, and
scenes from the stories of Our Lady, St. Anne, and the Passion are to be added.
The chancel screen is to be stencilled in various colours. The retable is to be
painted with the Trinity in the middle, and with St. Nicolas and St. Louis on
the side-leaves. The little oratory leading from the chapel is to be painted with
the Coronation of the Virgin *avec grant quantité d'angres* and the Annunciation,
with seven figures under arcades, and with coats of arms on the wooden wainscot
below.[3] The Coronation of the Virgin, indeed, was a favourite subject, and was
repeated on the tympanum of Charles V's chapel at the Louvre in 1366, with
angels censing and playing musical instruments and bearing shields of the arms

---

[1] In the church of Bourbon-l'Archambault.   [2] Fagniez, ii. 94.
[3] The contract lays down that it is all to be done in fine oil-colour on grounds of raised gold,
that Our Lady's vesture is to be of fine azure, and the whole well varnished and without fault. The
artist is to do it all and provide everything except firewood and beds for himself and his men, and to
receive the sum of 600 *moutons*.

of the king and queen.[1] His chapel at the Hôtel Saint-Pol imitated the Sainte Chapelle of Paris in having twelve statues of the apostles set round the walls; they were brightly coloured, with robes of blue and red and purple brocaded with gold, and their heads crowned by nimbuses a foot across, brilliantly painted with gold, green, red, and white.[2] This chapel, however, was eclipsed by that built by Louis II de Bourbon at his palace of the Petit Bourbon.[3] The vault was gilded, the ribs painted, the windows filled with glass of glowing colour, his arms painted and carved everywhere, and the great shields of his father, the Dauphin, himself, and his wife set in an oratory by the altar.

Such decoration was imitated by lesser men. The castle chapel at Brancion[4] was, about 1330, painted with the Nativity, the Resurrection of the Dead, the burial of a nun, a group of people listening to the reading of a sacred text, and pilgrims praying before the Sepulchre: scenes evidently chosen with a personal purpose now forgotten. The chapel of Jacques Cœur at Bourges is still beautified by the paintings of angels (Fig. 184) on the roof, holding scrolls inscribed with versicles from the Song of Songs and the *Gloria in Excelsis*.[5]

9. PSALTERS AND BOOKS OF HOURS

It was for use in the private chapels and oratories of castles that the most beautiful Psalters and Books of Hours of the Middle Ages were produced. The young Robert, son of Mahaut d'Artois, was given an illuminated book of *privées oroisons* soon after he had learnt to read, and in a few months they had to be provided with a little leather case to hold them when he travelled.[6] His sister was provided with a similar book; and, indeed, since women had more time for piety than men, more devotional books seem to have been painted for their use. Sometimes such books came near to being an expression of mere luxury. Eustache Deschamps makes a lady say:

> Heures me fault de Nostre Dame . . .
> Qui soient de soutil ouvraige
> D'or et d'azur, riches et cointes,
> Bien ordonnées et bien pointes,
> De fin drap d'or bien couvertes;
> Et quant elles seront ouvertes
> Deux fermaulx d'or qui fermeront.

The number of pictures seems generally to have been decided by the future owner; the painter was paid at piece-rates. In 1398, for example, the accounts of the Duchess of Orleans state that: 'Angelot de la Presse, paintre et enlumineur,

---

[1] Sauval, ii. 23.   [2] Ibid. 281.
[3] Ibid. iii. 25.   [4] Lemoisne, p. 30.
[5] The corbels of the vault are carved with angels holding shields of the arms of Cœur and allied families.   [6] Richard, p. 11.

à Blois, a reçu 12 liv. 10 s. t.[1] pour avoir fait vingt cinq histoires aux Heures en françois de Madame la duchesse, au pris de 10 sols t. pour chacune; pour deux lettres à vignettes, 10 s. t. et pour trois cent quatre lettres à deux points et entermellés, 12 liv. 16 s. 8 d. t.'[2]

The series of such books of private devotions begins with the Psalters illuminated for the ladies of the royal family in the thirteenth century; first the Psalter of Queen Ingeburge, wife of Philip Augustus,[3] with magnificent formal illustrations on a ground of burnished gold; then those of Blanche of Castille[4] and Jeanne de Navarre[5] with minute pictures arranged in medallions. Their illuminations at first usually consist in simple illustrations of Gospel scenes. Then gradually a new symbolic scheme is developed for the Calendar illustrations. For those painted by Jean Pucelle in the second quarter of the fourteenth century each month is identified with one of the Apostles, with one of the twelve articles of the Creed, and with an aspect of the teaching of St. Paul. Moreover, the whole year is made to symbolize the gradual supersession of the Old Law by the new. At the top of each page is one of the twelve gates of the Heavenly City. From its battlements the Virgin, 'par quoi nous fu la porte ouverte', waves a banner emblazoned with a device illustrating an article of the Creed. Below her is St. Paul, in January crouching beneath the hand of God, in the other months preaching. From the right side of the gateway springs an arch, showing the meridian altitude of the sun for the month. Beneath it is the zodiacal sign and a typical landscape: bare trunks and frost for January, rain for February, budding shoots for March, springing leaves for April. At the foot of the page is the Synagogue of the Old Testament, with a Prophet each month removing a fresh stone from it and handing it to an Apostle, in whose hands it becomes charged with an article of the Creed. Thus the Synagogue, complete in January, is pulled down throughout the year, until the Apostles can build the Church with its spoils.

The lay illuminators not only developed new schemes, but turned the old from formality to naturalism. The Psalters ordered by Saint Louis himself between 1253 and 1270[6] already show a greater liveliness of composition. The formal medallion scheme was being broken up; the scenes are true pictures, though they are set against an arcade framing a golden background. Then, apparently in the atelier of Jean Pucelle, light and shade was introduced, and air began to flow round the figures: a stage represented in the Psalter of Jeanne II de France, Queen of Navarre, who died in 1305.[7] Gradually even the divine figures became

[1] sols tournois.   [2] Laborde, iii. 174.
[3] Musée Condé, Chantilly. The Psalter is, of course, in Latin but the numerous pictures have French titles. See Delisle, Douze livres, p. 3.   [4] Paris, Arsenal 1186.   [5] Rylands Library, Manchester.
[6] Bib. Nat. lat. 10525, and another formerly in the Yates Thompson collection. The Breviary of Philippe le Bel (Bib. Nat. lat. 1023) has no architectural framing and lozenged grounds.
[7] Formerly Yates Thompson Collection.

moved by purely human feeling. In the *Bréviaire de Belleville*, for instance, painted about 1340, the Nativity is represented much as usual; but the Virgin, instead of looking away from the child in meditation, gazes at him as a mother would and strokes his head. Yet though naturalism crept into the figures, the backgrounds remained formal even in books as late and as accomplished as a Breviary copied for the use of Charles V.[1] It is only in the reign of Charles VI that Books of Hours—a form of prayer that was both cause and consequence of the development of castle chapels—came to approximate to the Romances in their landscape backgrounds and free compositions. For a time the two types of art continued side by side; those leaves of the Hours of the Duc de Berry known as the *Heures de Turin*, painted at Paris about 1390 (Fig. 185), still have impressive formal schemes for the larger miniatures: his *Très Riches Heures* painted just before 1416 not only lay as much stress on the Calendar illustrations of the duke's occupations (Fig. 150) as on scriptural subjects, but also set even such traditional themes as the Annunciation and Visitation against landscape backgrounds. These backgrounds might be purely romantic or exactly typographical: the Calendar scene for April—a betrothal—takes place just outside the walls of Dourdan, and the May Day party rides through the woods of Riom (Fig. 186). This change of background is paralleled by an equally striking change in composition; the illustrations are not only pictorial but picturesque. Even traditional schemes such as the Coronation of the Virgin (Fig. 187) are transformed into a new elegance; poetry is added to narrative, and humanity to symbolism. This curiously high standard, the reflection of an informed and elegant taste, could not be indefinitely maintained. The *Très Riches Heures* came to a premature end when the Duc de Berry died in 1416.[2] The tradition they established was carried on for a time. The Hours written for the Maréchal de Boucicaut between 1396 and 1421[3] have compositions and backgrounds as romantic if slightly less elegant than the *Très Riches Heures*. Their illuminator excelled in sky-painting: a noonday sky, deep at the zenith and very pale at the horizon, and a night sky of infinite depth, powdered with winking stars. Yet they shine on another world: July has succeeded to May.

Romance, indeed, could not endure for long; but topographical backgrounds and portrait figures continued in fashion. In the Hours which Foucquet painted for Étienne Chevalier just before 1461 it is Charles VII himself who appears as the first of the Magi, and his Château de Beauté that forms a background for the Nativity. Job lies on his dunghill by the road that leads to the castle of Vincennes, and Christ carries the cross along the banks of the Seine, with the Sainte Chapelle and the palace roofs behind Him.

[1] Bib. Nat. lat. 1052.
[2] They were completed about 1483 by Jean Combe for Charles, Duc de Savoie.
[3] Musée Jacquemart André, Institut de France.

With portraits and topography the heraldic decoration of civil life invaded Books of Hours; for example, the book of John, Duke of Bedford,[1] painted in France, probably as a wedding gift to his duchess Anne of Burgundy, has borders with little miniatures set against branches of his badge of juniper and scrolls of his motto *A vous entier* and her *J'en suis contente*. One miniature shows her kneeling before the Virgin and Child, against a tapestry background banded with her motto. The Hours of René of Anjou[2] include two pages which depict him praying, against a background of his arms, and on the opposite leaf a fine *Pietà*: both margins are powdered with his badges. Certain books of the time depict Solomon, Our Lady, and God the Father all enthroned beneath baldequins of the arms of France.[3]

This approximation to secular art was a natural consequence both of the tastes of the noble owners of such books, insensibly trained by the courtly atmosphere in which they lived, and of the fabrication of the books by laymen who divided their time between illustrating Books of Hours and illustrating Romances.

10. CHAPEL FURNITURE

The approximation to secular art is less manifest in the portable furnishings of castle chapels, though these were made by the same goldsmiths and ivory-carvers and tapestry-weavers as the adornments of the other rooms of the castle. Like other rooms the chapels had their sets of tapestries. Charles V had chapel hangings with the Passion of Christ, the Life of St. Denis, and the life of St. Theseus; the Duke of Anjou others with the Annunciation and the Adoration of the Magi, the Life of St. Catherine, and two of St. George; Philippe le Hardi tapestries of the Crucifixion and the Death of the Virgin; the Duke of Berri another Death of the Virgin, two of the Creed, the Coronation of the Virgin, and a Magdalene;[4] and Philippe le Bon a tapestry with Prophets and Apostles holding scrolls, the Prophets of their prophecies of the coming of Christ, and the Apostles of the articles of the Creed.[5]

These tapestries, like those of living-rooms, were closely based on illuminated manuscripts. Between 1375 and 1377 Jean de Bruges (more exactly Jean de Bondolf) painted an Apocalypse for the king's library at the Louvre.[6] In 1377 Louis I d'Anjou decided to have a set of tapestries made for his chapel in the castle of Angers: ninety panels joined into a series of bands some sixteen feet deep. The illustrations of the manuscript provided the subject, and Jean de Bruges produced cartoons drawn on linen based on them for the use of the weaver, Nicolas Bataille of Paris. The first three were finished in time for

---

[1] B.M. Add. MS. 18850.
[2] Bib Nat. lat. 1156 A, fols. 81[v] and 82.
[3] e.g. Bodleian MS. Rawlinson Liturg. e. 14.
[4] Guiffrey, p. 24.
[5] Bought in Paris from Jaquet Dordin in 1395. Laborde, ii. 273; iii. 109.
[6] The manuscript is now Cambrai 422. See Martin, *Min. franç.*, p. 59.

Christmas 1379. Like the illustrations of the manuscript the scenes are framed in imitation mullions of stone, and have backgrounds alternately of blue and red. These are brocaded in a lighter tint, powdered with flowers, with butter-flies charged with the arms of Anjou and Brittany, and with the initials of Louis and his wife Marie de Bretagne. In some places the double crosses of his Order are introduced. Originally there were inscriptions explaining the subjects woven at the bottom. After Louis's death they passed to René of Anjou, who, by his will of 1474, left to Angers Cathedral 'sa belle tapisserie en laquelle sont contenues toutes les figures et visions de l'apocalisse'.[1] Here they still remain; a few panels have disappeared, but sixty-nine are still in existence, from which we may still judge of the colour and beauty of a mediaeval castle chapel (Fig. 188).

Sometimes an illuminator worked yet more directly on chapel decoration. In 1481 Jean Bourdichon, the famous illuminator of the Hours of Anne de Bretagne, painted on the walls of Louis XI's country house of Plessis-lez-Tours scrolls inscribed *Misericordias Domini in aeternum cantabo*, upheld by three angels.[2] A similar scheme inspired the design of a set of chapel hangings woven in the valley of the Loire about 1515 for the widow of Pierre de Rohan. Against a charming verdure background angels stand bearing the instruments of the Passion (Fig. 189). Between them great scrolls are set inscribed with verses. A typical poem, set beside the angel with the Pillar and the Scourge, is this:

> Regarde en pitié et voy comme
> Benignement par la doulceur
> Tresdure angoisse por toy homme
> Voulut souffrir ton Créateur.
> En ceste atache a grant douleur
> Ou son benoist corps longuement
> Si quoy ne peult dire greigneur
> Endura non pareil tourment.[3]

The smaller hangings of castle chapels might also be of tapestry. Jean de Berri in 1402 owned no less than four altar frontals with the Coronation of the Virgin and musician angels.[4] More often, however, they were part of a set of vestments, known as a *chapelle*, for which painted or embroidered silk was more suitable than heavy tapestry.

None of these mediaeval *chapelles* survives in its entirety. The most interest-ing fragment that remains is that known as the 'Parement de Narbonne': a frontal of white silk painted in *grisaille*, representing a Calvary between symbolic figures of Church and Synagogue, with three scenes of the Life of Christ on

---

[1] Quatrebarbes, i. 85.　　　　　　　　　[2] Havard, *Dictionnaire d'ameublement*, s.v. 'Papier peint'.
[3] Part of another set of fifteenth-century chapel tapestries, with angels holding the instruments of the Passion against a brocaded background, are in Notre-Dame-de-Nantilly at Saumur.
[4] Guiffrey, ii. 162 et seqq.

either side. Charles V and his queen appear kneeling in adoration, and it was probably intended for one of his chapels (Fig. 190). Such colourless hangings and vestments were used in Lent; to paint them was one of the customary tasks of the king's painters.[1] The scenes the *Parement de Narbonne* portrays closely resemble those in a book of Hours painted for Queen Jeanne some years earlier: the Kiss of Judas, the Bearing of the Cross, and the Entombment, all offer close parallels.[2]

The greatest riches of the chapels, as of other rooms in the castle, lay in objects made from intrinsically precious materials. In them, as in secular objects of gold and silver, one great man vied with another in profusion and magnificence. Charles V had a superb gold cross set with 382 sapphires made for the Sainte Chapelle of Vincennes, and gave five golden statues of the Virgin to the Sainte Chapelle of Paris.[3] The Duke of Guyenne was described on his death in 1415,[4] at the age of nineteen, as 'moult curieux à magnificences d'abiz et joiaux *circa cultum corporis sui*, desirant grandeur et honneur de par dehors, et grant despensier à ornamens de sa chapelle privée, à avoir ymages grosses et grandes d'or et d'argent; qui moult grant plaisir avoit à sons d'orgues, lesquels entre les autres oblectations mondaines hantoit diligemment . . . '. His inventory reveals the details of this magnificence. He had a great crucifix with figures of Our Lady and St. John, altar candlesticks upheld by angels, and a 'tableau' of the Descent from the Cross, all of jewelled gold. Even the holy-water stoup and aspergil were of gold set with jewels. He had a great golden image of the Virgin seated in a silver-gilt chair, all jewelled, and a standing St. John Baptist of jewelled gold. The chapel of Charles the Bold was no less magnificently furnished;[5] the Duke of Berri had the very lectern of silver gilt.[6] When great men ate their daily bread off gold, nothing could be too precious to contain the sanctified bread and wine. Such a chalice, paten, and burette, probably made in Paris about 1333, still survive[7] to show what the yet more splendid riches of the inventories may have looked like. The burette (Fig. 191) is enamelled with scenes of the story of the Prodigal Son, evidently based on the illuminations of a manuscript. The grotesques on the foot and the games represented on the

[1] e.g. Richard, p. 209. 'Une chapelle de quaresme . . . en samit blanc . . . . A Pierre de Brusselle [a painter] pour pourtraire ladite chapelle de ymageries, xx lb.' 1328. The surviving frontal may be part of a *chapelle* attributed to the king's painter Maistre Girard in an inventory of Charles V. Labarte, *Inv. du mob. de Ch. V*, no. 1122.   [2] MS. Arsenal 2002. See Michel, iii. 119.

[3] Christine de Pisan, *Vie de Charles V*, pt. i, chap. xxxiii.   [4] Pannier in *Rev. arch.*, p. 161.

[5] Laborde, ii. 1. It contained some fourteen images of gold and silver gilt, a number of crosses and crucifixes, a ciborium, three paxes, six candlesticks, two holy-water stoups and aspergils, five basins, three sets of altar vessels, diptychs, books in gold covers, and a large number of reliquaries.

[6] Gay, *Glossaire*, s.v. 'aigle'.

[7] In the National Museum, Copenhagen. See Worsäe, *Nordiske Oldsager*, 1859; Molinier, iv. 213; Falke, *Deutsche Schmelzarbeiten*, p. 119, and Michel, ii. 982. The inscription on the paten indicates that the paten was given by an unknown Brother Petrus Regneri to an unknown church in 1333.

neck equally find parallels in marginal illustrations. The colouring likewise closely resembles that of manuscripts. The chief scenes are set against a background of translucent blue; the lesser fields have a background of red. The dresses are enamelled in pale green, crimson, violet, and various tones of yellow; the faces and hands are gilt.

For devotional images ivory was for long the most favoured material; at once delicate and monumental, beautiful in itself and susceptible of enrichment in gold and colour, it was particularly fitted to work on the comparatively small scale which the size of castle chapels demanded. For a great church a cult-image had to be of wood, painted or plated with metal, or of stone; such images had a prestige and legend which no private oratory could command.[1] Towards the end of the thirteenth century, however, the development of the cult of the Virgin introduced lesser images of Our Lady even into castle sanctuaries, and these were usually of ivory.[2] For them the ivory-carver developed a type of his own, less dependent than heretofore on illuminated manuscripts or monumental sculpture. Gradually the hieratic dignity of greater cult-images was made more human. An ivory Virgin in the convent of St. Mark at León[3] is still stiff in pose, but the Virgin smiles a remote and enigmatic smile. In another in the Martin le Roy Collection the pose is still formal, but the Virgin smiles and holds an apple to the Child, who stretches out His hands to play with it. The Virgin has a new grace and elegance; she is not only Mother, but also Queen. The figure may be compared in pose with the rather later figure at Villeneuve-lès-Avignon,[4] on which the robes of Virgin and Child are decorated with gold borders and embroideries. These courtly characteristics find their completest expression in the ivory Virgin added to the treasure of the Sainte Chapelle of Paris early in the fourteenth century[5] (Fig. 192). She is a smiling young mother; aristocratic, it may be, but without the austere nobility that would enable her to bear the sorrows to come. She has no prevision of them; no artist has created a Virgin more gay or more heartless.

The cult of the Virgin that introduced such statuettes into castle chapels likewise led to the fabrication of ivory 'tabernacles' in her honour that superseded the earlier diptychs of the Passion[6] (Fig. 193). These generally enshrine a central figure of Our Lady, with subordinate scenes of the Infancy of Christ.[7] More closely analogous with the sculptured tympana of the cathedrals are certain

---

[1] Exceptionally Enguerrand de Marigny ordered a painted wooden statue of Saint Louis for his castle chapel at Mainneville. It is now in the parish church.

[2] When such statues belong to a church they have usually come to it from a private chapel. Koechlin (i. 95) cites Guillaume de Hainaut, Bishop of Cambrai, who in 1296 gave one from his own chapel to the Carthusians of that city.   [3] Koechlin, xxviii.

[4] It probably dates from about 1335.   [5] Koechlin, i. 104.   [6] Ibid., i. 116.

[7] Jean le Scelleur made one for Mahaut d'Artois in 1325, but the type is found thirty years earlier. Koechlin, loc. cit.

ivory diptychs and triptychs (Fig. 194). The likeness, however, seems to be due less to direct imitation than to derivation from a common source in manuscript paintings. The ivories in particular[1] are in close connexion with the French royal psalters[2] and such illuminations as those of the Gospel-book of the Sainte Chapelle: even their colouring is similar.[3]

Towards the end of the thirteenth century ivory was employed for groups of statues, naturally of small size, that were set upon the altars of castle chapels, arranged against a background of wood, metal, or textile, to form a kind of retable.[4] Parts of two such groups survive[5] to show that the monumental dignity of cathedral sculpture could be transferred even to work on a small scale. One represents Christ crowning His Mother, with two enraptured angels; the dress patterns of fleurs-de-lis, towers of Castille, and barbel, the device of the House of Bar, are proof of its original royal ownership.[6] The figures may fairly be compared with those of the tympanum of Longpont, and with the gable sculptures of the same subject at Rheims; but their elegant compactness, which gives them an illusory air of simplicity, and their freedom from an elaborate background endows them with a lyrical poignancy of their own. This quality is yet more evident in the second group (Fig. 195) which represents Joseph of Arimathea and the Virgin receiving Christ's body as it is taken down from the Cross. In this a grand simplicity of line and a subtle and calculated treatment of drapery combine in a whole that is at once noble and exquisite.[7] A traditional stiffness prevents the hair of the dead Christ from hanging downwards as it would; yet Joseph of Arimathea has knotted his cloak round him apron-wise to be ready for his hard task. The figure of the Virgin is as static and dignified as any cult-image, but for the head and hands that move in a controlled agony of grief.

By the second half of the fourteenth century gold had taken the place of ivory as the favoured material for statuettes and tabernacles. The schemes and the subjects were commonly unchanged, but the different technique of goldwork made for greater elaboration in detail. Even the ivory diptychs of the Passion were reproduced in metal; in 1399 Charles VI bought a gold diptych with a *Pietà* on one side and an angel supporting the Virgin on the other.[8] More characteristic of gold-work were the tabernacles based on an architectural

---

[1] See Koechlin, i. 80.   [2] See p. 199.

[3] One of the Passion in the Salting Bequest has the architectural background picked out in green and red, the hair black or gold, and the lips red.

[4] Cf. such sculptured retables as that of the Sainte Chapelle of Saint-Germer-de-Fly.

[5] Both now in the Louvre.

[6] The figures all came to Paris in the nineteenth century from Savoy. See Molinier, *Ivoires*, p. 183. He compares the group with one described in the inventory of Charles V.

[7] The composition may be compared with a fragment of the Jubé of Bourges. Koechlin, i. 59.

[8] Laborde, p. 276.

scheme of niches and pinnacles. Sometimes the central part of one of these was shaped to contain the Host. One such is described in the inventory of Louis d'Anjou:[1] a 'très grant et très noble tabernacle d'or pour mettre, poser et porter le Corps de nostre Seigneur Jhesu Crist'; an elaborate architectural whole with scenes of the Life of Christ represented by figures in the round, statuettes of the four Doctors of the Church in niches, and the Virgin and Child with the duke and duchess and their patron saints at the top.

The free-standing statuettes of the Virgin lent themselves yet better to translation into gold. One such figure survives (Fig. 196) which was given to Saint-Denis by Jeanne d'Évreux, widow of Charles le Bel, in 1339. It may earlier have figured in his private chapel. It is infinitely more noble and dignified than the ivory Virgin of the Sainte Chapelle, yet the Child's lively gesture is anything but traditional.[2] The base is enamelled with scenes of the Passion; the fleur-de-lis that the Virgin holds was intended to contain relics.

Such images were soon multiplied. Charles V in 1380 had thirty-seven images and tabernacles of Our Lady in silver gilt[3] and nine in gold, besides many of other saints. Soon even gold was painted or enamelled in an effort after verisimilitude. The Duc d'Anjou had golden figures of Christ, the Virgin, St. John, and St. Peter, with painted hands and faces;[4] and an angel reliquary, once in the royal treasury, still exists[5] with face and hands enamelled in natural colour.

Both images and 'tabernacles' were often destined to serve as reliquaries. The Duke of Orleans, for example, owned a reliquary for a thorn from the Crown of Thorns in the Sainte Chapelle,[6] which still survives[7] (Fig. 197). It is shaped like a pax. The central panel is enamelled with a figure of Our Lord in high relief, seated on a rainbow with the orb of the world beneath His feet. The Virgin and St. John kneel below Him in adoration. A large sapphire serves as pedestal to the Thorn. This 'tableau' is framed in leafy scrolls of jewelled gold from which the heads of the apostles rise like flowers, and is surmounted by a seated figure of God the Father in a jewelled glory. On the foot angels sound the trump of Resurrection and the dead rise from their tombs. The base is a bastion with towers in each of which an angel blows a trumpet. Over the arches at the sides a coat of arms of France within a bordure gules indicates its

[1] Moranvillé, p. 18.

[2] M. Mâle points out (*Art rel. fin*, p. 127) that this is the first known instance of the Child being represented naked to the waist.

[3] Cf. the silver-gilt images of Charles the Bold's chapel: Our Lady, Saints Peter, Paul, John the Baptist, Louis, Antony, Philip, James, John the Evangelist and the rest of the Apostles, Barbara, Laurence, and George.   [4] Moranvillé, p. lxxvi.   [5] In the Louvre.

[6] F. M. Graves, *Deux inventaires de la Maison d'Orléans*, no. 366, p. 101.

[7] Waddesdon Bequest, British Museum. See Joan Evans, 'The Duke of Orleans's reliquary of the Holy Thorn', in *Burlington Magazine*, June 1941.

former ownership. The whole hierarchy of its personages and its richly coloured realism recall the scene of some fifteenth-century mystery play, magically transmuted into gold and jewels.

Sometimes the owners were represented even on such reliquaries. The Duc de Berri owned in 1416 a tabernacle called 'le joyau du mont Calvaire',[1] with figures of the duke and duchess under canopies and a Crucifixion above, 'et pendent au dit tabernacle deux petites fioles de cristal, en l'une desquelles a du sang de Nostre Seigneur et en l'autre du lait de Nostre Dame, prins en la Sainte Chapelle de Paris'. The 1321 inventory of the Sainte Chapelle of Paris[2] includes an image of Saint Louis of silver gilt between two angels, with a kneeling knight in silver on either side, one identified by his arms as Peter the Chamberlain[3] and the other as Pierre de Chambly. A splendid surviving 'tabernacle' of the kind is that now known as the *Goldene Rössel* in the treasury of Altötting (Fig. 198). It was given to Charles VI by his wife Isabel of Bavaria on New Year's Day, 1404.[4] His inventory, made the next year, thus describes it:[5] 'Un ymaige de Nostre Dame qui tient son enfant, assis en un jardin faict en manière de treille. . . . Et au dessoubz au bas de l'entablement a un cheval esmaillé de blanc, et a la selle et le harnois d'or et un varlet esmaillé de blanc et de bleu qui le tient par une main par la bride, et en l'autre mein un baston . . . .' It remains an astonishing piece, in its dramatic arrangement, that recalls that of the fifteenth-century stage, in the rich glow of its enamels and jewels, and in its curious mixture of the religious and the secular, the courtly and the naïve. No surviving object can better capture for us the atmosphere of a castle chapel of about 1400, of the years before war brought misery to France. The splendour of such work is a secular splendour, designed as much to enhance the glory of the owner of the chapel as of the God he worshipped. It represented no sacrifice and no unselfish devotion; but it brought both beauty and magnificence within the walls both of Saintes Chapelles and of the lesser castle oratories of the aristocracy.

11. PICTURES

It remains to consider the pictures painted for castle chapels, a kind of decoration that it is perhaps easier for posterity to appreciate than the unfamiliar glories of ivory and gold and jewels.

The earlier devotional pictures were as easily portable as the ivory diptychs which they succeeded. Like them they were generally two-leaved, and when shut with the delicate inner paintings face to face could safely be packed for

[1] Laborde, p. 264.   [2] Vidier, xxxiv. 203.

[3] See Joinville, *Histoire de Saint Louis,* chap. lxxvi.

[4] It was taken to Bavaria by her brother Louis of Bavaria in 1413. See Labarte, 'Le Rössel d'or d'Altoetting', in *Annales archéologiques,* xxvi, 1869, p. 204.

[5] Gay, *Glossaire,* i. 367, s.v. 'Cheval'.

travelling. Such pictures might be used in the castle chapel or in the bedroom of the owner; in 1397 the painter Colart de Laon was paid 'pour avoir fait pour Messire Loys de France un tableau où est en peinture Saint Loys de France et Saint Loys de Marseille, qui est attaché au chevet de son lit'.[1] They were often composed, as the Wilton Diptych is, of one leaf with a representation of the Virgin (Fig. 199) or the Trinity (Fig. 200) or a saint, and another representing the owner of the picture in adoration. In others the owner is indirectly represented by the figure of his patron saint.

A larger form of diptych was circular. In 1383, for example, Jean d'Orléans, the king's painter, made such a picture for Philippe le Hardi of Burgundy.[2] One side represented Christ rising from the sepulchre, with an angel to uphold Him; the other the Virgin supported by St. John. On the back were lesser pictures of St. Christopher and an *Agnus Dei*. The diptych had hinges and clasps of silver, and a felt-lined case for travelling. These circular diptychs, too, were sometimes designed with a picture of the owner in one half; René d'Anjou in 1471 owned 'ung tableau ront couplé à deux copplez dont en ung des costez est limage de nostre Dame qui tient son Enfant et de lautre costé y a la pourtraiture d'un ancien seigneur'.[3] Two fine circular pictures of the kind survive, but without the portrait of the owner. One represents the Virgin holding the dead Christ, between the Magdalene, St. John, Joseph of Arimathea, and another.[4] It is a small picture, such as probably had its own travelling-case and went everywhere with its owner. The second represents the Coronation of the Virgin with an admirable nobility (Fig. 202).

Besides such portable pictures castle chapels often contained large altar-pieces. In 1415, for example, Henri Bellechose made such a painting for the castle of Saulx, more than seven feet long, representing the Virgin and Child adored by Jean sans Peur and Philippe le Bon, presented by their patron saints St. John the Evangelist and St. Claude.[5] Usually such altar-pieces were planned as a triptych. On that painted for the chapel of the Palace at Paris about 1461[6] the centre is filled with a Crucifixion, while the wings have the patron saints of the royal family: St. Louis, St. John the Baptist, St. Denis, and St. Charlemagne. A similar royal commission must have been the origin of a splendid polyptych of about 1490 of which two panels are in the National Gallery. One represents the hunted doe taking refuge with the hermit St. Giles, the other (Fig. 201) the Mass of St. Giles. This is represented in the basilica of Saint-Denis with every detail of the retable given by Charles the Bald, the cross of Saint Éloi, and the base of the shrine of Saint Louis. Two other panels from the same picture[7]

[1] Koechlin, i. 25.   [2] Poëte, p. 36; Prost, ii. 1788.   [3] Gay, s.v. 'Tableau'.
[4] Another *Pietà* of the same kind of about 1400 is in the Museum at Troyes.
[5] Lemoisne, p. 50.   [6] Now in the Louvre.
[7] I do not know their present whereabouts; about 1938 they were in the Wildenstein Gallery, in New York.

P

represent Saint Rémy baptizing Clovis in the Sainte Chapelle and blessing the people from the steps of Notre-Dame de Paris.

Usually figures of the owners appeared with their patron saints on the leaves. The famous painting of the Burning Bush,[1] painted by Nicolas Froment for René of Anjou about 1475, shows on the left-hand leaf René presented by Saint Maurice and the Magdalene and on the right his wife Jeanne de Laval with St. Nicholas, St. Catherine, and St. John.[2] The loveliest of such altar-pieces is that painted by the Maître de Moulins for Pierre II de Bourbon and his wife Anne de Beaujeu about 1498[3] (Fig. 203). St. Anne presents Anne de Beaujeu and her daughter on one leaf, St. Peter Pierre de Bourbon on the other (Fig. 204). The pensive Virgin, the glorious rainbow that surrounds her, the effortless floating angels, and the careful portraits of the great people on the leaves, combine to give a complete expression to the glories, at once devotional and materialistic, of the end of the Middle Ages.

12. TOMBS

In the early Middle Ages sculptured tombs were the prerogative of saints. Then the honour was extended to abbots, who might one day be canonized. Laymen continued to lie beneath modest tomb-slabs, a knight's marked only by the incised representation of his sword. Such tombs, indeed, continued in use down to the middle of the thirteenth century, especially for knights of the Temple. A late example at Saint-Ouen de Rouen[4] was incised only with a knight's closed helm and an inscription giving his name.

Meanwhile kings and great lords were gradually assuming the right to tombs as splendid as those of saint or abbot. The right was at first acquired by their being buried in an abbey which they had founded: such seems to have been the justification for the splendid tomb of gilt and jewelled metal erected by his wife to Louis VII in the abbey of Barbeau, inscribed

GEMMIS ARTE NOVA PROFUSA ET AURO
QUONDAM MAGNIFICUM FIDELIS UXOR
SPONSA TOTA SUO REGENS ADELA
EREXIT LAPIDEM.

Another founder's statue may be that of a Vicomte de Beaumont dating from the beginning of the twelfth century and one of the earliest known.[5]

The most magnificent of these early tombs were all of copper, enamelled and

---

[1] Now in the cathedral of Aix-en-Provence.   [2] See Lemoisne, p. 82.

[3] Ibid., p. 107. Now in the cathedral of Moulins. The donors may be compared with another picture by the same hand in the Somzée Collection, Brussels.

[4] Bodleian Gaignières, vol. vii, f. 39: 'Dominus Johannes dictus de Monte Poignani miles.'

[5] Now in the Musée archéologique of Le Mans. Another from the abbey of Bonneval is portrayed among the Gaignières drawings in the Bodleian.

gilt. They were made, like other enamels of the kind, at Limoges; and though they were doubtless ordered specially, represented not a portrait of any particular knight or lord but a generalized type made recognizable by the heraldic decoration. One was set up between 1151 and 1160 to Geoffroi, Count of Anjou and Maine, in the church of Saint-Julien du Mans. The slab still survives (Fig. 205): it is like some full-page illustration of a manuscript turned into metal. It was set up by a bishop of Le Mans; the inscription reveals that the count figures here not as founder, but as benefactor. He is celebrated as the giver of peace to Anjou:

ENSE TUO, PRINCEPS, PREDONUM TURBA FUGATUR,
ECCLESIIS QUE QUIES, PACE VIGENTE, DATUR.

One of the richest tombs of the kind of which we have a picture and exact description is that erected to Henry the Liberal of Champagne,[1] who died in 1181, in the collegiate church of Saint-Étienne at Troyes which he had founded. He was represented in gilt bronze, lying under an arcaded altar-shrine of gilt and enamelled metal. The spandrels were filled with figures of angels holding inscribed scrolls,[2] and other verse inscriptions in turquoise-blue enamel on a gold ground commemorated the virtues of the count. It is hard now to realize how brilliant the whole must have been: as elaborate in its architecture and decoration as a Romanesque portal, and as rich in gold and colour as a twelfth-century manuscript.

This splendid tomb was soon rivalled by that erected in the same church by Blanche of Navarre to her husband, Thibault III of Champagne, after his death in 1201.[3] The figure was of silver, with fermail, cross, belt, buckle, and purse-mount all jewelled. Worldly vanity found fuller expression in it than in the shrine-like tomb of Count Henry. Round the tomb were set small silver statues of his ancestors Louis VII, King of France, and Henry II of Champagne, King of Jerusalem; of his father and mother; of his sisters, his wife, his son and daughter, and his father-in-law Sancho of Navarre, all with inscriptions in Latin verse to say who they were and what was the degree of their relationship to the dead man.[4]

Not even the royal family of France could rival such magnificence; from the little we know of them the enamelled tombs raised at Saint-Denis by Louis VIII to his father, who died in 1223, and by Blanche of Castille to her husband, who

[1] It was destroyed at the Revolution, but drawn a little before by Mouillefarine and engraved by Gaucherel. (See *Annales archéologiques*, xx. 8.) For a detailed description see Arbois de Jubainville, iii. 311. A few fragments survive in the Museum of Troyes.

[2] Cf. the angels above the Blessed on the tympanum of the portal of Conques.

[3] See Arbois de Jubainville, iv. 90.

[4] Cf. the thirty-six little figures with their names and relationships above on the enamelled tomb of Marie, Comtesse de Dreux, d. 1274, in Saint-Yved de Braisne. Bodleian Gaignières, 18346, i, fos. 78–80.

died in 1226, were less splendid versions of those at Troyes.[1] Parts of two
survive, commemorating a son and daughter of Saint Louis who died as children.
The heraldic dresses of the children, and the heraldic borders, are more modest
claims to nobility than the statues on the tomb of Thibault de Champagne.[2]
Beside the figures are little effigies of monks and angels. Each tomb was originally set in a niche with a more life-like representation of the dead child painted
on the wall: she serious in an embroidered dress and he with hawking-glove
and kestrel and a surcoat of fleurs-de-lis over a red robe.[3]

Such enamelled tombs continued to be occasionally preferred for the tombs
of great personages; a familiar example is that of William de Valence, who died
in 1296, at Westminster.[4] Yet even this is more remarkable for its stone setting
than for the actual figure, and the next great group of tombs are of carved stone.

Family pride was in the air, and even saints could be moved by it.[5] King
Louis IX, moved by *pietas*, or, it may be, by a politic desire to enhance the
prestige of the royal house, towards the end of his reign set up tombs to his
ancestors in the royal abbey of Royaumont. Such of these as survive[6] are perfect
examples of the stock figures of the monumental sculptors; they are kings and
queens more uncharacterized and impersonal than the kings and queens of
Israel and Judah on the portal of a cathedral. Such statues were still being used
for the tombs of people whose features and characteristics were known; the
tomb set up to Blanche of Castille at Maubuisson in 1255 was bought ready-
made at Tournai.[7]

The tomb of the saint's son Louis, who died in 1260, was made soon after
his death and marks a fresh stage. The figure (Fig. 206) is no longer stiff and
symmetrical; the hands are to one side, and one leg is slightly flexed. The long
face and high forehead make the head look like a portrait. The sides of the
tomb are decorated with a file of mourners: abbots and bishops, kinsmen in
mourning-hoods, officers of his household with purses and staves. At one end
is the coffin, borne by the kings of France and Hungary. The slightly later
tomb of Jeanne de Chastillon, a benefactress of the abbey, showed a file of its
monks as mourners.[8]

[1] Both were destroyed by the Huguenots in the sixteenth century.

[2] Cf. the heraldic decoration on the tombs of Alix of Brittany, d. 1221, and Pierre de Dreux,
d. 1250, at Saint-Yved de Braisne. Bodleian Gaignières, 18346, p. 99.

[3] See Bodleian Gaignières, ii. 26.

[4] Another example is that of Blanche de Champagne, Duchess of Brittany, d. 1283, from the
Abbaye de la Joie, Morbihan, now in the Louvre. They continued in fashion longer in the Limousin,
where there are records of as many as twenty-seven. As late as 1327 Hugues de Haric ordered two
tombs of *l'œuvre de Limoges* for himself and his wife. Ducange, s.v. 'Limogia'.

[5] Even the legendary sons of Clovis II had a magnificent tomb erected to them at Jumièges at this
time.   [6] They are now in Saint-Denis.

[7] *Tumba empta*. Prost in *G.B.A.* xxxvi. 235. It is of black marble and is now in Saint-Denis.

[8] She died in 1290. Bodleian Gaignières, 18347, p. 27.

In 1271 Isabella of Aragon, wife of Philippe le Bel, was killed in a travelling-accident at Cosenza in Calabria, where her tomb, evidently of French work-manship, still exists. It represents her and her husband kneeling on either side of a statue of the Virgin. The queen's face is scarred, distorted, and suffering; evidently it was copied from a death-mask. The king, still alive when the tomb was made, is much less strongly characterized. Yet the figure on his own tomb, made between 1298 and 1307 by Pierre de Chelles and Jean d'Arras, is a definite portrait, with a large thin mouth and a crooked nose (Fig. 211 A). The only conventional features are the eyes, which suggests that this head too may be based on a death-mask.

These attempts at portraiture, however, were almost entirely confined to the tombs of the royal family.[1] The tombs even of great lords and ladies continued to be works of art rather than chronicles of fact. On them, the dead were always represented young: a convention that to this day gives them a lyrical pathos. The convention was suited to an age of courtesy, and reflected the religious belief that when men rose again all would have the age of the per-fected Christ, thirty-three.[2] At Châlons a tomb represents a mother between her two daughters: all are portrayed as of the same age. Few tombs are more beautiful or more full of repose than those of the years round 1300 (Fig. 207). One of the loveliest of all probably commemorates Adelaïs of Champagne, Comtesse de Joigny. The effigy represents her robed for a journey: the long journey into another world. Her little dog sniffs lovingly at her feet. Round the tomb stand the mourners (Fig. 208): dressed not in mourning-hoods or heraldic robes, but in the ordinary clothes of civil life, cloaked and hooded for the road, holding a book, or with falcon on wrist, ready for the chase. The end of the tomb (Fig. 209) is carved with the figure of a youth standing in a tree and picking fruit, not knowing that two monsters are gnawing at its root: an alle-gory of time that gnaws at the roots of life, derived from the romance of *Barlaam et Josaphat*.[3]

Many of the finest tombs of the time seem to have come from the workshop of the Paris *tombier* Jean de Huy. When the husband of Mahaut d'Artois died in 1312 she ordered an alabaster tomb from him:[4] the contract makes clear how precise, and how impersonal, were the details demanded from the sculptor. 'Un ymage d'un chevalier armé, un escu, une espée, unes bracïeres entour ledite ymage, un lion souz les piez dudit ymage et deus angelos aus deus espaules qui tendront les mains à un orillier qui sera sous le chief dudit ymage, et lettres tout entour.' The sculptor evidently gave satisfaction, for when Countess Mahaut

---

[1] It is possible that they were influenced by the series of portrait statues of the kings of France in the great hall of the palace in Paris, begun by Philippe le Bel and added to on the death of every king. See Prost in *G.B.A.* xxxvi. 241.   [2] See Mâle, *Art rel. fin*, p. 434.
[3] See Mlle Pillion in *Rev. de l'art anc. et mod.*, 1910, p. 321.   [4] Richard, p. 313.

lost a young son three years later the tomb, this time of marble, was again ordered from him.[1] When he had carved it, it was painted by Jean of Rouen, and then packed into a case wrapped in linen and padded with cotton, and sent to the church of the Dominicans at Poligny where the child was buried. Jean de Namur, an assistant of Jean de Huy, went there from Paris on purpose to set it up.[2]

Many tombs of the time included subsidiary representations of religious subjects. The tomb of a woman of the middle of the thirteenth century at Nanteuil[3] represented her with a Virgin and Child, an angel, a bishop receiving the soul, and two other figures, all rather awkwardly and irregularly arranged. On the rather later tomb of Guillaume de Mussy and his wife at Mussy-sur-Seine, Abraham is represented behind the heads of the two couchant figures. With the help of two angels he holds up a winding-sheet containing their two souls, represented like children. The tomb of Enguerrand de Marigny, who died in 1315,[4] showed, besides the usual effigy in its niche, figures of a seated Christ with hands stretched out to show His wounds, a Virgin and St. John, and two figures of mourners kneeling. An early fourteenth-century tomb-niche in the abbey church of Évron has one gable carved with the knight dressed for a journey, on his heavily caparisoned horse; on the other he kneels before the Virgin, his travelling-scrip hung on a tree behind him. The abbot and two of the monks of Évron kneel on the other side.

By the middle of the fourteenth century the classic types of tomb were giving place to more elaborate forms, or were themselves being elaborated out of recognition.

Sometimes a sculptured tomb of the usual shape was transformed by being set under a canopy. One of the finest of these was that of Jean d'Artois, Comte d'Eu, who died in 1386 and was buried in the abbey of Notre-Dame d'Eu.[5] In form it was not unlike the tomb of William de Valence at Westminster; four pillars, themselves carved with canopied niches and surmounted by angels, supported a roof painted blue and powdered with fleurs-de-lis, resting on elaborately pierced stone gables. Charles, Comte d'Artois, who died in 1336, had a tomb with a catafalque canopy at Saint-Denis,[6] as had a few other members of the royal family.

Occasionally tombs represented the dead person not lying, but kneeling: a type of statue influenced by the familiar kneeling statues of donors.[7] An early

[1] Richard, p. 315. Another tomb bought from Jean de Huy is mentioned on p. 312.
[2] The district round Namur, where Huy is also situated, was famous for its marble-quarries and from there many sculptors came to Paris.
[3] Bodleian Gaignières, xii, fol. 33. She bore arms of France and Castille.
[4] Ibid., vii. 123. It was in the Collégiale of Écouis which he founded.
[5] Ibid., i. 57. Only the effigy survives, in the crypt.   [6] See Courajod, ii. 62.
[7] e.g. the kneeling statue of Mahaut d'Artois, sheltering a nun and offering a church, once in the abbey she founded at Thieuloye, c. 1325.

example is that of Pierre d'Orgemont, Chancellor of France, who died in 1389, which was once in the church of the Culture Sainte-Catherine at Paris.[1] In Notre-Dame, the kneeling effigy of Antoine des Essarts, seigneur de Glatigny, who died in 1442, combined the functions of a tomb-statue and a donor-statue; its inscription commemorated him and his gift of a great image of St. Christopher, before which the statue knelt.[2] A later tomb at Saint-Étienne de Sens showed a knight and his lady kneeling upon a high platform so that they could for ever see Mass celebrated at the altar they had endowed.[3]

Humbler tombs no longer were engraved only with the symbol of occupation but were incised with full-length figures of the dead set under canopies with an infinity of small ornamentation. Isabel de Labroce (Fig. 210), who died in 1316, lies under a slab as beautiful as any tomb sculptured in the round. Jehan, Sire de Montmorency, who died nine years later, rests at Conflans Saint-Honorine in chain-mail surcoat, a burly figure within an elegant niched canopy, all incised on marble and filled in with coloured mastic. The brasses of the time were no less magnificent, but nearly all were melted to make the cannon of the Revolutionary armies.[4]

Meanwhile in the more splendid portrait-tombs realism was increasing. An exactness in portraiture was coming into fashion; the statues[5] of Philip VI by André Beauneveu show him with small eyes too close together, a sharp nose, and a heavy jowl; that of Charles V, by the same artist, portrays him as whimsical and deprecatory. Charles V, indeed, who in many ways made his ancestor Saint Louis his model, followed him in his interest in tombs. He ordered from Beauneveu his father's tomb in 1364, his own and his wife's in 1367, and the great du Guesclin's just before his own death. This was executed by Robert Loisel and Thomas Privé, together with that of Louis de Sancerre, his friend, who was buried beside him. Literal realism could go no farther; du Guesclin was represented with his scarred eyeball (Fig. 211 c), and Sancerre with his squint. When Charles VI died in 1422 his painter François d'Orléans moulded the face and hands of the corpse for a wax effigy in real clothes to lie on the catafalque, and such moulds no doubt served as models to the sculptors who made his tomb after death.[6] Beauneveu's statues, indeed, are artistically

[1] Courajod, ii. 450.   [2] Bodleian Gaignières, iii. 3.
[3] Bodleian Gaignières, xi. 70. One of the rare kneeling figures to survive is that of Étienne Porcher in Saint-Thibault de Joigny.
[4] A magnificent one was that of Jean de Honnecourt, d. 1358, in the cloister of the abbey of Ourscamps. Bodleian Gaignières, xiii. 68: it was far more elaborate than the surviving English brasses.
[5] The Benedictines of Saint-Denis had an ancient and prescriptive right to bury the bodies of the kings of France. To evade this, and ensure commemoration in favoured if less ancient foundations, the bodies were sometimes divided. Thus Philip VI had two tombs, one of his entrails at the Jacobins (now in the Louvre) and one of the rest of his body at Saint-Denis. It is recorded that the Dominicans' statue represented him in youth, and the Benedictines' at the age at which he died.
[6] Courajod, ii. 127. The mask of Blessed Jeanne de France, founder of the Order of the

unsatisfactory, for their faces are over-lifelike for the smooth and formal folds of the drapery.

Such realism could not satisfy for long. When Philippe le Hardi of Burgundy had his tomb begun in 1383 he started[1] a new cycle of monuments remarkable less for realism than for artistic splendour. The tomb is a reflection of the time when the panoply and procession of the tournament had set new standards of magnificence for every aspect of courtly life, and even funerals were pageants. The tomb was intended to be the chief adornment of Philippe's Charterhouse of Champmol, which he had founded to serve as a mausoleum for his family.[2] It was begun in 1383 by Jean de Marville and a team of workmen that included Claus Sluter; six years later polishers came from Paris to finish it. It was still without its sculptures, which were only begun by Claus Sluter and his nephew Claus de Werve after Duke Philip's death in 1404. Towards the end of this year Sluter retired from the world to the cloister of Saint-Étienne de Dijon, and thus, though he designed the tomb, the greater part of it was executed by Claus de Werve. The alabaster effigy, with face and hands naturalistically tinted, and jewels and ornaments picked out in gold, rests on a slab of black marble. Two angels with wings of gilt bronze kneel at the head. Beneath the heavy cornice of the slab a peculiarly delicate and elaborate arcade runs round the tomb, with little figures of mourners of an extraordinary vitality. When Philippe le Hardi died he was followed to the grave by two thousand of the men of his household and Court; nobles, knights, pages, chamberlains, cooks and menials, valets; the bishops and abbots of his dominions, the monks of his foundations; all robed in mourning-mantles.[3] So they appear round the tomb; few in number in reality, but so strongly characterized that they epitomize the great procession. The tomb was partly destroyed at the Revolution, and when set up again the mourners were not all correctly placed; originally a bishop attended by deacons and acolytes headed the procession, and priests and monks ended it.[4]

So soon as the reigning duke, Jean sans Peur, saw the splendours of the tomb he began to bargain with Claus de Werve for his own sepulchre. But it had not been begun before he was murdered, and it was not taken in hand until after Claus de Werve's death in 1439. Four years after this the order was given to a

Annonciades, who died in 1505, still survives in the Archevêché at Bourges. *Rev. de l'hist. franciscaine*, viii, 1931, p. 56.

[1] It is possible that he followed the type of the tomb of Louis de Crécy, Count of Flanders, erected by his son in Saint-Donat de Bruxelles in 1354. The tomb is destroyed; its description indicates a black marble sarcophagus, a white marble effigy, with two angels, and twenty-four *pleurants* in an arcade. Pinchart, i. 127.　　　[2] See p. 154.

[3] Cf. those worn in the miniature of the funeral of Jean le Bon, Bib. Nat. MS. franç. 77.

[4] Some of the statuettes which were in America have lately been generously restored to the tomb.

wandering sculptor from Aragon named Juan de la Huerta. He was a rolling stone and absconded in 1457, leaving in his workshop most of the minor sculpture of the tomb—canopies, mourners, and angels—and two effigies of the duke and his wife which had been rejected as ill made. After his departure there was a pause, until in 1463 Antoine le Moiturier, a sculptor from Avignon who had already made a name for himself, was engaged to finish the tomb. It is a perfect pendant to the earlier tomb, though the double effigy and the more elaborate arcade make the composition more crowded; the artist strove to make the mourners yet more diverse than on the earlier tomb,[1] but many of them lost their dignity in the process.

These tombs were imitated in all the countries under Burgundian influence, from the Netherlands[2] to Spain.[3] Even in France their influence was quickly felt. When Jean de Berri planned his tomb in his Sainte Chapelle at Bourges, before 1438, he had Philippe le Hardi's tomb in mind;[4] the effigy and mourners were of the same type (Fig. 212). Anne, Duchess of Bedford, sister of the Duke of Burgundy, ordered Guillaume de Veluton to make her a tomb of the same kind at the Célestins in Paris.[5] When in 1448 the Bourbon tombs at Souvigny were ordered from Jacques Morel, it was specifically stated in the contract that they were to be like those of the Dukes of Burgundy at Dijon.[6] Morel was better than his word: no man of his time could carve drapery as he could,[7] and both the portrait heads and the robes are finer than those at Dijon[8] (Figs. 211 A, 213 A).

Other tombs continued and renewed the tradition of work in bronze.[9] Philippe le Bon in 1455 erected a bronze tomb to his great-grandfather Louis de Mâle, Comte de Flandre, in the Chapelle de Treille at Lille,[10] and this in its turn established a tradition. When in 1477 René II of Lorraine defeated Charles the Bold before Nancy, he erected a bronze tomb to his enemy who had been killed in the battle.[11]

When Louis XI first planned his tomb in 1474[12] Michel Colombe and Jean

---

[1] Though he copied some exactly: the monk with a hand in a half-open book, the *chappier*, the Carthusian seen in profile, a weeping monk, and a monk with a hand beside his head.

[2] e.g. Michelle de France at Saint-Bavon de Gand, 1436–42.

[3] Outside Burgos, for instance, the Cartuja contains a monument of about 1490, some eighty years later than the completion of the tomb of Philippe le Hardi, which in its contrast of black marble and white alabaster, its canopies, angels, and mourners, is obviously based on the Dijon tomb although it is by a Spanish sculptor and is octagonal in form.

[4] The effigy remains in the crypt of Bourges Cathedral, and some of the mourners are in the Musée du Berri.

[5] Other tombs showing Burgundian influence are those of Jean de Vienne, d. 1435, at Pagny, and of the Bâtard de Saint-Pol, d. 1466, at Ailly-sur-Noue.   [6] See Courajod, ii. 429.

[7] His hand seems visible in the draperies of the tomb of Agnès Sorel at Loches, but the head has been restored.   [8] The figures of mourners have disappeared.

[9] The trade of bronze-founding was still active at Paris. Jehan Morant, who signs the tomb of Armand de Barbazan, d. 1431, at Saint-Denis, was probably the founder. Courajod, ii. 435.

[10] Where it still exists.   [11] See Courajod, ii. 449.   [12] Laborde, p. 434.

Fouquet were ordered to prepare a drawing on paper for a stone monument, apparently of the Dijon type. Some eight years later the king fell seriously ill, and shut himself up at Le Plessis and tried to persuade the world that he was in excellent health. Once more, and this time more seriously, his thoughts turned to his tomb.[1] First his secretary had to write to a Paris painter:

'Mestre Colin d'Amiens, il faut que vous faciez la pourtraiture du roy nostre sire: c'est assavoir qu'il soit à genoux sus ung carreaul comme ycy dessoubz et son chien costé luy, son chappeaul entre ses mains jointes, son espée a son costé, son cornet pendant à ces espaules par darrière, monstrant les deux bots. Oultre plus fault des brodequins, non point des ouseaulx, le plus honneste que fere ce porra, habillé comme un chasseur, atout le plus beau visaige que pourrés fere, et jeune et plain; le netz longuet et ung petit hault, comme savez, et ne le faicte point chauve, le netz aquilin, les cheveux plus longs derrière . . .'

The drawing survives just as it was ordered, with plenty of hair. Then men had to be found to translate the design into bronze: not an easy task, for part was to be cast and part engraved. Robert le Noble, goldsmith of Paris, was first approached, but the negotiations fell through. At last the treasurer was able to sign a contract with Conrad of Cologne, a goldsmith, and Laurent Wrine, the king's cannon-founder, for making the statue in bronze, all gilt, with an enamelled cushion; and finally it was set up, to kneel[2] before the image of Notre-Dame de Cléry until it was destroyed by the Huguenots.

The disappearance of almost all the bronze tombs of the later Middle Ages in France makes it difficult to know how closely they followed these models. The stone tombs of the end of the Middle Ages, however, betray the influence of bronze in a certain dry precision of modelling and in a marked preference for free-standing figures. The tomb of the Sire de Chaource at Malicorne still follows the Dijon tradition in the main, but for the dramatic abundance of the Burgundian tradition it substitutes a slightly dry precision that evidently owes something to bronze. Philippe Pot (Fig. 213 B), Grand Seneschal of Burgundy, Ambassador to London, and the teller of fifteen of the remarkably coarse *Cent nouvelles nouvelles*, has a noble tomb that is so far inspired by bronze that its translation into stone is a *tour de force*. Eight men in mourning-hoods, with the shields of the dead man's eight degrees of noble descent, bear upon their shoulders a bier of stone on which the effigy of the dead man rests.[3]

---

[1] See Courajod, ii. 452 et seqq.

[2] A few other kneeling statues are recorded in the fifteenth century: Charles VIII, Louis XII; Jean Jouvenel des Ursins, d. 1431. Their approximation to the donor type of statue made them particularly suitable for use in chantry chapels.

[3] Philippe Pot died in 1494, but the epitaph, which begins *Cy demorra*, shows that the tomb was made in his lifetime, and it probably dates between 1477 and 1483. The only imitation of this tomb I know is that of Saint Ronan at Locronan, which dates from the sixteenth century and represents the saint on a bier upheld by statues of the Virtues.

The series closes with the effigies of Nicolas du Moustier and his wife in the church of Chaource (Fig. 214), that at once commemorates their gifts to the church and serves as their memorial. They kneel in their bright-coloured clothes, serious and life-like, for ever praying for the salvation of the mediaeval world that was so soon to end.

IX

THE CITIZENS

1. CITIES AND TOWNS

THE cities and towns of France lived obscurely, industriously, and as it were anonymously through the early Middle Ages. Apart from their cathedral, their monastery, or their feudal lord, their existence can only be guessed at. In certain cities Gallo-Roman traditions still lived, and the memory of a municipality endured. Sens, for example, once the capital of the Roman province of Senonia, continued as the capital of the ecclesiastical province of Sens, which was exactly conterminous with the Roman territory. Its oval walls, still largely Roman, strengthened by a Gallo-Roman tower, enabled it to resist attack: its bishop St. Loup defended the city against Clotaire II early in the seventh century, and his successor St. Ebbo led the resistance against the Saracens in 732. Sens survived, quiet and watchful behind its patched and ancient walls; and when the city was joined to the crown of France in 1020 it had vitality and tradition enough for its prosperity to blossom anew. The Gallo-Roman town of Semur-en-Auxois, safe behind the rocky barrier of its *castrum*, and strengthened by a communal charter, could even in 1478 refuse to accept French domination until it had been captured by force. Often, too, the memory of a Roman city remained in the division of a town. Toulouse, Rodez, Nîmes, Carcassonne, Périgueux, and other ancient *municipia* continued to consist in the Roman *cité* and a later *bourg* each enclosed in its own walls and usually separately represented on the city council. Even the little town of Chaource, once the Roman station Cadusia, kept apart from the rival settlement of Villeneuve that was established alongside it.

Already in the ninth century new towns were being formed round the abbeys or castles that provided a walled sanctuary for the inhabitants in times of danger. Abbeville was only a farm of the abbey of Saint-Riquier at the beginning of the ninth century, but by the reign of Hugues Capet it had its own ramparts. Such settlements were deliberately encouraged by their abbots and lords, for they paid dues. In 831 the town of Saint-Riquier was a feudal dependency of the abbey round which it had grown up.[1] Each trade had a street allocated to it, and each street paid dues. The street of grocers paid a vestment each month; the street of smiths forged the abbey's ironwork for nothing; the shield-makers bound the abbey books; the saddlers made the harness for the abbey horses; the bakers provided a hundred loaves a month, the butchers fifteen measures of dripping, the wine-sellers sixteen measures of wine and one of oil a week,

[1] Fagniez, i. xxv.

and the inn-keepers thirty measures of beer a day. The cordwainers provided the servants' shoes, the furriers the monks' pelisses, and the fullers all the cloth they needed. In 881, after the Normans had destroyed the abbey and town of Saint-Bertin, the abbot built a fortress and a wall and planned the dependent town anew, with accommodation again allotted according to trade.[1]

Such *burgi*, however, had no more than a few hundred inhabitants. Even the ancient *civitates* had only two or three thousand;[2] a cathedral city was the size of a small Cotswold town. The Ville Haute of Provins remains to give the scale of the metropolis of one of the great provincial fiefs. The church of Saint-Thibault, patron of the count's family, where the wagoners who brought their horses successfully up the steep ascent used to offer a horseshoe to the saint; the ancient hospital; the salt-barns; the public baths and the town well; the stones that mark the parish limits; the count's palace and its collegiate church; the Donjon and its prison; the mayor's house set on the walls; the little square tower where the executioner lived; the cross where the count's edicts were read; the house where his provost lived and the lesser pleas were heard; the great tithe barn; the two inns—all held within a pentagon of ramparts defended by gates and towers—form a feudal microcosm, astonishingly self-sufficing and with nothing metropolitan about it. It was by virtue of their tradition rather than their size that the cities were powerful, and gradually they leavened the life of lesser communities. By the twelfth century artisan labour was beginning to be established on a free rather than a servile basis;[3] travelling merchants, the *pedes pulverosi* of the mediaeval law-courts, were being brought within the orbit of city life.

With the growth of pilgrimages, fairs came into being at pilgrimage centres, and the right to hold them and to levy dues was soon confirmed to the churches by deed. The great fair of the Lendit was instituted at Saint-Denis 'out of honour and reverence for the holy relics of the Nail and Crown of Our Lord', according to a deed of 1124. The fair of Lagni[4] belonged to the abbey of Saint-Pierre de Lagni. At Chartres the first fairs were held in the cloister. Under Philippe le Bel more fair-privileges were granted, and Troyes, Provins, and Bar-sur-Aube joined Lagny in making Champagne one of the commercial centres of France. Cloth-making was recognized in seventeen towns, which were bound by law to send goods to the *Foires de Champagne*. Halls were built from which the merchants of Languedoc, the Low Countries, and the *Hanse de Londres* sold their goods: halls very like the merchants' khans of such cities as Damascus or Aleppo. The Burgundian fairs of Dijon (at Midsummer and All Saints'), of Autun, Auxonne, Châtillon, and Tonnerre, were usually

---

[1] 'Per ministeria disposuit.' Fagniez, xxxii.   [2] Pirenne, p. 70.
[3] Pirenne, p. 91; Acloque, p. 4.
[4] On this and other *foires de Champagne* see Bourquelot.

held twice in the year: a *foire chaude* in the spring or summer, and a *foire froide* in autumn or early winter.

While city trade was being developed, civic rights were being claimed and granted. The first mention of *burgenses* is in France and in 1007.[1] Yet even such cities as Rheims, which cherished a clear memory of its Roman status as a *municipium*, had to fight its archbishop to get its communal rights recognized. Dijon had a mayor by 1100; by 1108 Noyon had received a charter from its bishop,[2] and by 1111 Laon had bought one from its canons. Paris had maintained the tradition of a merchants' guild: their Roman predecessors dedicated an altar to Jupiter in the time of Tiberius. Under the name of the *Marchands de l'eau de Paris* they had the monopoly of carrying merchandise up the river and of levying toll on all goods that entered the city by water. The guild and its privileges were confirmed by Louis VII and became the nucleus of the municipality. Their badge, a ship, with the later motto *Fluctuat nec mergitur*, still appears as the arms of the city. In the *municipia* of the south the election of consuls and capitouls continued, but their rights were gradually confirmed and codified.

As cities and towns thus became integrated into the mediaeval system, feudal lords, both clerics and laymen, began to exploit their territories by the foundation of new towns. Some were founded alongside a castle, like Montauban, Montferrand, and the numerous Castelnaus of the south,[3] others were built *de novo* to make a new centre for a tract of undeveloped land. The map of France still shows more than 150 Neuvilles, more than 300 Villeneuves, and many Franchevilles, Montségurs, and other names indicative of new foundations.[4] The development of these new towns in the north was encouraged by Louis VII—who himself founded Villeneuve-le-Roi[5] near Sens, Villeneuve near Compiègne, Villeneuve-d'Étampes, and many others—and in Languedoc by the feudal lords and the officers of the Crown in an effort to repopulate a province ravaged by the Albigensian crusade.[6] The southern new towns often bore the

---

[1] Pirenne, p. 134.

[2] The chief grants of communal rights in the twelfth century were Saint-Quentin 1103, Amiens 1113, Eu 1151, Montreuil 1188, Nevers 1194, Montdidier 1195, Coucy 1197.

[3] Curie-Seimbres enumerates thirty-two; Longnon forty-three.

[4] Longnon, pp. 515 et seqq.

[5] Now Villeneuve-sur-Yonne.

[6] A dated list of a few *villes neuves* makes their extension plain:

    1125 Vaucresson, Seine-et-Oise.
    1144 Montauban, Tarn-et-Garonne.
    1163 Villeneuve-le-Roi (sur Yonne), Yonne.
    1168 Belleville, Saône-et-Loire.
    1175 Villeneuve (Pont-sur-Seine), Aube.
    1222 Cordes, Tarn.
    1239 Villefranche-d'Albigeois, Tarn.

name of *bastide* that like the more familiar *bastille* means a fortification. Some were set up by Edward I of England about 1270 to defend the marches of Guyenne.[1] Many were named after foreign cities, to make them more attractive.[2] Their construction ranges from the middle of the twelfth century to the middle of the fourteenth; the creation of new bastides by anyone but the king was forbidden in 1344.

All were uniformly planned. Four crosses were set up at the four cardinal points to serve as boundary stones, and the rectangular plan of the future town was traced on the ground, with two wide streets crossing at right angles to form a market square in the middle, and a criss-cross of lesser streets to break up the rest of the area into lots. The founder was responsible for the erection of the

1252 Villeneuve-d'Aveyron; Villeneuve-de-Rouergue.
1264 Villeneuve-sur-Lot, Lot-et-Garonne.
1265 Montségur, Gironde; Gimont, Gers; Villeréal, Lot-et-Garonne.
1269 Montflanquin, Lot-et-Garonne.
1270 Castelsagrat, Lot-et-Garonne; Réalmont, Tarn; Villefranche-de-Lauragais, Hte-Garonne.
1271 Eymet, Dordogne.
1272 Aigues-Mortes; Beaumont-du-Périgord, Dordogne.
1277 Bretenoux, Lot.
1280 Fleurance, Gers; Pampelonne, Aveyron.
1281 Pavie, Gers; Sauveterre-de-Guyenne, Gironde; Sauveterre, Aveyron.
1283 Villeneuve-de-Berg, in the Vivarais.
1284 Vianne, Lot-et-Garonne; Montpazier, Dordogne.
1285 Mirande (Lézian), Gers; Valence-d'Agen, Tarn-et-Garonne.
1286 Cologne, Gers.
1290 Grenade, Hte-Garonne; Briatexte, Tarn.
1306 Rabastens de Bigorre, Htes-Pyr.
1310 Réalville, Tarn-et-Garonne.
1322 Gimont, Gers.
1332 Revel, Gers.
1346 Labastide Clairence, Basses-Pyr.
[1] 1272 Beaumont-du-Périgord.
     1284 Monpazier.
     1285 Valence-d'Agen.
[2] Barbastro, Barbaste, Lot-et-Garonne.
    Barcelona, Barcelonne-du-Gers.
    Bologna, Boulogne-sur-Gesse, Hte-Garonne.
    Cologne, Cologne, Gers.
    Cordova, Cordes (Cordua), Tarn.
    Damietta, Damiatte.
    Florence, Fleurance, Gers.
    Granada, Grenade, Hte-Garonne.
    Pampelona, Pampelonne, Aveyron.
    Pavia, Pavie, Gers.
    Piacenza, Plaisance, Hte-Garonne.
    Tournai, Tournay, Htes-Pyr.
    Valencia, Valence-d'Albigeois, Valence d'Agen.
    Viterbo, Viterbe, Tarn—and even Lincoln (Longnon, p. 524).

walls and gates, the church and market hall, and the setting up of a forge and a baker's oven and weighing-place.[1] It was he, too, who established the customs of the town-to-be, by a charter that at once secured its administration and advertised its privileges.

In 1175, for instance, Henri, Comte de Troyes, granted a charter to his Villeneuve near Pont-sur-Seine. Every man living in it was to pay twelve deniers and a measure of barley each year as ground rent of his house, and four deniers a year for his allotment of land for cultivation outside the walls, if he wished to take it up. The tenant had the right to sell or otherwise dispose of his house and land, subject to these rents. The men of the town were to be free from the obligation of joining the count's army in the field unless he himself rode at their head. They were to have the right of electing six *échevins* to administer the town's affairs and to sit with the count's provost to hear pleas. No lord or knight could claim any inhabitant of the town as his unless he were a bondslave or owed him dues. The form continued in use with little change, though there were local variations in the number and name of the town councillors and in the conditions of tenure. Often a fine was imposed on those who failed to build their houses in an appointed time, usually three years. At Saint-Osbert the tenants were bound to build the façade of their houses in the first year, and the rest of it within three years.

A number of these new towns survive with little enough change to give us an idea of mediaeval town-planning. The walls of Aigues-Mortes (Fig. 215 A) were ordered by Philippe III in 1272 after his return from crusade;[2] the Genoese Boccanegra built them for 500 *livres tournois*, in a great parallelogram some 620 yards long and 330 wide. Similar walls, little less perfect, still surround Castelnau-de-Montratier, Monpazier, and Vianne. Cordes originally had three separate enceintes, with lists between. The fortified gateways of the *villes neuves* are their most striking architectural feature. The great gates of Villeneuve-lès-Avignon may stand as a type of entrance (Fig. 216), but they can be paralleled at Aigues-Mortes, and on a lesser scale at Monpazier, Domme, Villeneuve-d'Aveyron, and Castelnau-de-Montratier. At Villeneuve-sur-Lot the gates are surmounted by great square towers like belfries. The most familiar characteristic of the new towns is the arcades round the central market-place, that give shelter from sun and rain. They are found everywhere, from Carentan in the north—an old town, but rebuilt after a fire—to Monpazier in the west and innumerable *bastides* in the south.[3]

[1] See Mortet, ii. 60.

[2] Louis IX had bought the site from the monks of Psalmody and had built the Tour de Constance and dug a canal to Grau-Louis, its port, because he had no port on the Mediterranean that was his own property.

[3] An incomplete list includes Monpazier (1284), Libourne, Castelnau-de-Montratier, Mirepoix (wooden), Bretenoux, Villeneuve-de-Rouergue, Réalville, Sauveterre-d'Aveyron, Réalmont, Lisle-

The creation of new towns, with their fortifications and wide streets, was paralleled by improvements made at the same time to the older cities. Paris did not have new walls until the eleventh century, though little can have been left of the old after six successive sieges by the Northmen before 911 and the siege of Otto II in 978. Even then the new fortifications were built only to defend the island of the city. Not until 1180 did Philip Augustus plan a greater wall to include the suburbs on either bank of the river. It was begun in 1190 on the right bank with a round tower every sixty-five yards or so. The wall on the left bank was finished by 1209, with thirty-two little towers only ten feet in diameter and six fortified gates. The area enclosed on both banks was only 625 acres. The defences were completed by building the Louvre as a place of defence outside the enceinte.[1]

The lesser towns were similarly fortified. Noyers, near Chablis, that even now has little more than a thousand inhabitants, was protected at the end of the twelfth century by a wall and towers, of which sixteen still remain. In 1212 Hervé de Vierzon endowed Mennetou-sur-Cher with walls from twelve to sixteen yards high, with three gates each pierced through a square defensive tower. Lormes in the Morvan even now holds only two thousand souls; but when it got its charter in 1223 it promptly fortified itself with a wall and twenty-two towers. Saint-Sévère-sur-Indre, a town now of about a thousand inhabitants, had a triple enceinte of machicolated walls, although it was set on a hill above a river in a naturally strong situation.[2] Crécy-en-Brie, of the same size, has a double line of fortifications originally strengthened by no less than fifty-five towers. At La Couvertoirade in Aveyron the castle and the church are built into the fourteenth-century polygonal walls of the town.

Greater cities were fortified on an equally grand scale; a section of the fourteenth-century wall of Poitiers that survives at Pont-Achard shows it set thickly with round turrets, that serve at once as buttresses and as places of shelter for the defenders. A later section of the ramparts (Fig. 215 B) has a decorative cusped machicoulis like that of a fifteenth-century castle. Naturally the defences of older towns were often of many dates—the double enceinte and fifty-two towers of Carcassonne range from the fifth to the fourteenth century—but sometimes circumstances caused the fortifications of a large city to be wholly

---

sur-Tarn, Sauveterre-de-Guyenne, Villeneuve-sur-Lot, Montflanquin, Castelsagrat, Revel, Marciac, and Saint-Macaire. One of the largest is in an old city, Millau, Aveyron; its oldest arcades are of the thirteenth and its latest of the sixteenth centuries, whereas those of the *villes neuves* were mostly built in one piece.

[1] See Rochegude and Dumolin, p. 15.

[2] Sometimes the town walls were joined on to those of the castle, as at Fougères, which has ten towers to the castle's thirteen, and Coucy, with twenty-eight towers all told. Both sets of walls were built in the thirteenth century. At Dinan the oval donjon, built between 1382 and 1387, is set in the walls of the town, which originally had twenty-four towers and four gates.

Q

rebuilt. The exiled Popes rebuilt the walls of Avignon on a magnificent scale between 1349 and 1370, with beautifully corbelled machicolations (Fig. 217).

The gates of a city were no less vital to its defence than the walls. They naturally followed the general scheme of the entrances to castles, especially as the town wall was usually supplemented at these points by a moat or fosse to be crossed by a drawbridge. The earlier gates, such as those of Cluny, Provins, and Sens, are strong and simple. The Porte Saint-Jacques of Parthenay (Fig. 218) is one of the most monumental of the earlier period; its almond-shaped corner-towers and corbelled machicolations are plainly derived from contemporary castles. The great Porte du Croux of Nevers, built between 1393 and 1398, is a castle in itself, though pierced by a low gateway; it served to house part of the permanent garrison of the town. At Flavigny the fifteenth-century Porte du Bourg, which controlled a drawbridge over the moat, was flat with the wall, but the usual fifteenth-century plan for a large city gate was a double tower linked by a building beneath which the road passed. Monumental examples survive at Chartres,[1] Alençon, Barbezieux, and La Ferté-Bernard (Fig. 219).

Sometimes the situation of a town demanded fortifications of another kind. The harbour of La Rochelle is still defended by the Tour de la Chaîne, built about 1375, and the Tour Saint-Nicolas, built between 1350 and 1380; until lately there was a third, the Tour de la Lanterne, built between 1445 and 1468. Elsewhere a bridge was part of the town's defences; the Pont-Vieux of Albi, for example, first built in 1035, and the bridge over the Vienne at Saint-Junien, built in the thirteenth century and enriched by Louis XI with a chapel to the Virgin. In the fourteenth century such bridges were often heavily fortified, like the bridge of Montauban, built between 1303 and 1316, and the more famous Pont Valentré at Cahors (Fig. 220), of which the consuls of the town laid the first stone in 1308.[2]

2. TOWN HOUSES

The houses within the defending walls were infinitely varied. By virtue of the protection of the ramparts the citizens were free from the necessity of fortification, and could build for air and warmth and decorate for beauty at a time when the rich men living in castles in the country could think only of defence. For, as Fra Salimbene observed in the middle of the thirteenth century, 'In France only the townspeople live in the towns; the knights and noble ladies stay in their country houses and on their own domains.' It is only in the

---

[1] Severely damaged in the bombardment of 1944.

[2] It originally led to a fortified gate, now destroyed. The consuls were justifiably proud of it; it is represented on the town seal, and the architect was given a fine tomb in the Cordeliers at the town's expense.

south, where nobles did sometimes live in the towns, that a fortified house is found inside a city wall.[1]

A typical town house of the twelfth century was on three floors. One at La Chaise-Dieu may serve as an example. A low arch on the ground floor leads to a cellar. Alongside it a sculptured archway opens on to the stairs which lead to the chief room—the *avant-solier*—on the first floor, with a handsome arcaded window of two lights opening on to the street. The stairs continue to the smaller rooms above which served as sleeping-quarters. Houses of this type are found all over central France;[2] in the south—for instance at Saint-Gilles— stress is laid on string-courses rather than on arcades, giving a horizontal line to the whole façade.

Cluny used to be particularly rich in Romanesque houses, that were for the most part built after the great fire of 1159. A few still survive,[3] but the best general impression can be obtained from old engravings of the town (Fig. 221), which show how picturesque and rich was the effect of the sculptured arcades. The friezes and spandrels were often decorated with roundels of fantastic beasts; a frieze from Cluny has roundels with a monkey between two fishes, a boar with his foot in a platter, a deer-hunt, two wyvern-like monsters, and a tiger with a vine coming out of his mouth: decorative subjects that seem ultimately inspired by bestiary illustrations. Even artisans had houses decorated with sculpture; a late twelfth-century panel from a shoemaker's or leatherworker's at Cluny shows him seated at his bench between his apprentice and a client[4] (Fig. 222 B). It is significant that such figure-sculpture is hardly found except in places where the building of a great church had established a school of sculptors. At Rheims, for example, the tympanum of a house was carved with a beautiful trinity of Learning, Strength, and Love (Fig. 223 A).

In the thirteenth century the Romanesque scheme of ground-floor arcade, many-windowed *avant-solier*, and attics was retained, but was given a new aspect by the adoption of Gothic arches and window tracery.[5] A good example is the Hôtel Aubriot at Dijon,[6] built by a money-changer, Guillaume Aubriot, in the middle of the thirteenth century. The openings on the ground floor, closed at need by shutters, led to his warehouse. The *avant-solier* has round-headed traceried windows like a triforium; above are the usual attics. A similar scheme was followed at the Hôtel de Vauluisant at Provins (Fig. 224). Even

[1] There are some good examples at Périgueux, e.g. the Château Barrière.

[2] e.g. Vézelay, Cluny, Thiers.

[3] Rue de la République, rue d'Avril, rue du Merle, rue Joséphine Desbons, rue Lamartine (formerly Dauphine). See also Verdier and Cattois, *Arch. civile*, i. 69.

[4] The type may well be derived from such Gallo-Roman stelae as that of a carpenter in the Museum of Sens, no. 2783.

[5] The whole development may be followed in such ancient stone-built towns as Figeac, Brioude, and Chalard (Haute-Vienne).   [6] 40 rue des Forges.

as late as 1445 Jacques Cœur built himself a house at Montpellier on this traditional plan.[1] The three arches of the ground floor had sculptured spandrels: on one a sun charged with fleurs-de-lis, on one a moon surrounded by a crown of thorns, on the third a fruit-tree with a shield of Cœur's arms, and on the fourth his merchant's mark. At Cordes, a *ville neuve* in the Tarn, the fine 'Maison du Grand Fauconnier' has a second story of arcaded windows (Fig. 225), with a surprisingly decorative effect.

The thirteenth century was a great age of growth for towns. In Paris, for example, the streets were beginning to be replanned with a width of from fifteen to twenty-eight feet, to be paved and named. By the end of the century the city had 300 streets and covered 865 acres.[2] Here and in other towns, as building increased and street frontages grew more restricted, houses were sometimes built with the gable-end to the street. A good example at Saint-Benoît-sur-Loire[3] has three fine early Gothic windows under the gable. At this time ornamental chimney tops came into fashion, that served to prevent the chimney from smoking: in many districts—for example at Bayeux, Brantôme, and Figeac—these were elegant lanterns of carved stone; in Champagne they were of moulded terra-cotta. Sculptured decoration continued to be concentrated on the mouldings and cuspings of the *avant-solier*; exceptionally, a late thirteenth-century house at Rheims was adorned with statues of a harper, a fiddler, and a man playing the bagpipes.

The fourteenth century witnessed new growth in the larger cities. Between 1356 and 1358 Étienne Marcel, Provost of the Merchants of Paris, built a new wall that enclosed the Louvre, Bourg-l'Abbé, the priory of Saint-Martin-des-Champs, and the Temple within its boundary, and divided the city into administrative sections. Twelve years later Charles V began to extend the city wall on the right bank to follow the line of the present *grands Boulevards*, and strengthened both it and the old enceinte of Philip Augustus to resist artillery. In 1383, when the new wall was finished, the city enclosure covered 1,085 acres. Charles V had wearied of the Palais de la Cité and did not care to be at the Louvre within the city walls; so he built the Hôtel Saint-Pol for a residence on the confines of the city, with the Chastel Saint-Antoine[4] to defend it. This extension and this new building, in spite of the years of revolt, war, pestilence, and famine that followed, started the building of a whole series of fine town houses. Guillebert de Metz begins his description of them with the phrase 'en l'an quatorze cent quant la ville estoit en sa fleur . . .' and indeed 1400 marks the flowering-time of Paris as a city. The finest houses, apart from the palaces of the king and the royal dukes, were those of the prosperous lawyers and civil

[1] Bouvier, p. 67.   [2] Rochegude and Dumolin, p. 16.
[3] In 1931 the ironmonger's shop. Other early examples will be found at Thiers.
[4] Later called the Bastille.

servants. That which Guillebert de Metz admired most was the town house of maître Jacques Duchié, clerc du Roi en la Chambre des Comptes,[1] in the rue de Prouvelles. It was planned round a court, in which peacocks and other *oyseaux à plaisance* were kept. The first hall was decorated with *tableaux et escriptures d'enseignmens* hung on the walls; the next contained every kind of musical instrument, on which Maître Duchié used to play, and the next chess and backgammon boards and all sorts of games. There was a chapel panelled with marble, with carved desks and seats, and many other rich rooms. At the top of the house there was a solar, a great square room with windows on three sides from which to look over the city. Nothing remains of the Hôtel Duchié, but in the rue de Montmorency[2] the much more modest house of Nicolas Flamel, scribe, writing-master, and bookseller to the University, still exists. He bought the land in 1406, and began the house in the following year. When he died in 1418 he left it to the parish. The façade is enriched with incised sculptures under the cornice: angel musicians, a St. Christopher, and Flamel kneeling with his two sons before a crucifix with the Virgin and St. John. The inscription sums up the philosophy of the thrifty citizen:

Chacun soit content de ses biens
Qui n'a souffisance il n'a rien.[3]

Old engravings of Paris show many fifteenth-century sculptured stair-turrets in the districts on the right bank of the river; these, however, were nearly all destroyed when the new streets were made in the nineteenth century.[4] In several cases, for example in the house called that of Admiral Coligny in the Marais, these turrets were corbelled out to project over the street and give a little extra space to the house. The Hôtel de Sens survives, built between 1475 and 1519, with corbelled-out turrets at the corners, and high ornamental dormer windows.

Certain towns had a tradition of building in stone which brought their architecture under the influence of castle-building. An old saying declares, 'Qui a maison à Uzerche a château en Limousin.'[5] Sometimes, indeed, such town houses were built by noblemen, like that at Saumur[6] built by René of Anjou about 1450, with turrets and steep gables and a façade sculptured with a statue of the Virgin and the devices of René's Order of the Crescent. Burgundy is rich in stone-built towns: Autun, Avallon, Saulieu, Beaune. Dijon, which in

[1] Leroux and Tisserand, p. 199. [2] No. 51.
[3] A second inscription reads: 'Nous hommes et femmes laboureurs demourans ou porche de ceste maison qui fu faicte en l'an de grace mil quatre cens et sept sommes tenus chascun en droit soy dire tout les jours une patenostre et .1. Ave Maria en priant Dieu que de sa grace face pardon aux povres pecheurs trepassez. Amen.' [4] See, e.g., Verdier and Cattois, *Arch. civile*, ii. 19.
[5] Other Limousin stone towns are Brive and Aubusson.
Called 'Maison de la reine de Sicile'.

the fifteenth century had as many as twelve thousand inhabitants, has a series of late-mediaeval town houses, of which the Hôtel Chambellan may serve as an example. Tours and Toulouse[1] have others in brick. All are built on a court-yard scheme, and show a development of the windows from a Gothic arch through an ogival form to a square mullion. At Montferrand, a fine stone town, the houses are remarkable for their sculptured doorways, generally carved with the heraldic or merchant's device of the owner (Fig. 226). At Chinon there is a multiplicity of turrets. In the south, too, many plainer houses were built of stone in such towns as Périgueux, Lauzerte, and Sarlat, often on too restricted a site to permit of a courtyard, but usually with a sculptured door-way or a stair-turret or *échauguette* to give them grace.

In most towns, however, houses were built of timber and plaster. A fifteenth-century manuscript of Froissart[2] shows the Place de Grève at Paris surrounded by timber-and-plaster houses. Even when stone was used instead of plaster in combination with wood, most of the expense of such a house lay in the timber-work. The bill for building one at Douai in 1459[3] has items totalling 586 livres to Pierre Merel, Maslen de Cambray, and Collart Goden, carpenters, for the woodwork of roof and walls and stairs and windows, and others of only 20 livres to two masons for stones, with other items for the wind-vanes, pulleys, hinges, and door-knocker.

In Normandy, for example at Rouen, Caen, Louviers, Caudebec, and Lisieux, the system of timbering has parallel uprights with an occasional diagonal strengthening-piece[4] (Fig. 227). Farther south, for example at Chartres, Sens, Joigny, Clamecy, Bourges, and Moulins, and as far south as Périgueux and Lusignan, the timbering is arranged in a criss-cross fashion (Fig. 228). Towards the end of the Middle Ages the timbering was often sculptured. A fifteenth-century house at La Ferté-Bernard[5] has three caryatid figures sculptured under the cornice, representing St. Stephen and two grotesque figures stoning him, and four more under the projection of the second floor: a fool, a pilgrim, a mer-maid, and a Moor. At Joigny[6] a house has a fine Tree of Jesse carved on the angle-post; another,[7] probably once a draper's, a St. Martin dividing his cloak, and two other saints under canopies; and a third the Angel and the Virgin and the lily-pot of the Annunciation on the three posts that support the projecting upper floor.[8] At Sens the Maison d'Abraham, built at the beginning of the sixteenth century by Nicolas Mégissier, has a fine Tree of Jesse at the angle, and a representation of the owner's tanner's tools by the door. At Nogent-le-

---

[1] e.g. Hôtel Saint-Germain, Hôtel Bernuy.   [2] B.M. Harl. MS. 4379, fol. 64.
[3] Gay, s.v. 'Architecture privée'.
[4] Most of these houses have been destroyed in the recent War.
[5] In 1938 the Boucherie Chevaline.
[6] Corner of Grand-rue and rue Montant-au-Palais.   [7] Maison Toulouse.
[8] Cf. a house, 10 Place Billard, Chartres.

Rotrou a house of the same date[1] has a group of the Stoning of St. Stephen on the corner-post. At Bourbon-Lancy a house[2] built partly of stone and partly of wood, has kept all the mouldings and cuspings, corbels and cornice, of its ancient timbering. It may be compared with a staircase turret[3] at Chartres which still has charming little figures of angels to guard its summit.

Besides such decorations all the streets of shops were gay with signs, that hung out at right angles. Paris still has streets named after them: du Chat qui Pêche, du Coq-Héron, des Marmousets, des Trois Poissons, des Trois Canettes, des Trois Visages, du Pied de Bœuf. At Beauvais[4] a fifteenth-century sign survives of a draper who had a large equestrian statue of St. Martin dividing his cloak for his device, and two inn-signs, *Aux Quatre Fils Aymon* and *Le Dauphin*. At Besse a butcher's shop still has a niche above the door where an image of the butcher's patron saint once stood.

3. THEIR FURNISHINGS

We know surprisingly little of the furnishings of mediaeval town houses. Their hangings were usually not of enduring tapestry, but of serge; their benches and cupboards, tables and chests, were of a kind that when they went out of fashion would be worn out in the kitchen rather than kept in the attic because of their beautiful workmanship. Their pottery would be broken, and their pewter and bronze refounded when the king's enamelled gold or the knight's silver gilt might become an heirloom. The lesser mediaeval fairs of France, though their pottery and pewter might be better shaped than the cheap china and enamelled ware of to-day, dealt as little in works of art as the market-stalls of Sous-Préfectures do now. By the end of the Middle Ages some of the needs of the bourgeois were already being met by manufacture on a comparatively large scale in centres of specialized industry. By the time of Charles VII ironwork was to some extent localized at Abbeville, with its hall-mark of 'A' in a double circle; in the fourteenth and fifteenth centuries Beauvais was a centre for the manufacture of pottery of all kinds; glass was being made at various centres where there was a forest for the furnaces and access to the buying public;[5] cheap tapestries were woven at Felletin, La Marche, and Saint-Yrieix, furnishing-serges at Rheims and the other towns of Champagne,[6] and bronze and latten were cast at Paris and other centres as well as at Dinant.[7] It was the

---

[1] Café Française.   [2] Called 'La Maison de Madame de Sévigné'.
[3] Called 'L'Escalier de la reine Berthe'; 35 rue Saint-Éman.   [4] In the Museum.
[5] e.g. in the Argonne, and at Aubigny, Châtillon-sur-Indre, the forest of Chevreuse, La Fontaine de Houx, Fougères, La Roche-sur-Yon.
[6] On these and other textiles see Bourquelot, p. 224.
[7] There is a record of the dues paid at Lagny by 'cil de Dynant, qui vendent pots et paelles'. Bourquelot, i. 304.

industries of bourgeois luxury, such as gold-work, that were to be found in every large city, for it was such work that continued to be made to order under the eye of the patron. Rodez and Villefranche-de-Rouergue, Aurillac and Toulouse, Le Puy and Avignon, had flourishing goldsmiths who carried on their trade from generation to generation.[1]

A few inventories remain to give some idea of the equipment of a bourgeois house. In 1318 the goods of Firmin the shoemaker of Amiens in his house *Aux Quatre Fils Aymon*[2] included bed-covers of fur and stuff; vessels and ornaments of pewter and brass; lanterns; saucepans and other kitchen gear; five 'huches' or coffers and three chests; trestle-tables, benches, and a writing-desk; a suit of armour, a saddle, and clothes; and his bench and tools put away in the attic, for he was an old man past work when he died.

Little of such household gear survives. The only things that can claim to be works of art are the candlesticks, ornaments of latten or bronze (Fig. 229). For the rest we have such things as skillets and waffle-irons,[3] and pilgrims' signs —little emblems of base metal sold outside pilgrimage churches and worn in the hat in token of pilgrimage accomplished.[4] The work specially made to the order of citizens was most often devotional in its inspiration. The richer citizens imitated their betters in owning Books of Hours. In 1399, for example,

'Maistre Jean de Molin, escripvain de forme, demorant à Dijon, fait marchief et convenances à honorable homme Philippe Juliot, bourgeois de Dijon, de faire et parfaire un messaul . . . et sera de tel lettre et de tel longuour comme ce qui est ja fait par devers ledit Maistre Jehan en son parchemin . . . et fera en icellui ung kalendrier aussi une majesté et un crucifil qui seront de colour et seront les grosses lettres tournées d'azour et de vermillon et devront être les grosses lettres des bonnes festes d'or floretées . . . et sera couvert de roige cuer emprainté . . . pour le priz de seze frans d'our et d'un meui de vin.'[5]

Such bourgeois missals as survive are rather more perfunctory in execution and a little less rich in ornament than those made for noble owners, but offer no particular originalities. About 1414 Jehan de Langres, enameller of Paris, asked the king's scribe Raoulet d'Orléans to write a Boethius in French for him. The book[6] is well written but in no wise remarkable. In 1489 Jacques de Besançon illuminated a missal for Pierre Malhoste, merchant and bourgeois of Melun. The book[7] is definitely poor in quality compared with that painted by the same artist for the Sainte Chapelle two years later.

---

[1] e.g. families of Ito, Hot, Provins, and Rayronie at Rodez, Pierre Frechrieu at Villefranche. Plate was also sold at the fairs of Champagne.   [2] Fagniez, ii. 37.

[3] A fine collection is in the Musée de la Seine-Inférieure at Rouen.

[4] Collections in the Musée de Cluny, Musée de la Seine-Inférieure, Musée historique d'Orléans, &c.

[5] Gay, s.v. 'Calendrier'.   [6] Bib. Nat. fr. nouv. acq. 1982; Delisle, p. 78.

[7] Bib. Nat. lat. 880; Durrieu, p. 35.

4. GUILDS AND CONFRATERNITIES

By mediaeval custom, men of the same trade or calling lived in the same street. As early as the twelfth century the Cité island at Paris had its rues de la Draperie and de la Pelleterie and a quarter of Apothecaries' shops. Goldsmiths and money-changers congregated on the Grand Pont; mercers in the rue Saint-Denis; and grocers on the island and the right bank. The Halles quarter of Paris[1] still has, or had till lately, its rue de la Sellerie, originally occupied by the saddlers, de l'Aiguillerie by the needlers, its rues de la Ferronnerie and des Forges by the smiths, de la Corderie by the ropemakers, de la Saulnerie by the drysalters, and des Orfèvres and the rue à Petits Souliers by the goldsmiths. In the quarter of Saint-Martin and Saint-Merri[2] are the rue de la Tacherie, where the makers of *ataches* or clasps were congregated, the rue de la Coutellerie for the cutlers, de la Tableterie for the workers in ebony and ivory, de la Haumerie for the armourers, de la Vannerie for the basket-makers, and so on. There were more than three hundred trades represented in Paris at the end of the thirteenth century, and nearly all of them had a recognized district. The booksellers were congregated in the rue neuve Notre-Dame,[3] the illuminators and parchment-sellers in the rue Érembourc de Brie[4] and in the rues des Écrivains, des Enlumineurs, and de la Parcheminerie, which were in the university quarter on the left bank.

The artists' and artisans' quarter of Paris was near the Porte Saint-Denis, called in consequence the Porte aux Peintres.[5] The painters were congregated in the rue Mauconseil, and the ivory-workers in the rue de la Tableterie. Elsewhere craftsmen of the luxury trades tended to live in the same house. The *Livre de la Taille* of 1292[6] shows Richardin, the enameller of London, in the same house in the rue Saint-Germain as Thomas the figure-sculptor and Climençon de Troyes the painter. Alain the *entailleur d'ymages* lived next door, with several leather-workers, and a few houses away several goldsmiths were established. The *Livre de la Taille*, indeed, paints an extraordinarily vivid picture of a city resembling in its economy the Rive Gauche of Paris some fifty years ago: craftsmen of every kind living on the top of each other with their families about them; a few foreigners and an inordinate number of provincials; and the familiar scheme of the great trades of food and dress and luxury maintaining the *menu peuple* who served their requirements. Already, too, the *métiers* were strictly subdivided; by 1268 it needed four separate kinds of workmen to deal with the Paris trade in rosaries, according to whether they worked in bone and horn, in coral and mother of pearl, in amber, or in jet. Ivory was handled by the 'ymagiers tailleurs et ceux qui taillent cruchefix' and by the makers of combs, lanterns,

[1] Rochegude and Dumolin, pp. 161 et seqq.
[2] Ibid., pp. 47 et seqq.
[3] Richard, p. 104.
[4] Géraud, p. 156.
[5] Koechlin, i. 14.
[6] Géraud, p. 23.

knife-handles, chess-boards, and rosaries, all different crafts.[1] The regulations of the crafts show how near one another they lived. It is laid down that the journeymen shield-makers are to stop work in Lent as soon as the bell of Saint-Merri rings for compline, and outside Lent 'si tost come il voit passer le segont crieur pardevant soi du soir'. Similarly the carpenters were to stop work on Saturday when the great bell of Notre-Dame rang for nones.[2]

The congregation of artisans and craftsmen into groups working at the same trade naturally led to their organization into trade guilds. As naturally such organizations had a religious basis, for religious confraternities were in being before the trades were organized. As early as 852 Hincmar, Archbishop of Rheims, was trying to restrain the abuses of the bodies 'quas geldomas vel confratrarias vulgo vocant'.[3] Such brotherhoods might be religious, charitable, or social, or combine these aspects. They began to be important towards the end of the twelfth century; at Le Puy, for example, a confraternity was founded to keep the peace, and at Limoges another to maintain the lights before the altar.[4] By the time that the statutes of the Paris craftsmen were drawn up under Étienne Boileau in 1268 the trade guilds were organized and were already in some instances religious confraternities as well; the statutes of the bakers, shield-makers, masons, and *tabletiers* indicate the patron saint of the guild.[5] The gold-smiths alone came to have five religious brotherhoods: that of Saint Éloi, which maintained a hospital; that of Saint Denis, which made pilgrimages to Montmartre and interested itself in various good works; that of Notre-Dame de Blancmesnil, which made pilgrimages to that church; that of Saint Marcel, which carried his shrine in procession; and the Confrérie du Mai, founded in 1448, that at midnight before May morning set up a green tree as a maypole before the great door of Notre-Dame de Paris.

Their services, naïve and pious, brought their trade into direct relation with Heaven. In the hymn sung at the goldsmiths' Mass in Paris from the twelfth century to the Revolution God becomes the divine smith, the forger of the world. Saint Éloi, it declares,

> . . . in arte mirifica
> Fabrum contemplans omnium
> Rerum, videt in fabrica
> Trinitatis vestigium.
>
> Faber et Fabri filius,
> Fabrum creans Eligium
> Nobis adsit propitius
> Per hujus Fabri studium.

---

[1] Koechlin, i. 1 et seqq.   [2] Fagniez, i. 220.   [3] Ibid., i. 52.   [4] Lasteyrie, p. 252.
[5] Cf. the Guilds of Dijon; A. Chapuis, in *Mém. de la Soc. bourguignonne de géog. et d'hist.* xxii, Dijon, 1906, p. 5.

Their religious spirit, however, was indicated less by devotional exercises than by a lofty standard of professional honour. The statutes of the *imagiers*, drawn up in 1391, impose the production of a 'master-piece' upon those desiring admission to the guild and forbid their members to sell work made 'en Allemagne ou ailleurs' unless it has been passed by the wardens.[1] The 1485 statutes of the ivory-carvers[2] are full of regulations to ensure good work. No carving is to be done at night 'a chandaile, quar la clartez de la nuit ne soufist au mestier'. Any work not executed in accordance with the regulations is to be broken and burnt, except religious images, 'pour les reverances des saints et des saintes en qui remembrances elles sont faites'.

At Limoges the butchers have lived in the rue de la Boucherie since the castle of Limoges was built in the tenth century. For almost as long they have constituted a confraternity of St. Aurelian that is at once a religious brotherhood and a trade guild. Their eighty meat-stalls are still divided among some half-dozen families. In the middle is the chapel of St. Aurelian, rebuilt by his confraternity in 1475, with a Cross and a statue of the Virgin before it. One house has four corbels rudely carved in granite with Hercules leaning on his club, a bull, a lion, and a pig; otherwise there is no attempt at architectural display or decoration. The whole is as dark, sordid, and picturesque as the butchers' quarter of an Eastern *souk*: a little world at first sight unlikely to produce any form of art. Yet such trade guilds and the religious confraternities of humble citizens were patrons of art, if on a modest scale. The needs of their own services had to be met. Their books were simple; the office for St. John Baptist written for the confraternity of the 'Libraires jurez, escrivains, enlumineurs, hystorieurs, parcheminiers et relieurs de livres' in the church of Saint-André-des-Arts at Paris, in 1485, has only two small miniatures, though it came from the workshop of the famous Jean de Besançon.[3] Their banners and staves, as we know them, were equally humble; even their pews did not receive much ornament, though the confraternity of St. Stephen in Toulouse Cathedral had theirs carved with the preaching, arrest, and stoning of the saint.[4]

Every guild, however, strove to have a statue of its patron to adorn its chapel or some part of the church where the community heard Mass. Some such forgotten donation is the *raison d'être* of many of the fifteenth-century statues of saints in French churches: statues that may be clumsy country work, or as exquisite as the St. Martha (Fig. 230) which is said to have been given to the Madeleine at Troyes by a guild of maid-servants.[5] The saint is represented

---

[1] Poëte, p. 22. [2] Koechlin, i. 17.
[3] MS. Mazarine 461; Durrieu, *Jean de Besançon*, p. 10.
[4] Fifteenth century; now in the Musée Reymond.
[5] See Koechlin and Marquet de Vasselot, p. 96. The statue retains its original colouring; the face is naturally tinted, the dress and cloak are white lined with blue.

sprinkling holy water on the dragon beneath her feet, but she does it with the gesture of a woman sprinkling water on the floor to lay the dust before she sweeps it. Each time they cleaned a room the maids of Troyes had cause to remember the statue of their patroness. Sometimes a professional desire for exactness turned a religious subject into a genre scene: the painted stone group of the arrest of St. Crispin and St. Crispinian in Saint-Pantaléon at Troyes must have greatly pleased the cobblers who gave it.

Glass windows, too, were commonly given by guilds and confraternities, alike to the great cathedrals and to humbler churches. Chartres Cathedral has no less than forty-three windows given by guilds of local artisans.[1] The main subjects of the windows are the lives of saints and Bible stories in accordance with the usual scheme of iconography of the Church; but men of the guilds who gave them are in most instances represented at the bottom of the window. There are bakers, kneading and baking, making waffles, carrying bread-baskets on poles, and selling bread; butchers slaughtering beasts and cutting up meat; innkeepers selling wine; masons with hammers and plumb-lines; sculptors carving a cornice and an effigy; the coopers—who gave the Noah window— making their barrels; a turner with his lathe; basket-makers selling their wares, and a whole series representing the different branches of the main industries of the place, cloth and hides.[2] Such windows continued to be given by guilds to churches all through the Middle Ages. Semur-en-Auxois has one given by the drapers at the end of the fifteenth century that tells the story not of any life of a saint but of the whole process of finishing cloth: fulling, carding, dyeing, facing, and folding. Other windows show the brotherhood marching in procession in honour of the saint whom the painted glass commemorates.[3]

The part the guilds played in architectural decoration was less important. At Rheims, however, the mullion of the north door rises from a pedestal carved with scenes from a draper's shop, and the whole door was probably given by a guild of the weavers of the serges for which the city was famous. Exceptionally, too, members of a guild might build a church or chapel for common

---

[1] For a detailed list see Acloque, p. 313.

[2] Besides these there are farriers, armourers, grocers, buckle-makers, money-changers, porters, and water-carriers. The linen-weavers' window shows by its inscription that they were incorporated as a guild of St. Vincent. At a rather later date all the Chartres guilds had their patron saints: the porters St. Christopher, who carried Christ; the cooks St. Laurence who was grilled on a gridiron; the cutlers St. John Baptist, whose head was cut off; the parchment-sellers St. Bartholomew, who was flayed; the carpenters St. Joseph, the painters St. Luke, who had followed their trades, and so on. The tapestry-makers had St. Francis, whose cult had come in at about the same time as their craft. Acloque, p. 58. All had their banners and devices.

[3] Mâle, *Art rel. fin*, p. 177. Window of Saint Pourçain, Saint-Martin de Laigle, early sixteenth century; of Saint Jacques, Lisieux, 1527; of the Holy Sacrament and Saint Ouen, Pont-Audemer, c. 1530.

use. The butchers' chapel of St. Aurelian at Limoges has already been mentioned; and in 1330 two jongleurs of Paris, Jacques Grure and Hugues le Lorrain, founded the church of Saint-Julien-des-Ménétriers in a street in which a corporation of jongleurs already existed.[1] Less rarely a guild would add a chapel to an existing church. In the fifteenth century, for example, the crossbowmen of Châlons-sur-Marne added a chapel of St. Sebastian to the church of Saint-Jean-Baptiste and those of Montreuil gave another, powdered all over with crossbows and their motto PAR AMOUR, to their parish church.

The purely religious confraternities did as much or more for art than the trade guilds. Their chief activities were literary or dramatic, but through these the visual arts were influenced. At Amiens, for example, a *Puy Notre Dame* was founded in 1388 as a confraternity in honour of the Virgin. Every year the master set a phrase, *le palinod*, in her honour as the refrain for a poem, and gave a prize to the successful competitor, and every year after 1452 the master gave a picture, generally illustrating the *palinod* of the year, to be hung as a votive offering in the cathedral.[2] The results are surprisingly fanciful; one of the finest surviving (Fig. 231), given by Jean du Bos, mercer, in 1437,[3] represents the Virgin as High Priest, for she gave form to God and offered him upon the altar of Calvary. It illustrates the 'palinod' *Digne vesture au prestre souverain*, which may have reference to the donor's trade. In 1470 Jehan le Barbier, pastry-cook, gave a picture illustrating *Harpe randant armonie souveraine* (Fig. 232); in 1471 Jean de Béry, seigneur d'Esserteaux, gave a Virgin standing in a forest full of birds, to illustrate *au pélican forest silencieuse*. Not only is the iconography of these pictures recondite and poetical but their execution is far above the level that one might expect from the brotherhood of a provincial town.

More often the Puy or confraternity commissioned a play and acted it.[4] The drama was either a *miracle*—the dramatization of some astonishing escape brought about by the intervention of the Virgin or a saint—or a Passion play. The *Mystère de Saint Louis* was written for a Paris confraternity of masons and carpenters who met in a chapel of the saint in the church of Saint-Blaise. The *Mystère de Saint Crépin et Saint Crépinien* was written for their guild of shoe-makers in Notre-Dame de Paris. *Mystères* of the Passion were written for many

---

[1] Petit de Julleville, i. 413.

[2] Many of these were destroyed by order of the canons in 1723. Those that survive are in the Musée de Picardie at Amiens. Fig. 232 is taken from the contemporary copies in Bib. Nat. MS. fr. 145. They usually show the *palinod* on a scroll and the master kneeling as donor. A similar Puy existed at Abbeville, but only one of their pictures survives.

[3] Other dates and arms were added later. See Sterling, p. 135; *Bull. des Musées de France*, Dec. 1938, p. 162.

[4] See Petit de Julleville, i. 115, 345, 355.

confraternities, especially in Paris and Burgundy and Champagne;[1] in 1402 Charles VI issued letters patent recognizing these confraternities of the Passion and their plays.[2] The plays date from the end of the fourteenth to the beginning of the sixteenth century, and were nearly all written by clerics.[3] They were, however, performed by laymen; the mystery of the *Actes des Apôtres*—a drama of 16,908 lines of verse—was, as its rhymed prologue declares, produced by a lawyer, a tapestry-weaver, a butcher, and a seedsman.[4] The *mystères* appealed to every class, and could command an audience of fifteen or twenty thousand people.[5]

The mysteries influenced religious iconography of the fifteenth century as the liturgical drama of the eleventh and twelfth centuries had influenced the imagery of Romanesque sculpture. In many forms of art, especially stained glass, a crowded composition reflected the innumerable personages of dramas that deliberately set as many actors on the stage as it would hold. The actual story told was taken directly from the mysteries: the Saint-Denis window at Bourges, for example, derives its story from the *Mystère de Saint Denis* and not from the Golden Legend.[6] The rudimentary scenery found its way into art; the wattle hut of the Nativity, the brocade[7] (Fig. 233) and tapestry[8] backgrounds of the stage. Fouquet represents the Martyrdom of Sainte Apolline in the Hours of Étienne Chevalier, painted in the middle of the fifteenth century, against a background of the 'mansions' of a *Mystère*, with the ladder going up to Paradise guarded by angels, Hell-mouth full of demons with extra faces painted on their bodies, and the throne for God the Father over all.

It was the confraternities of the Passion and their plays that had the strongest influence on the visual arts. The figure of Christ crowned with thorns, with His nailed hands helpless before Him, appears on a relief dedicated at the Abbaye du Trésor about 1400 (Fig. 234 B); it is adored by a donor, his wife, and their seven sons and three daughters. Behind them stand their patron saints St. Michael and St. William of Aquitaine who was both monk and knight. This representation of Christ is itself an innovation, but it was but the first step. The continuous drama of the Passion which the confraternities performed brought into view new aspects of the death of our Lord: moments passed over

---

[1] See G. Frank, *Passion d'Autun*, S.A.T.F., 1924, p. 23.

[2] See Koechlin and Marquet de Vasselot, p. 26.   [3] See Petit de Julleville, i. 314.

[4] Mâle, *Art rel. fin*, p. 186.

[5] Lavisse iv². 19.   [6] Petit de Julleville, i. 365.

[7] e.g. the brocade held by angels to form a background to the Virgin of Pity, St. Michael, and St. Stephen on a tapestry altar-frontal in the cathedral of Sens, *c.* 1520.

[8] Some painted linen cloths with the Story of Susanna, and scenes from the Passion and Resurrection, belonging to Rheims Cathedral, seem to have been used as a back-cloth for mystery plays. See Sartor, Fig. 4.

in silence in the Gospel narratives and their amplifications, that were suddenly found to be intensely moving when seen upon the stage. One of these moments was that when Christ was seated, bound, waiting while the Cross was being set up. All over France images of this waiting Christ were dedicated in churches,[1] often by the dying wish of some member of a confraternity of the Passion.[2] Some, like that at Saint-Nizier de Troyes (Fig. 235), are fine works of art; others, like that at Sormery, no more than the touching attempts of an unskilful country carver to interpret a tragic theme. All show an intense sympathy with a Man who, like all men, suffers and waits for death.

The second great moment of which the mystery plays revealed the tragedy[3] was that when the body of Christ was taken from the Cross and laid across the knees of His Mother: a scene of that Passion of Mary that was found to play itself out alongside the Passion of Christ.[4] There were, indeed, confraternities of Notre Dame de la Pitié which enjoyed special indulgences; and it was no doubt their members who gave, corporately or individually, the many sculptures of the subject which are to be found in French churches.[5] Before Michelangelo interpreted the theme in marble the humble sculptors of the French provinces had already turned it into tragic beauty in stone. The *Vierges de Pitié* of Senlis and Bayel[6] (Fig. 236) and Prémery can stand comparison in all but technical execution with the masterpieces of the Italian sculptors of the Renaissance. Nor was it in sculpture alone that the *Pietà* was represented; the parish church of Nouans still owns a painting (Fig. 237) with the Virgin of Pity surrounded by Joseph of Arimathea, St. John, the Holy Maries, and the donor.

Such figures standing round the Virgin with the dead Christ insensibly bring us to the next scene of the drama of the Passion: the Entombment. The scene was already being represented at Saint-Étienne de Troyes in an Easter sepulchre

[1] Salives, Côte d'Or; Venizy, Yonne; Sormery, Nièvre; Saint-Pourçain, Allier; Guerbigny, Somme (dated 1475); Saint-Nizier de Troyes. Bas-relief, Saint-Urbain de Troyes; glass, Maizières, Aube, hospital of Châlons-sur-Marne. See Mâle, *Art rel. fin*, p. 87.

[2] Some confraternities, for example one at Clamecy, were called 'Confréries de l'Ecce Homo'.

[3] It seems probable that the subject is related to the institution of the feast of Corpus Christi in 1264, but direct evidence of this in art is lacking.

[4] See Mâle, *Art rel. fin*, pp. 30, 119, 122, and Wilmart, pp. 505 and 519, for the early history of this conception.

[5] The earliest recorded was of wood, made for the chapel of the Hôtel d'Artois in 1388 (Koechlin, i. 25). Those that survive are all of the fifteenth century or early sixteenth century: Moissac, dated 1476; Bayel, Aube (from the priory of Belleröi); Mussy-sur-Seine, Aube; Autrèche (Touraine); Moutier d'Ahun, Creuse; Vernou, Indre-et-Loire (bas-relief); Conches, Eure; Senlis Museum; Amiens Museum; Saint-Ayoul, Provins (1510); Saint-Pierre, Bar-sur-Aube; N.-D. du Bout des Ponts, Amboise; Montpezat, Lot; Saint-Agnan, Dordogne; Prémery, Nièvre; Rozier-Côtes-d'Aurec, Loire (1493); Saint-Nazaire, Carcassonne; Lavaudieu, Toulouse; Musée des Augustins, &c. The parish church of Bec-Hellouin has in the choir a fifteenth-century group of the Trinity in which God the Father holds Christ, not as usual on the Cross, but lying in His arms.

[6] Probably by the master of the Sainte Marthe of Troyes, as is that at Villeneuve-l'Archevêque.

play in 1371.[1] By 1410 Christine de Pisan was writing a devotional poem on the subject, that implies that she has the scene in her mind's eye.

> ... Pour les larmes qui respandues furent
> Sevelissant et oignant ton corps saint
> Et pour ta mère et ceulx qui pitié eurent,
> Dieu, fay mon cuer d'ycelle pitié çaint.[2]

Already there were confraternities of the Holy Sepulchre, brotherhoods of men who hoped one day to make the pilgrimage to Jerusalem,[3] but it was not until the drama had made the Entombment visible that it was represented in art with the same personages as in the mysteries: St. Joseph of Arimathea and another old man, St. John, the Virgin, and the three Maries.[4] The earliest Entombment known to us is that set up at Sainte-Catherine-du-Val-des-Écoliers in 1407;[5] the earliest dated ones surviving are those at Langres, of which Christ in the tomb alone remains, from a group of 1420, and that in the hospital of Tonnerre, given by a citizen, Lancelot Buronfosse, in 1454. Some of the undated examples are probably as early or earlier.[6] They show at once an astonishing consistency and an astonishing variety in their composition; nothing like mass-production was reached until in the sixteenth century a certain number of identical terra-cotta statues were turned out from moulds in Touraine. The Entombments, indeed, remain one of the most interesting sculptural creations of the late Middle Ages; nowhere else are the rich robes and dramatic gestures of the mystery plays more effectively commemorated. The most beautiful of all is that given by Nicolas du Moustier and his wife to the church at Chaource (Fig. 238): dignified, tragic, and noble, it shows what a provincial sculptor could achieve in the service of a country gentleman for the glory of his modest church.[7]

---

[1] Laborde, iii. 464; and again in 1380, iii. 467. One of its earliest appearances in art is on the 'Parement de Narbonne', c. 1370. It appeared again on a reliquary of Charles VI in 1399. Laborde, p. 351.

[2] *Une Oroyson de nostre Seigneur*, S.A.T.F. iii. 25.

[3] Mâle, op. cit., p. 130.

[4] Ibid.

[5] Guillebert de Metz, in Le Roux de Lincy and Tisserand, p. 192.

[6] Some surviving examples are those at Semur-en-Auxois; Saint-Nizier de Troyes; N.-D. de l'Épine, Châlons-sur-Marne; cathedral of Nevers; Souvigny (bas-relief); Thouars; Saint-Trophime, Arles; Saint-Pierre, Avignon; Toulouse Cathedral (now Musée des Augustins); Joigny, Yonne; Verneuil, Eure; Saint-Germain, Oise; Agnetz, Oise; Saint-Phal, Aube; Salers, Cantal (given in 1496 by the priest); Châtillon-sur-Seine (Franciscans); Carennac, Lot; Amboise, Indre-et-Loire; Saint-Valery, Somme; Villers-Bocage, Somme; Montdidier, Somme; Poissy, Seine-et-Oise; Louviers, Eure; La Chapelle-Rainsoin, Mayenne; Auch, Gers; Saint-Germain, Amiens; Millery, Rhône; Bessey-lès-Cîteaux, Côte-d'Or; Rosporden, Finistère; Solesmes, Sarthe. See Mâle, *Art rel. fin*, pp. 133-5. There are many more. Exceptionally they were placed in private chapels, for instance in that of René d'Anjou at Angers (Courajod, ii. 526) and in that of Louis d'Amboise, Bishop of Albi, at Combéfa (Bévotte, p. 10). The subject was occasionally represented in church tapestries (see Farcy, p. 6).

[7] A variation is sometimes found representing the Entombment of the Virgin: Fécamp, by

5. COMMUNAL BUILDINGS

The échevins of a town formed a guild like any other confraternity. It was the merchant *confrérie* of Mantes that gave rise to the commune of Mantes. In the time of Saint Louis the confraternity of Saint Hilaire at Poitiers was confined to the hundred men who formed the corporation; it was in fact the municipality, though its statutes were like those of any other pious brotherhood of the time.[1] The communal authorities, however, had not so much leisure to devote to the arts as the other confraternities. It needed the deliverance of the city of Orleans by St. Joan to stimulate a civic body to patronage of the arts. In her honour the one civic play, the *Mystère du Siège d'Orléans*, was written, and in her honour the city in 1457 raised a monument of bronze. In the centre was a Virgin of Pity, with her dead Son across her knees; to one side knelt St. Joan, and to the other Charles VII.[2]

Yet if the municipalities were not usually patrons of art, necessity made them builders. At first the communal authorities did not have buildings of their own. At Nîmes the consuls of the city met in the Maison Carrée; at Albi the communal elections were held in the cathedral; at Beauvais the échevins' quarters formed part of Saint-Étienne. As late as 1247 even the communal banquet was held in Notre-Dame de Melun.[3] It was not long before the échevins needed a *parloir aux bourgeois* of their own. One of the earliest surviving is that at La Réole (Fig. 239), built at the end of the twelfth century over an arcaded market hall.[4] This disposition apart, its simple double windows and corbelled cornice are like those of a town house of the period. At Trie-Château, again, the communal house built about 1170 is as plain as a merchant's house; and the same is true of the rather later buildings of Boulogne and Saint-Guilhem-le-Désert. At Saint-Antonin, indeed, a town house was bought from the family that built it and used by the échevins.

The *villes-neuves* commonly set the *parloir aux bourgeois* over the arcades of the market square; Libourne remains an excellent example. At Domme, however, an ordinary town house with its gable to the road served for their deliberations. As town houses grew more pretentious, so did town halls. Instead of a *parloir aux bourgeois* over the market, cities demanded a more ambitious building, a true civic mansion. In 1355 Étienne Marcel, Provost of the Marchands of Paris, bought for 2,400 gold florins the Maison aux Piliers in the Place

Desaubeaux, *c.* 1495; Gisors, 1510, by the same sculptor, given by the confrérie de l'Assomption of Gisors; Courtisols, near Sainte-Ménéhould, from the Franciscan church of Châlons-sur-Marne.

[1] It seems, too, as if like other confraternities they had statues of their patron saints. The Musée de Picardie at Amiens has a fifteenth-century statue of Saint Yves *en Mayeur d'Amiens*.

[2] Courajod, ii. 136.   [3] Enlart, *Arch. civile*, p. 327.

[4] It was restored in the nineteenth century.

de Grève to take the place of the old *Parloir aux Bourgeois* on the south wall of
the city. Even small towns began to have similar pretentions; the fourteenth-
century Hôtel de Ville at Martel is built round a courtyard, with elegant
traceried windows and a crenellated tower. At Sarlat, again, the fourteenth-
century Maison Consulaire[1] is a town house of the same type.

In the fifteenth century, at a time when the great Flemish cities such as Douai
and Arras were building the most splendid town halls in Europe, the French
cities continued to follow on a more modest scale the type of town-house plan
established by the Hôtel Saint-Pol and continued by such houses as that of
Jacques Cœur at Bourges. The Maison des Échevins at Bourges itself[2] (Fig.
240), built between 1489 and 1491, follows the Hôtel Jacques Cœur in its courtyard plan and in its fine sculptured turret. Inside, the door to the *Parloir aux
Bourgeois* is sculptured with the legend of the town's patroness, Sainte Solange,
and the chimney-piece with a formal pattern of the sheep which made Berri
rich, and the town's arms upheld by a shepherd and a shepherdess. The Hôtel
de Ville at Noyon[3] is likewise built round a courtyard with an ornamental stair-
turret. Another such sculptured turret, this time set on the street, forms the
Tour des Échevins at Brive. Even when the Palais de Justice of Rouen (Fig.
241) was built between 1499 and 1509 to the designs of Roger Ango and
Roland de Roux, to combine in one building a merchants' exchange,[4] the
Exchequer court of Normandy,[5] a *Parlouër aux Bourgeois*,[6] and a town prison,
it imitated the courtyard of a contemporary castle such as Josselin rather than a
Flemish town hall. The parlour, which dates from 1493, was set above the prison,
with gables to north and south, and octagonal turrets. Before its destruction in
1944 it had a fine wooden barrel-roof, and traceried windows with niches
between four statues of saints.

The real sign of a town's independence, however, was not the meeting-place
of the municipality but the belfry of the commune. It might be the tower
of a fortified church, as at Marciac, or a tower over one of the town gates, as
at Villefranche-sur-Lot and other *villes-neuves*. Certain old towns, such as
Avallon[7] and Saint-Fargeau, had the belfry over a gate within the walls. The
Trinité at Vendôme has an early tower which served at once as a donjon, a
town belfry, and a church tower. Towards the end of the fourteenth century,

---

[1] Now the Maison Plamont, rue Gambetta.
[2] Now Petit Collège. M. Enlart ascribes its design to Jacques Gendre.
[3] Built between 1485 and 1523.   [4] Later the Salle des Pas Perdus.
[5] Few other mediaeval courts exist, but at Mantes the Auditoire Royal had an elegant traceried
door with the hedgehog of Louis XII, and the arms of France, Brittany, and Mantes over the windows,
until it was destroyed by an American aerial attack in 1944.   [6] Later the Salle des Procureurs.
[7] Built in 1456. On the first floor is the Salle des Échevins, where they met till 1772. Other such
belfries over a street are to be found at Amboise, Auxerre, Besse-en-Chandesse, Bordeaux, Déols,
Évreux, Lezoux, Loches, Lucheux, Parthenay, and Vierzon.

however, the growing importance of the towns made the citizens demand a more imposing structure. At Rouen the belfry was rebuilt in 1389 to house the curfew bell, cast in the thirteenth century,[1] and the other bells and a fine clock made for it by Jean de Felains. Such clocks, indeed, were among the glories of the greater towns. The Gros Horloge of Caen, set up in 1314, was inscribed:

> Puis qu'ainsi la ville me loge
> Sur ce pont pour servir d'auloge
> Je feray les heures ouir
> Pour le commun peuple esjouir.[2]

Dijon, which had furnished a thousand men-at-arms to the Duke of Burgundy to fight the rebellion in Flanders in 1380, received in reward a famous clock that he had taken from Courtrai. The Belfry of the commune of Moulins still has a clock with mechanical figures, set up in 1455, which every passer-by stops to look at as they strike the hours.

After the courtyard plan was adopted for town halls, there was no longer the arcaded lower floor of the earlier communal house to provide a covered market. Separate market halls were therefore commonly built even in small towns. That at Saint-Pierre-sur-Dives is among the earliest.[3] It is divided into three by wooden pillars, and has a good wooden roof resting on gables of masonry. The fourteenth-century market hall at Nolay is all of wood; but for the gable that built at Thilly in 1479 is all of chestnut. None of them have any architectural pretensions.

The other public buildings of the towns were little more ambitious. One of the most marked contrasts between fourteenth-century France and fourteenth-century England lies in their university buildings. The English college, with its great hall with screens and dais and oriel, approximates to the type of a noble house; the French college is based on the scheme of a poorly endowed monastery, and never enriches it. The early colleges at Paris[4] were little more than hospices for poor clerks, and were as plain as possible.[5] The accounts survive for the Collège de Beauvais,[6] built in 1387 with funds bequeathed by a bishop of Beauvais. They show Maître Raymond du Temple, the architect, tied down by a contract that the college authorities felt a protection; they reveal all the usual delays in building: days when so many wagons of stone came at

[1] La Rouvel rang till 1904, when it cracked. The task was then taken up by the contemporary bell, La Cache-Ribaud, hanging alongside.   [2] Gay, i, s.v. 'Horloge'.

[3] They were originally built in the thirteenth century but were considerably modified in the fifteenth.

[4] Collège des Dix-huit, twelfth century; Saint-Thomas-du-Louvre, c. 1186; Bons-Enfants-Saint-Honoré, 1208; Bons-Enfants-Saint-Victor, 1248; Sainte-Catherine-du-Val-des-Écoliers, 1229; Prémontré, 1252; Collège du Trésorier, 1268; in all some sixty between 1137 and 1360.

[5] The students' books were equally plain, though Daniel de Morley and the Bolognese jurist Odofredo complain that some had books with gilded letters. Michel, ii. 330.   [6] Fagniez, ii. 128.

once that time was wasted, days when the bishop's surveyor came about the alinement of the building, days too cold for work, and days when *pour oster escandle* the workmen had to be given drinks. There were the usual misunderstandings between the clerk of the works and the masons, the usual last thoughts of the college committee, the usual visits of the architect too late to prevent a mistake. Finally, the architect dined with the college authorities and the building was finished. Throughout the course of the building there is no mention of any ornamental feature, or any concern but with the barest practical necessities. What little we know of the other mediaeval colleges of Paris confirms the impression of bareness and simplicity. The fourteenth-century refectory of the Collège des Bernardins in the rue de Poissy is a simple aisled room, over cellars of the same plan, indistinguishable from the refectory of any small Cistercian house. Old engravings of the Collège de Cluny show it to have been no less plain; a turret at the angle and simple rose windows in the gable were its only architectural features. Its chapel, however, is said to have been only less lovely than the Sainte Chapelle from which it was imitated. The door of the Collège de Bayeux is preserved in the Musée de Cluny; it is no more pretentious than the entrance to a citizen's house. The Collège de Navarre, founded in 1304 with a richer endowment, had a more elaborate entry with figures of the Virgin, Saint Louis, and Jeanne de Navarre, its foundress, over the gateway, while its library, if plain, had yet the dignity of noble scale and fine proportion; yet even here the dorters were as bare as in any poor monastic house.

Even in the fourteenth century Paris had no university buildings apart from the colleges. The Faculties and Nations met in some borrowed church or monastery.[1] The famous schools of the rue de Fouarre were only built in the fourteenth century. The earliest surviving university building in Paris is the fifteenth-century School of Medicine:[2] a room like the refectory of a poor monastery, with plain columns down the middle, pointed windows, and a wooden roof.

In provincial cities it was usually the municipality who provided the university buildings, as that of Poitiers did in 1448. At Caen they adjoined the Halles. The only surviving building of the kind is the library of Orleans University,[3] built between 1444 and 1450. It has traceried windows, a central row of polygonal columns, and a ribbed vault resting on consoles, set rather high to give room for cupboards beneath. The brackets are carved, two with angels, six with prophets holding scrolls, and four with the Evangelists.

The other public buildings of a town, the hospitals, were usually the fruit of private munificence. Some had been founded in the great cities of Paris, Lyons,

---

[1] See Rashdall, ed. Powicke and Emden, i. 406.   [2] 13 rue de la Bûcherie.
[3] Now called the Salle des Thèses, in the rue Pothier; severely damaged during the 1939–45 War.

Autun, Arles, and Rheims in the sixth, seventh, and eighth centuries. Then comes a gap; the earliest mediaeval hospitals date from the eleventh century.[1] In 1200 Philip Augustus decreed that all hospitals and hospital funds should be administered by the bishop or his deputy, and endeavoured to bring order into their administration. This ruling was followed by the formal endowment by bishops of hospitals to take the place of earlier, more casual charity: Guillaume, Archbishop of Rheims, in 1201 built a hospital 'pour y recevoir et nourrir à perpétuité vingt pauvres languissans', and Hugues de Morville, Bishop of Coutances, founded the Hôtel-Dieu there in 1209.[2] The royal house and other feudal lords, too, fulfilled their duty by founding hospitals. About 1069 Berthe, Countess of Maine, founded 'l'aumône Notre-Dame' at Chartres; and the Hôtels-Dieu of Abbeville, Bar-sur-Seine, Les Montils, and the Maison du Saint-Esprit at Dijon were all founded by members of the royal house. As riches became more diffused, men of all classes joined in such foundations. In 1328 two minstrels, shocked by the sight of a paralysed woman begging from a barrow in the street of Saint-Martin-des-Champs at Paris, where they lived, founded the small hospice of Saint-Julien at Paris.

Such hospitals were as inclusive as an old-fashioned workhouse: they housed pilgrims and travellers, the old and the homeless, the sick and the needy. Often, indeed, they had been founded specifically as hospices for pilgrims. The Dômerie or Hôpital de Notre-Dame-des-Pauvres at Aubrac (Aveyron) was founded in 1120 to shelter those who travelled over the mountains, especially pilgrims to and from Rocamadour and Compostella.[3] Near Notre-Dame-du-Puy is another pilgrims' hostel of the kind. Its entrance-door has two Romanesque sculptured capitals; on one 'Karitas' gives the pilgrim bread, and on the other the weary traveller rests in bed. At Levroux, near Châteauroux, a wooden house still stands which once served as a hospice for pilgrims going to Compostella. Elsewhere hospitals show by their dedication to St. James that they were the foundation of guilds of his pilgrims. The ancient hospital of Nogent-le-Rotrou, founded in 1190, is Saint-Jacques de l'Aumône; the Hôtel-Dieu-Saint-Jacques of Toulouse was founded in 1258 by the confrérie Saint-Jacques; and the thirteenth-century Hôtel-Dieu at Dammartin-en-Goële is dedicated to St. James and has a statue of the saint on its façade. As late as the fourteenth century the Hôpital Saint-Jacques was founded at Cordes and the Pèlerins de Saint-Jacques of Paris built a hospital between the rue Saint-Denis and the rue Mauconseil.[4]

[1] Laon, Provins (1050), Vienne, Romans.

[2] Other hospitals under the chapter of the cathedral existed at Vannes, Tours, Clermont-Ferrand, Autun, and elsewhere. Lallemand, iii. 61.

[3] It was rebuilt in the fifteenth century and destroyed at the Revolution.

[4] It was finished in 1324. Excavations have revealed statues of the apostles there, in a style that is an old-fashioned continuation of that of the Sainte Chapelle. See Michel, ii. 696.

Other hospitals were founded by men returning from crusade.[1] The Maison-Dieu at Montmorillon, for example, was built by Robert Dupuy when he came back from the First Crusade. The small octagonal kitchen and a tower remain, together with a sepulchral chapel, likewise an octagon, on two floors. The chapel has a cupola, and the choir a pyramidal roof ending in a *lanterne des morts* in which a lamp was always kept burning. Four Virtues and Four Vices are carved over the door;[2] the interior was originally painted. Such decorations were sometimes the gift of a returned pilgrim: Joinville, who went to Egypt and Syria with Saint Louis, gave a new chapel to the Hôtel-Dieu which a crusading ancestor had founded when he came back, with wall-paintings illustrating events from his life abroad which had justified his faith.[3]

The earliest hospitals, in the modern sense of buildings reserved for the care of the sick, were lazar-houses in which lepers could be both tended and segregated. By the end of the reign of Saint Louis there are said to have been eight hundred of them in France; by the middle of the fourteenth century there were fifty-nine in the diocese of Paris alone. These were built like a charter-house, with separate little dwellings for the lepers and a small house for those who looked after them.[4] One of the earliest recorded is the Hospice-Saint-Gilles at Surgères, which is said to have been founded in the eleventh century and endured until the Revolution. The donations made by Hugues de Champagne to the Maladrerie-des-Deux-Eaux show that besides the little cells it had a communal kitchen and a church of Saint-Lazare. A nun and a chaplain looked after the physical and spiritual needs of the lepers. The Maladrerie-de-la-Madeleine at Boulogne, founded in 1125, originally[5] had twelve little houses, communicating only by slits with the outside world, but by small windows to the common court; it had a chapel and a house for the chaplain that also served as a porter's lodge. The Maladrerie du Tortoir[6] has three buildings in a quadrangular enclosure: a ward on two floors, each lit by eight traceried windows to the east, with turrets in the angles and great chimneys, and movable wooden screens between the beds; a chapel; and a two-storied building that housed the staff and the kitchen.

The chapels of lazar-houses were commonly decorated with paintings:

[1] Jean de Beaumont came back from the First Crusade with relics of St. Cosmas and his brother St. Damian acquired in Rome. He built a church at Luzarches to hold them, and since the saints were patrons of medicine, their confraternity in Paris sent practitioners twice a year to Luzarches to examine and operate upon the citizens.

[2] They may be compared with Patience treading on Anger and Charity on Avarice on capitals from the Hôtel-Dieu of Chartres, *c.* 1230, now destroyed. *Bull. Soc. Nat. Ants Fr.,* 1925, p. 221.

[3] See Bib. Nat. nouv. acq. fr. 4509; Bib. Nat. lat. 11907, fol. 231; and Delaborde and Lauer in *Mon. Piot,* xvi, 1909, p. 61.

[4] The *Life* of Robert d'Arbrissell describes his lazar-house *et suas mansiunculas* soon after 1100. Mortet, i. 311.   [5] It was rebuilt in the seventeenth century. Enlart, *Arch. civile,* p. 48.

[6] Tollet, p. 61; near Saint-Nicolas, Aisne.

paintings which must have become a very part of the minds of the poor out-
casts who worshipped there. The lepers' chapel of Saint-Romain de Colbosc,
between Bolbec and Harfleur, still has remains of such decoration; that at
Lamarche-sur-Sâone has the figure of a sainted abbot. The chapel of Saint-
Julien at Le Petit-Quevilly,[1] a lazar-house outside Rouen, founded by Henry II
of England in 1183[2] for lepers of noble family, has paintings of the Birth and
Baptism of Christ, the Adoration of the Magi (Fig. 242), and the Flight into
Egypt, arranged in medallions like those of painted glass, set above a simple
arcade that runs round the aisleless chapel. The chapel of St. Laurence in the
lazar-house at Loroux-Bottereau has paintings of the lepers' patron, St. Giles.[3]

Lazar-houses continued to be founded in the thirteenth century,[4] but the need
for them was growing less. The house of the Magdalene and Saint Ladre outside
Amiens, indeed, had, by the fifteenth century, so few inmates on whom to spend
its revenues that it turned them to the beautification of the church. In 1476
Maître Jean de Pois was commissioned to make a great carved retable for the
altar, and a group of the Magdalene meeting Christ in the Garden was set up
outside the church.[5]

Meanwhile Hôtels-Dieu for the sick and aged were developing as a result of
the institution of nursing Orders. These commonly followed the Rule of St.
Augustine; as the lightest of the monastic Rules it was peculiarly fitted to men
and women who had a hard task of nursing to perform in addition to the *Opus
Dei*. *Chanoinesses hospitalières* were instituted in 1158 to serve the Hôtel-Dieu
of Abbeville, in 1167 at Beauvais, and in 1171 for the Hôtel-Dieu-Saint-
Gervais, and in 1188 for the Hôtel-Dieu-Saint-Opportune at Paris.[6] The Ordre
Hospitalier du Saint-Esprit was founded at Montpellier about 1195 to tend the
sick, the poor, foundlings, pilgrims, and strangers; by 1198 it had six or seven
daughter houses.[7] Funds were secured by sending brethren round with relics
which were shown to the faithful in churches, displayed in special flat travelling-
reliquaries with folding doors showing the double cross of the Order on their
leaves.[8]

[1] The church is aisleless, with an old-fashioned barrel-vault.
[2] He also founded a lazar-house outside Caen in 1161.
[3] The Musée de la Grand' Barre at Poitiers has a twelfth-century capital sculptured with monsters
from the lazar-house of Poitiers.
[4] e.g. Louvres, Seine-et-Oise, founded by Blanche of Castille, *c.* 1240; Léproserie Saint-Lazare at
Allonne, Oise, of which the church and barn survive; and the lazar-house founded by Saint Louis
at Sarlat.
[5] Durand in *Bull. Mon.*, 1932, p. 9.
[6] See Hélyot in Migne, xx, col. 789. Another community was that of the Religieuses hospitalières
de la Charité Notre-Dame, founded at the end of the thirteenth century by Gui de Joinville. They
became Augustinian in 1347. Ibid., col. 833.
[7] A later example from the Vaucouleurs house is now in the hospital of Neufchâteau, Vosges.
[8] See P. Brune, *Histoire de l'Ordre hospitalier du Saint-Esprit,* Lons-le-Saunier and Paris, 1892. About

At Montreuil-sur-Mer the hospital is still served by the same Augustinian sisterhood as was instituted when it was founded in 1200. Others were attached to the hospital founded by Saint Louis at Pontoise in 1258 and to the Hôtel-Dieu at Paris when he re-endowed it in 1258.[1] Some forty Filles-Dieu nursed here, with twenty-five men to help them and two canons to serve the chapel. By a natural analogy these monastic Hôtels-Dieu were built like the infirmary of a monastery, on a church-like plan with nave and aisles, with an altar at the head of the building. Angers, Pons, and Coeffort, all founded by Henry II of England about 1180; the Hôtel-Dieu-de-Gallande at Senlis, of the thirteenth century, and the Hôtel-Dieu of Pont-Lieue near Le Mans, all resemble the great infirmary of such a monastery as Ourscamps[2] (Fig. 69). At Angers the great hall, nearly 200 feet long and more than 70 wide, is remarkable for its tall columns, its high-pitched rib vaults, its sixteen windows, and its light and elegant proportions.[3] The men patients occupied the right aisle, the women the left, and the middle aisle was empty. The tombs of the founders were set near the door, and there was a great statue of the bound Christ awaiting death. A cloister opened out of it, giving on to a small frescoed chapel. Near by still stand the great barns of the hospital, likewise Cistercian in plan, and quarters for the staff.[4]

Such hospitals were abundantly decorated. A record remains[5] which shows that the Hôtel-Dieu of Chartres, rebuilt after a fire in 1134, had the capitals of its double row of columns carved with foliage, and the consoles of the roof carved with the symbols of the evangelists and the traditional figures of Hope praying, Despair killing himself, Charity giving alms, and Avarice clasping his money-bags. The walls were painted with the Labours of the Months.

At the end of the thirteenth century this monastic plan was changed in favour of a new scheme which combined ward and chapel in a single room. When Margaret of Sicily, widow of Charles d'Anjou, founded the hospital at Tonnerre in 1292, she had it built like the great hall of a castle, buttressed outside, nearly 330 feet long and nearly 60 wide. It is lighted by large pointed windows high up in the walls, which once had a wooden gallery where the patients might walk and get sun and air.[6] Where the chimney and dais would have been in a

1095 the Order of the Hospital of St. Antony was founded in the Dauphiné to tend those who suffered from the *mal des ardents*.

[1] It had been built by Saint Landry, Bishop of Paris, and belonged to the bishop until in 1097 it was given to the canons. Hélyot, op. cit., col. 466. See also Dorothy Mackay Quinn, 'A Medieval Picture of the Hôtel-Dieu of Paris', in *Bull. of the History of Medicine*, xii, 1942, p. 118.

[2] Other hospitals on this plan were built at Falaise, Caen, Rheims, Soissons, and Chartres. Enlart, *Arch. civile*, p. 46.   [3] It is now the Musée Saint-Jean.

[4] See C. Tollet, *Les Édifices hospitaliers*, 1892, p. 125.

[5] Tollet, p. 136.

[6] A similar gallery ran round the ward at Charlieu. Lallemand, iii. 154.

hall there is a triple apse with an altar[1] behind a fine wooden rood-screen. As in a hall the chief light falls on the dais, so here it is concentrated on this sanctuary. The windows were originally filled with plain glass leaded in patterns, with a little colour introduced in the portraits and arms of the foundress and her husband. The plan became classic in the fourteenth century,[2] and is followed in the most perfect surviving mediaeval hospital, that of Beaune, dedicated to the Virgin and St. Antony. Nicolas Rolin, its founder, was a man 'sprung from little people' who rose to be Chancellor of Philippe le Bon. Chastellain said of him that he always harvested upon earth as though the earth were to be his abode for ever. With some of his harvest, however, he founded in 1443 the Hôtel-Dieu at Beaune and endowed it with the vineyards from which it still draws its revenues. The sisters that serve it still follow the Rule and wear the habit of the Sœurs hospitalières of Valenciennes whom he brought there in 1449.[3] His architect, Jehan Rateau, built it like a great town house, with a canopied doorway to the street and an arcaded courtyard within (Fig. 243), not of stone and slate, as that of a noble house would have been, but of timberwork and bright glazed tiles. The hospital was originally divided into two *Chambres des povres* for men and women, and an *enfermerie des povres malades en danger de mort*. On the first floor of one wing were single rooms for those who could pay for them. Each *Chambre des povres* was built like the Hôtel-Dieu of Tonnerre as a great hall with a chapel at the end (Fig. 244). The keeled wooden roof and its beams were brightly painted and the floors set with tiles ornamented with Rolin's motto SEULLE and his initials.[4] Above the door was set a wooden statue of the seated Christ, crowned with thorns and awaiting death. Like a great house the hospice had its tapestries—still hung out for the feast of Corpus Christi—of red woven with doves and with the arms and initials of the founder and his wife. Originally these were used on feast days to cover the beds nearest to the chapel in the ward.[5] The altar had a magnificent retable of the Last Judgement by Roger van der Weyden. The *povres malades* had at least colour to help them through their troubles; no modern hospital is so beautiful and few as cheerful as the Hospice de Beaune.

The Order of the Holy Ghost remained faithful to the plan with a separate chapel. Their hospital at Dijon, founded in the same year as Beaune, had a fine church in a courtyard. A hospital building on two floors, with a ward below and rooms for children and sisters above, a separate building for the brethren,

---

[1] It once also contained the bronze tomb of the foundress.

[2] e.g. Dracy-Saint-Loup, Chartres, Brie-Comte-Robert.

[3] The whole building was modelled on the hospital of Valenciennes, though the workmen were local. It was finished in 1451.

[4] Some remain in the Salle des Archives.

[5] Cf. the two tapestries 'semées de verdure et plusieurs bestes et oyseaulx' which Nicole Jourlaine left to the hospital of Saint-Jacques-aux-Pèlerins at Paris in 1512. Lallemand, iii. 81.

and another for stores, completed the quadrangle. Over the portal was inscribed

> Ut rosa flos florum, sic est domus ista domorum:
> Nam pupillorum est cibus, et requies miserorum.[1]

The final mediaeval development of the ward-plan was reached at Issoudun in 1502. There the two wards for men and women are linked by an arcaded screen-wall, so that both can see the chapel at the end of the smaller room. This, too, is full of decoration: the rafters are sculptured, the windows are filled with stained glass, and in each corner is a great stone panel delicately and elaborately carved with the Tree of Jesse.

6. TOWN CHURCHES

The town churches of France were less important, architecturally and historically, than the abbeys, the cathedrals, and the collegiate churches. They had neither their antiquity, their prestige, nor their endowments. Their foundation was not systematically organized before the year 1000; the first legal steps towards such organization were taken at the Council of Limoges in 1032.[2] It was therefore natural that the parish churches should rarely initiate in their architecture or decoration, and that they should tend to take their colour from the greater churches of the locality.[3] Served only by one or two priests, they could hardly be centres of learning or spiritual revival. They were often old-fashioned. Zigzag, chevron, and billet mouldings were still carved for them when the abbeys had given them up; at Thury-Harcourt a Norman bird-head moulding adorns a pointed arch of mature Gothic style. At Hagetmau the crypt combines Romanesque capitals not unlike those of Moissac with a high-pitched Angevin rib-vault.

The parish churches in Romanesque or early Gothic style are often of the simplest kind, constructions of the feudal lord, the corporation, or the abbot who was responsible for the spiritual welfare of the town but did not fulfil that duty in any over-generous spirit. It is only in the later Middle Ages, and in the richer towns in districts such as Brittany and Champagne that were not too severely tried by the hazards of war, that churches at all comparable with those intended for monastic or collegiate use were built.

Yet the town churches must not be, as they often are, ignored. They were

[1] Brune, p. 121.

[2] In certain cities, for instance Albi, some of the parishes appear to be of Carolingian institution; but Moulins had no town parishes until after the Revolution, the two town churches being dependencies of the rural parishes of Yseure and Saint-Bonnet.

[3] Certain curious exceptions are no doubt explicable by historical circumstances now forgotten. The church of Saint-Paul-Serge at Narbonne, for instance, begun in 1229, is in pure Gothic with a false triforium in the Rouen manner.

extraordinarily numerous: in such cities as Laon, which in the Middle Ages had sixty-three churches, Rouen, which up to 1940 still had eighteen Gothic churches, and Dijon, apart from the cathedral and a few monastic churches the churches were parochial. Through these churches, many of which have no recorded history, the tide of the city still ebbs and flows; in them we feel ourselves closer to the daily religious life of the ordinary man, merchant or artisan, citizen or servant, than we can be in a monastic church or even in a great cathedral.

Their origins are extraordinarily diverse. A considerable number were founded by the Benedictine abbeys which owned the towns. At Cluny, for instance, all the town churches were built by the abbey, and continued to be in the abbey gift. Saint-Nicolas in Caen was built in 1083 by the Benedictines of the Abbaye-aux-Hommes. It resembles the abbey in its general proportions, but offers a marked contrast in its extreme plainness of style: a contrast that is equally evident in the town churches at Cluny. Saint-Nicolas seems originally to have followed the Benedictine plan of five parallel apses.

Some of the richly decorated parish churches of the south-west were equally dependent on the neighbouring abbey. The parish churches of Maillezais and Thouars (Fig. 245), for example, have richly sculptured Romanesque façades of a splendour due to their Benedictine owners.

Others depended upon a cathedral chapter and were built or rebuilt out of its revenues. Aulnay, for example, has one of the finest Romanesque churches of any small town in France; it was rebuilt between 1119 and 1135, just after possession of the living had passed to the chapter of Poitiers cathedral. Its quadrilobed piers, its cruciform plan, its pointed arches, its deep choir, and the extreme richness of its sculptural decoration (Fig. 246) make it comparable with the abbey and priory churches of Saintonge.[1] To this day it remains disproportionately splendid for the little town it serves. Another unexpectedly splendid church is that of Larchant, with a tympanum sculptured with the Last Judgement and a rich and unusual east end. It was the property of the chapter of Notre-Dame de Paris, who built it on a scale heightened by that of the cathedral they served.

Other churches, again, were due to the munificence of feudal lords. Notre-Dame-de-la-Coudre at Parthenay, which has a west doorway comparable with that at Aulnay, is the church dependent on the Lusignans' castle there. Many were built to house relics brought back from the crusades. Longpré-les-Corps-saints, for example, owes its name to relics brought from the Holy Land by Alléaume de Fontaine, who built the church to enshrine them in 1190. Sainte-Croix de Provins was built to contain a relic of the True Cross brought back from the Holy Land by Thibault IV of Champagne, after the Damietta

[1] For a fuller account see Gardner, p. 138.

expedition. Notre-Dame de Lamballe was partly rebuilt in 1371 by Charles de Blois when he endowed it with a relic of Saint Yves.

Some churches were converted, or partly converted, from earlier buildings. The Madeleine-de-la-Cité at Paris was the successor of a church created by the conversion of a synagogue to Christian use when Philip Augustus drove out the Jews in 1183. The church of Saint-Sylvain de Levroux, near Châteauroux, was built on the ruins of the palace of the Roman governor of the district in the thirteenth century.

Other churches were due to royal munificence. In 1240, for example, Blanche of Castille ordered the church of Saint-Gervais and Saint-Protais at Gisors to be begun, with an aisled choir and a flat chevet in the style of the Cistercians whose patroness she was. After the devastations of the Hundred Years War Charles VII rebuilt several churches in his domains: Beaune-la-Rolande, for instance, fortified with a drawbridge at the foot of the tower. The rebuilding of Saint-Maclou at Rouen was begun in 1437 and finished in 1521, at the expense of the two Cardinals of Amboise.

The building of a church was a necessary part of the foundation of a *ville-neuve*, but it was an obligation usually met in an economical spirit. When Edward I, as Duke of Guyenne, founded Beaumont-de-Périgord, the church was built without apse or aisles, and so highly fortified as to form a donjon in case of need. Even the later *ville-neuve* churches tend to have the chief emphasis laid on a fortified tower: Villefranche-de-Lauragais, for example, has a church built in 1271 in the local brick, without aisles or transepts, with two tall turrets joined by a fortified wall-belfry.[1]

Sometimes it was by the generosity of the citizens themselves that a church was built or rebuilt. That at Neuilly-sur-Marne was erected through the efforts of its priest, Foulques, who preached the Fourth Crusade. Chénerailles in the Creuse contains the tomb-slab of the priest Barthélemy de la Place, in a form which suggests that he founded or rebuilt the church.[2] The architecturally unusual church of Notre-Dame de Dijon (Fig. 247), with a high flat façade adorned with arcading and gargoyles, was rebuilt by the citizens to house a black wooden statue of the Virgin, Notre Dame du Bon Espoir, which is still venerated there; work was begun after a fire in 1240 but it was eighty years before it was finished. Saint-Maclou at Mantes was built a century later from the proceeds of the tolls on boats passing under the town bridge on Sundays and holidays. In the fourteenth and fifteenth centuries churches were occasionally

---

[1] For other southern *bastide* churches see R. Rey, *Arch. goth. midi*, p. 140.

[2] Lasteyrie, *Gothique*, ii. 538. It is divided into three friezes. On the lowest the priest's funeral is represented. On the middle compartment are the Virgin and Child with the priest kneeling before them with St. Bartholomew and Saint Aignan, with the martyrdom of St. Cyriacus and St. Julitta to one side. At the top the priest kneels before a Crucifixion, with Longinus and the Virgin and St. John. The tomb must have been erected in the priest's lifetime, for the date of death is left blank.

built as, or grew out of, the chapels of confraternities. As late as the end of the fifteenth century the shipbuilders of Honfleur constructed their church of Sainte-Catherine, all but the base, of sound timber like their ships. The very tower is of wood; the nave is double, with aisles beyond, and there is a double apse with a spire over it. Town churches, often built on a constricted site, offer variety rather than novelty in their plan. In the late twelfth and early thirteenth centuries a certain number in the provinces under English domination—Normandy, Bordeaux, and Anjou—show the rectangular chevet of the English style.[1] Yet the ensemble is not English; Saint-Jean at Saumur, for instance, combines the English chevet and an English elaboration of rib vaults into a scheme which has no exact English parallel. At Saint-Macaire in the Gironde, the church, built early in the thirteenth century, has three equal eleven-sided apses, two of which are set to form a transept. Gradually the plan of churches in the larger towns came to be influenced by that of the churches of Friars Preachers. A second nave was sometimes added, as at Notre-Dame-de-Froide-Rue at Caen,[2] with a second and sometimes quite disparate apse. The fifteenth-century church of Saint-Gilles at Malestroit in Brittany was planned with two almost equal naves. Saint-Michel-des-Lions at Limoges is planned as a great rectangle, with three naves of equal height, and windows at either end. In other places[3] a confined site led to a church being built as a shapeless labyrinth of columns; its only aim was to hold as many people as possible.

The iconography of town churches is little more original. Aulnay has extraordinarily rich capitals, with lions and devils and monsters and donkeys and elephants, but their like are to be found in Benedictine abbeys; the Zodiac and Seasons and Virtues, and the seated Christ of its tympana, fine though they are, come likewise from the monastic cycle. The chief originality lies in the representation of the Crucifixion of St. Peter, which is not a successful composition. Enpezat has an interesting capital with a usurer held by demons, his money-bag still slung about his neck;[4] but there are similar capitals in the abbey of Orcival and the collegiate church of Notre-Dame-du-Port.[5] At Champeix the portal has a shorthand representation of the Trinity: a lamb and cross, a *Manus Dei*, and a dove, inscribed TRES TRINVM SIGNANT: POLLEX PECCVS ATQ: COLV(M)BA. At Martel (Fig. 248) there is a representation of Christ on the tympanum, with traces of the nails in His hands, showing the wound in His side; angels behind Him bear lance and crown. It is an excerpt from a greater scheme of Judgement. In the Gothic period, parish churches occasionally stole their subjects for

[1] e.g. Saint-Seurin, Bordeaux; Vieux Saint-Étienne, Caen; Louviers; Saint-Serge, Angers.
[2] Now Saint-Sauveur.
[3] e.g. Saint-Aspais at Melun, Notre-Dame at Étampes, and Saint-Jean-au-Marché at Troyes.
[4] Inscribed CANDO VSVRAM ACCEPIST(I) OPERA MEA FECISTI.
[5] Clermont-Ferrand, see Bréhier, p. 226. They have different inscriptions.

sculpture from secular imagery. The capitals of the nave of Saint-Étienne at Caen are carved with subjects not only from the bestiaries but also from the romances: the hunted unicorn taking refuge with a maiden; Lancelot crossing the Sword Bridge and undergoing *l'épreuve du lit*; Gawain with the lion; Aristotle and Campaspe; and Virgil the necromancer. The rather later capitals at Presles are carved with fools and other burlesque figures. The fine windows in parish churches often represent the lives of saints and were probably the gift of confraternities; at Salvic, for example, there are late fourteenth-century windows of the Trial and Martyrdom of St. Eutrope, and at Saint-Saens rather later representations of the Passion and of the life of Saint Louis.

The devotional statues of town churches are often on a high level, for they came from the workshops of such centres as Paris and Troyes.[1] Such a statue as the St. John Baptist from Mussy-sur-Seine evidently comes from a Paris atelier, and is a later member of the same series as the Apostles of the Sainte Chapelle. We do not know from what church in Champagne came the noble painted Virgin in the Louvre (Fig. 249); the skill of its balance and drapery has no country clumsiness about it, though the Virgin's serious simplicity is not quite that of the capital. But the Virgin of Magny (Fig. 250) is altogether Parisian. A slightly later stone Virgin from the chapel of Notre-Dame-de-la-Bonne-Nouvelle at Toulouse[2] shows how much such statues depended upon colour for their effect. The hair is gilt, the dress red, the veil bordered with gold and scattered with flowers, the mantle brocaded with blue peacocks and roses and lined with dark blue powdered with fleurs-de-lis. Usually, however, the Virgins of the parish churches in country towns are commonplace enough: those in the Victoria and Albert Museum, said to come from Écouen and from a chapel near Abbecourt, and that in Saint-Nicolas at Coutances may stand as examples.[3]

In the earlier centuries the town churches were great patrons of the enamellers of Limoges; their reliquaries are admirable examples of the stock productions of these workshops.[4] In the fourteenth and fifteenth centuries they depended more on local goldsmiths and became more old-fashioned; the late bust reliquaries usually come from town churches.[5] Their tapestries, again, offered no great originality of subject. The church of Saint-Sépulcre at Paris in 1379 owned a set with the usual cycle of the Childhood and Passion of Christ, with only the addition of a tapestry of the Invention of the Cross to differentiate it

[1] Some seventy Gothic Virgins survive in Champagne, and almost all of these seem to have been made at Troyes. Koechlin and Marquet de Vasselot, p. 6.

[2] Musée des Augustins, no. 511.   [3] Gardner, plate xciii and figs. 384 and 391.

[4] e.g. those of Saint-Maurice at Sens, Saint-Dulcissime at Chambert, Saint-Exupère at Toulouse, Saint-Étienne at Guriel, and others at Bonsbecque (Nord) and Lieutadès.

[5] e.g. that of copper gilt of Saint-Ferréol, Nexon, Haute-Vienne, ordered by the priest from Aimery Chrétien of Limoges, 1346. See Michel, ii. 959.

from dozens of others.[1] Sometimes, however, even a town church had a set made to its order. In 1425 the parish of the Madeleine at Troyes embarked on the project of such a set. Brother Didier the Dominican summarized and set down the history of St. Mary Magdalene. Jacquet the painter made sketches on paper to illustrate the story. Then Poinsète the dressmaker and her assistant sewed linen sheets together for the cartoons. These were painted by Jacquet and Simon the illuminator, with the Dominican dropping in at intervals to see that they had kept to the story. Finally the cartoons were ready to be sent to the weaver.[2]

Towards the end of the fifteenth century, however, one composition of real originality was achieved. It represents the different orders of society, popes and cardinals, bishops and monks, men and women, helping Christ to carry His cross: the sick man, the leper, the prisoner, the pilgrim, the labourer, and the child are all there.[3] Even in this instance its source, however, is not to be sought in the towns. All the surviving examples are in parish churches; but the subject is taken from a poem by René of Anjou, and is first found on a linen hanging recorded in an inventory of his castle of Angers.

In their turn the bourgeois tombs of the town churches are much less remarkable than those of the knightly and noble classes or even of the churchmen. Nearly all were flat tombs either of incised stone or brass. Usually the deceased was represented under a gabled canopy, with censing angels above.[4] There is little variation in those from districts within reach of Paris; all must have come from one workshop, active for more than a century after about 1245. The merchants who were purveyors to the king had the ground powdered with fleurs-de-lis; a grocer would show his scales,[5] a haberdasher his merchant's mark.[6] The king's verderer wore his hunting-horn and held his dog in leash.[7] Architects were represented with the instruments of their craft: Hugues Libergier in Saint-Nicaise at Rheims with his measuring-staff and a model of the church; Alexandre de Berneval and his brother at Saint-Ouen de Rouen with compasses and designs for rose windows.[8] Professors were shown in gown and hood lecturing to serried ranks of students, with an assistant with a rod standing beside them.[9] Exceptionally the persons commemorated were

[1] Guiffrey, p. 25.   [2] Mâle, *Art rel. XIIIe siècle*, p. 437.
[3] See C. Urseau, *La Peinture décorative en Anjou*, Angers, 1920, p. 14. The subject occurs at Montrion, Saint-Aubin at Les Ponts-de-Cé, Le Lion-d'Angers, and Chauvigny.
[4] A number were in the Chartreuse of Paris. Bodleian Gaignières, v. 108 et seqq. See also the tomb of Jehan Sarrazin, drappier, ibid. v. 71.   [5] Richard l'Espicier, ibid. v. 29.
[6] Jehan Laurent, ibid. iv. 90.
[7] Guillaume Maleceneste, ibid. xiii. 104.
[8] Gaignières, vii. 23: dated 1411.
[9] Jean Guimet, Professor of Medicine, d. 1481, Gaignières, iii. 107; Hugues Chabert, Doctor of Laws, d. 1352, ibid. v. 88; Étienne de Sainte Croix, church of Sainte-Croix (Saône-et-Loire); Guibert de Celsoy, d. 1394, Celsoy (Haute-Marne).

represented kneeling before the Virgin and Child.[1] The inscription was usually
a bare record of identity and a prayer or request to the reader to pray for the
soul of the dead person. Exceptionally Simon Marmion the painter, who died
in 1489, had an epitaph which may serve for all the dead artists of the Middle
Ages.[2]

> Les yeulx ont prins douce réfection
> En mes exploicts tant propres et exquis
> Qu'ils ont donné grande admiration,
> Riant objet et consolation,
> Aux empereurs, rois, comtes et marquis.
> J'ay décoré par art et sens acquis
> Livres, tableaux, chappelles et autels
> Telz que pour lors ne sont guerre de tels.
> Peintres mortels qui prenez patronnaige
> Sur mes couleurs, vertes, noires et blanches,
> Quand vous avez pourtraict vos personnaiges
> Après les miens dont sont grand les sommaiges
> Octroyez nous les doulces bienveuillances,
> Priez aux saincts dont j'ai fait les semblances
> Que l'Eternel peintre pardon me face
> Sy que lassus je tire après sa face . . . .

[1] Arnoul de Puisseux, d. 1400, Gaignières, xii. 53; Symon le Turc, d. 1449, ibid. vi. 10; Marie le Goupel, ibid. vii. 97.   [2] Laborde, ii, p. xxvii.

X

THE VILLAGERS

FRENCH mediaeval civilization rested on a basis of peasant agriculturists. The church of France ultimately depended on the thousands of village churches scattered over the entire country. Yet, because France had created a feudal and aristocratic society, for every civilizing influence and every artistic stimulus she depended upon the king and his court, the nobles and their families, the great abbeys and cathedrals that in virtue of their possessions ranked with the aristocracy. The villagers and farmers set little store and spent less money on art; their contribution to the beauty of France was the orderly country-side, the well-kept forests, the neatly stooked corn, the apple-orchards of Normandy, the vineyards of the south, the meadows of Burgundy where autumn crocuses grow like mauve shadows on the grass. They had little else that was beautiful as their heritage: their strong, plain farms, with a moulding or two round door or window; a few salt-mills carved out of the local granite; benches and tables plainer than those of a monastery; hangings spun by their own womenfolk and woven by the village weaver; pots and pans bought at the local fair; a stick calendar, scratched with a saint's attribute—arrow or sword or key—to mark his feast day.[1] When Arnoul Gréban in his *Passion*, written before 1452, makes the shepherds discuss what presents to take to the new-born Christ, he reveals the poverty of their possessions. Shall it be a crook, or a wreath, or the sheep-dog? Brown bread, or roast chestnuts? No, a new penny whistle, or a rattle:

> Si très bien faite que merveille,
> Qui dira clic clic à l'oreille;
> Au moins quand l'enfant pleurera
> La hochette l'apaisera
> Et se taira pour une pause.

Even such things as were industrially produced were rarely designed expressly for peasant use. It is exceptional to find floor-tiles painted with a labourer coming back from work, with a heavy load, and the legend *grant poine*, or with a ploughshare ironically set on a shield, with the motto *vive labeur* beneath.[2] Usually the wares intended for peasant use were merely old-fashioned. Everything, however simple, has the style of an age; but in the Middle Ages the possessions of the poor had the style of an age that had just passed away. A girl's dowry would contain a ring, a circlet, and a brooch of gold or silver or base

---

[1] A fourteenth-century example is in the Bibliothèque Nationale.
[2] Fifteenth century. Musée de Dijon; Musée Rolin, Autun.

S

metal,[1] that would serve her all her life; but even at the end of the fifteenth century the brooch would be the *fermail* that great ladies had worn in the thirteenth century and citizens' wives in the fourteenth.

The decrease of tillage after the Hundred Years War increased the yield of timber: 'les bois sont venus en France avec les Anglais.' Consequently farmers at last began in the sixteenth century to have rather more elaborate furniture, carved chests and cupboards and such-like; but they were modelled on bourgeois types of the previous century.

In many parts of France one can date the moment when the local style of architecture became fixed.[2] In the charming but rather backward villages of Auvergne, the Cantal, and Périgord it is still not hard to imagine that one is living in the fifteenth century.

When any fine building or unnecessary ornament was attempted on a French farm in the earlier Middle Ages, it was the work not of peasant or farmer but of church or monastery. All the finest barns of France are monastic.[3] Even the best farms were abbey property. The farm of Meslay, near Tours, was built between 1211 and 1227 by Hugues de Rochecorbon, Abbot of Marmoutier, in an enclosure protected by a crenellated wall, a monumental gateway, and a porter's lodge. The farm buildings huddle inside, with a dovecote and an immense five-aisled barn nearly two hundred feet long. No feudal landlord would build on that scale for his tenant's benefit, and no farmer could afford to for his own. The very landmarks of abbey estates were sculptured. When in 1288 the abbey of Sainte-Seine had settled a dispute over boundaries with Flavigny, the abbot set up *bornes* to mark them carved with figures of St. Sequanus and St. Peter. The Prior of Figeac a little later marked the limits of the priory lands by graceful obelisks crowned by a cross. To this day the villagers of Magnac-Laval, once part of the estate of the collegiate church of Le Dorat, make the 'Procession des Neuf Lieues' on Whit Monday, round the forty-eight crosses that mark the boundary: a course of more than thirty miles. The route runs over hill, over dale, through fields and meadows, across a temporary bridge, and through a house.

The host of crosses that starred the country-side—at cross-roads, in cemeteries, at the boundaries of church property—were nearly all destroyed at the Revolution. Their number is incalculable. The parish of Clamecy, for example, had thirteen crosses, to one of which in turn a procession was made after vespers between Easter and Ascension. Only a few remain to show that these, too, brought monastic art outside the cloister. The monks of Tiron set one up at

---

[1] See Laborde, p. 312.

[2] See J. Brunhès in Hanotaux, i. 411 et seqq., for a sketch of the distribution of roof styles and cottage types.

[3] e.g. those of the abbey of Perrières, Calvados; Maubuisson, Seine-et-Oise; and Saultan, Nord.

the boundary of some of their property near Chartres:[1] an early fourteenth-century crocketed cross with a pierced quatrefoil at the crossing. Inside this is carved the founder of Tiron on his death-bed, with two of his monks in attendance; on the other side he is shown surrounded by angels. A fifteenth-century cross survives in the cemetery of Aulnay-de-Saintonge, its shaft carved with figures of Saints Peter, Paul, James, and John; it was doubtless ordered by the monks of Saint-Cyprien de Poitiers who owned the place.

Less remains of the purely feudal buildings of the villages: the lord's mill and oven and weigh-house and dovecote: successive revolutions have seen to that. A few bridges, where the seigneur's tolls were taken, and a few mills, where his tenants' corn had to be ground, alone survive. At Bagas in the Gironde, for example, there is a fifteenth-century mill fortified at each angle by an octagonal échauguette; at Barbaste one with four square towers (Fig. 251). At Boucieu-le-Roi, near Tournon, there are still the administrative buildings of the royal bailiff who administered the property: a bridge, a mill, and a house with a delightful turret for the bailiff to live in.

The villager did not enjoy the citizen's freedom; some degree of servitude was his normal lot. Communal rights were rarely achieved for a village, though in Ponthieu and the Laonnais certain groups of villages succeeded in obtaining collective rights. The only hope of obtaining or keeping such rights lay in combined action; all the rural communes that existed owed their origin to a religious confraternity. It was with reason that everything in village life centred in the church and the local saint and his confraternity and his feast. To this day the village feasts of the Limousin are called 'frairies', though now the confraternity may be no more than a memory and the celebration only a bourrée to the bagpipes and a long monotonous hymn about the local saint or the fairies. To this day the members of the confraternity of Saint Léonard in his village[2] ride at the quintain and demolish a cardboard castle with three pigeons inside it, and the corporation of the mariners of the Loire bear their model boat from the little church of Cuffy[3] to the junction of the Loire and the Allier at the feast of St. Nicholas.

The village churches were as diverse in origin as those of the towns. Such a church as that of Saint-Just at Valcabrère[4] links the Middle Ages with Roman times. It became a parish church in the fourth century; when it was rebuilt in the twelfth century some of its ancient stones were re-used. Other churches grew up, and their villages with them, round a saint's tomb that became a place of pilgrimage. The village of Sainte-Maignance thus arose between Avallon

---

[1] Now in the Chartres Museum. Others survive at Saint-Cirgues and Fontfroide (Lasteyrie, Gothique, ii. 531), and two others, now destroyed, are illustrated by Viollet-le-Duc, Dict. iv. 434 and 437.

[2] Saint-Léonard, Haute-Vienne; it is now a town. It grew up round the saint's tomb.

[3] Near Saincaize.

[4] Basses-Pyrénées.

and Saulieu round the tomb of one of the five Roman ladies who brought back the body of Saint Germain from Ravenna to Auxerre and died on the way. She lies in a sculptured tomb of the twelfth century, that represents her as a pilgrim, and portrays her death and the vision of the man who rediscovered her body. Saint-Céneri-le-Gérei, between Le Mans and Alençon, grew up round the tomb and oratory of a hermit saint who died in 669. The Romanesque church has its apse decorated with frescoes of the saint's death and funeral. Saint-Viâtre[1] had the sixth-century tomb of the saint in the crypt; there was a local pilgrimage, and in the fourteenth century an arcaded stone altar was built at the other end of the village street on which his relics were exposed at his festival. Tournemire,[2] again, owed its comparative prosperity to a pilgrimage to a thorn from the Crown of Thorns brought back from Crusade by Rigald de Tournemire in 1101. The church of Notre-Dame-de-Liesse was built in 1134 to receive a wooden statue of the Virgin miraculously brought back from the Holy Land by the local lord and two of his friends; the village grew up round the church. This was rebuilt about 1380, but the Virgin is still above the altar.

One of the most splendid village churches in France is that of Saint-Sulpice de Favières,[3] an enormous building in a village that has never had more than three hundred inhabitants. It owned, however, the body of Saint Sulpice, Bishop of Bourges, and it was rebuilt as a great aisled church of six bays about 1260 to house his shrine and the pilgrims that came to it. The portal has a gable carved with angel musicians, a tympanum with a Judgement,[4] door-jambs with medallions of the saint's life, and the mullion adorned with his statue.

Other churches were built by great lords and great abbots, often in the attempt, which was general in the eleventh century, to turn a sprawling farm into a village community. Such an abbey as Cluny owned an enormous number of such churches,[5] some given by its benefactors, some built by the abbey on its lands, for the most part in the eleventh and early twelfth centuries. These churches are simple enough, but the very fact that they are vaulted, that they have comparatively lofty towers and comparatively developed apses, betray the influence of a community accustomed to think in terms of fine architecture.[6] Chapaize, of which the nave and tower were built before 1020, Blanot, with a tower at the crossing, and Farges, of much the same date, still give a curiously

[1] Loir-et-Cher.
[2] Cantal.
[3] Seine-et-Oise. See *Bull. mon.* ciii, 1944, p. 246.
[4] Christ stands upright, holding the chalice in one hand and blessing with the other.
[5] For a list, see Joan Evans, *Rom. Arch. Ord. Cluny,* Appendix B; for a detailed study of some of these, J. Virey, *Les Églises romanes de l'ancien diocèse de Mâcon,* and M. and C. Dickson, *Les Églises romanes de l'ancien diocèse de Chalon,* Mâcon, 1935.
[6] See, for contrast, the record of a church, originally of stone, rebuilt in wood between 1013 and 1022. Mortet, i. 17.

vivid impression of the decency and simplicity of village life at the beginning
of the Middle Ages. It was not until the second half of the twelfth century that
sculpture began to overflow from the abbeys even on to the parish churches of
the monastic domains. Champagne in the Ardèche, a church of very early
foundation, has a tympanum of the late twelfth century carved with a Crucifixion that recalls that of the abbey of Saint-Gilles.[1] The rural churches of
Saintonge, that astonish us with the richness and beauty of their façades and
portals[2] (Fig. 252), were often monastically owned, and faintly reflected the
glories of such abbeys as Saint-Eutrope de Saintes. Trois-Palis, not far from
Angoulême, imitates the façade of its cathedral on a small scale; Civray, that
belonged to the abbey of Nouaillé, has a splendid portal with the Assumption,
the Wise and Foolish Virgins, and the Labours of the Months, in the best monastic style. The village churches of Berri imitate, *longo intervallo*, the city churches
of Bourges. Saint-Ursin had a cross with a Paschal Lamb carved on its gable
about 1100; the unusual feature reappears a little later on the small parish
churches of Jussy-Champagne, Avor, Vorly, and Charost.[3] The same design,
bordered by medallions with busts of saints, was painted in the choir of the
village church of Chalivoy-Milon, which belonged to the abbey of Saint-
Sulpice de Bourges. The wooden Virgins of the country churches of Auvergne,
seated, hieratic, veiled, and uncrowned, are all ultimately derived from the
famous tenth-century gold Virgin of the cathedral of Clermont.

The finest parish churches of the Gothic period were often monastically
owned. Saint-Sauveur du Petit-Andely, for example, which depended on the
adjacent monastery of Le Grand-Andely, is the work of a first-rate architect
who, in 1197, planned a seven-sided apse within a semicircular ambulatory.
Later a sculptured Christ was set against the mullion of the door. The most
splendid of all is perhaps the church of Saint-Père-sous-Vézelay (Fig. 253), a
tiny village where the first monastic establishment of the district had been
founded by Girart de Roussillon to commemorate his victory over Charles the
Bald. That monastery was destroyed by the Normans, but the village continued to depend on the abbey re-established on the hill-top above. The monks
rebuilt the village church at the end of the thirteenth century. They were adding
a great false gable decorated with statues to the west front of their own church,
and they copied it on a slightly smaller scale on the front of the parish church
below. Christ occupies the summit of the gable, with two angels holding a
crown over His head. The Virgin and the Magdalene stand on either side, with
St. Benedict below. On either side are three apostles. The portal is preceded
by a most graceful porch in which are two standing figures of a man and a

---

[1] It is signed GIRBERTVS.
[2] e.g. Mandé, Cintré, Saint-Gemmes, Saint-Martin le Beau, all in Charente-Maritime, and Chenay
(Deux-Sèvres). [3] See *Cong. arch.*, 1931, p. 304.

woman holding a church; the absence of any arms or inscription suggests that these are the legendary Girart de Roussillon and his wife Bertha rather than any contemporary donors.

The plan of village churches was likewise often affected by local monastic influences. Usually aisleless and of great simplicity, they could not vary much; but it is noteworthy how many of them have a flat chevet when there is a Cistercian abbey church of that form in the neighbourhood. Donnemarie-en-Montois, near the Cistercian house of Preuilly, and Chartrettes and Héricy, near the Cistercian abbey of Barbeaux, may serve as examples. In the anglicized districts of Saintonge and northern Normandy it may have been English influence which caused the plan to be adopted, as it is at Grand-Jean, near Taillebourg, and at Sainte-Mère-Église and Montebourg[1] between Bayeux and Valognes.

Too much rural and monastic history has been lost or forgotten for the character of many village churches to be explicable. Why should that of Thaon in Normandy, in a village so small that the church is now shut, still present a splendidly monumental aspect even though it is now bereft of its aisles (Fig. 254)? Why should Chars, near Pontoise, have a beautiful Romanesque façade, fine sculptured capitals, and a Gothic apse with crockets? Why is Jazeneuil, near Lusignan, budded over with ball-flower decoration? The problems are infinite, and infinitely interesting. The problems of their sculpture are no less absorbing, for their capitals are often unusual (Fig. 255). The omissions from their imagery are equally interesting. As early as the eleventh century Rupertus declared that the Labours of the Months were particularly suitable for the decoration of village churches: 'illas cum observet rusticana plebecula magis ad serviendum Deum religiosam considerat ecclesiam.' [2] Yet such representations occur not in the villages but in the great abbeys, cathedrals, and collegiate churches. It was not until the end of the thirteenth century that the figure-sculpture of greater churches was imitated in a simplified form. Even so it was old-fashioned in design. The village church of Saint-Eugène near Condé-en-Brie has a tympanum of the Last Judgement, of that date, on which Christ still appears with the evangelistic beasts of the Romanesque tradition, and the angels who bear the sun and moon are crowded among the Elect.[3]

Nor did the village churches have an iconography of their own. Quite exceptionally that of Mervilliers,[4] now destroyed, had a unique tympanum of the early twelfth century which survives; but this represents no religious scene, but the donation of lands to the church. A kneeling knight, with his horse and squire behind him, presents the deeds to the priest of the place, while a canon—the church belonged to the chapter of Sainte-Croix d'Orléans—blesses him and

[1] This, however, has rectangular chapels in the transept on the Cistercian plan.
[2] Le Sénécal, p. 51, n. 7.   [3] See Lefrançois-Pillion, *XIIIe siècle*, p. 241.
[4] Eure-et-Loir. See *Cong. arch.*, 1900: Chartres, p. 97.

a scribe registers the donation. An inscription gives the names of the donors and explains the scene. The top of the lunette is filled with figures of Christ and two censing angels, but all the interest is focused on the human personages.

A considerable number of village churches still retain their mediaeval wall-paintings. These range through the centuries. Brinay[1] has good twelfth-century frescoes of gospel scenes, prophets and evangelists, and a calendar with figures of the months. The paintings of about 1135 in the church of Saint Gilles at Argenton-Château[2] are yet more complete. They include six pairs of Virtues and their opposing Vices and the Wise and Foolish Virgins—subjects also found in the sculpture of the district—a Zodiac, the Months, and a fine Last Judgement. A late twelfth-century fresco of the Crucifixion at Saint-Jacques-les-Guérets[3] is rather crude and evidently based on a manuscript painting of an earlier date. Chalivoy-Milon[4] has early thirteenth-century paintings of the Resurrection of Lazarus and scenes of the Infancy and Passion of Christ. The apse originally had a *mappa mundi* with the Creation, the Four Rivers, and the strange people of distant lands that appeared nearly a century before on the portal of Vézelay.[5] Fine late fourteenth-century paintings adorn the walls of the church of Saulcet.[6] There is a Christ in Majesty[7] in a mandorla held by four angels, with the four Evangelists; and representations of the Legend of St. James that seem to show the influence of castle paintings in their elegant ladies and forest backgrounds.

The chapel of Kernascleden, near Le Faouet in Brittany, was entirely painted about 1455. In the south transept is a Dance of Death, in the north a choir of angels; in the sanctuary twenty-four scenes of the Life of the Virgin. All are of great beauty, and seem to be the work of a skilful artist.[8] More often the frescoes of a village church are of varying dates. The small church of Pritz, near Laval, has thirteenth-century paintings of the Legend of St. Catherine and the Labours of the Months, a St. Christopher of about 1500, and sixteenth-century paintings, still Gothic in style, of St. Hubert and St. Agatha.[9] Occasionally, too, fifteenth-century panel-paintings are to be found in village churches. Crocq,[10] for example, has a retable of 1410 with seven panels, painted with the life of Saint Éloi.

It is, perhaps, the statues of wood which are most characteristic of mediaeval

[1] Cher.　　　　[2] Deux-Sèvres. See Sanoner in *Rev. d'art chrét.* xlvi, 1903, p. 397.
[3] Loir-et-Cher.　　　　[4] Cher.
[5] See p. 39. Chalivoy-Milon, though a village church, belonged to the Benedictine abbey of Saint-Sulpice de Bourges.
[6] Allier: a village church that belonged to the priory of Saint-Pourçain.
[7] Represented as an ageing man with grey hair and beard. See *Cong. arch.*, 1938, p. 355.
[8] See Lemoisne, p. 92.
[9] The little altars have fifteenth-century panel-paintings, and the rood-screen large fifteenth-century figures of the Crucifixion, with the Virgin and St. John.　　　　[10] Creuse.

village churches, that could afford only them when the chapels of the nobles
had ivory and gold and the richer churches marble and alabaster:

> Li un fisent ymages d'or
> Qu'il pendoient en leur tresor,
> L'un de keuvre, d'estain, d'argent,
> Celes de fust la povre gent.[1]

A church near Sens could show a wooden Crucifixion most moving in its
simple dignity;[2] Humbert, in the Pas-de-Calais, two angels of great beauty
which must once have formed part of a larger group. Duclair still has its early
fifteenth-century Calvary, Notre-Dame d'Avenières its imperial Saint Sauveur
and colossal St. Christopher.[3] Usson[4] has an equestrian statue of St. Maurice;
Écouis an *Ecce Homo* (Fig. 256 A). Notre-Dame-de-la-Brune near Tournus has
a seated Virgin that reproduced in wood the pose of the great golden Virgins
of the pilgrimage churches.[5] Few museums are without some wooden
Virgin of which a church has been bereft (Fig. 256 B). Such statues were often
numerous: Lyons-la-Forêt, for example, the small church of a small village,
has a St. Christopher, a St. Martha, and a St. Anne of wood, and a Virgin of
Pity in alabaster; Rouvres-Plaine[6] two enormous St. John Baptists, as well as
a Virgin between two St. Johns over the altar.

The stone images of the village churches tend to be poor versions of those in
greater places. The finest, such as those at Nanteuil-le-Haudouin and Bouée
near Nantes, are good examples of the stock types turned out by city workshops;
the more characteristic, like those of Saint-Béat and Sautron,[7] the grotesque
attempts of country carvers to achieve what was beyond their powers.

The villages were not fortified,[8] and many had no castle to offer a refuge in
time of war. As early as the Albigensian Crusade the Seneschal of Rouergue
reported to Alphonse of Poitiers that the peasants had no other place of refuge
than their churches, and in time of war brought their chests of corn and clothes
there for storage.[9] About this time Najac had its windows filled with stone slabs
pierced with quatrefoils, to fortify them, and rather later[10] the fine Romanesque
tower of Saint-Hippolyte was built into a great oblong donjon. The necessity
for such defences continued. In 1358 Jean de Vinette recorded: 'Many villages
which possessed no fortifications made true strongholds of their churches.

---

[1] Söhring, p. 571.   [2] Now in a chapel of Sens Cathedral.
[3] Another St. Christopher, with the arms of the Bourbons d'Archambault, is at Saint-Christophe,
Sarthe.   [4] Puy-de-Dôme.   [5] See *Cong. arch.*, 1850, p. 105.
[6] See *Cong. arch.*, 1928, p. 441. Every district can show some: e.g., in Eure, La Bonneville and
Barc.   [7] Loire-Inférieure.
[8] The few exceptions, such as Saint-Haon-le-Châtel, can be explained by the fact that the villages
lay actually within a castle enceinte; or, like Puycelci (Tarn), they are fortress villages dominating a
strategic position.
[9] See *Bull. mon.* xxiii. 24.   [10] Before 1319; see Virey, 2nd ed., p. 382.

Moats were dug to surround the sacred buildings, and the towers and belfries were furnished with stones and engines of war.'[1] It was, however, during the Hundred Years War that the fortification of churches was most general. In the south, as at Tarjac in the Dordogne and Rudelle in the Lot; in the centre of France, as at Royat; in the Limousin, as at Le Dorat and Compreignac; in the west, as at Charras (Fig. 257) and Esnandes and Angoulins and Le Boupère, new and old churches were strengthened by crenellations and machicoulis and defensive turrets; sometimes merely disfiguring the earlier design, sometimes achieving a new and austere architectural beauty.

The village churches had fewer fine tombs than those of the towns and cities. They were not, however, unmindful of their dead. In hundreds of village churchyards rose a *Lanterne des Morts*: a hollow column, more or less decorated, with a pierced top from which the light which was set within it every evening could shine out over the quiet graves.[2]

[1] Quoted Lavisse, iv, pt. 1, p. 132.
[2] See Peter the Venerable, *De miraculis*, book ii. Examples may be seen at Château-Larcher (monastic); Fenioux; Antigny, near Saint-Savin-sur-Gartrempe; Culhat, near Lezoux; Felletin, Creuse; La Souterraine (monastic); Mauriac, Cantal; and in many other places in the Limousin and south-west.

XI

THE END OF THE MIDDLE AGES

1. THE HUNDRED YEARS WAR

THE Middle Ages ended in a long-drawn series of disasters: plague, pestilence and famine, battle, murder and sudden death. Against each catastrophe France struggled manfully: from each she rose magnificently, but the effort was too prolonged and at the end she knew exhaustion. When that came her unique mediaeval civilization, and the arts that were a part of it, could no longer withstand the influences of other countries that had been less cruelly tried.

The first disaster, the Hundred Years War, fell on France with her invasion by Edward III of England in 1339. Nine years later, *la tierce partie du monde mourut*. The Black Death ravaged every province of France, abbeys, cities, towns, and villages. In Burgundy they still remember

En mil trois cent quarante et huit
A Nuits de cent restèrent huit;

while at Beaune

En mil trois cent quarante-neuf
De cent ne demeuraient que neuf.

Another widespread outbreak of bubonic plague in 1360–1 was especially virulent in Burgundy, where it carried off the duchess and half the court.

Plague and pestilence, indeed, continued to ravage France, and their toll was nowhere higher than in the crowded dorters of the monastic houses. The tide of war in its turn wrecked their very buildings:[1] Notre-Dame de Saintes, Saint-Jean-d'Angely, Poitiers, Ligugé, Saint-Lucien de Beauvais, Saint-Germer-de-Fly, Saint-Riquier, Saint-Josse, and hundreds more. Other abbey churches fell down for want of men and money to repair them. For the monasteries knew poverty such as they had not known since the eighth and ninth centuries. Agricultural France lay waste and their estates brought them no revenues; the roads were dangerous and no pilgrims came to their shrines. Instead, English armies came to sack their barns and even their sacristies: yet still the royal officers demanded forced contributions from them. Jean Molinet the poet summed up what war had done to the abbeys:

Je laisse aux abbaies grandes
Cloistres rompus, dortoirs gastés,
Greniers sans bled, troncqs sans offrandes,
Celiers sans vins, fours sans pastés,

---

[1] For a list of abbeys burnt or destroyed in the war, see Denifle, ii. 19 et seqq.; it is much too long to quote here.

Prelats honteux, moisnes crottés,
Pertes de biens et de bestaille,
Et, pour redressier leurs clochés
Sur leur dos, une grande taille.[1]

After Crécy Philippe de Valois asked the Abbot of Saint-Denis to give him Suger's great gold cross; Charles VII demanded it later. Both could only be refused because a pope had once given sentence of excommunication against anyone who should take it.

The abbey was looted by English and Picards in 1411, and by Burgundians in 1418. The monks succeeded in hiding the treasure, but in 1418 the gold shrine, given by Charles VI only twenty-five years before, had to be melted down and coined for his benefit. In 1419 there was a bad fire in the monastery buildings; in 1429 and 1436 the English came again.[2] Then Dunois seized even the silver dishes from the monks' refectory.

The story is the same everywhere. At Saint-Martial de Limoges the buildings were damaged, the farms and vineyards were laid waste, the houses were burnt and every source of revenue made dry.[3] Popes and bishops, kings and lords, made claims that there were none to oppose. By 1439 there were only thirty monks left, and not enough money to feed them. For a time the abbey was deserted; then a few monks returned to live without a Rule, with a bourgeois family called Jovion holding all the offices and drawing what little revenue there was. The abbey never wholly recovered, and was secularized in 1535. In 1404 there were only fifteen monks left at Saint-Benoît-sur-Loire; at Moissac only twenty, instead of a hundred and twenty; in 1424 Conques was secularized because only twenty-nine monks were left. It is fair to say that monasticism in France never recovered from the Hundred Years War.

The story of the cities and towns is no more happy, though only within their walls could there be a shadow of security. Yet they were not strong enough to hold back the forces of destruction indefinitely. Few of the greater towns of France escaped from being taken by assault, pillaged, and burnt between 1337 and 1453. In 1435 only five people were left living in all Limoges. If the smaller towns suffered less, it was because they offered less resistance. In 1438, after a hard winter made worse by an epidemic of smallpox, wolves were seen outside the gates of Paris. In that year it was sixteen years since Paris had ceased to be the real capital of France. The next year grass grew in its streets.

Rouen, that early in the thirteenth century had had nearly fifteen thousand inhabitants, had barely six thousand. In 1442 the population of Avallon consisted in five households able to pay their taxes, thirty-six misérables, and eleven

[1] Written between 1478 and 1482. Champion, *Hist. poét. XV*e *siècle*, ii. 343.
[2] See Denifle, i. 63.
[3] See Lasteyrie, p. 157.

beggars. In 1444 Senlis, Saint-Nicolas, Gournay, Avilly, Saint-Firmin, Apre-
mont, Malassise, Rieux, La Noël-Saint-Martin, Bray, Montlévêque, and Oirry
la-Ville were entirely deserted. The Fairs of Champagne, Lyons, and Paris were
no longer held; the merchant class was ruined. The enamel-trade of Limoges
was almost at an end in the last quarter of the fourteenth century. Provins, that
once had had 3,200 cloth-looms, lay empty while its weavers tilled the fields
outside the walls. By the end of the fourteenth century Eustache Deschamps
was complaining that at Paris

> Il n'a ouvrier à Paris qui ne pleure
> Car riens ne font . . .
> Ni les brodeurs n'ont gaires à broder,
> Les orfèvres n'ont pas trop à dorer,
> Les cousturiers n'ont gaires à ouvrer;
> Sellier n'y a qui petit ne labeure . . .[1]

After 1407 there is a strange pause in artistic creation. By 1420 the great
Paris trade of tapestry-weaving had moved to the rich towns of Flanders; its
ivory-carving had already practically come to an end.[2] The only merchants
who had any trade were those who braved the dangers of the roads and peddled
their goods.[3] There were many wanderers upon the road, and as many Calvaries
where alone they could find consolation. 'O vos omnes qui transitis per viam,
attendite et videte si est dolor sicut dolor meus.'

Even the great stores of treasure of the king and the royal dukes were lost or
diminished. All the vast treasures of Louis d'Anjou went to pay for the Sicilian
Expedition. In 1411 all the works of art collected by the Duc de Berry and
housed in his castle of Bicêtre were pillaged and destroyed by the Cabochiens;
in 1420 the English found the Sainte Chapelle of Vincennes, once one of the
richest of royal chapels, empty but for an old chair and a ragged altar-cloth.
The greater part of such portable treasures as had been saved from spoliation
had to be sold to pay their owners' ransoms after the successive English victories.

The chief work in architecture and sculpture accomplished between 1338 and
1360, the first acute stage of the war, and again between 1415 and 1429, the
second and worse, was necessarily in the few parts of France that were least
engaged. In 1351, for example, Pope Clement VI from the sanctuary of Avignon
could plan his tomb and give orders for its execution at La Chaise-Dieu.[4] In
their uninvaded duchy the Dukes of Burgundy could build the charterhouse of
Champmol and plan its sculptures and their tombs. In Brittany, at peace and
practically independent, architecture could flourish as it never had before; towns

---

[1] Œuvres, ed. Queux de Saint-Hilaire (S.A.T.F.), v. 123.
[2] See Koechlin, i. 32.
[3] M. Koechlin cites Mougny Ferry, *marchand passant pays* from whom the Duke of Orleans bought
three expensive ivory combs in 1455.
[4] It was carved by Pierre Roye assisted by Jean David and Jean de Santolis.

could be walled, houses, churches, and cathedrals built. Duke John IV had money and leisure to build a nobler tower than that of Saint-Pierre de Caen at his chapel of Le Kreisker; his successor could see the cathedral of Saint-Pol-de-Léon finished and that of Nantes begun. Such examples fired the Bishop and Chapter of Le Mans to go on building even though the English were in Maine and Bedford was striving to bleed it white.[1] The magnificent windows of the north transept date from 1430; the Grosse Tour was finished in 1433; the statues of Louis II of Sicily and his wife were set up by the great southern rose in 1439. The English did nothing to help; all was done by the King of France and the nobles and citizens of Maine: a magnificent demonstration that they were not conquered.

2. PEACE

Charles VII was a physically feeble and wretched man, the eleventh child of a madman and of an unhealthy woman who had hated her husband with a deadly hatred. Yet he had foresight, astuteness, and political skill; with St. Joan to lead his armies he turned the tide of invasion, and by his own diplomacy he gradually won back France. His reign had seen not only the victorious armies of England, but every kind of civil disaster: riots in the cities, brigands on the roads, civil war between Burgundians and Armagnacs, treachery by the Duke of Burgundy, by his mother, by his son. Yet at the end of the war in 1453 England held no French soil but Calais and the Channel Islands; and France was united by the strong saving sense of nationality that comes from the knowledge of enemies conquered.

All that men asked for was peace. The tapestries of the story of St. Peter given to Beauvais by Bishop Guillaume de Hellande in 1460 and those of Saints Gervais and Protais given to Soissons about the same time have their grounds scattered over with little scrolls inscribed *Paix*. It was at once a thanksgiving and a prayer.

Yet peace had been too long in coming. Creation might begin again, but the rhythm of life had been broken and could not be repaired. Exhaustion lay over the land like a cloud:

> Toute léesse deffaut,
> Tous cuers ont prins par assaut
> Tristesse et merencolie.

The *Grandes Heures de Rohan*[2] that date from this time are remarkable for the extraordinary intensity and violence of emotion that inspires their illustrations; it is no convention but the creation of an artist who has known suffering and

[1] See Luce, i. 335.
[2] Bib. Nat. lat. 9471. One page is reproduced in Sterling, fig. 98.

death at close quarters, for a patron who is no less familiar with their horrors and their grandeur.

For a time it seemed as if the dominant Christian thought was no longer love, but suffering.[1] The very representation of the Crucifixion was changed: Christ wore the Crown of Thorns even on the Cross, and hung a dead weight by His pierced hands.[2] Tombs that had once shown a man young, serene, and beautiful, suddenly began to show him horrible in death. Some might only hint at horror in a shrouded figure (Fig. 258 B); others would exploit it to the full by the representation of the corpse in decay (Fig 258 A). The earliest tombs of the kind are those of Guillaume de Harcigny, doctor to Charles VI, who died in 1393, at Laon,[3] and of Cardinal de Lagrange, who died in 1402, at Avignon.[4] They are only the beginning of a series that continues right through the fifteenth century.[5] In the first half of the sixteenth century—an added horror— the corpse has no name. At Moulins one such tomb is only inscribed:

Olim formoso fueram qui corpore, putri
Nunc sum. Tu similis corpore, lector, eris.[6]

From such memorials it was an easy transition to *memento mori* art. The church of the Celestines at Avignon had a wall-painting of a woman enveloped in a shroud, with verses ascribed to René of Anjou:

Une fois sur toute femme belle
Mais par la mort suis devenue telle.
Ma chair estoit tres belle, fraische et tendre,
Or est elle toute tournée en cendre . . . .
En grand palais me logeois à mon vueil
Or suis logée en ce petit cercueil.
Ma chambre estoit de beaux tapis ornée
Or est d'aragnes ma fosse environnée.[7]

Such subjects even invaded the habitations of the living.[8] A house at Le Fay near Yvetot has its chief chimney-piece carved with a death's-head and cross-bones with the legend: 'Pensez à la mort — mourir convient — peu en souvient — souvent avient. Ces cheminées fit faire Robert Beuvry, pour Dieu, pour les trépassés, 1503.'

This morbid preoccupation with the horrors of death found its fullest expression in the *Danse macabre*. It seems to have grown out of a late thirteenth-century poem, *Le Dit des trois morts et des trois vifs*: a story of a king and two of

[1] See Mâle, *Art rel. fin*, p. 76.
[2] Ibid., p. 84. One of the earliest of such representations is on the 'Parement de Narbonne', *c.* 1370.
[3] Now in the Musée lapidaire.　　　　　　　　　　[4] Now in the Musée Calvet.
[5] e.g. Gilles de Rennepont, d. 1445, Saint-Maclou, Bar-sur-Aube; the wife of Jacques Cœur, d. 1457.　　　　　　[6] Mâle, op. cit., p. 380, cites others at Gisors and Clermont-sur-Oise.
[7] Huizinga, p. 127. Cf. the crowned Death in his Book of Hours (B.M. Egerton MS. 1070, fol. 43b), possibly painted by himself.　　　　　　[8] Mâle, op. cit., p. 381.

his nobles who met three skeletons and found they were themselves. The manuscripts of the story are illustrated[1] and provided models for other arts; in 1408 Jean de Berri had 'ymaiges des trois vifs et des trois mors' set up on the portal of the cemetery of the Innocents at Paris.[2]

The idea was developed at the moment when the English were in occupation of the city. The Dance of Death was enacted in the cemetery in 1422, some say by order of the Duke of Bedford, in grim celebration of his victory,[3] and again in 1424. A year later the theme was painted round the cloister that enclosed the cemetery, beneath the open ossuaries in which skulls and bones were piled. Pope, emperor, cardinal, king, patriarch, archbishop, constable of France, bishop, knight, squire, abbot, bailiff, lawyer, burgess, canon, merchant, Carthusian, sergeant, monk, usurer, doctor, lover, barrister, minstrel, priest, labourer, friar, child, and hermit were represented, each led by Death to his inevitable end. It was no dance, but a dreadful procession of unwilling victims. Death called each from the delights of the world, and each went mourning but the hermit and the friar.[4] Even the labourer was half-hearted in accepting the call:

> La mort ay souhaité souvent
> Mais volentier je la fuïsse.
> J'amasse mieulx feist pluye ou vent
> Estre es vignes ou je fouisse . . . .

Everywhere that the *Danse macabre* was acted, it entered art; Nicaise de Cambrai, the duke's painter, and his companions enacted it before the Duke of Burgundy[5] and it was painted on the walls of his Sainte Chapelle at Dijon.[6] In 1460, or possibly earlier,[7] it was painted in three long panels in the church of La Chaise-Dieu (Fig. 259): so far as we may judge this followed the model of the paintings at the Innocents.[8] A shorter version appeared a little later on the walls of the church of Kermaria-Nisquit in Brittany. Not till the sixteenth century did men rebel against the assertion of Death's supremacy. A chest of about 1540 from the Palais des Marchands at Angers[9] represents all the personages of the *Danse macabre* having their revenge and shooting with bows and arrows against the central figure of Death.

---

[1] e.g. B.M. Arundel MS. 83, f. 127. See H. Martin, *Min. franç.*, p. 17.

[2] It is also represented in the Chapel of the Virgin at Rocamadour, *c.* 1485. The subject is found in French engraving by 1485.

[3] See Langlois, *Essai sur les danses des morts*, p. 131.

[4] For the text see Abbé V. Dufour, *La Danse macabre*, 1891.

[5] Laborde, i. 393.　　　　　　[6] Lemoisne, p. 81.　　　　　　[7] Ibid.

[8] Single subjects from the dance were also represented. The 1471 inventory of René of Anjou's castle of La Ménitré includes in the chapel 'un tableau de toille paincte . . . ouquel est la mort qui picque l'amoureux', *Mém. soc. impériale d'agriculture, de sciences et d'arts d'Angers*, viii, Angers, 1865, p. 99.

[9] Now in the Musée Saint-Jean.

Gradually, too, the Church became afraid of such fatalism and despair. It strove to counteract it on the one hand by such devotional books as the *Ars moriendi* and on the other by the encouragement of confraternities to succour the sick and dying. In many cemeteries crosses were set up, to bring hope of salvation.[1] In the cemetery of Semur there is no *Danse macabre*, but a statue in painted stone of Christ showing His wounds; two angels hold back His mantle of imperial purple. The base is inscribed 'Domine, adjuva me'.

3. PRINTING AND ENGRAVING

At the same time a great change was coming over the religious imagery of France. Its basis hitherto had been the illuminated manuscripts, and now these were giving way before the new inventions of printing[2] and engraving: inventions that depended on the use of paper, of which France had begun to produce a considerable quantity by the end of the fourteenth century.[3] The earliest known French engraving is the famous 'Bois Protat', a fragment of a wood-block engraved for printing on both sides, that appears to date from between 1370 and 1380.[4] On one side it is engraved with part of a Crucifixion, on the other with the kneeling angel of the Annunciation: both are linear drawings of the utmost simplicity. Many such wood-blocks must have existed, and the engravings from them have been distributed through churches and monasteries and country fairs. Prints from some of them still exist, with many of the stock subjects of religious iconography:[5] Christ bearing the Cross, St. Christopher, scenes from the Passion, the Virgin (Fig. 260), the Christ of Pity, the Apostles, the Creed and Commandments, the Last Judgement, and the Death of the Virgin. A local pilgrimage is suggested by one of Saint Bénigne of Dijon, the influence of the friars by another with St. Francis showing his stigmata. All that the poor people who bought such cheap substitutes for devotional pictures asked of them was that they should conform exactly to tradition. It was not long before their manufacture had become a new trade. The 1465 statutes of

[1] Such crosses survive at Saint-Cirgues (Puy-de-Dôme); Fontfroide (Aude); Musée de Rouen; Léry (Eure); Royat; Aulnay de Saintonge, &c. There were no less than five in the Cemetery of the Innocents at Paris.

[2] In 1458 Charles VII commissioned one of the engravers of the Paris mint, N. Jenson, to study printing at Mainz. He went instead to Venice. In 1469 two doctors of the University of Paris sent for German printers who worked actually in the Sorbonne until 1473. The craft spread rapidly: Lyons 1473, Angers 1477, Poitiers 1479, Caen 1480, Troyes 1483, Rennes 1484, Abbeville 1486, Toulouse 1488, Orleans 1490, Dijon and Angoulême 1491, Nantes 1493, Limoges 1495, Tours 1496, &c.

[3] The earliest French watermark known, that of Ville-sur-Saulx in the Duchy of Bar, dates from 1348. Paper-mills were soon established in Champagne, Burgundy, Dauphiné, and the Île-de-France.

[4] It was found at La Ferté-sur-Grosne, near Dijon. It seems to have been too large for the size of paper then made, and may have been used to print textile banners. My thanks are due to Monsieur Émile Protat for allowing me to see it. See Blum, p. 20.

[5] Blum, pp. 22 et seqq. The only secular subjects are the Nine Worthies and the Planets.

the card-makers of Toulouse[1] state that 'tous les membres de la communauté ont la faculté de faire naips ou cartes, enseignes et images sur papier, à l'honneur de Dieu, des saints et confreries existant à Toulouse'. By the end of the century the new process had so developed that it was possible to make wood engravings of considerable size and complication: a *Passion* exists of about 1490 that is like the illustration of a mystery play, with as many as two hundred and fifteen personages.[2]

The early French engravings were intended for those who could afford nothing better. The early French engraved books that began to appear in the middle of the fifteenth century were a cheap substitute for illuminated manuscripts, intended, as the prologue of one of them states,[3] for the *clercs povres*. It seems likely that some of them—the *Ars Moriendi*, an Apocalypse, and the *Biblia Pauperum*—were produced at the instance of some of the Burgundian abbeys, who helped to market them.[4] Their pictures are naturally based on earlier illuminations. A printed book published at Abbeville in 1486 exactly reproduces in its illustrations the scheme of pictures of an earlier manuscript of Augustine's *City of God*.[5]

Similarly the two most important engraved books, the *Biblia Pauperum* and the *Speculum Humanae Salvationis*, went back both for text and illustrations to manuscript versions. The *Biblia Pauperum* first appeared in manuscript at the end of the thirteenth century, though much of its matter came directly from earlier sources. Intended for the layman who could read little, it always had very little text and a great many pictures.[6] It told of the Childhood of Christ, His Passion, and His Second Coming, in a series of composite pictures. Each scene was brought into relation with two events in the Old Testament that prefigured it, and with four prophets holding scrolls of the relevant prophecies. The *Speculum Humanae Salvationis*, first found in manuscript in 1324, was a book of the same kind, but with more text. It told the stories of the Virgin and of Christ, with three parallels from the Old Testament for each episode; and included the Seven Sorrows of Mary, paralleled by the Seven Joys and the Seven Stations of the Passion.

Printed and engraved books, that had originally been intended as cheap substitutes for manuscripts, fit for *povres clercs*, soon strangled the production of finer books. They came at a time when even the rich were a little weary of colour,[7] and they spread in a world which was becoming increasingly incapable of aristocracy. It was the first victory of mass-production over individual crafts-

---

[1] Blum, p. 37.   [2] Ibid., p. 35.   [3] *Speculum humanae salvationis*.   [4] See Blum, p. 50.

[5] Laborde in Blum, p. vi. See also Gertrud Bine, 'The Apocalypse Block Books and their Manuscript Models', in *Journal of the Warburg and Courtauld Institutes*, v, 1942, p. 143.

[6] The first printed edition, c. 1450, had forty plates; another ten were added between c. 1470 and c. 1480.

[7] There was a tendency for grisaille to come in even in illuminations. Brit. Mus. Roy. 17 E. vii,

T

manship. Had not linen grown cheaper in the fourteenth century, so that even poor men had shirts, from the rags of which paper could be made; had not the production of paper encouraged the development of printing and engraving; had not everyone been impoverished by the long war; had not Louis XI, a man without magnificence, ruled in France at precisely the moment when the new inventions were coming into general use, the tradition of mediaeval art might not have been weakened so early, and the French Renaissance might have taken another artistic form.

The astonishing success of printed books dealt a mortal blow to the craft of illumination. For a time, it is true, a few fine books printed on vellum were adorned with paintings. Jacques de Besançon, one of the most eminent Parisian illuminators of his day, in 1492 could not meet his debts, and entered the shop of the Paris printer Antoine Vérard to earn his living painting such miniatures. His new work, however, was by no means so finely executed as his old.[1] It was soon realized that an engraving was more congruous with a printed book, and few new illuminators arose. Those that survived tended to come down to the level of the lesser art; Bourdichon, that accomplished and unimaginative painter, repeated his compositions without compunction in the series of Books of Hours he painted for the Royal Family between 1494 and 1500.[2]

It is an astonishing fact that the engraved book-illustrations had as profound an influence on art in the fifteenth and sixteenth centuries as the painted illuminations of manuscripts had had in the Romanesque and Gothic periods.[3] They were in the main traditional in subject: they were of little enough value to be easily acquired and freely lent by craftsmen; and their technique necessitated a simple linear picture which could be made to serve as a working drawing for almost any craft. They even served as models for the surviving illuminators. A written Book of Hours of about 1500 exists[4] with illuminations copied from the engravings of the *Speculum Humanae Salvationis*. The great tapestries of the Life of Christ given to La Chaise-Dieu by Jacques de Senecterre, abbot from 1491 to 1518, have all their compositions taken straight from the printed *Biblia pauperum* and *Speculum Humanae Salvationis*; the richest tapestries of Rheims Cathedral, the seventeen panels of the Life of the Virgin given by Robert de Lenoncourt in 1530, have seven based on the *Biblia Pauperum* and the rest on the illustrations of the *Speculum Humanae Salvationis* and printed Books of

a Bible of 1357, has grisaille illustrations. In 1416 the Duke of Berry bought 'unes petites heures de Notre Dame . . . enluminées de blanc et de noir', and in 1454 the Duke of Burgundy paid an illuminator 'pour avoir fait de blanc et de noir deux cent trente histoires'. Laborde, ii. 191. The *Miracles de Notre Dame* translated by Jean Miélot (Bib. Nat. franç. 9198) is entirely illustrated in grisaille.

[1] Durrieu, *Jacques de Besançon*, p. 40.

[2] No doubt a sketch often served as a model for more than one Book of Hours at this time. Once engravings appeared such sketches were no longer needed. See H. Martin in *Rev. arch.*, 4th ser., iv, 1904, p. 17.   [3] See Mâle, *Art rel. fin*, pp. 244 et seqq.   [4] Cherbourg, MS. 5.

Hours.[1] When the enamel industry of Limoges revived towards the end of the fifteenth century its craftsmen used few designs that were not based on engravings.[2] A late ivory casket with scenes of the Childhood and Passion of Christ, with their Old Testament prototypes, is directly inspired by an early edition of the *Biblia Pauperum*.[3]

In glass-painting the influence of engraved pictures was more prevalent than in any other art. Some late fifteenth-century windows of the Passion in the Archevêché at Rouen imitate engravings even in being without colour.[4] A great number of windows of the early sixteenth century are directly inspired by woodcuts. The Virgin's window at Conches is after an engraving from the Hours of Geoffroy Tory; the story of the Cross on a window in Troyes Cathedral is copied from an engraving, and part of the story of Joseph comes from the *Speculum Humanae Salvationis*; the two great windows in the Sainte Chapelle of Ville-Comte from the *Biblia Pauperum*.

Such borrowings did much to weaken the traditions of the craft. The windows of the first half of the sixteenth century may be splendid in colour and magnificent in composition, but they are no longer *sui generis*. Not only is there something stereotyped about them, but also they are derivative. They are no longer designed in direct relation to their tracery; the stained glass is thought of as a translucent tapestry hung behind the stonework, a picture that bears no relation to its architectural frame.

4. THE DECLINE OF MEDIAEVAL ART

Such borrowings from a restricted cycle of wood-engravings helped to break the creative impulse in art. Already, too, the lucid iconography of the earlier Middle Ages was beginning to become so familiar that it was accepted without comprehension. Curious admixtures of secular and religious themes were tolerated even at the end of the fourteenth century. The Duke of Anjou, for example, had a great jewelled silver-gilt tabernacle in his chapel, borne by two greyhounds with their heads lifted in adoration. At each corner was a kneeling prophet bearing a scroll, not of prophecy, but of teaching from the *Enseignements des Sages*: such feudal moralizings as

> N'est pas sire de son pays
> Qui de ses hommes est hays,

and

> Bien doit estre sire clamez
> Qui de ses hommes est amez.[5]

[1] See Sartor, p. 68. For other examples, Mâle, op. cit., p. 253. R. Schneider, 'Note sur les livres à gravures et la décoration de la Renaissance en Normandie', in *Mélanges offerts à M. Henri Lemonnier*, 1913, p. 127.   [2] J. J. Marquet de Vasselot, *Émaux limousins*, p. 6.

[3] In the Musée de Cluny; Koechlin, ii. 353.

[4] Cf. a window of 1532 in Saint-Alpin, Châlons-sur-Marne.   [5] Moranvillé, p. 122.

Above this was elaborate arcading holding figures of St. George and the Dragon, the Virgin and Angel of the Annunciation, and our Lord showing His wounds with angels holding the instruments of the Passion. The whole was crowned with enamelled groups of the Death and Coronation of the Virgin, and completed by smaller enamels of the Life of Christ, St. Thomas of Canterbury, St. Christopher, and St. Leonard. Yet more incongruous was the mixture on a coffer of silver gilt set with crystal and jet.[1] Behind the crystal were paintings of the Childhood of Christ. The coffer was inscribed:

> En bien tousdis u que je soie
> Voel ma vie user en joie.

A more insidious decay was invading the imagery even of the great cathedrals. Donor and saint, who had already been represented on an equal scale, were now represented on an equal footing, each under a canopy (Fig. 261). Soon the representation of the saint came to approximate to that of the donor. The late fifteenth-century bust reliquaries of Saint Étienne de Mûret[2] and St. Mayeul[3] are as much portraits as any tomb effigies of the period. In other work, by a strange and degenerate fancy, the saint was represented as physically like the man he protected. The diptych of the Virgin with Étienne Chevalier and St. Stephen, painted by Foucquet about 1464, shows the saint as a younger and better-looking version of the donor; the brow, eyes, ears, and bony structure are precisely the same, although the saint is represented in the flower of his age, and Chevalier is tired, wrinkled, and melancholy. The same likeness is visible in the leaf of a picture (Fig. 262) by the Maître de Moulins, showing an elderly woman with the Magdalene as her protectress. The saint is young, but her slanting eyes, irregular nose, marked upper lip, and small chin are precisely those of the elderly donor.[4]

The very scheme of Gothic iconography was beginning to break up. The rebuilding of Saint-Vulfran d'Abbeville was begun in 1488, with a magnificent Gothic façade enriched with many statues of prophets and saints. These, however, are not arranged according to any scheme,[5] but seem to represent the patrons of the numerous confraternities who gave them. The same confusion is evident in the sculptures on the façade of Saint-Riquier, rebuilt after the last of many fires in 1487.

The monastic orders were losing their austerity, and with it their individuality. The rich Benedictine abbeys were beginning to be held *in commendam* by great ecclesiastics who were often not even monks; their benefactions might be

---

[1] Moranvillé, p. 543.   [2] Now at Saint-Sylvestre; from the treasure of Grandmont.
[3] At Veurdre, Nièvre.
[4] A similar likeness exists between St. Maurice and the donor in the noble picture by the same artist now in the Glasgow Gallery.
[5] See Mâle, *Art rel. fin*, p. 236. They were damaged in the late War.

splendid, but they could not bear the stamp of Benedictinism. The other Orders, in losing their characteristic needs in a general relaxation, lost too their characteristic arts. Rodez Cathedral, the charterhouse of Villefranche-de-Rouergue, and the collegiate church of that city all had very rich stalls carved by the same team of workmen in the last quarter of the fifteenth century. Any set of them might be exchanged for another; and even those made by the same craftsmen for the Cistercian abbey of Loc-Dieu[1] are hardly simpler. The Cistercian abbey of Cadouin built a new cloister about 1468 (Fig. 263) with an elaborate vault, a carved frieze, frescoes, and a carved chair for the abbot on the sunny side. It is not hard to imagine what St. Bernard would have thought of it.

An inevitable decay was creeping in. Nowhere is it more evident than in Étienne Chevalier's *Virgin* (Fig. 264):[2] surely the most sensual Madonna that the Middle Ages produced. She is a woman of fashion, with a court mantle and a rich crown; she has the fashionable shaven forehead and high waist: she is a woman with a face at once empty and vicious. In the sixteenth century rumour declared that the picture was a portrait of Agnès Sorel, the king's mistress, whom Étienne Chevalier too had loved. A touch of this same degenerate quality, here rather weak than corrupt, may be seen even in provincial work. The bronze bust reliquary of Sainte Fortunade (Fig. 265) represents no saint, but is a subtle and slightly decadent study of a child. The statue at Toulouse of Notre Dame de Grâce[3] (Fig. 266) represents no Queen of Heaven but a smiling girl, almost a child, sweet, gentle, and untragic, with her thoughts on anything but the Child beside her, who seems a young brother she has been told to mind rather than her Son. Yet more strangely, the mother of the Virgin herself appears at Bordeaux as a child (Fig. 267), although her daughter stands at her knee. Something of this gracious weakness may sometimes be seen in Foucquet's illuminations; much of it is evident in Bourdichon's. They have a kind of lazy facility; their very easiness betrays a want of life.

When provincial art escaped from this sweet weakness it was by virtue of a bourgeois realism. Such a *Visitation* as that of Saint-Jean de Troyes (Fig. 268) portrays nothing but a decent woman of Troyes, in her best clothes, visited by her daughter.[4] On one of the stalls at Montréal[5] the Holy Family is represented simply as a carpenter with his wife and child; the panel is surmounted by a

[1] Now in the church of the Pénitents noirs at Villefranche.
[2] The picture is commonly ascribed to Foucquet, but Comte P. Durrieu (in Michel, iv. 731) ascribes it rather to Piètre André, a painter of Tours attached to the household of the Duke of Orleans, who is recorded to have painted a Virgin with a background of red and blue angels.
[3] Musée des Augustins. Possibly from the abbey of Les Hautes-Bruguières (Haute-Garonne). A more serious Burgundian version of the type is in the Metropolitan Museum of New York.
[4] It may be ascribed to Nicolas Haslin. It enjoyed a great success and was freely copied, even in a glass window at Saint-Étienne near Arcis-sur-Aube. See Koechlin and Marquet de Vasselot, p. 140.
[5] By the brothers Rigoley of Nuits-sous-Ravières, 1522.

group of topers helping themselves out of an enormous jug. A sculptured group of St. Martin and the beggar from Arcenant in Burgundy represents St. Martin in ordinary travelling-dress on a poorish horse. The beggar has a gloved hand to hold his crutch, but no shoes. It is a group which might have been seen on any roadside at the end of the Hundred Years War.

This bourgeois tendency, indeed, is characteristic of the time. Paris was no longer the metropolis of art: the king lived in Berry or Touraine, Charles VII at Chinon, Bourges, and Loches, Louis XI at Le Plessis-lès-Tours. In the time of Charles VIII the most prosperous part of France was probably Champagne, in that of his successor probably Brittany. Something provincial crept into art; and the provincial is the negation of the courtly. Louis XI was a *roi bourgeois* such as France was not to see again until the reign of Louis-Philippe. While he contented himself with images for his chapel, not of gold but of painted wood,[1] his people were beginning to realize that money might do a man more good than birth. 'Il n'est chose qu'argent ne face', declares the *Mystère de la Passion*. The rich merchants ventured to buy fiefs and build country houses: the fine château de Martainville was built in 1485 by the bourgeois family of Le Pelletier of Rouen. The finest late Gothic glass at Bourges is the gift not of king or noble or confraternity, but of the bourgeois families of Aligret and Tullier. The finest windows at Troyes were given by the citizen families Dorigny, Marisy, and Huyard.[2] Most of the Champenois sculpture of the early sixteenth century was likewise made to the order of ordinary citizens.[3] They owned the fiefs in the surrounding country-side, and enriched the rural churches as well as those of the towns. By the time of Louis XII observers noted that citizens and even farmers were beginning to use silver plate.[4] The *bourgeoisie* dominated art as they did literature. Tournaments and jousting were going out of fashion; Commines, for example, no longer spends time in describing them. The pedigrees and armorial bearings of the castles were being used more and more to decorate not the houses of the aristocracy but the churches of the citizens. Trees of Jesse came everywhere into fashion: in sculpture at Beauvais, in glass at Beauvais and Évreux, in tapestry in hangings now in Notre-Dame-de-Nantilly at Saumur. The royal fleurs-de-lis ceased to have any great significance and became a commonplace of decoration: in window tracery at Saint-Florentin and Troyes Cathedral, in sculpture on the choir screen of the Madeleine de Troyes.

The piety of the age was undoubted; there was no department of life which remained unaffected by it. But it was a religiosity which had it in an element

---

[1] e.g. a St. Martin carved by François Jacquet and painted by Bourdichon in 1478. Courajod, ii. 559.

[2] Koechlin and Marquet de Vasselot, p. 38.

[3] Ibid., p. 23.

[4] Claude de Seyssel, *Histoire singulière du roi Louis XII*, Paris, 1508; Jean de Saint-Gelais, *Histoire de Louis XII*, p. 63.

of decadence. There were so many churches, so many festivals, so many devotions, so many images of so many saints, that they lost the clear significance they had had in the great age of faith.

5. FOREIGN INFLUENCES

While the indigenous tradition of art was thus weakening, foreign influences were creeping in. The art of the Low Countries, of England, and of Italy in turn invaded the territory of French Gothic; each in its turn was transmuted and absorbed, but each affected the purely national character of French art.

Flemish influences over plastic art were felt earliest, through the exploitation for monumental sculpture of the black and white marbles of the valley of the Meuse. Yet such artists as Jean Pépin de Huy, who was working in Paris before 1320, André Beauneveu of Valenciennes and Jean de Liége, who worked for Charles V and Charles VI, were trained in the French tradition, worked in Paris, and count as essentially French. Of the eighty-nine sculptors of Champagne in the fourteenth and fifteenth centuries of whom the name is known, twenty-two were Flemish,[1] yet it is not easy to distinguish any strong Flemish strain in the Champenois art of the time. Flanders, indeed, was at this time a province so strongly under French influence that it was hardly likely to have a dominating effect on French art.

In the time of Charles VI, Paris was the natural centre of all art west of the Rhine. The painters who came there from Flanders and Artois, Alsace, Hainault and Holland, Liége and Cologne, came as provincials to the artistic capital of northern Europe.

It was not until the Hundred Years War had weakened the vitality of France that the situation was reversed. Philippe le Hardi, Duke of Burgundy, had succeeded in marrying one of the greatest heiresses of the time, in the person of Margaret, daughter of Louis de Male, Count of Flanders, Nevers, and Rethel, and widow of Philippe de Rouvre. On the death of her father in 1384 his lands thus came to be joined with those of Burgundy, and the Burgundian court came to outshine the war-worn court of France.

Naturally workmen from the Low Countries tended to gravitate to Dijon, though even so a certain distinction must be made between men like Jean Malouel of Guelderland, who settled permanently in France and became part of the French School, and Flemings like Melchior Broederlam, who seems only to have spent two or three years of his maturity in Paris. Jean de Marville, Claus Sluter, and Claus de Werve had qualities in their art which are not French. Claus Sluter's statue of Philippe le Hardi and Marville's Virgin are in a different

[1] Koechlin and Marquet de Vasselot, p. 7.

language from the almost contemporary statues of the Poitiers chimney-piece. They are no longer planned as part of a decorative whole, but are conceived as free standing figures in the round. It is as if their vitality and realism had forced them out of an architectural frame into independent life.

With the assassination of Jean sans Peur in 1419, Burgundy turned away from France in all her art, both visual and literary. Sculptors and painters came from the Netherlands and followed Netherland ways; such pictures as the Virgin which Jan van Eyck painted for the Chancellor Rolin, as the Last Judgement which Roger van der Weyden painted for the hospital at Beaune (both in the second quarter of the century), such sculpture as the wooden retable which Michel de Chaugy left to Ambierle in 1476, cannot by any stretching of fact be considered French.

Such work, however, exercised a certain influence in France, especially over sculpture. The crowded and confused compositions found in French stone reliefs of the late fifteenth century are obviously taken over from the Low Country retables of painted wood.[1] They represent a true decline in French sculptural tradition: a decline felt as far south as Rodez, where it is evident in a panel of Christ in the Garden of Gethsemane of about 1470, and as far north as La Neuville-sous-Corbie, where the church has a great sculptured relief over the door that is pictorial in composition and over-moulded in style. It was felt even by the sculptors of the French court, for nowhere is it more evident than on the lintel of Charles VIII's chapel of St. Hubert at Amboise:[2] a piece of carving of fantastic skill, which denies every mediaeval sculptural tradition of style and composition.

The defeat and death of Charles the Bold before Nancy in 1477 ended the Flemish-Burgundian supremacy in art. What riches remained in the Burgundian treasury were dissipated during the minority of Philippe le Beau, and with them went the craftsmen of the Burgundian court. Such Teutonic influences as continued to be felt in France were derived rather from engravings than from larger works of art. Dürer's Apocalypse inspired the design of Champenois glass at Chavanges, Granville, Saint-Martin-des-Vignes at Troyes, and at Notre-Dame de Châlons-sur-Marne, and even influenced windows in the royal chapels of La Ferté-Milon and Vincennes; yet, Dürer apart, the Germanic influence on French art of the end of the Middle Ages is remarkably small.

English influence on French mediaeval art was much slighter and not much more prolonged. The wine-boats that traded from the Gironde to England, the craft that traded in salt fish from Rouen, did not return empty. Besides

[1] These were often acquired by French churches. An example survives at Ternant, and one from Mesnil-le-Hurlus is in the Museum of Châlons-sur-Marne.

[2] Severely damaged in the War of 1939-45.

English wool they occasionally brought back the sculptured alabasters carved at Nottingham and, perhaps, elsewhere in England. A considerable number of them remain in the Bordeaux district,[1] in the Limousin,[2] in the *villes-neuves* of the Marches,[3] and in Normandy,[4] and some exist as far afield as Burgundy[5] and Languedoc.[6]

French sculpture, however, was too accomplished to be susceptible to the influence of English alabasters. It is very rarely, and that, so far as I know, only in the Bordeaux district, that the faintest trace of such an influence can be perceived. On the other hand, the prolonged English occupation of Normandy inevitably caused a certain infiltration of English architectural style. The upper part of the cathedral of Rouen, of which the rebuilding was begun in 1370,[7] the chapel of St. John Baptist in the cathedral of Amiens, begun in 1375, the church of Saint-Maclou at Rouen, begun in 1432 (Fig. 272), all show in certain features the line of double curvature that dominated the Decorated style, which had been for fifty years the architectural mode in England. Similar influences are shown at a rather later date in churches in other towns occupied by the English: in the cathedrals of Bordeaux and Évreux, and in the transept of Le Mans.[8] They show it, however, with a difference. The strong keynote of such English decoration as the Lady Chapel at Ely is its conception in three dimensions and its consequent freedom from the plane of the wall. In France, however, the plane of the wall is as dominant a factor as it is in English Perpendicular. Thus it may fairly be said that the French Flamboyant style combines both the Decorated and Perpendicular styles of England: the curves and counter-curves of its window traceries find parallels in the Decorated style which was passing out of fashion in England, and its treatment of walls, its use of arcaded and panelled decoration, the liernes and tiercerons of its vaults and the complexity of its mouldings, in the Perpendicular style which was coming into vogue. It is as likely that the likenesses are those of parallel development as that they are of direct derivation.

The characteristics of the Flamboyant style[9]—the complex ogival vaults, the wide arches, the doorways *en anse de panier*, the ogival arcades and traceries, the small importance of the capitals, the elaborate and often interpenetrating mouldings[10]—were not based on any constructive principle capable of development.

[1] e.g. the chapel of Notre-Dame-de-la-Rose in Saint-Seurin de Bordeaux.
[2] e.g. Saint-Léonard (Haute-Vienne).   [3] e.g. Montpezat, Quercy.
[4] e.g. Louviers (Eure).   [5] e.g. Montréal (Yonne): a very fine specimen.
[6] e.g. that from Rabastens (Tarn), now in the Musée Reymond, Toulouse.
[7] John Wyllemer, an English mason employed by the Duke of Bedford, superintended the work.
[8] The fifteenth-century church of Notre-Dame-de-la-Couture at Bernay has elaborate wooden ceilings of an English type.
[9] The best analysis remains that of C. Enlart in *Bull. mon.* lxx, 1906, p. 43.
[10] At Saint-Saulge (Nièvre), the mouldings of the column bases are so complicated as to have become a meaningless basket-work; and instances could be multiplied.

The style was essentially sterile: it came at the end of a series which it closed. Few kinds of architecture are harder to date exactly. It was in use, in a developed form, for a century, from about 1420 to about 1520, and in the absence of a history the building must be dated chiefly from the elements of the styles that preceded and followed it that may be detected in the Flamboyant whole. Because of this limitation of possible development there is an element of weariness in Flamboyant decoration. Much of it looks as if it had been bought by the yard; and accounts reveal that this was sometimes true. Since its decorative elements were constant, there was no development of provincial variations; but it remains in its most characteristic form a creation of northern France.

The style was not English enough to be discarded when English domination ceased; indeed, its establishment and dissemination was largely due to its employment in the churches that had to be rebuilt after the Hundred Years War. In the Amiens diocese, for example,[1] almost all the parish churches of the city and most of the houses of Religious Orders in the district were rebuilt between 1470 and 1490. Before the First World War there were some two hundred and eighty late fifteenth-century churches still existing in the department of the Somme: churches that in size, richness, and uniformity of style invited comparison with their Perpendicular contemporaries across the Channel.

The Flamboyant was a style of extraneous decoration, with no constructive principle to dictate innovations in plan. Normally the plans of Flamboyant churches are of an extreme simplicity: exceptionally they have a real elegance. One of the most interesting from this point of view is Notre-Dame de Caudebec, built between 1426 and 1515 from the plans of Guillaume Letellier.[2] It has rectangular chapels beyond the aisles, and an ambulatory composed of a hexagonal apse with a square chapel with a triangular apse on either side; the high vault of the sanctuary is two-sided with an angular termination. At Moulins the choir of the collegiate church[3] begun in 1465 has a flat chevet and a rectangular ambulatory, but the sanctuary and the high vault above it is polygonal. At Pouzauges in the Vendée the large square choir is aisled like the nave.

The style, however, is best seen in façades, porches, and other unstructural parts. The great façades of Tours, Troyes, Rouen (Fig. 269), and Vendôme remain to show how well it could be employed on the grand scale, and such porches as those of Louviers, Argentan, and Alençon display its richness on a lesser scale. It is perhaps seen at its best in towers: in the perpendicular fretwork of Clamecy (Fig. 270), in the less rigid grace of the cathedral of Nevers and, best of all, in the metallic richness of the Tour de Beurre at Rouen[4] (Fig. 271).

---

[1] See Durand in *Bull. mon.*, 1931, p. 334.   [2] Badly damaged in the late War.
[3] Now the cathedral. The architect was named Musnier.
[4] Another tower of the same kind at Verneuil-sur-Aire was also built with the proceeds of dispensations in Lent.

It is perhaps in such cloisters as those of Cahors[1] and Cadouin that English influence is most evident, for their style is dominated by the liernes and tiercerons of the vault. Flamboyant decoration is, on the other hand, most elegant and most French in the many choir and chapel screens of wood and stone in north France[2] and in such staircases as that of Saint-Maclou (Fig. 273).

The beauty of Flamboyant architectural decoration applied to an earlier building can best be seen at Albi. The body of the cathedral had been begun as a fortress of orthodoxy at the end of the thirteenth century. Like a fortress it has no windows for a great height; its bell-tower looks like a donjon and its pinnacles like turrets. It is all of rosy brick, and is yet far more threatening than a northern cathedral of the greyest stone. It received a new prestige when Cardinal Joliffroy brought the relics of St. Cecilia to it from Rome in 1468.[3] Its chief beautification resulted from the benefactions of Bishop Louis I d'Amboise, partly in his lifetime and partly under his will: a great silver-gilt retable (now destroyed), the superb choir-screen, and the frescoes and porch that were only completed under his successor.

The screen runs right round the choir to form a false ambulatory.[4] The part that divides the choir from the nave (now bereft of nearly all its statues) is a magnificent variation on the familiar Flamboyant theme[5] (Fig. 274). The exterior of the rest of the enclosure is, to the aisles, an exceedingly rich Flamboyant arcade, with statues between the arcatures, and, to the choir, a series of canopies of an extreme elegance, crowning the stalls beneath (Fig. 275). The statues of the exterior are those of the Prophets, of the interior, of the Apostles, according to the familiar scheme; the rood-screen to the nave has on the reverse the patron, St. Cecilia. Behind the Virgin is Simeon, for he too bore the Child in his arms. It is a superb expression of French Gothic in its old age; nothing remains of English influence but the ogival line of the arcading.

The third influence, that of Italy, was more lasting and more deadly in its effect. The arts of Flanders and England were at least Gothic; they represented provincial varieties of the national style of France, rather than truly alien arts. Italy, which had never absorbed the Gothic style which had been brought into the country by the French Cistercians, had turned instead to the classical past.

---

[1] Begun soon after 1493, when permission was given to use half the revenues of the vacant benefices of the diocese for its construction.

[2] e.g. Guern and Le Faouet (Morbihan); cathedral of Saint-Pol-de-Léon.

[3] The festival was crowned by *tableaux vivants* of the life of the saint. Petit de Julleville, ii. 197.

[4] Mlle de Bévotte (*Sculp. dans la région de Toulouse, d'Albi et de Rodez, 1400–1520*, p. 64) stresses Spanish influence in the conception of the choir. The Spanish *coros* may have played some part in the inspiration of the great choir-enclosures of Amiens, erected between 1489 and 1530, Chartres, begun in 1514, and Albi, but even this is not certain, and I cannot see anything characteristically Spanish at Albi. The wooden choir-stalls at Auch, however, do seem Spanish, and may well be the work of a craftsman from across the frontier.

[5] Analysis reveals that all its elements are to be found in such work as the Tour de Beurre at Rouen.

Italian style, when it at last came to influence France, was wholly alien: its system of construction, its repertory of decoration, its imagery, were all conceived in another language. Moreover, though it served a Christian Church, it was not Christian in inspiration.

Italian merchants who dealt in silks had long been established in Paris. The French occupation of Genoa between 1396 and 1409 had brought knowledge of other forms of Italian art, and early in the fifteenth century some of the Italian merchants of Paris had begun to import classical medals, and modern imitations of them, wherewith to tempt such collectors of rare and beautiful things as the Duke of Berry. In 1402 the duke purchased from a Florentine merchant established in Paris medals of Constantine, Heraclius, Caesar and Octavian, Tiberius and Faustina set in jewels.[1] At the same time the duke patronized Italian arts in other fields. At the end of the fourteenth century he had commissioned from Italian sculptors a great retable in ivory[2] as a present to his niece, Marie de France, who was a nun at Poissy. The Duke of Burgundy commissioned two more retables for Champmol.[3] The first portrait of Louis XI is a medal by the Italian Francesco Laurana, made about 1461,[4] who remained in France long enough to carve an entirely Italian tomb[5] for Charles IV of Anjou, Count of Maine, after his death in 1472. In 1468 the Florentine Nicolo Spinelli was employed as seal-cutter and medal-maker by Charles the Bold.[6] Louis XI owned a Bellini of the dead Christ, and Benedetto Ghirlandaio is known to have travelled in France and to have worked for the king and his family. A picture by him, which has been at Aigueperse since it was painted, is signed 'A Bourbon, la maison de Monseigneur le dauphin d'Auvergne'.

A similar shift of interest was evident in both literature and painting. Charles the Bold, for example, ordered no single romance of a mediaeval cycle to be transcribed or rewritten, but encouraged the production of romances and compilations derived from the literature of the ancient world.[7] Italian compositions gradually crept into northern art. Jacques Raponde, who directed one of the most important workshops for illuminated manuscripts in Paris early in the fifteenth century, was half-Italian.[8] The miniature of the Purification in the Duke of Berry's *Très Riches Heures* is almost identical with Taddeo Gaddi's fresco in Santa Croce, and Jean le Bon in 1420 had a tapestry with the Petrarchan subject of the Triumph of Fame.[9]

Between 1445 and 1447 Foucquet visited Italy. The miniatures he painted for the Hours of Étienne Chevalier some ten years later are full of marble backgrounds in the Florentine manner; the Trinity sit to crown the Virgin on jewelled thrones like Italian canons' stalls of Renaissance design.

[1] Guiffrey, *Inv.* i. 70.   [2] The 'Retable de Poissy' now in the Louvre.   [3] Courajod, ii. 505.
[4] Ibid., ii. 534.   [5] In the cathedral of Le Mans.   [6] Courajod, ii. 534.
[7] Doutrepont, p. 69.   [8] Ibid., p. 13.   [9] Laborde, ii. 269.

The defeat and death of Charles the Bold in 1477 ended the glory of the House of Burgundy and greatly diminished the force of Flemish-Burgundian influence. The artistic centre of France was transferred with the royal court to the valley of the Loire; and here, in a school of sculpture which seems to have been dominated by Michel Colombe, something Italianate was for the first time fused into the French tradition of Gothic sculpture. Colombe had early worked with Claus de Werve on the Dijon tombs, but gradually lost any Flemish flavour in his style; we know little of his work before the end of the fifteenth century, but can detect in the sculpture of Touraine of about 1480 a rather conscious sweetness and grace, a slightly sentimental elegance, which seems to betray the influence of contemporary Florentine style. At the same time, the importation of engravings from Italy brought Italian influences to bear on other circles than those of the court. By 1486 Renaissance architectural backgrounds began to appear in the votive pictures of the Puy-Notre-Dame of Amiens.

In the autumn of 1494 the army of France invaded Italy, and found it a terrestrial paradise. Florence charmed them more than Amboise, and the Louvre was forgotten in the sunshine of Naples. When Charles VIII came back from Italy in 1495 he came with a train of Italian artists[1] and nearly forty tons' weight of Italian works of art. His kinsmen and captains likewise brought their share of Italian beauty: Gilbert de Montpensier, for example, had acquired a Gonzaga bride and a Mantegna, which is still at Aigueperse. For the first time a king of France ordered his tomb from a foreign sculptor; and when the Neapolitan Guido Mazzoni had finished the memorial of Charles VIII he stayed to make two equestrian statues of his successor.

From the time of the invasion of Italy the progress of the Italianate style in France was increasingly rapid.[2] The Italianate palace of Gaillon, begun by the Archbishop of Rouen in 1501, marks an epoch. More insidiously, Italianate motives were being included even in Gothic themes. The Sibyls of the Italian engravers[3] appear on the Tour de Beurre of Rouen, finished in 1508; the figures of the Liberal Arts in a contemporary painting in the Chapelle des Reliques at Le Puy are Italianate. A definite shift from Gothic to Renaissance design is evident if the details of the Palais de Justice at Rouen, of which the most important parts date from between 1499 and 1509, are compared with those of the Hôtel de Bourgtheroulde in the same city, begun in 1501 and finished in 1547. Two important royal tombs were set up by French sculptors in the first decade of the sixteenth century: that of Francis II of Brittany and his wife at Nantes, carved by Michel Colombe and his assistants Régnault and Jean de Chartres between 1502 and 1507, and that of the children of Charles VIII at

[1] e.g. Domenico da Cortona and Paganino.
[2] For its progress in Burgundy see H. David, *De Sluter à Sambin*, vol. ii.
[3] Illustrations of Filippo Barbieri's book on Jerome and Augustine.

Tours, carved by Jean Juste and Guillaume Regnault in 1506. Both are entirely of the Renaissance in their design; their sculptors' Gothic training may betray itself in the treatment of heads and drapery, but the ensembles are denials of the tradition which they had inherited.

6. THE LAST STRUGGLE

Mediaeval art had received mortal wounds, but it did not die without a struggle. The position of French artists was still unchanged, and the needs of their patrons as yet only superficially modified by changes of fashion. Sculptors and painters were still craftsmen, and their pay still bore more relation to the cost of their materials than to their skill. In 1492 Jean Copain was paid 35 *livres tournois* for painting with blue and fine gold the St. Michael on the gable of Troyes Cathedral, whereas Odard Colas only got 10 *livres* for carving it.[1] Painters still painted furniture and banners, and designed embroideries and brocades and tapestries, and did, in fact, whatever their employers asked of them. The prestige of the artist, who must follow the dictates of his inner consciousness or starve, had not yet been achieved.

The hierarchy of patrons was still unchanged. The great Benedictine abbeys, under commendatory abbots, might play a less important part in the life of the Church, but they still employed artists in their service. The magnificent portal of Sainte-Radegonde at Poitiers, built at the end of the fifteenth century, has a finely suitable iconographic scheme: Our Lady, with Sainte Radegonde and St. Hilary of Poitiers beside her, and Radegonde's companions St. Agnes and St. Disciole on either hand.[2] In 1504 Pierre de Montarley gave twenty-two pictures of the life of Saint Seine to his abbey, completed by one of himself being presented to the Virgin by the saint. Even those given to the abbey in 1521 by Claude de Durestal, a monk, were still Gothic in their iconography: St. Christopher, St. Bartholomew, the Virgin surrounded by the symbols of the Litany, and a tree of Jesse. Whole abbeys could still be rebuilt, even early in the sixteenth century, as Montier-de-la-Celle was rebuilt, as a Gothic building, that is to say, adorned with Gothic sculpture. There was still life in the monastic houses of France; new Orders could still be introduced, like the Mendicant Minimes whom Louis XI brought to France in 1482 and Charles VIII established at Les Montils; and new Orders could still be founded, like the Religieuses de l'Annonciade established by Jeanne de Valois at Bourges in 1501.[3]

[1] Koechlin and Marquet de Vasselot, p. 41.
[2] Cf. the silver-gilt shrine with panels of the life of Saint Florent given by Louis XI to the abbey of Saint-Florent de Saumur in 1480. See C. Port, *Les Artistes angevins,* Paris and Angers, 1881, p. 20.
[3] Hélyot in Migne, xx, col. 227.

The cathedrals were already built, it is true, but they were not all finished. That of Nantes, begun in 1434, was only finished in 1508. The great Flamboyant façade of Clermont was only designed in 1495.[1] The south portal of Sens was finished, and the transept façade begun, in 1501: a magnificent piece of architecture, pure Gothic alike in its architecture and its iconography.[2] Its great rose window, filled with glass between 1516 and 1519, represents the triumph of Christ in Paradise with no single Renaissance detail.[3] Even southern France was still Gothic in its architecture; the chapel of St. Joseph in the cathedral of Lavaur, built between 1500 and 1514 to the orders of Bishop Pierre du Rozier, has nothing Italianate in it. The cathedral canons still watched over the iconography and saw that no unauthorized novelty crept in. In 1517 the painter Jean Briaix had to make black and white drawings of figures of God the Father and St. Paul for the portal of Troyes Cathedral, for the canons, 'pour savoir s'ils seront bons patrons'.[4] Cathedral interiors were still being enriched by such choir screens and stalls as those of Le Mans, planned in 1495,[5] Amiens, begun in 1489, and Chartres, begun in 1514: work in which Renaissance influence creeps in, and that only in the details, after the work has progressed some way. The richest tapestries of the cathedrals, such as those of the Perfections of Mary at Rheims, and of the life of Saints Gervais and Protais at Le Mans, were planned in the first decade of the sixteenth century, on traditional Gothic lines.

Pilgrimage churches still flourished. The late fifteenth-century façade of the Chapelle du Saint-Esprit at Rue is carved with the Life of Christ and with the history of the miraculous Cross of Rue, that was found under the gate of Golgotha and arrived on the French coast in a boat without rudder or pilot on the first Sunday in August 1101. The Treasury to receive the gifts of the pilgrims, adorned with delicate sculptures of the Life of Christ, was built between 1505 and 1509.

Collegiate churches were still being founded and adorned. That at Blainville-Crevon in Normandy, founded in 1489 by Jean d'Estoutteville, was built in good Flamboyant style, with fine Gothic stalls of sculptured wood, wooden statues of St. Michael, St. Anne and the Virgin, and God the Father with the body of His Son. In 1497 the inhabitants of Clamecy began to rebuild their Collégiale of Saint-Martin, founded in 1076.[6] The collegiate church of Beaune was enriched in 1500 by the gift from its archdeacon, Hugue le Coq, of its chief treasure: the tapestries that are still hung in the church for the feasts of the

[1] Drawing in the Archives Départementales, Clermont-Ferrand.
[2] It was paid for by gifts from the faithful: brefs de quête to invite subscriptions were printed in Paris in 1490.
[3] Cf. the fine rose window in Notre-Dame de Montferrand, later than 1517.
[4] Koechlin and Marquet de Vasselot, p. 43.
[5] A contemporary design for it on parchment is in the Musée archéologique, Le Mans.
[6] See J. Charrier, Notice historique sur la Collégiale de Saint-Martin de Clamecy, Nevers, 1887.

Virgin, that tell all her life with such an extraordinary vernal beauty of colour that even at Candlemas they seem to bring spring into the church.

Knights, nobles, and princes still built castles in the mediaeval manner, with Gothic chapels. Even at Amboise the chapel is still northern, Gothic and French. The Sainte Chapelle at Champigny-sur-Veude, built between 1508 and 1543, is entirely mediaeval in feeling if not in architecture. Louis de Bourbon and his wife were both descendants of Saint Louis, and their chapel at Champigny is in his honour. The story of his life fills the windows, and his descendants kneel below. Everything is Gothic: vaulting, mouldings, canopies, sculpture; the only Renaissance detail occurs in the arcaded backgrounds of the kneeling figures in the glass and in the use of Roman letters for their inscriptions. Even the covered gallery outside is flamboyant in its design; the only new feature is the use of round instead of ogival arches for the arcade.[1]

All over France the mediaeval tradition of castle-building lived on into the sixteenth century. The castle built at Meillant by Admiral Charles d'Amboise between 1500 and 1510 is fortified outside; though the interior courtyard is richly ornamented with sculpture there is hardly anything Italianate in its decoration. L'Isle-Savary, rebuilt about 1500, is equally of the Middle Ages, with moat, drawbridge, and donjon. Bazouges-sur-Loir, built by Baudoin de Champagne, chamberlain to Louis XII and Francis I, still has machicolated towers of defence, an octagonal staircase-turret, gabled windows, and a fortified gateway. The great donjon of Saint-Agil, begun in 1510, is entirely mediaeval, with the traditional machicolations and *chemin de ronde*.[2] The entrance-pavilion of Carrouges, built in the middle of the sixteenth century (Fig. 276), continues the architectural tradition of Martainville, built some seventy years before. Even when Renaissance ornament was adopted, the plan remained Gothic. Chambord is a masterpiece of the French Renaissance; but seen in silhouette, against an evening sky, it appears a building of the Middle Ages.

Italianate arabesques might adorn the castle chairs and chests, but their early sixteenth-century tapestries—such as the famous set of *La Dame à la Licorne*—remained mediaeval. Outside tapestries there is little life in the Gothic genres of decoration; yet in the art of portraiture an unknown painter, sometimes thought to be Bourdichon, produced a new genre in some exquisite child

---

[1] The almost contemporary Sainte Chapelle, built at Vic-le-Comte by Jean Stuart, Duc d'Albany, is hardly less Gothic in its general scheme, though a little more Italianate in detail. Its sculptures, like those of the Sainte Chapelle at Paris, still represent the twelve apostles, and its windows depict the familiar scheme of the prophecies of the Life of Christ and their fulfilment.

[2] At Goulaine, not finished until about 1520, there is no imitation of Italy in the smallest detail. Javarzay, begun in 1514 by François de Rochechouart with a Tours architect, Alexandre Robin, has a great square donjon with corbelled-out angle-turrets and a squat entrance-tower: it was originally defended by twelve towers. The castle of Laxion in the Dordogne, built in the middle of the sixteenth century, is still a fortress, with four great machicolated towers at the corners and a barbican.

portraits (Fig. 277) that owe nothing to Italy in their colouring or characterization.[1]

The towns were no less conservative in their traditions.[2] The Hôtel de Ville of Saumur, built as part of the city wall early in the sixteenth century, has the mullioned windows and octagonal machicolated turrets of the Gothic style ; the belfry of Dreux, begun in 1512, still has elegant ogival decoration. It is only its upper story, begun in 1520, that shows Italianate detail. Such town houses as those at Le Mans, built by Échevin Robert Véron between 1490 and 1515,[3] and by Dr Jean de l'Épine between 1520 and 1525,[4] are entirely of the Middle Ages. The town churches, too, continued to be built in mediaeval style. The choir of Notre-Dame-des-Marais at La Ferté-Bernard (Fig. 278), built between 1500 and 1596, is still Gothic in all its fundamentals. The lower gallery is completed by statues of the King of France and his peers, and the seven planets. The balustrades, it is true, are carved in Renaissance fashion to form inscriptions: but the legends are the mediaeval anthems to the Virgin, *Regina Coeli* and *Ave Regina Coelorum*.[5]

The cities still had their patron saints to honour : a late Gothic window at Saint-Sauveur de Dinan has the local saints Mathurin, Armel, Yves, and Brieuc to balance the panels representing the evangelists. The patron saints of the Diocese of Sens were painted in the clerestory windows about 1516. There were still guilds and confraternities to make gifts. A sixteenth-century window at Saint-Nicolas de Châtillon-sur-Seine was given by a confraternity of pilgrims and portrays a pilgrimage to Compostella; and a window of the Life of Saint Claude was given to Gisors in 1526 by the corporation of tanners.

The sculptors were equally tenacious of mediaeval tradition. The Chaource Entombment[6] (Fig. 238) and portrait statues (Fig. 214) of 1515 and 1518 remain a perfect expression of the mediaeval genius. A statue of St. Anne (Fig. 267) recaptures the nobility of age. Such *plates tombes* as the brass of Martial Formier, Abbot of Saint-Jean-d'Angely, who died in 1513,[7] and the incised

---

[1] A delightful example of his work is the collection of the Society of Antiquaries of London.

[2] When new towns were founded, even in the seventeenth century (e.g. Brouage and Henrichemont, 1608), they followed the familiar mediaeval plan of a *ville-neuve*.

[3] Now known as the 'Maison de la reine Bérangère'.

[4] 'Maison d'Adam et d'Ève.'

[5] The church of Nonancourt, begun in 1511, has flying buttresses and gargoyles; and the churches of Notre-Dame-du-Paradis at Hennebont, built between 1513 and 1530, and of Arques-la-Bataille, begun in 1515, are no less Gothic in construction and decoration.

[6] The Entombment at Doullens, although it is dated 1583, still has strong reminiscences of the mediaeval tradition; yet the slightly earlier groups at Pontoise and Saint-Jean de Troyes are altogether Italianate. It must be remembered, too, that the subject is entirely French and mediaeval, yet it remained in use until the seventeenth century. The Sepulchre at Thèneville, Creuse, is dated 1692.

[7] At Saint-Junien, Vienne.

U

stone of Jean de Hazeuille, who died in 1518,[1] are completely mediaeval. Even when the widow of Raoul de Lannoy, who died in April 1513, commissioned the Milanese Antonio della Porta and his nephew Pace Gazzini to make a tomb for them both, she set it under a flamboyant canopy.

The erection of fine choir-screens in the town churches had become a matter of civic pride. That of the Madeleine at Troyes (Fig. 280) was begun in 1508, by the mason and carver Jean Gailde, who was the accredited *maître d'œuvre* of the church.[2] His employers were none too generous; in winter they gave him 5 *sous* 6 *deniers* instead of his regular 6 *sous* 3 *deniers*, 'à cause de . . . fournir les chandoilles pour ouvrer et le charbon pour . . . chauffer'. By 1512 the screen had progressed far enough for the priests and others to help to move the great stones into place, and to be regaled by an elegant meal of wine and tarts at the chapter's expense. On Christmas Eve, 1517, the jubé was finished, and Jean and his workmen stayed up to set the last statues in place and dust it all, for its formal inauguration on Christmas Day. When Jean Gailde died he was buried beneath it, secure in the knowledge that it was strong enough to shelter him until the Day of Judgement. For all the daring of its hanging arches, it still stands, bereft of its statues but one of the last perfect expressions of the mediaeval genius of France. Yet the Italian style was winning an inevitable victory, with fashion on its side.

The Concordat of 1516, by which the Pope granted to Francis I the right of nominating bishops and many abbots, ended the great age of the Gallican church and of French church architecture. Francis I was a monarch of the Renaissance, and without the protection of a Court that had come to dominate the Church the mediaeval style could not long survive. Even at Troyes the great fire of 1524 ended the Middle Ages; what was rebuilt after it was more Italianate, and the shift to the new style was finally confirmed when Domenico Fiorentino settled in the city in 1541.[3]

Already the institutions and customs of the Middle Ages were dying out. In 1507 the guild of the *imagiers* of Paris was driven out of separate existence by the rival company of goldsmiths, and had to be amalgamated with the confraternity of the *tabletiers* and comb-makers. In 1548, the Parlement of Paris forbade the representation of sacred subjects in drama, and the long cycle of *Mystères* and *Miracles*, that had proved so fertile an inspiration to art, came to an end. The Reformation set the Catholic Church on its defence, and the Council of Trent in 1545 made that unconstructive point of view the official inspiration of its art. The natural development of mediaeval imagery was at an end. The last real tournament in France was held in 1559, when Henri II died jousting

---

[1] At Gadancourt (Seine-et-Oise).
[2] For a full account, see Koechlin and Marquet de Vasselot, pp. 31, 47 et seqq., 63.
[3] See Koechlin and Marquet de Vasselot, p. 158.

against the Comte de Montgommery. With the end of jousting, vitality left the arts of heraldry. The green May-Day livery was given for the last time in 1560. By then men had rather wear city silks in formal gardens or dance pavanes in candle-lit galleries than ride in good new cloth through the spring woods and picnic under the hawthorns to the songs of minstrels. The Middle Ages were over.

7. CONCLUSION

The test of a civilization is its power of synthesis. Only by integrating the disparate elements of knowledge, faith, and feeling into a system, whatever the basis of that system, can a true synthesis be created. Such a synthesis, on a basis of Christian learning, was achieved in the narrow frame of Benedictine cloisters in the eleventh century. By the twelfth century it had expanded to include the cathedrals and lesser churches, by the thirteenth the feudal world. In the four-teenth century relief and shadow were added to the picture. Courtly luxury balanced cloistered austerity, romantic fantasy counterpoised formal icono-graphy, and deliberate realism the stylization of hieratic art. In the fifteenth century, this bright bubble of civilization trembled before the winds of plague and war. It shivered, but it did not break. Yet, when it once more glowed, round and iridescent, its colours had changed. The synthesis had now come to include the money world of the great cities and the lesser towns. For the first time the force and weight of numbers had entered it: crowds of people, quanti-ties of money. Quality was gradually giving place to quantity; the basis of the world was changing. For the basis of the mediaeval world was aristocracy: an aristocracy of the soul, in the cloister; an aristocracy of birth, of courage, and of land, in feudalism; an aristocracy of the mind, in the universities. Only the towns and the parish churches had tried to open their doors to all men; and, significantly enough, it was not within them that the most characteristic mediaeval creations had been wrought.

The mediaeval subordination of the artist's personality to the needs of his patron, and of the writer's to his audience, meant that the arts of the Middle Ages were completely included within this synthesis. Mediaeval art is above all a social art, and can only be understood in relation to the society for which it was created. The requisites of its creation were two: first, a relative security, and second, a clear purpose, whether that purpose were the pursuit of holi-ness, the worship of God, the pursuit of glory, or the earning of a livelihood and contentment. Art, then as always, was a part of life, and thus a part of history.

The world of France after the Hundred Years War was still a synthesis, but a synthesis with its parts no longer inevitably bound together. It could no longer withstand indefinitely the shock of new ideas: ideas that set the individual above his position, experiment above authority, representation above symbolism, success above endurance, glory above Redemption. The bubble broke; the synthesis disintegrated. Men turned to build another, with a basis not of religion but of humanism. Its art was an individual art that can only be understood in relation to the men who created it: but the study of their lives belongs to the history of another age.

LIST OF BOOKS CONSULTED

IT would obviously be impossible to give a complete bibliography of the subject: the following is rather a list of the books and papers that have been consulted for the matter of this book, with the addition of certain works (marked *) which were not available when it was written.

Unless otherwise stated, French books are published in Paris and English in London.

ACKERMAN, P. 'Recently Identified Designers of Gothic Tapestries', in *Art Bulletin*, ix, 1926, p. 142.

ACLOQUE, G. *Les Corporations, l'industrie et le commerce à Chartres.* 1917.

ADHÉMAR, J. *Influences antiques dans l'art du moyen âge français.* London, 1939.

ANDROUET DU CERCEAU, J. *Les Plus Excellents Bastiments de France.* 1576.

ANFRAY, M. *L'Architecture normande.* 1939.

ANGLÈS, A. 'L'Abbaye de Silvanès', in *Bull. mon.* lxxii, 1908, p. 41.

ARBOIS DE JUBAINVILLE, H. D'. *Études sur l'état intérieur des abbayes cisterciennes et principalement de Clairvaux au XIIᵉ et au XIIIᵉ siècle.* 1857.

—— *Histoire des ducs et des comtes de Champagne.* 7 vols. 1859–69.

ASSIER, A. *Comptes de l'œuvre de l'église de Troyes au XIVᵉ siècle.* 1858.

Association bourguignonne des sociétés savantes. Congrès de 1927. *Saint Bernard et son temps.* 2 vols. Dijon, 1928.

AUBERT, M. 'La Maison dite de Nicolas Flamel, rue Montmorency, à Paris', in *Bull. mon.* lxxvi, 1912, p. 305.

—— *French Sculpture at the Beginning of the Gothic Period, 1140–1225.* Florence and Paris, 1929.

*—— *L'Architecture cistercienne en France.* Paris, 1943. 2 vols.

*—— and Verrier, G. *L'Architecture française des origines à la fin de l'époque romane.* 1941.

AUBERTIN, C. *Notice sur la Chapelle des Chevaliers du Temple à Beaune.* Beaune, 1886.

AURIOL, A., and REY, R. *La Basilique Saint-Sernin de Toulouse.* Toulouse and Paris, 1930.

BAUM, J. *Romanesque Architecture in France.* 2nd ed. 1928.

—— *La Sculpture figurale en Europe à l'époque mérovingienne.* 1937.

BENGY-PUYVALLÉE, M. DE. 'Les Tombeaux de la Chapelle de Saint Jean Baptiste à Saint-Denis', in *Bull. Mon.* lxxi, 1907, p. 113.

BENOÎT, C. 'La Peinture française à la fin du XVᵉ siècle', in *Gaz. Beaux-Arts*, xxvi, 1901, pp. 90, 308, 368; xxvii, pp. 65, 239.

BERGER, S. *La Bible française au moyen âge.* 1884.

—— and DURRIEU, P. 'Les Notes pour l'enlumineur dans les manuscrits du moyen âge', in *Mém. soc. nat. ants France*, liii.

BÉVOTTE, M. DE. *La Sculpture à la fin de la période gothique dans la région de Toulouse, d'Albi et de Rodez, 1400–1520.* 1936.

BISHOP, E. *Liturgica historica: Papers on the Liturgy and Religious Life of the Western Church.* Oxford, 1918.

BLUM, A. *Les Origines de la gravure en France.* Paris and Brussels, 1927.

—— and LAUER, P. *La Miniature française aux XIVe et XVe siècles.* Paris and Brussels, 1930.

BOSSEBŒUF, L. *A Fontevrault: son histoire et ses monuments.* Tours, 1890.

BOUILLET, A., and SERVIÈRES, L. *Sainte Foy, vierge et martyre.* Rodez, 1900.

BOURQUELOT, F. 'Études sur les foires de Champagne', in *Mém. de l'Acad. des Insc. et Belles-Lettres*, 2nd series, v, 1865.

BOUVIER, R. *Un Financier colonial au XVe siècle: Jacques Cœur.* 1928.

BRÉHIER, L. *L'Homme dans la sculpture romane.* n.d. (1927).

—— *L'Art chrétien: son développement iconographique des origines à nos jours.* 2nd ed. 1928.

—— *L'Art en France des invasions barbares à l'époque romane.* n.d. (1930).

—— Le Style roman. 1941.

BRUEL, A. *Romans français du moyen âge.* 1934.

BRUNE, P. *Histoire de l'Ordre hospitalier du Saint Esprit.* Lons-le-Saulnier and Paris, 1892.

CARLIER, A. *L'Église de Rampillon.* 1930.

CARRIÈRE, M. B. *Les Jacobins de Toulouse.* 2nd ed. Toulouse, n.d. (*c.* 1865).

CARTELLIERI, O. *The Court of Burgundy.* 1929.

CHABEUF, H. 'La Sainte Chapelle de Dijon', in *Rev. de l'art chrét.* lxi, 1911, p. 177.

CHAMPEAUX, A. DE, and GAUCHERY, P. *Les Travaux d'art exécutés pour Jean de France, duc de Berry.* 1894.

CHAMPION, P. *Vie de Charles d'Orléans 1394-1465.* 1911.

CHAPUIS, A. 'Les Anciennes Corporations dijonnaises', in *Mémoires de la société bour-guignonne de géographie et d'histoire*, xxii, Dijon, 1906, p. 5.

CHARRIER, J. *Notice historique sur la Collégiale de Saint-Martin de Clamecy.* Nevers, 1887.

CHÉNESSEAU, G. *L'Abbaye de Fleury à Saint-Benoît-sur-Loire.* 1931.

CLAPHAM, A. W. 'The Renaissance of Architecture and Stone-carving in Southern France in the Tenth and Eleventh Centuries', in *Proc. Brit. Acad.*, 1932, p. 45.

COHEN, G. *Le Théâtre en France au moyen âge.* 2 vols., 1928-31.

—— La Grande Clarté du moyen âge. 1945.

CONWAY, W. M. 'The Abbey of Saint Denis and its Ancient Treasures', in *Archaeo-logia*, lxvi, 1915, p. 103.

COOK, T. A., and WARD, W. H. *Twenty-five Great Houses of France.* n.d. (*c.* 1930).

COULTON, G. G. *Five Centuries of Religion.* 3 vols. Cambridge, 1923-36.

—— *The Chronicler of European Chivalry* (Froissart). 1930.

COURAJOD, L. *Leçons professées à l'école du Louvre.* 2 vols., 1899-1901.

COX, T. *Jehan Foucquet, native of Tours.* 1931.

CROZET, R. *L'Abbaye de Noirlac et l'architecture cistercienne en Berry.* 1932.

CURIE-SEIMBRES, M. A. *Essai sur les villes fondées dans le sud-ouest de la France au XIIIe et au XIVe siècle sous le nom générique de bastides.* Toulouse, 1880.

DAVID, H. *De Sluter à Sambin: essai critique sur la sculpture et le décor monumental en Bourgogne au XVe et au XVIe siècles.* 1932.

DELABORDE, H. F., and LAUER, P. 'Un Projet de décoration murale inspiré du Crédo de Joinville', in *Mon. Piot*, xvi, 1909, p. 61.

DELISLE, L. *Mélanges de paléographie et de bibliographie*. 1880.

—— *Notice de douze livres royaux du XIIIᵉ et du XIVᵉ siècle*. 1902.

—— *Recherches sur la librairie de Charles V*. 1907.

DENIFLE, H. *La Désolation des églises, monastères et hôpitaux en France pendant la guerre de Cent Ans*. 2 vols., 1897–9.

DESCHAMPS, P. 'Autel roman de Saint-Sernin de Toulouse et sculptures du cloître de Moissac', in *Bull. arch.*, 1923, p. 239.

—— *French Sculpture of the Romanesque Period, Eleventh and Twelfth Centuries*. Florence and Paris, 1930.

DICKSON, M. and C. *Les Églises romanes de l'ancien diocèse de Chalon*. Mâcon, 1935.

DOUËT D'ARCQ, L. *Comptes de l'argenterie des rois de France au XIVᵉ siècle*. 1851.

—— *Comptes de l'hôtel des rois de France aux XIVᵉ et XVᵉ siècles*. 1865.

DOUTREPONT, G. *La Littérature française à la cour des ducs de Bourgogne*. 1909.

*DOYEN, G., and HUBRECHT, R. *L'Architecture rurale et bourgeoise en France*. 1942.

DUPIN, H. *La Courtoisie au moyen âge*. n.d. (*c.* 1930).

DUPONT, J. *Les Primitifs français*. n.d. (1937).

DURAND, G. *Tableaux et chants royaux de la confrérie du Puy Notre-Dame d'Amiens*. Amiens and Paris, 1911.

—— 'Monuments figurés du moyen âge exécutés d'après les textes liturgiques', in *Bull. mon.* liv, 1888, p. 521.

DURRIEU, P. *Un Grand Enlumineur parisien au XVᵉ siècle: Jacques de Besançon et son œuvre*. 1892.

—— *Les Antiquités judaïques et le peintre Jean Foucquet*. 1908.

—— 'Un Siècle de l'histoire de la miniature parisienne à partir du règne de Saint Louis', in *Journ. des Savants*, Jan. 1909, p. 5.

EBERSOLT, J. *Orient et Occident: recherches sur les influences byzantines et orientales en France avant les Croisades*. Paris and Brussels, 1928.

ENLART, C. 'Origines anglaises du style flamboyant', in *Bull. mon.* lxx, 1906, p. 38.

—— *Manuel d'archéologie française*. I. *Architecture religieuse*. 2nd ed. 1927; II. *Architecture civile*, 1929.

—— 'L'Émaillerie cloisonnée à Paris sous Philippe le Bel et le maître Guillaume Julien', in *Mon. Piot*, 1928.

—— *Monuments religieux de l'architecture romane . . . dans la région picarde*. Amiens and Paris, 1895.

EVANS, JOAN. *Life in Medieval France*. Oxford, 1924.

—— *Monastic Life at Cluny, 910–1157*. Oxford, 1931.

—— *Pattern: a Study of Ornament in Western Europe from 1180 to 1900*. Oxford, 1931.

—— *The Romanesque Architecture of the Order of Cluny*. Cambridge, 1938.

—— *Romanesque Art of the Order of Cluny*. Cambridge (in the press).

FAGNIEZ, G. *Documents relatifs à l'histoire de l'industrie et du commerce en France*, 1898.

*FARAL, E. *La Vie quotidienne au temps de Saint Louis*. 1944.

FARCY, L. DE. *Histoire et description des tapisseries de la Cathédrale d'Angers.* Lille and Angers, n.d.

FELS, F. *Die altfranzösischen Bildteppiche.* Berlin, n.d.

FOCILLON, H. *L'Art des sculpteurs romans: recherches sur l'histoire des formes.* 1931.

—— *Art d'Occident: le moyen âge roman et gothique.* 1938.

—— *Peintures romanes des églises de France.* 1938.

FODÉRÉ, J. *Narration historique et topographique des convens de l'Ordre S. François et monastères S. Claire erigez . . . en Bourgogne . . . .* Lyon, 1619.

FONTAINE, G. *Pontigny, abbaye cistercienne.* 1928.

FOVILLE, J. DE, and LE SOURD, A. *Les Châteaux de France.* n.d. (*c.* 1912).

FRIMMEL, T. *Die Apokalypse in den Bilderhandschriften des Mittelalters.* Vienna, 1885.

GAIGNIÈRES, R. DE. MS. Collections, Bodleian Library, Oxford.

GARDNER, A. *Mediaeval Sculpture in France.* Cambridge, 1931.

—— *An Introduction to French Church Architecture.* Cambridge, 1938.

GAY, V. *Glossaire archéologique.* 2 vols., 1888 and 1928.

GÉRAUD, H. *Paris sous Philippe le Bel.* 1837.

GILLET, L. *Histoire artistique des Ordres Mendiants.* 2nd ed., 1939.

GODEFROY, T. *Le Cérémonial français.* 2 vols., 1649.

GUÉRIN-BOUTARD, J. G. and A. *Les Églises romanes de l'ancien diocèse d'Angoulême.* 1898.

GUIBERT, L. *L'École monastique d'orfèvrerie de Grandmont.* Limoges, 1888.

GUIFFREY, J. 'Inventaire des tapisseries du roi Charles VII vendus par les Anglais en 1422', in *Bibl. de l'École des Chartes*, xlviii, 1887, pp. 59, 396.

—— *Les Tapisseries du XIIᵉ à la fin du XVIᵉ siècle.* n.d. (*c.* 1910).

HACHETTE, ed. *Les Guides Bleus* (various dates).

HAHNLOSER, H. R. *Villard de Honnecourt.* Vienna, 1935.

HALPHEN, L. *Le Comté d'Anjou au XIᵉ siècle.* 1906.

HASKINS, C. H. *The Renaissance of the Twelfth Century.* Cambridge, Mass., 1927.

HÉLYOT, P. 'Dictionnaire des ordres religieux, 1714–1719', in Migne, *Encyclopédie théologique*, vols. xx–xxiv, 1847.

HOFFBAUER. *Paris à travers les âges.* 2 vols., 1875.

HOUVET, E. *Monographie de la ville de Chartres.* n.d.

HUBERT, J. *L'Art pré-roman.* 1938.

HUIZINGA, J. *The Waning of the Middle Ages.* 1924.

*JACQUES, C. *Les Peintres du moyen âge.* 1946.

KATZENELLENBOGEN. *Allegories of the Virtues and Vices in Mediaeval Art.* 1939.

KERVYN DE LETTENHOVE. *La Toison d'Or.* Brussels, 1907.

KILGOUR, R. L. *The Decline of Chivalry as shown in the French Literature of the Late Middle Ages.* Cambridge, Mass., 1937.

KLEINCLAUSZ, A. *Claus Sluter et la sculpture bourguignonne au XVᵉ siècle.* 1905.

KOECHLIN, R. *Les Ivoires gothiques français.* 3 vols., 1924.

—— and MARQUET DE VASSELOT, J. J. *La Sculpture à Troyes et dans la Champagne méridionale au seizième siècle.* 1900.

LABARTE, J. *Inventaire du mobilier de Charles V roi de France.* 1879.

LABORDE, CTE DE. *Les Ducs de Bourgogne: études sur les lettres, les arts et l'industrie pendant le XVᵉ siècle.* Part II: *Preuves.* 3 vols., 1849–52.

—— *Notice des émaux, bijoux et objets divers exposés dans les galeries du Musée du Louvre.* Part II: *Documents et glossaire.* 1853.

LA CURNE DE SAINTE-PALAYE. *Mémoires sur l'ancienne chevalerie.* 3 vols., 1781.

LAFARGUE, M. *Les Chapiteaux du Cloître de Notre-Dame-la-Daurade.* 1940.

—— Art roman du Roussillon. Lanzac, 1947.

LAFOND, J. *Un Livre d'heures rouennais enluminé d'après le 'Speculum humanae salvationis'.* Rouen, 1929.

LALLEMAND, L. *Histoire de la Charité.* Vol. iii : *Le Moyen Age.* 1906.

LALORE, C. *Le Trésor de Clairvaux.* Troyes, 1875.

LA MARCHE, O. DE. 'L'Estat de la maison du duc Charles de Bourgogne dit le Hardy', in Michaud and Poujoulat, *Nouv. coll. des mém.,* iii, 1837, p. 549.

*LAMBERT, É. 'L'Église et le couvent des Jacobins de Toulouse', in *Bull. mon.* civ, 1946, p. 141.

LAMBERT, V. 'L'Église des Templiers de Laon', in *Rev. arch.,* 1926, July–Dec., p. 224.

LASTEYRIE, C. DE. *L'Abbaye de Saint-Martial de Limoges.* 1901.

—— 'Études sur la sculpture française', in *Mon. Piot,* viii, 1902.

LASTEYRIE, R. DE. *L'Architecture religieuse en France à l'époque romane.* 2nd ed., 1929.

—— (ed. M. Aubert). *L'Architecture religieuse en France à l'époque gothique.* 2 vols., 1926.

LAUER, P. *Les Enluminures romanes des manuscrits de la Bibliothèque Nationale.* 1927.

LAVISSE, E. *Histoire de France illustrée depuis les origines jusqu'à la Révolution.* Vols. ii–iv, 1911.

LEBEUF, ABBÉ (ed. H. Cocheris). *Histoire de la ville et de tout le diocèse de Paris.* 3 vols., 1863.

LECGER, A. 'Histoire de l'abbaye de Grandmont', in *Bulletin de la Société historique du Limousin,* tomes lvii–lx. Limoges, 1907–10.

LECOY DE LA MARCHE, A. *Œuvres complètes de Suger.* 1867.

LEFÈVRE-PONTALIS, E., and AUBERT, M. (edd.). *Petites monographies des grands édifices de la France.*

—— *L'Architecture religieuse dans l'ancien diocèse de Soissons au XIᵉ et au XIIᵉ siècle.* 2 vols. 1894.

LEFRANÇOIS-PILLION, L. *Les Sculpteurs de Reims.* 1928.

—— *Les Sculpteurs français du XIIᵉ siècle.* n.d. (1931).

—— *Les Sculpteurs français du XIIIᵉ siècle.* 2nd ed., n.d. (1931).

LEJEUNE, M. J. *Histoire . . . de l'Ordre des Chevaliers du Temple de Jérusalem, dits Templiers.* Paris, 1789.

LEMOISNE, P. A. *Gothic Painting in France. Fourteenth and fifteenth centuries.* Florence and Paris, 1931.

LE ROUX DE LINCY and TISSERAND, L. M. *Paris et ses historiens aux XIVᵉ et XVᵉ siècles.* 1867.

LESNE, E. *Histoire de la propriété ecclésiastique en France.* Vol. iii. Lille, 1936.

L'ESPINASSE, R. DE. *Les Métiers et corporations de la ville de Paris.* 2 vols., 1886–93.

LONGNON, A. (ed. P. Marichal and L. Mirot). *Les Noms de lieu de la France.* 1920–9.

LOOMIS, R. S. 'Origin and Date of the Bayeux Tapestry', in *Art Bulletin*, vi, 1923, p. 3.

LOT, F. *Études sur le règne de Hugues Capet et la fin du Xe siècle.* 1903.

LUCE, S. *La France pendant la guerre de Cent Ans.* 2 vols., 1890.

LUTZ, J., and PERDRIZET, P. *Speculum Humanae Salvationis.* Mulhouse. 2 vols., 1907.

MAILLARD, E. *Les Sculptures de la cathédrale de Saint Pierre de Poitiers.* Poitiers, 1921.

MÂLE, E. *L'Art religieux du XIIIe siècle en France.* 2nd ed., 1902.

—— *L'Art religieux en France de la fin du moyen âge.* 1908.

—— *L'Art religieux du XIIe siècle en France.* 1922.

—— *Art et artistes du moyen âge.* 1927.

MARQUET DE VASSELOT, J. J. 'Le Trésor de l'abbaye de Roncesvaux', in *Gaz. des Beaux-Arts*, 1897, xxxix, pp. 205 and 319.

—— *Les Émaux limousins de la fin du XVe siècle et de la première partie du XVIe.* 2 vols., 1921.

MARTIN, H. *Les Peintres de manuscrits et la miniature en France.* 1909.

—— *Les Miniaturistes français.* 1906.

—— *La Miniature française du XIIIe au XVe siècle.* Paris and Brussels, 1923.

MAUMENÉ, C., and HARCOURT, CTE LOUIS DE. *Iconographie des rois de France.* Soc. de l'hist. de l'art français, Archives, N.S., xv, 1928.

MÉLY, F. DE. *Le Trésor de Chartres.* 1886.

MICHEL, A. (ed.). *Histoire de l'art.* Vols. i–iii, 1905.

MOLINIER, E. *Les Ivoires.* 1896.

—— *L'Orfèvrerie religieuse et civile du Ve à la fin du XVe siècle.* n.d. (c. 1898).

MONGET, C. *La Chartreuse de Dijon.* 3 vols. Montreuil-sur-mer, 1898.

MONTFAUCON, B. DE. *Les Monumens de la monarchie françoise.* 5 vols., 1720–3.

MORANVILLÉ, H. *Inventaire de l'orfèvrerie et des joyaux de Louis I, duc d'Anjou.* 1906.

MOREY, C. R. 'The Sources of Romanesque Sculpture', in *Art Bulletin*, ii, 1919, p. 10.

MORTET, V. 'La Fabrique des églises cathédrales et de la statuaire religieuse au moyen âge', in *Bull. mon.* lxvi, 1902, p. 216.

—— *Recueil de textes relatifs à l'histoire de l'architecture et à la condition des architectes en France au moyen âge.* Vol. i, XIe et XIIe siècles, 1911; vol. ii (with P. Deschamps), XIIe et XIIIe siècles, 1929.

—— 'Hugues de Fouilloi, Pierre le Chantre, Alexandre Neckam', in *Mélanges Bémont*, 1913, p. 105.

—— and BELLANGER, J. 'Un Très Ancien Devis français', in *Bull. mon.* lxii, 1897, pp. 232 and 397.

*MOUREY, G. *Tableau de l'art français des origines à nos jours.* 1938.

NEUSS, W. *Die Apokalypse des Hl. Johannes in der altspanischen und altchristlichen Bibel-illustration*, 2 vols. Münster in Westphalia, 1931.

OURSEL, C. *La Miniature du XIIe siècle à l'abbaye de Cîteaux.* Dijon, 1926.

—— *L'Art roman de Bourgogne.* Dijon and Boston, 1928.

PANNIER, L. 'Les Joyaux du duc de Guyenne', in *Rev. arch.*, N.S., xxvi, 1873, pp. 158, 209, 284, 306.

*PANOFSKY, E. *Abbot Suger on the Abbey Church of St.-Denis and its Art Treasures.* Princeton and London, 1946.

PAUL, G. and P. *Notre-Dame du Puy.* Le Puy and Paris, 1926.

PETIT DE JULLEVILLE, L. *Les Mystères.* 2 vols., 1880.

PINCHART, A. *Archives des Arts, Sciences et Lettres.* 1st series, 2 vols., Ghent, 1860.

PIRENNE, H. *Les Villes du moyen âge.* Brussels, 1927.

POËTE, M. *Les Primitifs parisiens.* 1904.

PORTER, A. K. *Romanesque Sculpture of the Pilgrimage Roads.* 10 vols., Boston, 1923.

PROST, D. 'Quelques documents sur l'histoire des arts en France', in *Gaz. des Beaux Arts,* xxxv, 1887, p. 322, and xxxvi, 1888, p. 235.

—— *Inventaires mobiliers et extraits des comptes des ducs de Bourgogne de la maison de Valois, 1363–1477.* 2 vols., 1902–4.

PROU, M. *La Gaule mérovingienne.* n.d. (c. 1897).

QUATREBARBES, CTE DE. *Œuvres complètes du roi René.* 4 vols., Angers, 1845.

QUÉTEY, A. (ed.). *Journal d'un bourgeois de Paris, 1405–49.* 1881.

*REAU, L. *La Peinture française du XIVᵉ au XVIᵉ siècle.* 1939.

*—— *L'Art religieux au moyen âge.* 1946.

REY, R. *La Sculpture romane languedocienne.* Toulouse and Paris, 1936.

—— *Les Vieilles Églises fortifiées du Midi de la France.* 1925.

—— *L'Art gothique du Midi de la France.* 1934.

*—— *L'Art roman et ses origines.* Toulouse, 1945.

RICHARD, J. M. *Mahaut, comtesse d'Artois et de Bourgogne, 1302–1329.* 1887.

ROCHEGUDE, MARQUIS DE, and DUMOLIN, M. *Guide pratique à travers le vieux Paris.* 1923.

ROHAULT DE FLEURY. *Gallia Dominicana: les couvents de Saint Dominique au moyen âge.* 2 vols., Paris, 1903.

SARTOR, M. *Les Tapisseries, toiles peintes et broderies de Reims.* Reims, 1912.

Société française d'archéologie. *Congrès archéologiques.*

SOHRING, O. 'Werke bildender Kunst in altfranzösischen Epen', in *Romanische Forschungen,* xii, Erlangen, 1900, p. 490.

STEIN, H. *Les Architectes des cathédrales gothiques.* n.d. (c. 1910).

—— *Le Palais de Justice et la Sainte-Chapelle de Paris.* 1912.

STERLING, C. *La Peinture française: les primitifs.* 1938.

SWARTWOUT, R. E. *The Monastic Craftsman.* Cambridge, 1932.

TOLLET, C. *Les Édifices hospitaliers depuis leur origine jusqu'à nos jours.* 1892.

TROESCHER, G. *Claus Sluter.* Freiburg-im-Breisgau. n.d. (1932).

VALLERY-RADOT, J. *Églises romanes: filiations et échanges d'influence.* n.d. (c. 1930).

VAN MARLE, R. *Iconographie de l'art profane au moyen âge et à la Renaissance.* 2 vols., The Hague, 1931–2.

VERDIER, A., and CATTOIS, F. *Architecture civile et domestique.* 2 vols., 1855.

VIARD, J. *Les Journaux du Trésor de Philippe VI de Valois.* 1899.

VIDIER, A. 'Le Trésor de la Sainte-Chapelle', in *Mém. de la Soc. de l'hist. de Paris et de l'Île de France,* xxxiv–xxxvii, 1907–10.

VIELLIARD, J. *Le Guide du Pèlerin de Saint-Jacques de Compostelle.* Mâcon, 1938.

VIREY, J. *Les Églises romanes de l'ancien diocèse de Mâcon: Cluny et sa région.* 2nd ed. Mâcon, 1935.

VITRY, P. *Michel Colombe et la sculpture française de son temps.* 1901.

—— *La Cathédrale de Reims.* 2 vols., n.d. (1919).

—— *French Sculpture during the Reign of Saint Louis, 1226–1270.* Florence and Paris, n.d. (c. 1930).

WARD, C. *Mediaeval Church Vaulting* (Princeton Monographs in Art and Archaeology V). Princeton, 1915.

WATSON, A. *The Early Iconography of the Tree of Jesse.* Oxford, 1934.

*WESCHER, P. *Jean Fouquet and his Times.* Basle, 1947.

WILLEMIN, H. *Monuments français inédits, pour servir à l'histoire des arts.* 2 vols., 1806.

WILMART, DOM A. *Auteurs spirituels et textes dévots du moyen âge latin.* 1932.

YOUNG, K. *The Drama of the Mediaeval Church.* Oxford, 1933.

ILLUSTRATIONS

1. Benedictine Abbey of Jumièges, Seine-Inférieure. The Western Towers. *c.* 1065.

(Phot. Archives Photographiques.)

2. Benedictine (Cluniac) Priory of Champvoux, Nièvre. The Sanctuary. First half of the
eleventh century.

(Phot. Archives Photographiques.)

3. Benedictine Abbey of Jumièges, Seine-Inférieure. The Nave. Middle of the eleventh century.

(Phot. Archives Photographiques.)

4. Benedictine (Cluniac) Priory of La-Charité-sur-Loire, Nièvre. Consecrated 1107. The East End (the lower chapels added later).

(Phot. Delayance, La Charité.)

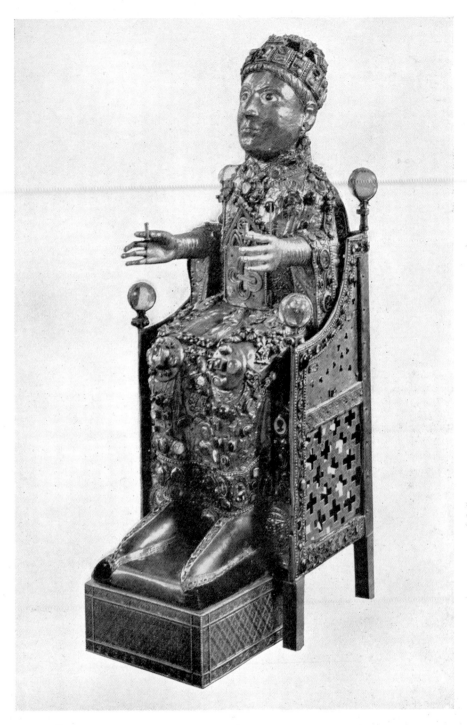

5. Benedictine Abbey of Conques, Aveyron. Reliquary Statue of Sainte Foy.
Made for Abbot Stephen, 940–84.

(Phot. Archives Photographiques.)

6 *a*. Phylactery Reliquary of the Tooth of Saint Maclou. *c.* 1190. Now at
Saint-Maclou, Bar-sur-Aube.

(*Phot. Archives Photographiques.*)

6 *b*. Benedictine (Cluniac) Priory of Volvic, Puy-de-Dôme. Capital showing
the donor, Gulielmus de Bez, giving the column to the Prior. Early twelfth
century.

(*Phot. Joan Evans.*)

7. Benedictine Abbey of Saint-Sernin, Toulouse. The Nave. Begun 1077.
(Phot. Lévy et Neurdein.)

8. Benedictine (Cluniac) Abbey of Saint-Martin-des-Champs, Paris.
Virgin of gilt and painted wood. *c.* 1130. Now in Saint-Denis.

(Phot. Giraudon.)

9. Benedictine Abbey of Grandselve. Reliquary of Sainte Libaude. Twelfth century. Now in the Church of Bouillac, Tarn-et-Garonne.

(Phot. Archives Photographiques.)

10. Benedictine Abbey of Fleury (Saint-Benoît-sur-Loire), Loiret. The Choir from the Ambulatory. Begun between 1067 and 1080.

(*Phot. Archives Photographiques.*)

11. Benedictine Abbey of Cluny, Saône-et-Loire. The Interior of the Abbey Church. Begun in 1088. Reconstruction by Professor K. J. Conant.

(Courtesy of Professor Kenneth Conant.)

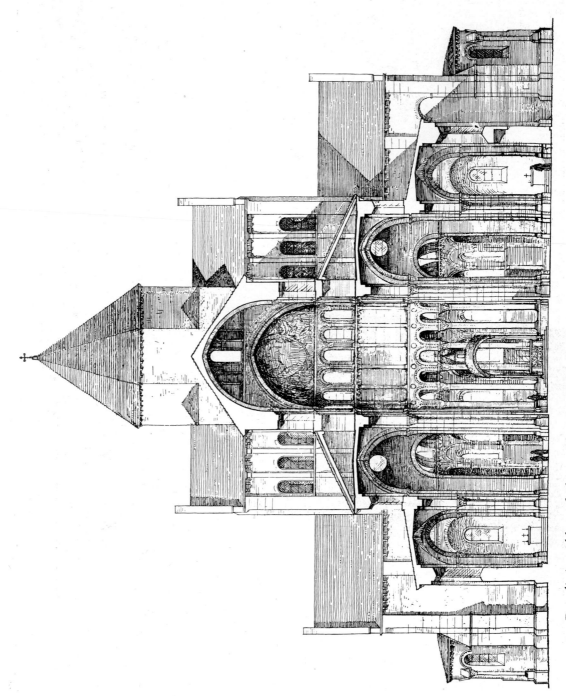

12. Benedictine Abbey of Cluny. The Third Abbey Church. Transverse section at the Transept. Begun 1088, the Altars dedicated 1095, the Church dedicated 1130. Reconstruction by Professor K. J. Conant.

13. Benedictine Abbey of Saint-Savin-sur-Gartrempe, Haute-Vienne. The Nave. *c.* 1080.
(*Phot. Archives Photographiques.*)

14. Benedictine (Cluniac) Abbey of Vézelay, Yonne. The Nave. Begun in 1089.

(Phot. Lévy et Neurdein.)

15. Benedictine (Cluniac) Priory of Paray-le-Monial, Saône-et-Loire. The Apse, before restoration. *c.* 1100.

(*Phot. Archives Photographiques.*)

16. Benedictine Abbey of Saint-Pierre de Chauvigny, Haute-Vienne. The Apse. *c.* 1100.
(*Phot. Archives Photographiques.*)

17. Benedictine (Cluniac) Abbey of Vézelay, Yonne. The Galilee. Begun *c.* 1120, dedicated 1132.
(*Phot. Archives Photographiques.*)

18. Benedictine Abbey of Charroux, Vienne. The Central Lantern of the Rotunda.
Consecrated 1095.

(Phot. Archives Photographiques.)

19. Benedictine (Cluniac) Priory of Retaud, Charente-Maritime. The Apse. *c.* 1150.

(*Phot. Archives Photographiques.*)

20. Abbaye-aux-Dames, Saintes, Charente-Maritime. Detail of the façade, built by Abbess Sibylle de Bourgogne between 1119 and 1134.

(*Phot. Archives Photographiques.*)

21. Benedictine (Cluniac) Abbey of Saint-Gilles, Gard. The southern half of the Portal. *c.* 1140.
(Phot. Archives Photographiques.)

22. Benedictine (Cluniac) Priory of La Charité-sur-Loire, Nièvre. La Tour Sainte-Croix.
Middle of the twelfth century.

(Phot. Delayance, La Charité.)

23 *a*. Benedictine Abbey of Saint-Aignan d'Orléans. Capital of the Crypt. 989–1029.
(Phot. Archives Photographiques.)

23 *b*. Benedictine Priory of Thil-Châtel, Côte-d'Or. Corinthian Capital of the Nave.
c. 1100.
(Phot. Archives Photographiques.)

23 *c*. Benedictine Abbey of Cluny, Saône-et-Loire.   Corinthian Capital.   *c.* 1096.
Musée Ochier, Cluny.
(Phot. Archives Photographiques.)

23 *d*. Benedictine (Cluniac) Abbey of Mozac, Puy-de-Dôme. Capital with Winged Genii.
c. 1125.
(Phot. Archives Photographiques.)

24 *a*. Oriental Silk that wrapped the relics of Saint Josse, in the Church of Saint-Josse-sur-Mer, Pas-de-Calais.   Tenth century.

(Phot. Archives Photographiques.)

24 *b*. Benedictine (Cluniac) Priory of Montierneuf, Poitiers. Capital with elephants.
c. 1085.

(Phot. Archives Photographiques.)

25. Initial Q from Josephus, *De Bello Judaico*. Manuscript written in the Benedictine (Cluniac)
Abbey of Moissac, Tarn-et-Garonne. *c.* 1070. Bib. Nat. lat. 5058, fol. 7.
(Phot. Catala.)

26 *a*. Benedictine (Cluniac) Priory of Layrac, Lot-et-Garonne.
Built 1072–85. Capital.

(*Phot. Joan Evans.*)

26 *b*. Benedictine Abbey of Fleury, Saint-Benoît-sur-Loire. Capital of Porch.
Second half of the eleventh century.

(*Phot. Archives Photographiques.*)

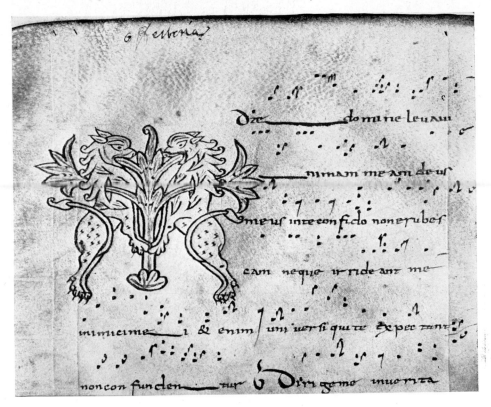

27 a. Initial A from the Antiphonal of the Benedictine Abbey of Cluny. *c.* 1000.
Bib. Nat. lat. 1121, fol. 90.

(*Phot. Catala.*)

27 b. Benedictine Abbey of Fleury (Saint-Benoît-sur-Loire). Capital.
Second half of the eleventh century.

(*Phot. Joan Evans.*)

28. Initial P. Martyrology of Cluny. Bib. Nat. lat. 3779, fol. 121ᵛ. *c.* 1100.
(*Phot. Catala.*)

29 a. Benedictine Abbey of Saint-Aignan
d'Orléans. Capital of the Crypt. c. 1100.
(*Phot. Archives Photographiques.*)

29 b. Benedictine Abbey of Saint-Andoche
de Saulieu, Côte-d'Or. Capital of the Nave.
Consecrated 1119.
(*Phot. Archives Photographiques.*)

29 c. Benedictine Abbey of Saint-Germain-
des-Prés, Paris. Engaged Capital. c. 1100.
(*Phot. Archives Photographiques.*)

29 d. Benedictine Priory of l'Île-Bouchard,
Indre-et-Loire. Capital of the Apse. c. 1100.
(*Phot. Archives Photographiques.*)

30 *a*. Initial D from the Psalter of the Benedictine (Cluniac) Abbey of Saint-Martial de
Limoges. *c.* 1095. Bib. Nat. lat. 11550, fol. 169.
(Phot. Catala.)

30 *b*. Benedictine (Cluniac) Abbey of Sainte-Marie-la-Daurade, Toulouse, Tarn-et-Garonne.
Twin Capital from the Cloister. *c.* 1115–25.
(Phot. Giraudon.)

31. Initials PRE from a manuscript Life of St. Martial, from the Benedictine (Cluniac) Abbey of Saint-Martial de Limoges. *c.* 1100. Bib. Nat. lat. 5296 A, fol. 2ᵛ.

(Phot. Catala.)

32. Benedictine Abbey of Saint-Denis. Detail of the columns of the façade. 1137–44.
(*Phot. Archives Photographiques.*)

33 *a*. Initial L and St. Matthew from the Bible of the Benedictine Abbey of Saint-Martial de Limoges. *c.* 1070. Bib. Nat. lat. 254, fol. 10.
(*Phot. Catala.*)

33 *b*. Sculptured column from the Benedictine Abbey of Souillac, Lot. *c.* 1115.
(*Phot. Archives Photographiques.*)

34. Benedictine (Cluniac) Abbey of Moissac, Tarn-et-Garonne. The Tympanum. c. 1110.

(Phot. Archives Photographiques.)

35 *a*. Rough sketch of *Majestas Domini nostri Jhesu Christi* on the end-leaf of a manuscript of Caesar from Fleury. *c.* 1100. Bib. Nat. lat. 5763.

(*Phot. Catala.*)

35 *b*. Rough sketch of *Angelus Domini* in a blank space of a manuscript from Saint-Martial de Limoges. *c.* 1100. Bib. Nat. lat. 2826, fol. 157.

(*Phot. Catala.*)

36. Benedictine (Cluniac) Grange of Berzé-la-Ville, Saône-et-Loire.
Wall-painting of the Apse: Christ in Glory. Before 1109.

(Phot. Archives Photographiques.)

37 *a*. Christ upheld by Angels. Beatus of the Abbey of Saint-Sever, Landes. Copied between 1028 and 1072. Bib. Nat. lat. 8878, fol. 215ᵛ.

(Phot. Catala.)

37 *b*. Benedictine Priory of Perrecy-les-Forges, Allier. Tympanum of the Portal. *c.* 1110.

(Phot. Archives Photographiques.)

38 *a*. Benedictine Priory of Saint-Julien-de-Jonzy, Loire. Tympanum of the Portal. *c.* 1160.
(*Phot. Archives Photographiques.*)

38 *b*. Benedictine (Cluniac) Priory of Montceau-l'Étoile, Saône-et-Loire. Tympanum of the
West Door. The Ascension. *c.* 1115.
(*Phot. Archives Photographiques.*)

39. Benedictine Abbey of Saint-Bénigne de Dijon. Tympanum, now in the Musée Lapidaire. *c.* 1120

(Phot. courtesy of Monsieur P. Lebel, Dijon.)

40. Benedictine Abbey of Conques, Aveyron. Tympanum of the Portal. *c.* 1120.
(*Phot. courtesy of Arthur Gardner, Esq., F.S.A.*)

41. Benedictine (Cluniac) Abbey of Vézelay, Yonne. The Portal. *c.* 1120–32.
(Phot. Neurdein.)

42 *a–b*. Benedictine (Cluniac) Abbey of Mozac, Puy-de-Dôme.
Capital with the Three Maries and the Angel at the Sepulchre.
c. 1130.
(*Phot. Archives Photographiques.*)

43 *a*. Benedictine (Cluniac) Priory of Sainte-Marie de Donzy-le-Pré, Nièvre. Tympanum.
c. 1130.
(*Phot. Archives Photographiques.*)

43 *b*. Benedictine Abbey of Saint-Pierre de Chauvigny, Vienne. Capital: Adoration of the Magi.
c. 1110.
(*Phot. Joan Evans.*)

44. Benedictine (Cluniac) Priory of La Charité-sur-Loire, Nièvre. The Portal. The Transfiguration. *c.* 1110.

(Phot. Delayance, La Charité.)

45. Benedictine Abbey of Cluny, Saône-et-Loire. Capital of the Choir: the Four Rivers and the Four Trees. *c.* 1096. Musée Ochier, Cluny.

(*Phot. Archives Photographiques.*)

46. Benedictine Abbey of Cluny, Saône-et-Loire. The Four
Virtues and the Four Seasons: Prudence. Musée Ochier, Cluny.
(Phot. Archives Photographiques.)

47. Benedictine Abbey of Cluny, Saône-et-Loire. The Second
Tone. Musée Ochier, Cluny.
(*Phot. Archives Photographiques.*)

48. Benedictine Abbey of Saint-Denis. Detail of Window given by Abbot Suger. *c.* 1145.
a. Quod Moyses velat Christi doctrina revelat.
Denudant legem qui spoliant Moysem.
b. God bestowing the Seven Gifts of the Spirit on Church and Synagogue.
(*Phot. Archives Photographiques.*)

49. Benedictine Abbey of Souillac, Lot. The Prophet Isaiah, from the Portal. *c.* 1110.
(*Phot. Archives Photographiques.*)

50. Benedictine Priory of Notre-Dame de Corbeil, Seine-et-Oise. Statues of Solomon and the Queen of Sheba from the Portal rebuilt by Suger before 1152. Musée du Louvre.

(Phot. Giraudon.)

51. Benedictine Abbey of Saint-Aubin d'Angers, Maine-et-Loire. Arcade to the Chapter House.
Middle of the twelfth century.

(Phot. Archives Photographiques.)

52 *a*. Benedictine (Cluniac) Abbey of Moissac, Tarn-et-Garonne. The Cloister.
1100 (the arcade reset later).
(*Phot. Archives Photographiques.*)

52 *b*. Benedictine Abbey of Saint-Hilaire, Aude. The Cloister. Fourteenth century.
(*Phot. Archives Photographiques.*)

53 *a*. Benedictine Abbey of Chamalières, Haute-Loire. Sculptured Pier from the Cloister, now in the Church. *c.* 1120.

(*Phot. Archives Photographiques.*)

53 *b*. Benedictine Abbey of Saint-Guilhem-le-Désert, Hérault. Statue-pier from the Cloister. Middle of the twelfth century.

(*Phot. Archives Photographiques.*)

54. Benedictine (Cluniac) Abbey of Vézelay, Yonne. The Choir. Begun 1170, finished 1201.
(Phot. Lévy et Neurdein.)

55. Benedictine Abbey of Saint-Rémi de Reims. The Choir. Rebuilt between 1170 and 1190.
(Phot. Archives Photographiques.)

56 *a*. Benedictine Abbey of Mont-Saint-Michel, Manche. The Cloister. Finished 1228.
(*Phot. Archives Photographiques.*)

56 *b*. Benedictine Abbey of Mont-Saint-Michel, Manche. The Refectory. 1225.
(*Phot. Archives Photographiques.*)

57. Benedictine (Cluniac) Abbey of Saint-Germain d'Auxerre, Yonne. Chapel of the Ambulatory. Fifteenth century.
(Phot. Archives Photographiques.)

58. Benedictine Abbey of La Chaise-Dieu, Haute-Loire. The Stalls. End of the fourteenth century.

(Phot. Archives Photographiques.)

59. Benedictine Abbey of Montmajour, Bouches-du-Rhône. Ciborium of Limoges enamel, now in the Louvre. Signed MAGISTER G. ALPAIS ME FECIT LEMOVICARVM. Late twelfth century.

(Phot. Archives Photographiques.)

60. Benedictine Abbey of Saint-Jean-des-Vignes, Soissons. The Cloister. *c.* 1300.
(*Phot. Archives Photographiques.*)

61. Benedictine Abbey of Saint-Bénigne de Dijon. The Refectory. Early thirteenth century.

(Phot. Archives Photographiques.)

62. St. James and Queen Esther. Bible of Stephen Harding, Abbot of Cîteaux, 1098–1109. Dijon MS. 14, fol. 110, and 15, fol. 83.

(Phot. courtesy of Monsieur Oursel, Dijon.)

63. Cistercian Abbey of Fontenay, Yonne. The Church. Consecrated in 1147.
(Phot. Archives Photographiques.)

64. Cistercian Abbey of Pontigny, Yonne. The Ambulatory. *c.* 1170.
(*Phot. Archives Photographiques.*)

65. Cistercian Abbey of Le Val, Meriel, Seine-et-Oise. The Church. *c.* 1200.

(Phot. Archives Photographiques.)

66 *a*. Cistercian Abbey of Fontenay, Yonne. The Cloister. *c.* 1150.
(*Phot. Archives Photographiques.*)

66 *b*. Cistercian Abbey of Bonport, Eure. The Refectory. *c.* 1250.
(*Phot. T.C.F. (Abbé Bretocq).*)

67. Cistercian Abbey of Fontenay, Yonne. The Chapter House. *c.* 1150.

(Phot. Archives Photographiques.)

68. Cistercian Abbey of Royaumont, Oise. The Refectory. *c.* 1250.
(*Phot. Archives Photographiques.*)

69. Cistercian Abbey of Ourscamps, Aisne. The Infirmary. *c.* 1230.

(*Phot. M. Henri de Segogne.*)

70. Cistercian Abbey of Vauclerc, Aisne. The Dorter. *c.* 1200.

(Phot. Archives Photographiques.)

71. Cistercian Abbey of Vauclerc, Aisne. Interior of Dorter. *c.* 1200.
(*Phot. Archives Photographiques.*)

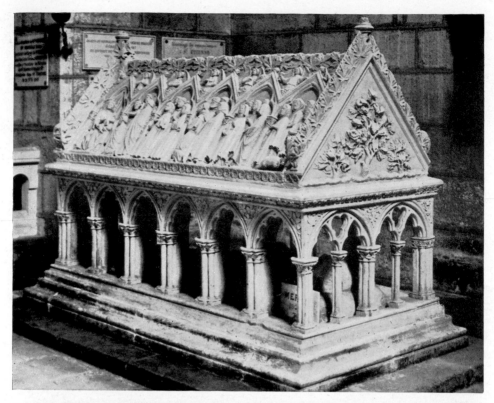

72. Cistercian Abbey of Aubazine, Corrèze. Shrine of Saint Étienne. Middle of the thirteenth century.

(Phot. courtesy of Arthur Gardner, Esq., F.S.A.)

73. The Templars' Church, Rampillon, Seine-et-Marne. The Portal. *c.* 1240.
(*Phot. Archives Photographiques.*)

74. Cathedral of Saint-Trophime, Arles. The Cloister. Begun *c.* 1160.
(Phot. Jean Roubier.)

75. Detail of the façade of the Cathedral of Angoulême, Charente. *c.* 1140.
(*Phot. Archives Photographiques.*)

76. Cathedral of Langres, Haute-Marne. Detail of the Apse. Middle of the twelfth century.
(*Phot. Archives Photographiques.*)

77. Cathedral of Notre-Dame de Chartres. Column Figures of the Royal Door. *c.* 1155.
(Phot. TEL, Paris.)

78. Cathedral of Bayeux, Calvados. 'La Toile de Saint Jean.' First half of the twelfth century.

(Phot. Lévy et Neurdein.)

79. Cathedral of Noyon, Oise. The Interior. Begun soon after 1131.
(Phot. T.C.F. (Abbé Bretocq).)

80. Cathedral of Laon, Aisne. The Nave. Second half of the twelfth century.

(*Phot. Archives Photographiques.*)

81. Cathedral of Laon, Aisne. The Towers. Last quarter of the twelfth century.
(*Phot. Archives Photographiques.*)

82. Cathedral of Bourges, Cher. Begun in 1192, the Nave finished in 1266.

(*Phot. Archives Photographiques.*)

83. Cathedral of Chartres, Eure-et-Loir. Begun 1194, finished 1260.
(Phot. courtesy of Service cinématographique de l'air.)

84. Cathedral of Amiens, Somme. The Façade. *c.* 1245. (The top of the Towers and Façade 1529.)
(*Phot. Yvon.*)

85. Cathedral of Le Mans, Sarthe. The Apse. Begun 1217. Consecrated 1254.
(Phot. T.C.F. (Burthe d'Annelet).)

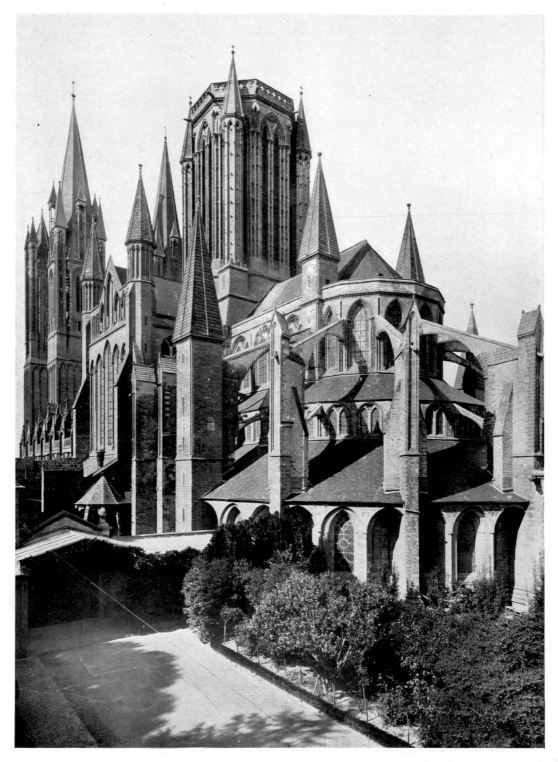

86. Cathedral of Coutances, Manche. The Apse. Begun *c.* 1220.

(Phot. Archives Photographiques.)

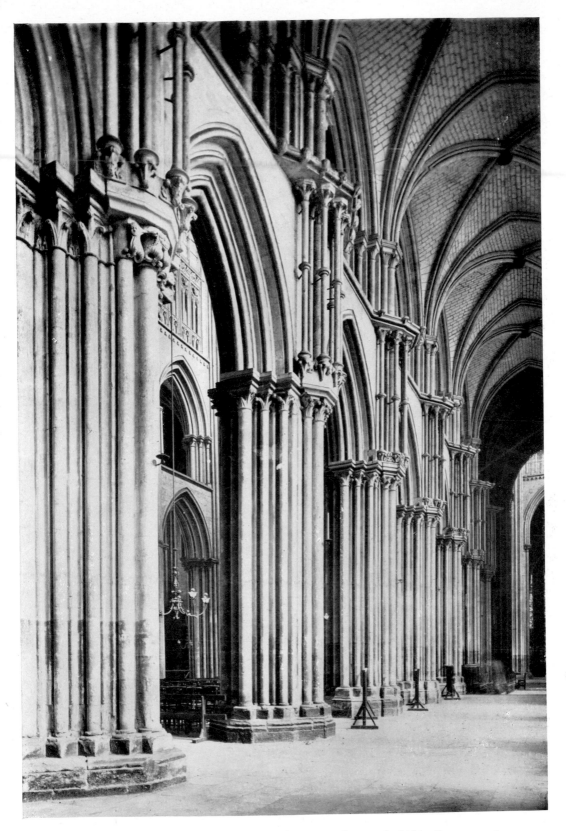

87. Cathedral of Rouen, Seine-Inférieure. The South Aisle. Begun 1206.

(Phot. Archives Photographiques.)

88. Cathedral of Beauvais, Oise. The Choir. Begun 1247, finished 1272.
(*Phot. Bulloz.*)

89. Villard de Honnecourt: Drawing of Seated Figure. Bib. Nat. MS. franç. 19093.
(Phot. Hahnloser, Vienna.)

90 *a*. Cathedral of Rheims. Capital of the Triforium. *c.* 1240.
(*Phot. Archives Photographiques.*)

90 *b*. Cathedral of Rheims. Panel of Sculptured Stone. *c.* 1280.
(*Phot. Archives Photographiques.*)

91. Cathedral of Notre-Dame de Senlis, Oise. Detail of the Virgin's Door: Resurrection of the Virgin c. 1190.

(Phot. Archives Photographiques.)

92. Cathedral of Chartres. The South Porch. *c.* 1230.

(Phot. Lévy et Neurdein.)

93. Cathedral of Chartres. South Portal: the Last Judgment. *c.* 1230.
(Phot. TEL, Paris.)

94. Cathedral of Bourges. Detail of the Judgment Portal: the Blest. *c.* 1300.
(*Phot. Giraudon.*)

95. Cathedral of Amiens. South Transept: the Virgin. Middle of the thirteenth century.
(Phot. Jean Roubier.)

96. Cathedral of Sens, Yonne. West Door: St. Stephen.

(Phot. Archives Photographiques.)

97. Cathedral of Rheims. Statues of the West Front. The Visitation: Central Bay, West Porch.
c. 1250.
(*Phot. Archives Photographiques.*)

98. Cathedral of Poitiers. Central part of the East Window. Given by Eleanor of Guienne and Henry II of England. *c.* 1180.

(*Phot. Archives Photographiques.*)

99 *a*. Cathedral of Rouen. Canopy work of a window in the Lady Chapel. End of the fourteenth century.

(*Phot. Archives Photographiques.*)

99 *b*. Cathedral of Évreux. Portrait of Pierre de Navarre, Comte de Mortain, as donor of a window. *c.* 1390.

(*Phot. Archives Photographiques.*)

100. The Nativity, by the Maître de Moulins, given to the Cathedral of Autun by Cardinal Jean Rolin, Bishop of Autun. Musée d'Autun. *c. 1470.*

(*Phot. Bulloz.*)

101. Cathedral of Sens. 'La Sainte Coupe'. Silver gilt. *c.* 1200.
(Phot. courtesy of Monsieur Pierre Verlet.)

102. Cathedral of Rheims. Reliquary of Saint Samson. End of the twelfth century.

(*Photo. Giraudon.*)

103. Cathedral of Rheims. Chalice of Saint Rémi. Twelfth century.
(Phot. Giraudon.)

104. Cathedral of Cahors, Lot. The Cloister. *c.* 1500.
(*Phot. Archives Photographiques.*)

105. Palace of the Popes, Avignon. The Hall of Audience. Middle of the fourteenth century.
(Phot. Lévy et Neurdein.)

106. Palace of the Popes, Avignon. Fresco of Hawking. 1343.
(*Phot. Lévy et Neurdein.*)

107. Collegiate Church of Les Aix-d'Angillon, Cher. The Apse. *c.* 1110.
(*Phot. Archives Photographiques.*)

108. Collegiate Church of Bénévent-l'Abbaye, Creuse. The Interior. *c.* 1140.
(*Phot. Archives Photographiques.*)

109. Collegiate Church of Saint-Junien, Vienne. Middle of the twelfth century.
(*Phot. Archives Photographiques.*)

110. Fontevrault, Maine-et-Loire. The Interior. Middle of the twelfth century.

(Phot. Archives Photographiques.)

111. Collegiate Church of Tour-en-Bessin, Calvados. The Choir. Fourteenth century.
(Phot. Archives Photographiques.)

112. Augustinian Convent, Toulouse. The Cloister. Begun in 1396.

(*Phot. Lévy et Neurdein.*)

113. The Canons' Tithe Barn, Provins, Seine-et-Marne. The Ground Floor. End of the twelfth century.

(Phot. T.C.F.)

114. Collegiate Church of Notre-Dame-du-Port, Clermont-Ferrand, Puy-de-Dôme. Capital of the Choir: *Largitas* and *Caritas* pierce the Vices beneath their Feet; *Ira* kills himself because Patience will not give battle. *c.* 1140.

(Phot. Archives Photographiques.)

115. Rose Window with the Wheel of Fortune. Saint-Étienne de Beauvais. *c.* 1130.
(*Phot. Archives Photographiques.*)

116. Collegiate Church of Saint-Urbain de Troyes. Tympanum of the West Door. End of the thirteenth century.

(Phot. Giraudon.)

117. Collegiate Church of Notre-Dame-la-Grande, Poitiers. Detail of the Façade. *c.* 1140.

(*Phot. Archives Photographiques.*)

118. Collegiate Church of Villeneuve-l'Archevêque, Yonne. The Portal. End of the thirteenth
century.
(*Phot. Archives Photographiques.*)

119. Copper-gilt Reliquary of Saint Étienne de Muret from
Grandmont. Thirteenth century. Les Billanges, Haute-Vienne.
(*Phot. Archives Photographiques.*)

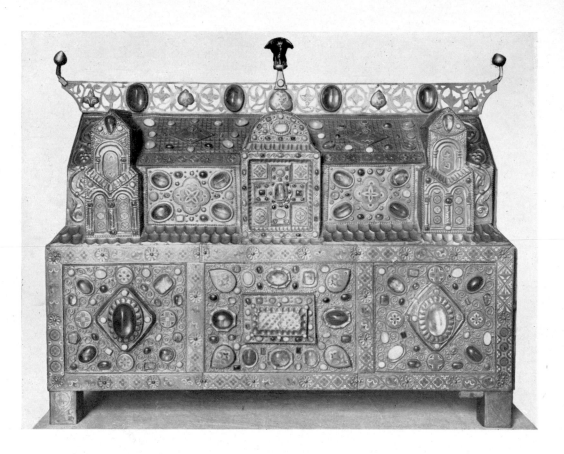

120. Reliquary of the Theban Legion, from Grandmont. Copper gilt, enamelled and set with crystals. Thirteenth century. Ambazac, Haute-Vienne.

(Phot. Archives Photographiques.)

121. Leaf of a Diptych: the Virgin presenting the Augustinian Donor to the Christ of Pity. c. 1400.
Deutsches Museum, Berlin.

(Phot. Giraudon.)

122. Collegiate Church of Écouis, Eure. Statue of St. Veronica. Early fourteenth century.
(Phot. Bulloz.)

123. Franciscan Nunnery, Provins, Seine-et-Marne. The Cloister. End of the fifteenth century.

(Phot. Archives Photographiques.)

124. Reliquary of St. Francis, copper gilt and enamelled. Louvre. *c.* 1250.
(Phot. Giraudon.)

125. Franciscan Convent of Toulouse. Chapelle des Rieux. Statue of St. Paul given by Bishop Jean Tissandier to his Funerary Chapel. *c.* 1330. Musée des Augustins, Toulouse.

(Phot. Bulloz.)

126. Dominican Church of the Jacobins, Toulouse. Begun 1260, finished 1304.
(Phot. Jean Roubier.)

127. Dominican Church of the Jacobins, Toulouse. Crucifix from the Choir Screen
given by Cardinal Godin in 1385. Musée Raymonde, Toulouse.

(Phot. Guitard, courtesy of Monsieur Élie Lambert.)

128. Tomb of the Heart of Thibault de Champagne, d. 1270. Formerly in the Dominican Church
at Provins. Hôpital Général, Provins, Seine-et-Marne.

(Phot. Archives Photographiques.)

129. Virgin of Mercy, painted by Enguerrand Charenton and Pierre Villate for Pierre Cadart, Seigneur du Thor, 1452. Musée Condé, Chantilly. (Figures of Donors at sides omitted.)

(Phot. Giraudon.)

130. Carmelite Monastery, La Rochefoucauld, Charente. The Cloister. Late fifteenth century.

(Phot. Archives Photographiques.)

131. Carmelite Monastery, Paris. Processional Cross. *c.* 1500. Musée de Cluny, Paris.
(Phot. Giraudon.)

132. The Charterhouse of Villefranche-de-Rouergue, Aveyron. The Lesser Cloister. *c.* 1460.

(Phot. Archives Photographiques.)

133. Charterhouse of Villefranche-de-Rouergue, Aveyron. The Chapel in the Cloister. *c* 1460.

(Phot. Archives Photographiques.)

134. Charterhouse of Villefranche-de-Rouergue, Aveyron. The Stalls. 1462–79.
(*Phot. Archives Photographiques.*)

135. Chartreuse du Liget, Chemillé-sur-Indrois, Indre-et-Loire. Frescoes: the Virgin and
Jesse; the Death of the Virgin. End of the twelfth century.

(Phot. Archives Photographiques.)

136. Circular devotional picture of the Trinity with the arms of France and Burgundy on the back.
Probably by Jean Malouel. *c.* 1420. From the Chartreuse de Champmol. Louvre.
(Phot. Giraudon.)

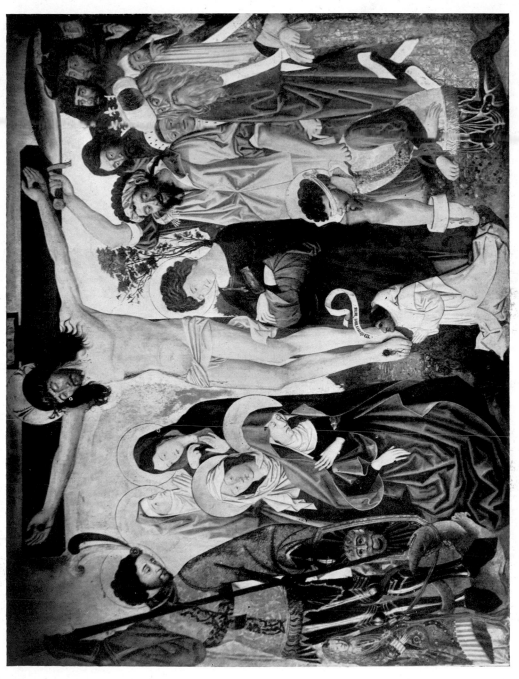

137. Chartreuse de Champmol. Picture of Christ on the Cross and St. George, with a Carthusian donor.
? Henri Bellechose. *c.* 1410. Louvre.

(Phot. Giraudon.)

138. Chartreuse de Villeneuve-lès-Avignon. Saints in Paradise. Detail of the Picture of the Coronation of the Virgin by Enguerrand Charonton given by Jean de Montagnac in 1453. Musée de l'Hospice, Villeneuve-lès-Avignon.

(Phot. Giraudon.)

139. Chartreuse de Champmol, Côte-d'Or. Figure of Christ by Claus Sluter. *c.* 1398. Dijon Museum.

(Phot. Bulloz.)

140. Chartreuse de Champmol, Côte-d'Or. Base of Crucifix by Claus Sluter. 1397–1405. Zechariah, Daniel, and Isaiah.

(Phot. Giraudon.)

141. Chartreuse de Thuison. Detail of Altar-piece, Virgin
and Child. Amiens School. Late fifteenth century. Ryerson
Collection, Art Institute of Chicago.

(Courtesy of the Art Institute of Chicago.)

142. Chartreuse de Thuison. Detail of Altar-piece. St. Hugh
of Lincoln. Amiens School. Late fifteenth century. Ryerson
Collection, Art Institute of Chicago.

(Courtesy of the Art Institute of Chicago.)

143. Folding Retable from the Chartreuse de Champmol. End of the fourteenth century. Deutsches Museum, Berlin.

(Phot. courtesy of Christopher Norris, Esq.)

144. Chartreuse de Villeneuve-lès-Avignon. *Pietà. c.* 1440. Louvre.
(Phot. Bulloz.)

145. Town House of Archambaud de Saint-Antonin. 1120–5.
Saint-Antonin, Tarn-et-Garonne.
(*Phot. Archives Photographiques.*)

146. Statue of Charles V. From the Portal of the Chapelle des
Quinze-vingts. *c.* 1375. Musée du Louvre.

(Phot. Bulloz.)

147. The Louvre in the time of Charles V. *Très Riches Heures*.
1416. Musée Condé, Chantilly.
(*Phot. Giraudon.*)

148. Castle of Mehun-sur-Yèvre, built by the Duc de Berry between 1367 and 1390.
Très Riches Heures. Musée Condé, Chantilly.

(*Phot. Giraudon.*)

149. Palace of Jean, Duc de Berry, Poitiers. Chimney-piece in the Great Hall. Made in 1384–6 by Guy de Dammartin.

(Phot. Giraudon.)

150. The Duc de Berry at Table. *Très Riches Heures*. 1416. Musée Condé, Chantilly.
(*Phot. Giraudon.*)

151. Palace of Jean, Duc de Berry, Poitiers. Detail of the Head of Queen Jeanne de Bourbon.
c. 1385.
(Phot. Giraudon.)

152. Palace of the Duc de Berry, Poitiers. Room in the Tour Maubergeon. 1386–95.
(*Phot. Jean Roubier.*)

153. Château de la Ferté-Milon, Aisne. The Entrance Towers. 1392–1407.
(Phot. Archives Photographiques.)

154. Château de la Ferté-Milon, Aisne. Bas-relief of the Assumption of the Virgin over the entrance. 1392–1407.

(Phot. Giraudon.)

155. Château de Combourg, Ille-et-Vilaine. Chiefly *c.* 1420.

(Phot. Joan Evans.)

156. Statue of a Lady, perhaps from a chimney-piece. Early fifteenth century.
Musée de Graville-le-Havre.

(Phot. Giraudon.)

157. House of Jacques Cœur, Bourges. The Courtyard. 1443–51.
(*Phot. Archives Photographiques.*)

158. House of Jacques Cœur, Bourges. The Chapel Staircase. 1443–51.
(*Phot. Archives Photographiques.*)

159. House of Jacques Cœur, Bourges. A room on the first floor. 1443–53.
(*Phot. Archives Photographiques.*)

160. Château du Lude, Sarthe. Bronze Wind-vane. Signed on back of
wing: 'LE XXVIIIᴱ JOUR DE MARS LAN MIL CCCCLX+XV JEHAN BARBET
DIT LE LION FIT CEST ANGELOT.' 1475.

(*Phot. Giraudon.*)

161. Château de Cherveux, Deux-Sèvres. Fifteenth century.

(Phot. Archives Photographiques.)

162. Manoir de Courtangis, La Ferté-Bernard, Sarthe. End of the fifteenth century.
(Phot. Archives Photographiques.)

163. Château de Frazé, Eure-et-Loir. The Entrance Gate. *c.* 1486.

(Phot. T.C.F.)

164. Château de Martainville, Calvados. 1485.

(Phot. Archives Photographiques.)

165. Château de Josselin, Morbihan. 1490–1505.
(Phot. Archives Photographiques.)

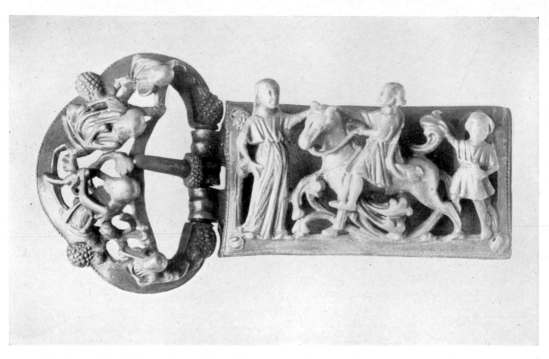

166 *a*. Silver Clasp. Late thirteenth century. National Museum, Copenhagen.

166 *b*. Casket of copper, gilt and enamelled. Probably made at Limoges for William de Valence, Earl of Pembroke, 1290–6. Victoria and Albert Museum.

167. Miniatures from René d'Anjou's *Le Cœur d'amour épris*. *c.* 1470–80. Vienna, Imperial Library MS. 2597. *a.* The God of Love draws out the heart of Cœur and gives it to Désir. *b.* Cœur reads an inscribed stone in the light of dawn while Désir sleeps.

(*Phot. courtesy of E. K. Waterhouse, Esq.*)

168. Detail of Tapestry with scenes from the *Chanson de Roland*. Fifteenth century. Musée du
Cinquantenaire, Brussels.

(Phot. courtesy of Musée du Cinquantenaire.)

169. Tapestry with Portrait Figures, made for Charles VII. *c.* 1430. Metropolitan Museum, New York.

(Phot. courtesy of Metropolitan Museum.)

170. Tapestry with Figures of the Duke and Duchess of Orleans. *c.* 1400. Musée des Arts décoratifs, Paris.

(*Phot. Giraudon.*)

171. Tapestry with the Heraldic Beasts of Charles VII. Middle of the fifteenth century. Musée des Antiquités de la Seine-Inférieure, Rouen.

(*Phot. Moreau, Paris.*)

172. One of a set of Tapestries of 'La Dame à la Licorne' made for a member of the family of
Le Viste of Lyons. *c.* 1510. Musée de Cluny.

(*Phot. Archives Photographiques.*)

173 *a*. Carved Oak Chest. *c.* 1480. Musée des Arts décoratifs, Paris.
(Phot. Giraudon.)

173 *b*. Carved Oak Chest. *c.* 1470. Musée de Cluny, Paris.
(Phot. Giraudon.)

174. Ivory Mirror-case carved with the Siege of the Castle of Love. *c.* 1360. Victoria and Albert Museum.

(Crown copyright.)

175. The Royal Gold Cup made for the Duc de Berry. *c.* 1380. British Museum.
(Phot. courtesy of Trustees of the British Museum.)

176. Reliquary of St. Ursula, formerly a Nef belonging to Anne of Brittany. End of the fifteenth century. Tours hall-mark. Given by Henri III to the Cathedral of Rheims.

(Phot. Giraudon.)

177. Painting of an Enamelled Cup. *c.* 1400. Bodleian Library, Gaignières MS. 18361, fol. 63.

178. Lid of a Covered Cup in Mazer Wood. *c.* 1470. Victoria and Albert Museum.
(Crown copyright.)

179. Portrait of Jean le Bon. Probably by Girart d'Orléans. *c.* 1359. Louvre.
(Phot. Giraudon.)

180. Portrait of Louis II d'Anjou. *c.* 1400. Paris, Cabinet des Estampes.
(Phot. Giraudon.)

181. Portrait of an Unknown Man. School of Tours. 1456. Liechtenstein Gallery, Vienna.
(*Phot. Giraudon.*)

182. The Sainte Chapelle, Paris. The Apse. Begun 1243, dedicated 1248.
(Phot. Giraudon.)

183 *a*. Statue of Dunois, Chapel of the
Castle, Châteaudun. *c.* 1451.

(*Phot. Archives Photographiques.*)

183 *b*. Statue of Louis de Châtillon. From
the Sainte Chapelle, Bourges. *c.* 1405.
Church of Marognes, Cher.

(*Phot. Archives Photographiques.*)

184. House of Jacques Cœur, Bourges. The Chapel Ceiling. *c.* 1453.
(Phot. Giraudon.)

185. God the Father. *Heures de Turin*. Painted in Paris for the Duc de Berry. *c.* 1390.
(*Phot. Giraudon.*)

186. Riding in May. *Très Riches Heures* of the Duc de Berry. 1416. Musée Condé, Chantilly.
(Phot. Giraudon.)

187. Coronation of the Virgin. *Très Riches Heures* of the Duc de Berry. 1416.
Musée Condé, Chantilly.
(*Phot. Giraudon.*)

188. Detail of the Tapestry of the Apocalypse, made for the Chapel of the Castle of Angers.
c. 1379. Designed by Jean de Bruges and woven by Nicolas Bataille, for Louis I d'Anjou.
Musée de l'Évêché, Angers.

(Phot. Archives Photographiques.)

189. Chapel Tapestry with Angels bearing the Instruments of the Passion. Woven in the valley of the Loire for the widow of Pierre de Rohan. Musée de l'Évêché, Angers. c. 1515.

(Phot. Archives Photographiques.)

190. *Parement de Narbonne*. Detail of Lenten altar frontal of painted silk. Made for the Chapel of Charles V between *c*. 1374 and 1378. Louvre.

(*Phot. Giraudon.*)

191. Altar Burette of enamelled silver gilt. *c.* 1333. National Museum, Copenhagen.
(*Phot. courtesy of National Museum, Copenhagen.*)

192. Ivory Virgin from the Sainte Chapelle of Paris. Early fourteenth
century. Louvre.

(*Phot. Giraudon.*)

193. Ivory Tabernacle of the Virgin. First half of the fourteenth century.
Victoria and Albert Museum.
(Crown copyright.)

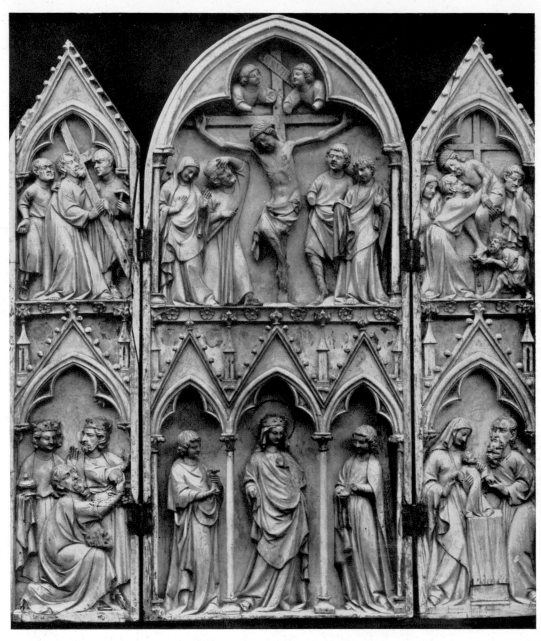

194. Ivory Triptych. Early fourteenth century. Musée de Cluny, Paris.
(*Phot. Giraudon.*)

195. Descent from the Cross. Ivory. End of the thirteenth century. Louvre.
(Phot. Giraudon.)

196. Golden Virgin, belonging to Jeanne d'Évreux in 1339 and given by her to the
Abbey of Saint-Denis. Louvre.

(Phot. Giraudon.)

197. Reliquary of the Holy Thorn. Made for Louis, Duc d'Orléans, between 1389
and 1407. Waddesdon Bequest, British Museum.

(Phot. courtesy of the Trustees.)

198. Tabernacle for the Altar given to Charles VI by his wife Isabel of Bavaria on New Year's Day, 1404. Treasury of Altötting.

(Phot. Schöning & Co., Lübeck. Courtesy of C. C. Oman, Esq.)

199. Virgin and Child with Four Angels. Maître de Moulins. *c.* 1490. Brussels Museum.
(Phot. Giraudon.)

200. Leaf of a Diptych. The Trinity. *c.* 1410. National Gallery.
(Phot. courtesy of National Gallery.)

201. Leaf of a Diptych. The Mass of St. Giles. *c.* 1495. National Gallery.

(Phot. courtesy of National Gallery.)

202. Circular Devotional Picture. Coronation of the Virgin. *c.* 1380.
Deutsches Museum, Berlin.

(Phot. Giraudon.)

203. The Virgin Enthroned. Painted for Pierre II de Bourbon and his wife Anne de Beaujeu by the Maître de Moulins. *c.* 1498. Cathedral of Moulins.

(Phot. Giraudon.)

204. Pierre II de Bourbon and his wife Anne de Beaujeu. Side-leaves of the previous picture.
Maître de Moulins. *c.* 1498. Cathedral of Moulins.

(Phot. Giraudon.)

205. Enamelled Copper Tomb-slab of Geoffroi, Count of Anjou and Maine, from
the Tomb erected in the Church of Saint-Julien du Mans between 1151 and 1160.
Musée archéologique, Le Mans.

(*Phot. Giraudon.*)

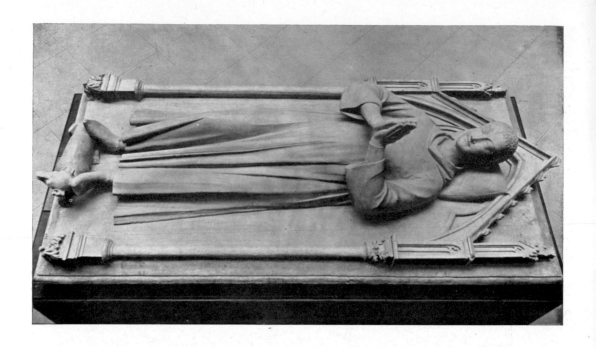

206. Tomb of Louis of France, d. 1260, from the Abbey of Royaumont.   Saint-Denis.
a. The Effigy.   b. The Mourners.
(Phots Giraudon.)

207 a. Statue from the Tomb of Jeanne de Flandres, wife of Enguerrand IV, Sire de Coucy. c. 1300. Cathedral of Laon.

207 b. Statue from a Tomb in the Abbey of Pont-aux-Dames, Seine-et-Marne. Early fourteenth century. Louvre.

(Phots Giraudon.)

208. Detail of the Mourners round a Tomb, probably of Adelaïs of Champagne, Countess of Joigny. *c.* 1290. Saint-Jean de Joigny, Yonne.

(Phot. Archives Photographiques.)

209. Detail from a Tomb, probably of Adelaïs of Champagne, Countess of Joigny.
c. 1290. Saint-Jean de Joigny, Yonne.
(Phot. Giraudon.)

210. Incised Tomb-slab of Isabel de Labroce, d. 1316. Saint-Sulpice de
Favières, Seine-et-Oise.

(Phot. Archives Photographiques.)

211 a. Philippe le Bel, by Pierre de Chelles and Jean d'Arras. 1298–1307. Saint-Denis.

211 b. Jean d'Artois, Comte d'Eu, d. 1402. Saint-Laurent d'Eu.

211 c. Bertrand du Guesclin, by Thomas Privé and Robert Loisel. 1390–7. Saint-Denis.

211 d. Louis II de Bourbon, by Jacques Morel. 1448. Souvigny, Allier.

(Phots Archives Photographiques.)

212. Mourners from the Tomb of the Duc de Berry at Bourges, by Jacques Morel. *c.* 1449.
Bourges Museum.
(Phot. Bulloz.)

213 *a*. Tomb of Charles de Bourbon and Agnès de Bourgogne, by Jacques Morel. 1448.
Souvigny, Allier.

(Phot. Archives Photographiques.)

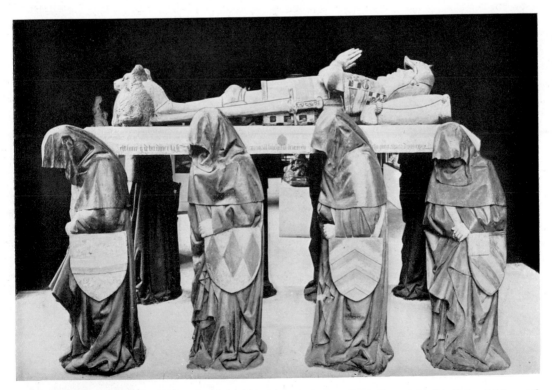

213 *b*. Tomb of Philippe Pot, Grand Sénéchal de Bourgogne. 1477–83. From the Abbey of
Cîteaux. Louvre.

(Phot. Giraudon.)

214. Nicolas du Moustier and his wife. 1518. Church of Chaource, Aube.

(Phot. Archives Photographiques.)

215 *a*. The Walls of Aigues-Mortes, Gard. Built by Philip III in 1272.

215 *b*. Bastion of the Walls of Poitiers. Fifteenth century.
(*Phots Archives Photographiques.*)

216. The Gate of Villeneuve-lès-Avignon, Gard. *c.* 1300.
(*Phot. Lévy et Neurdein.*)

217. The Walls of Avignon. 1349–70.

(Phot. Archives Photographiques.)

218. Porte Saint-Jacques, Parthenay, Deux-Sèvres. End of the thirteenth century.
(*Phot. Archives Photographiques.*)

219. La Ferté-Bernard, Sarthe. The Town Gate. Fifteenth century.
(Phot. Joan Evans.)

220. Pont Valentré, Cahors, Lot. Begun 1308.
(*Phot. Joan Evans.*)

Une Rue de Cluny

221. Romanesque Houses, Rue Dauphine (now Lamartine), at Cluny, Saône-et-Loire.
(*From a lithograph by Sagot, 1838.*)

222 *a*. Sculptured Frieze from a Romanesque House at Villemagne, Hérault.

222 *b*. Carved Stone Panel from a Shoemaker's House at Cluny,
Saône-et-Loire. Twelfth century. Musée Ochier, Cluny.

(Phots. Archives Photographiques.)

223 *a*. Tympanum of a House at Rheims. Learning, Strength, and Love. *c.* 1186.

223 *b*. Carving over the Door of the Maison aux Licornes, Montferrand, Puy-de-Dôme.
c. 1500.
(*Phots. Archives Photographiques.*)

224. Hôtel de Vauluisant, Provins, Seine-et-Marne. Second half of the thirteenth century.
(*Phot. Archives Photographiques.*)

225. House called 'La Maison du Grand Fauconnier', Cordes, Tarn. End of the thirteenth century.
(Phot. Yvon.)

226. Hôtel d'Albiat, Montferrand, Puy-de-Dôme. *c.* 1500.
(*Phot. Archives Photographiques.*)

227. Le Logis Saint-Romain, Rouen
(*Phot. Archives Photographiques.*)

228. Timbered Houses, Bourges, Cher.
(*Phot. T.C.F. (Burthe d'Annelet*).)

229. Candlestick of Bronze. End of the thirteenth century. Now in the Treasury of Rheims Cathedral.
(*Phot. Giraudon.*)

230. Statue of St. Martha in painted stone, said to have been given by a guild of
maidservants. La Madeleine de Troyes. *c.* 1515.

(Phot. Bulloz.)

231. Picture given by Jean du Bos, mercer, to Notre-Dame d'Amiens in 1437.
'Digne vesture au prestre souverain.' Louvre.

(Phot. Giraudon.)

232. Picture given by Jean le Barbier, pastrycook, to Notre-Dame d'Amiens in 1470.
'Harpe randant armonie souveraine.' Bib. Nat. MS. franç. 145.

(Phot. Bib. Nat.)

233. Virgin and Child with St. Anne. Church of Saint-Jean de Joigny, Yonne.
Late fifteenth century.
(*Phot. Archives Photographiques.*)

234 *a*. Bas-relief of Entombment. Souvigny, Allier. Fifteenth century.
(*Phot. Archives Photographiques.*)

234 *b*. Christ of Pity adored by Donors with St. Michael and St. William of Aquitaine.
From the Abbaye du Trésor. *c.* 1400. Church of Écos, Eure.
(*Phot. Giraudon.*)

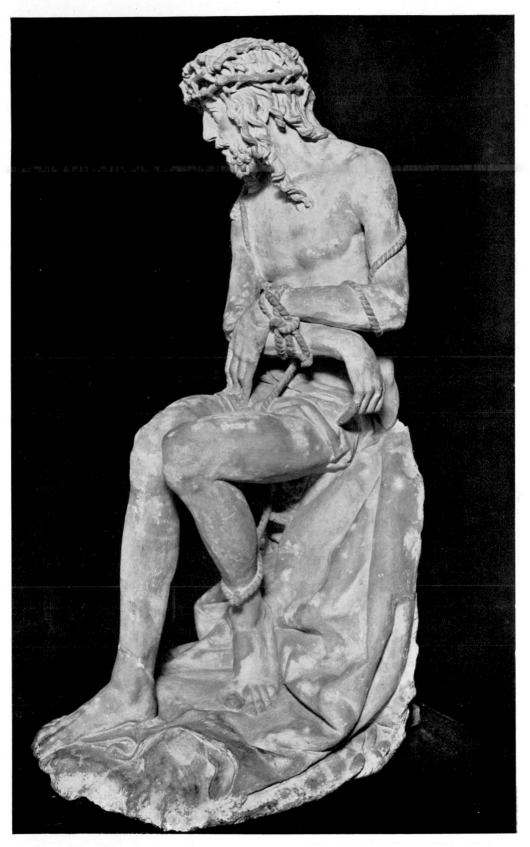

235. Christ awaiting Death. Saint-Nizier de Troyes. *c.* 1500.
(*Phot. Giraudon.*)

236. Virgin of Pity, from the Priory of Belleroc. Bayel, Aube. End of the fifteenth century.

(Phot. Bulloz.)

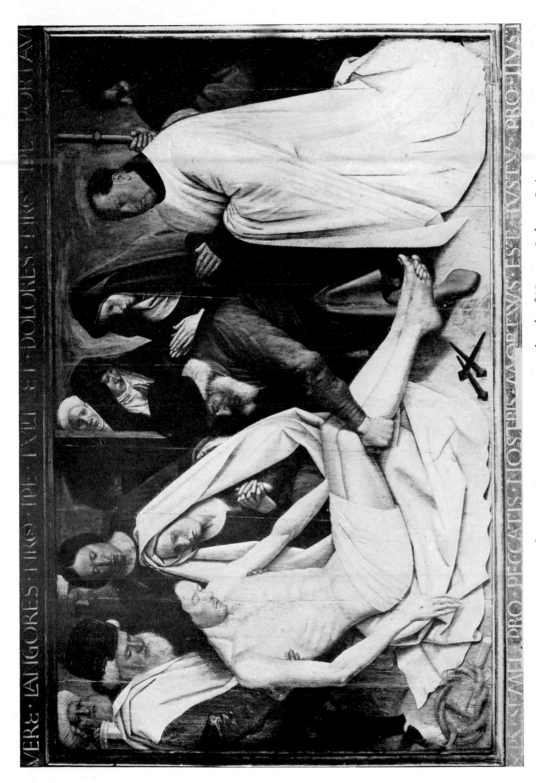

237. Virgin of Pity. Votive painting. *c.* 1470. Church of Nouans, Indre-et-Loire.

(Phot. Bulloz.)

238. Entombment Group given to the Church of Chaource, Aube, by Nicolas du Moustier and his wife Jacqueline de Laignes. 1515.

(Phot. Archives Photographiques.)

239. Hôtel de Ville, La Réole, Gironde. Thirteenth century.
(Phot. Archives Photographiques.)

240. Maison des Échevins, Bourges. 1489–91.
(*Phot. Archives Photographiques.*)

241. Palais de Justice, Rouen. Designed by Roger Ango and Roland le Roux. 1499–1509.
(Before 1944.)

(Phot. Archives Photographiques.)

242. Chapel of Saint-Julien, Lazar-house of Le Petit-Quevilly, Seine-Inférieure. · Late twelfth
century. From a drawing by L. Yperman.

(Phot. Archives Photographiques.)

243. Hospital of Beaune, Côte-d'Or, founded by Nicolas Rolin. 1443–9. The Courtyard.
(*Phot. Jean Roubier.*)

244. Hospital of Beaune, Côte-d'Or, founded by Nicolas Rolin. 1443–9. 'La Chambre des Povres.'

(*Phot. P. Hainaux.*)

245. Church of Saint-Médard, Thouars, Deux-Sèvres. Middle of the twelfth century.

(Phot. Archives Photographiques.)

246. Parish Church of Saint-Pierre d'Aulnay, Charente-Maritime. 1119-35.
(Phot. Archives Photographiques.)

247. Notre-Dame de Dijon. *c.* 1240.
(Phot. Yvon.)

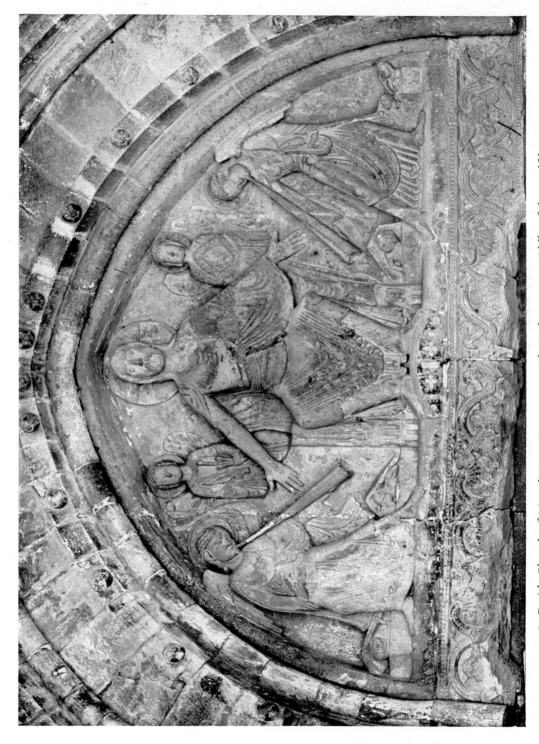

248. Parish Church of Martel, Lot. Tympanum: The Judgement. Middle of the twelfth century.
(*Phot. Archives Photographiques.*)

249. Virgin of painted stone. School of Champagne. Early fourteenth century. Louvre.
(*Phot. Giraudon.*)

250. Stone Statue of the Virgin. Church of Magny, Seine-et-Oise. Fourteenth century.
(*Phot. Bulloz.*)

251. Fortified Mill, Barbaste, Lot-et-Garonne. Fifteenth century.

(Phot. Archives Photographiques.)

252. Parish Church of Lichères, Charente-Maritime. The Portal. Twelfth century.
(Phot. Archives Photographiques.)

253. Parish Church of Saint-Père-sous-Vézelay, Yonne. End of the thirteenth century.
(Phot. Archives Photographiques.)

254. Parish Church of Thaon, Calvados. Twelfth century.

(Phot. Archives Photographiques.)

a.

b.

c.

255. Sculptured Capitals from Village Churches. *a.* Arthies, Seine-et-Oise. Eleventh century. *b.* Bussy-le-Grand, Côte-d'Or. Twelfth century. *c.* Bury, Oise. Twelfth century.
(Phots. Archives Photographiques.)

256. Wooden Statues. Fifteenth century. *a. Ecce Homo*. Écouis, Eure.
b. Virgin from a Crucifixion Group. Tours, Musée des Antiquités.

(Phots Giraudon.)

257. Fortified Church, Charras, Charente-Maritime.
(*Phot. Archives Photographiques.*)

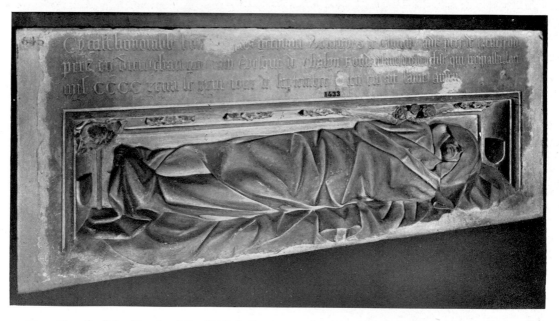

258. *a.* Detail of the Tomb of Cardinal de Lagrange, d. 1402. Musée Calvet, Avignon. *b.* Tomb of Jacques Germain, Bourgeois de Cluny, d. 1424. Musée de Dijon.

(*Phots Archives Photographiques.*)

259. Details of *Danse macabre*. La Chaise-Dieu, Haute-Loire. *c.* 1460.

(Phot. Archives Photographiques.)

260. Engraving of the Death of the Virgin. End of the fifteenth century. British Museum.

(*Phot. courtesy of the Trustees.*)

261. St. John the Baptist and Jean Bureau, Sire de la Rivière. Cathedral of Amiens. 1373–5.
(Phot. Giraudon.)

262. A Donor and St. Mary Magdalene, by the Maître de Moulins. End of the fifteenth
century. Louvre.

(Phot. Brückemann, Munich.)

263. Cistercian Abbey of Cadouin, Dordogne. The Cloister. Begun c. 1468.
(Pho.: Archives Photographiques.)

264. The Virgin of Melun. Painted by Jean Foucquet for Étienne Chevalier. *c.* 1464.
Antwerp Museum.

(Phot. Bulloz.)

265. Reliquary of Sainte Fortunade. End of the fifteenth century. Sainte-Fortunade, Corrèze.

(Phot. Bulloz.)

266. Notre Dame de Grâce, Toulouse. Middle of the fifteenth century. Musée des Augustins, Toulouse.

(Phot. Giraudon.)

267. St. Anne. Cathedral of Bordeaux. *c.* 1480.
(*Phot. Archives Photographiques.*)

268. The Visitation. Perhaps by Nicolas Haslin. *c.* 1520. Saint-Jean de Troyes.
(Phot. Guérinet.)

269. Façade of Rouen Cathedral. Built between 1509 and 1514. (Before 1944.)

(Phot. Archives Photographiques.)

270. Tower of Saint-Martin de Clamecy, Nièvre. Begun 1497.

(*Phot. Archives Photograp'iiques.*)

271. 'La Tour de Beurre.' Cathedral of Rouen. Built 1485–1507 from money received for
dispensations to eat butter in Lent.
(*Phot. Yvon.*)

272. Saint-Maclou, Rouen. Façade. Begun 1432. (Before 1944.)

(Phot. Archives Photographiques.)

273. Staircase to Organ-loft, Saint-Maclou, Rouen.
By Pierre Gringoire. *c.* 1500.
(*Phot. Archives Photographiques.*)

274. Cathedral of Albi, Tarn. The Choir Screen. 1473–1502.

(*Phot. Lévy et Neurdein.*)

275. Cathedral of Albi, Tarn. Stone canopy work of the Choir. 1473–1502.
(*Phot. Archives Photographiques.*)

276. Carrouges, near Argentan, Orne. The Entrance-pavilion. Middle of the sixteenth century.
(*Phot. Archives Photographiques.*)

277. Portrait of a Child. *c.* 1495. Louvre.
(*Phot. Giraudon.*)

278. Notre-Dame-des-Marais, La Ferté-Bernard, Sarthe. The Choir. 1500–96.

(Phot. Archives Photographiques.)

279. Statue of St. Anne. Beginning of the sixteenth century. Louvre.
(Phot. Bulloz.)

280. Sainte-Madeleine de Troyes, Aube. Detail of the Choir Screen by Jean Gailde. 1508–17.

(Phot. Archives Photographiques.)

INDEX

PRINTED IN
GREAT BRITAIN
AT THE
UNIVERSITY PRESS
OXFORD
BY
CHARLES BATEY
PRINTER
TO THE
UNIVERSITY